# THE BATTLE OF MIDWAY

PIVOTAL MOMENTS IN AMERICAN HISTORY
*Series Editors*
David Hackett Fischer
James M. McPherson
David Greenberg

James T. Patterson
*Brown v. Board of Education: A Civil
Rights Milestone and Its Troubled Legacy*

Maury Klein
*Rainbow's End: The Crash of 1929*

James McPherson
*Crossroads of Freedom:
The Battle of Antietam*

Glenn C. Altschuler
*All Shook Up: How Rock 'n' Roll
Changed America*

David Hackett Fischer
*Washington's Crossing*

John Ferling
*Adams vs. Jefferson:
The Tumultuous Election of 1800*

Joel H. Silbey
*Storm over Texas: The Annexation
Controversy and the Road to Civil War*

Raymond Arsenault
*Freedom Riders: 1961 and the Struggle
for Racial Justice*

Colin G. Calloway
*The Scratch of a Pen: 1763 and the
Transformation of North America*

Richard Labunski
*James Madison and the
Struggle for the Bill of Rights*

Sally McMillen
*Seneca Falls and the Origins of the
Women's Rights Movement*

Howard Jones
*The Bay of Pigs*

Elliott West
*The Last Indian War:
The Nez Perce Story*

Lynn Hudson Parsons
*The Birth of Modern Politics:
Andrew Jackson, John Quincy Adams,
and the Election of 1828*

Glenn C. Altschuler and
Stuart M. Blumin
*The GI Bill: A New Deal for Veterans*

Richard Archer
*As If an Enemy's Country: The British
Occupation of Boston and the Origins of
Revolution*

Thomas Kessner
*The Flight of the Century: Charles
Lindbergh and the Rise of American
Aviation*

CRAIG L. SYMONDS

# THE BATTLE OF MIDWAY

OXFORD
UNIVERSITY PRESS

# OXFORD
## UNIVERSITY PRESS

Oxford University Press is a department of the University of Oxford.
It furthers the University's objective of excellence in research, scholarship,
and education by publishing worldwide.

Oxford    New York
Auckland    Cape Town    Dar es Salaam    Hong Kong    Karachi
Kuala Lumpur    Madrid    Melbourne    Mexico City    Nairobi
New Delhi    Shanghai    Taipei    Toronto

With offices in
Argentina    Austria    Brazil    Chile    Czech Republic    France    Greece
Guatemala    Hungary    Italy    Japan    Poland    Portugal    Singapore
South Korea    Switzerland    Thailand    Turkey    Ukraine    Vietnam

Oxford is a registered trade mark of Oxford University Press
in the UK and certain other countries.

Published in the United States of America by
Oxford University Press
198 Madison Avenue, New York, NY 10016

First issued as an Oxford University Press paperback, 2013.

Library of Congress Cataloging-in-Publication Data
Symonds, Craig L.
The Battle of Midway / Craig L. Symonds.
p. cm.—(Pivotal moments in American history)
Includes bibliographical references and index.
ISBN 978-0-19-539793-2 (hardcover); 978-0-19-931598-7 (paperback)
1. Midway, Battle of, 1942.
2. World War, 1939–1945—Naval operations, American.
3. World War, 1939–1945—Naval operations, Japanese. I. Title.
D774.M5S93    2011
940.54′26699—dc22    2011010648

Printed in Canada

*For my grandson,*
*Will Symonds*

# CONTENTS

# MAPS

# EDITOR'S NOTE

In a matter of eight minutes on the morning of June 4, 1942, three of the four aircraft carriers in Japan's principal striking force were mortally wounded by American dive bombers. The fourth would follow later that day. The Japanese Navy never recovered from this blow. These pivotal minutes—the most dramatic in World War II, indeed perhaps in all of American history—reversed the seemingly irresistible momentum toward Japanese victory and started the long comeback of American forces from the disasters at Pearl Harbor and the Philippines six months earlier.

Craig Symonds begins the riveting story of the Battle of Midway with the arrival of Admiral Chester Nimitz at Pearl Harbor on Christmas Day, 1941, to start the planning for the counteroffensive that led to those climactic moments near Midway Atoll, a thousand miles west of Hawaii. American aircraft carriers had been absent from Pearl Harbor when the Japanese struck on December 7, 1941. That fortuitous absence seemed to make little difference at the time, for in the ensuing four months Japanese forces advanced from one triumph to the next until they had conquered Malaya and Singapore, the Dutch East Indies, the Philippines, and Indochina. Japan thereby created its Greater East Asia Co-prosperity Sphere, which stretched from China to the mid-Pacific and almost from the borders of Alaska to Australia. So easy were these conquests that they led to an overweening disdain for their enemies—especially the United States—which Japanese historians subsequently and ruefully labeled "the victory disease."

One Japanese leader who did not suffer from this disease was Admiral Yamamoto Isoroku, commander in chief of Japan's combined fleet and the architect of the Pearl Harbor attack. The survival of America's small fleet of carriers enabled the United States to begin a series of counterthrusts in early 1942, including the Doolittle raid over Tokyo, culminating in the Battle of Coral Sea in May. Yamamoto was determined, in Symonds' words, "to eliminate the threat of more carrier raids by engineering a climactic naval battle somewhere in the Central Pacific that would destroy those carriers once and for all." He designed a campaign by Japan's large striking force of four carriers and numerous battleships, cruisers, destroyers, and submarines, designated the Kidō Butai, to draw out the American carriers (only three were available) defending the outpost on Midway Atoll. Yamamoto planned for his superior force to pounce and sink them.

In the event, however, it was the Americans who did the pouncing and sinking. This victory is often described as "the miracle at Midway," a success that depended on the lucky timing of the dive-bomber attack that screamed down from the sky at precisely the moment when Japanese fighter planes (the famous Zeroes) were preoccupied with shooting down the hapless American torpedo planes, whose only accomplishment—though it was a crucial one— was to distract the fighters. Symonds makes clear that while luck played a part, the American victory was mainly the result of careful planning, the effective use of radar (which the Japanese did not have), and superior intelligence. The Americans had partially broken the Japanese naval operations code, which gave them timely intelligence of Japanese intentions and actions. Symonds gives much credit to Joseph Rochefort, an unsung hero of the battle, who as head of the Combat Intelligence Unit was principally responsible for decoding and interpreting Japanese communications.

One of the many great strengths of this book is its emphasis on the important "decisions made and actions taken by individuals who found themselves at the nexus of history at a decisive moment." Symonds' vivid word portraits of these individuals—Japanese as well as Americans—their personalities, their foibles and virtues, are an outstanding feature of *The Battle of Midway*. Readers will come away not only with a better understanding of the strategies, operational details, and tactics of this pivotal battle but with greater appreciation for the men whose decisions and actions made it happen.

James M. McPherson

# THE BATTLE OF MIDWAY

# INTRODUCTION

I n a series that focuses on historical contingency, it is appropriate, perhaps even essential, to include the Battle of Midway, for there are few moments in American history in which the course of events tipped so suddenly and so dramatically as it did on June 4, 1942. At ten o'clock that morning, the Axis powers were winning the Second World War. Though the Red Army had counterattacked the Wehrmacht outside Moscow in December, the German Army remained deep inside the Soviet Union, and one element of it was marching toward the oil fields of the Caucasus. In the Atlantic, German U-boats ravaged Allied shipping and threatened to cut the supply line between the United States and Great Britain. In the Pacific, Japan had just completed a triumphant six-month rampage, attacking and wrecking Allied bases from the Indian Ocean to the mid-Pacific following the crippling of the U.S. battle fleet at Pearl Harbor. Japan's Mobile Striking Force (the Kidō Butai) was at that moment on the verge of consolidating command of the Pacific by eliminating what the strike at Pearl Harbor had missed: America's aircraft carriers. The outcome of the war balanced on a knife-edge, but clearly leaned toward the Axis powers.

An hour later, the balance had shifted the other way. By 11:00 a.m., three Japanese aircraft carriers were on fire and sinking. A fourth was launching a counterstrike, yet before the day was over, it too would be located and mortally wounded. The Japanese thrust was turned back. Though the war had three more years to run, the Imperial Japanese Navy would never again initiate a strategic offensive. Later that summer the battle for Stalingrad began. The Atlantic sea lanes remained dangerous, but the convoys continued, and Britain survived. The war had turned.

In 1967, a quarter century after Midway, Walter Lord published a history of that battle entitled *Incredible Victory*. The title's assumption is that the odds against the Americans at Midway were so long that their ultimate triumph defied comprehension. So dominant was this perception that when the national memorial to the Second World War was unveiled in Washington, D.C., in the spring of 2004, a sentence from Lord's book was chiseled into its marble façade in letters six inches high: "THEY HAD NO RIGHT TO WIN, YET THEY DID, AND IN DOING SO THEY CHANGED THE COURSE OF THE WAR." Similarly, when Gordon Prange's long-awaited book on Midway came out in 1982, brought to press by two of his former graduate students after his death, it bore the title *Miracle at Midway*. Once again, the implication was unmistakable.

Embedded in these books' titles, and in their conclusions as well, is the supposition that the American victory at Midway was the product of fate, or chance, or luck, or even divine will. In fact, sixty years after the battle, when a group of Midway veterans conducted a survey asking who had played the most decisive role on the American side, one veteran insisted that, as in the days of the ancient Greeks, this improbable earthly event could be explained only as the result of divine intervention.[1]

In *War and Peace*, Leo Tolstoy argues that great historical events, including (maybe even especially) great military events, are the product of historical forces only dimly understood. The great drama of the Napoleonic Wars, Tolstoy wrote, "came about step by step, incident by incident, moment by moment, emerging from an infinitely varied set of unimaginably different circumstances, and was perceived in its entirety only when it became a reality, a past event." To him, individuals were not the prime movers of history but its victims, subject to "a boundless variety of infinitesimally small forces"—little more than chaff blown by a storm.[2]

Certainly chance—or luck—played a role at Midway, but the outcome of the battle was primarily the result of decisions made and actions taken by individuals who found themselves at the nexus of history at a decisive moment. In short, the Battle of Midway is best explained and understood by focusing on the people involved. Tolstoy insists that *chance* determines events, but it is *people* who make history, and this book is about the individuals who made history in that perilous spring of 1942. The list is a long one. A Japanese admiral (Yamamoto Isoroku) decided that a battle must be fought and not only initiated the planning but insisted that it go forward in spite of—indeed, almost because of—considerable opposition within his own service. An American admiral (Chester Nimitz) decided that the gauntlet that had been thrown down must be picked up, and he devised a plan of his own. A group of dedicated code breakers, and in particular Lieutenant Commander Joseph Rochefort, supplied the information that ended up giving the Americans a crucial edge. And combatants on both sides—admirals and captains, commanders and lieutenants, petty officers and enlisted men—determined the timing, the course, and ultimately the outcome of the fight. Midway might have ended differently. That it didn't was the result of these men and the decisions they made.

Essential to understanding those decisions is an appreciation of the culture that informed these individuals, for while they were free agents, they were also products of their society, and their actions were shaped and constrained by the world in which they operated. For that reason, a history of what is perhaps the most pivotal naval battle in American history necessarily must explore the culture of both the U.S. Navy and the Imperial Japanese Navy, as well as the politics and technology of the age. It does not detract from the drama of the event, nor diminish its significance, to acknowledge that in light of these factors, the outcome of the Battle of Midway was less incredible and less miraculous than it has often been portrayed.

# 1

# CinCPac

An hour after dawn on Christmas morning in 1941, a lone PB2Y-2 Coronado flying boat circled slowly over the fleet anchorage at Pearl Harbor, Hawaii, at the end of a seventeen-hour flight from San Diego. From inside her fuselage, 56-year-old Admiral Chester Nimitz peered out the window at the devastation below. Even dressed as he was in civilian clothes, he would have prompted a second look from strangers on the street, for his face had been weathered by years at sea and he had snow-white hair, which led a few of his young staffers to call him "cottontail"— but only behind his back. His most arresting feature, however, was his startling light-blue eyes, eyes that now scanned the scene below him. As the four-engine Coronado approached the harbor, its pilot, Lieutenant Bowen McLeod, invited Nimitz to come up and take the copilot's seat to get a better view. Through a steady rain that added to the pall of gloom, Nimitz saw that the surface of the water was covered with black fuel oil. From that oily surface, the rounded bottoms of the battleship *Oklahoma* and the older *Utah* protruded like small islands. Another, the *Nevada*, was aground bow first near the main entrance channel. Other battleships rested on the mud, with only their shattered and fallen superstructures extending above the water. Here was the U.S. Navy's vaunted battle fleet that Nimitz had been sent halfway around the world to command.[1]

Nimitz made no comment, only shaking his head and making a soft clucking sound with his tongue. While en route by rail from Washington to San Diego on the Santa Fe "Chief" to catch the flight to Hawaii, he had studied the reports of the devastation that had been wrought by the Japanese in their attack three weeks earlier on December 7. The reports could not convey the extent of the destruction. Even the photograph he had seen of the battleship *Arizona* engulfed in black smoke did not prepare him for the scene that now met his eyes. The seaplane splashed down and slowed to a stop on the oily surface of the roadstead. The doors were thrown open and the powerful odor of fuel oil, charred wood, and rotting flesh hit him like a fist. It was the smell of war.[2]

The reserve that Nimitz normally displayed in moments of crisis had earned him a reputation as unemotional; at least one officer described him as "coldly impersonal." Nimitz was certainly undemonstrative, able to maintain an astonishing coolness under pressure. Even as a midshipman, his quiet reserve impressed classmates, who described him in the Naval Academy yearbook, the *Lucky Bag*, as one who "possesses that calm and steady-going Dutch way that gets at the bottom of things." As an example of that, a quarter century later, during his command of the heavy cruiser *Augusta*, he had directed Ensign O. D. Waters (inevitably nicknamed "Muddy") to "bring the ship to anchor." Perhaps nervous with the captain's eyes on him, Waters brought the big cruiser into the anchorage too fast, overshot the mark, and had to order the engines full astern while paying out ninety fathoms of anchor cable before the ship finally came to a stop. Nimitz remained silent throughout. Only when the *Augusta* was securely at anchor did he remark, "Waters, you know what you did wrong, don't you?" Waters responded: "Yes, sir, I certainly do." To which Nimitz replied, "That's fine." While Nimitz was not cold—he was a great teller of jokes and fond of terrible puns—he did keep his emotions under control, rarely betraying them to others. His most confrontational response was generally "Now see here."

That ability to remain calm under pressure would be severely tested over the next six months, and indeed throughout the Pacific war.[3]

Before he stepped out of the flying boat and into the launch that had come out to greet him, Nimitz turned and shook hands with every member of the seaplane's crew, apologizing for keeping them from their families on Christmas Day. His first question to the officer on the launch was about Wake Island, a tiny outpost of coral and sand two thousand nautical miles to the west. When he had left California, Wake's small Marine garrison was still holding out against a Japanese invasion, and an American relief force was steaming toward it at best speed. Told now that Wake Island had surrendered and that the relief expedition had been recalled, Nimitz said nothing, staring out silently over the rain-spattered surface of the harbor for several minutes, his expression unreadable. As the launch headed for shore, he could see several small boats moving about the roadstead. They were fishing the bodies of dead servicemen from the water.[4]

Nimitz had been ordered to Pearl Harbor as commander in chief, Pacific (CinCPac), because Washington had concluded that keeping Admiral Husband Kimmel in charge after the disaster of December 7 was politically impossible. On December 9, Secretary of the Navy Frank Knox had left Washington for Pearl Harbor to assess things for himself. Arriving two days later, the wreckage still smoldering, Knox was appalled by what he saw. He was also appalled that no one seemed able to explain to him why the Japanese had achieved such complete surprise. His annual report, issued the previous summer, had asserted that "the American people may feel fully confident in their navy." Just three days before the attack, Knox had spoken at a small dinner party in Washington in honor of Vice President Henry Wallace. "War may begin in the Pacific at any moment," he had warned the assembled guests. "But I want you to know that no matter what happens, the United States Navy is ready. Every man is at his post, every ship is at its station. The Navy is ready. Whatever happens, the Navy is not going to be caught napping." Yet within seventy-two hours of those assurances, the Navy was caught almost literally napping. Little wonder that Knox was furious.[5]

The 66-year-old Knox had been an unlikely choice as secretary of the navy. A lifelong newspaperman, he was also a lifelong Republican, and had been Alf Landon's running mate on the Republican presidential ticket in the 1936 election. In that role he had been a virulent critic of President Roosevelt and the New Deal. Despite that, after Germany's invasion of Poland and the onset of war, Roosevelt sought to build a bipartisan administration dedicated to rearmament by naming several prominent Republicans to the cabinet. His first thought was to ask both Landon and Knox, the defeated Republican ticket, to join the cabinet, with Landon as commerce secretary and Knox as navy secretary. Landon, however, insisted on a pledge that Roosevelt would not seek a third term as a condition of his acceptance, so Roosevelt instead picked another Republican, 73-year-old Henry L. Stimson, who had been secretary of state under Hoover, to head the War Department. He did, however, ask Knox to take over the Navy Department, announcing both appointments on June 20, 1940, two days before France formally surrendered to the Nazis.[6]

FDR may have been attracted to Knox because the jowly, round-faced newspaperman had been a Rough Rider under Franklin's "Uncle Teddy" in the Spanish-American War. For his part, Knox remained suspicious of the New Deal, but he was foursquare behind FDR on the question of national preparedness, and he admired Roosevelt's get-tough policies toward Hitler's regime. He was also a man of quick decision. As publisher of the *Chicago Daily News*, he had a hardnosed management style, guided by facts and deadlines, that made him impatient with delay or uncertainty. ("All my life I have been fighting against time," he declared during his confirmation hearing.) Roosevelt's deputy chief of staff Harold Ickes thought him "impetuous" and "inclined to think off the top of his head." That impetuosity was evident as the grim-faced Knox toured the wreckage of the Pacific Fleet at Pearl Harbor on December 11. When he got back to Washington, he reported to Roosevelt that the Japanese had achieved surprise at Pearl Harbor because of "a lack of a state of readiness," and the blame for that, in his view, fell squarely on the shoulders of the commanding officers, Lieutenant General Walter C. Short of the Army and Admiral Husband Kimmel of the Navy. Eventually a lengthy investigation headed by Supreme Court justice Owen Roberts would come to a similar conclusion and declare that Short and Kimmel were guilty of "a dereliction of duty." However fair or unfair that conclusion, the political reality was that neither man could be retained in his position.[7]

Once it was clear that Kimmel would have to go, Roosevelt and Knox discussed who should replace him. On December 15, they sent for Admiral Ernest J. King, the talented but abrasive commander of the Atlantic Fleet. While King had compiled an impressive service record during his forty-one years in the Navy, his personality was scandalous. He tended to be abrupt and dismissive when dealing with subordinates, and he did not suffer fools gladly, whatever their status. When introducing himself to a group of young officers in Hawaii, he declared, "I'm Ernest King. You all know who I am. I'm a self-appointed son of a bitch." He asserted his privileges of rank as a matter of course. One officer recalled, "You could be halfway through a haircut and he decided that he wanted a shave. You got out of the barber chair and waited until he was shaved." His personal life was notorious. Though he foreswore drinking during the war, he had a well-earned reputation as a heavy drinker and womanizer. What FDR and Knox wanted now, however, was not a role model but a warrior, and King was arguably the most aggressive senior officer in the Navy. When King arrived in Washington on December 16, Knox told him that the president wanted him not merely for the Pacific

■ The tough-minded and tough-talking Admiral Ernest J. King wielded unprecedented authority over the U.S. Navy during World War II as both commander in chief (CominCh) and chief of naval operations (CNO). (U.S. Naval Institute)

command but for the more powerful position of commander in chief of the U.S. Fleet (CinCUS), with authority over both the Atlantic and Pacific and all Navy commands worldwide.[8]

FDR made the formal offer that afternoon. King was willing to accept— he made no secret of his lifelong ambition to "get to the top"—but he had three conditions: first, he wanted his abbreviated title changed from CinCUS (which sounded too much like "sink us") to CominCh; second, he wanted a promise that he would not have to hold press conferences or testify before Congress unless absolutely necessary; and third, he wanted authority over the various navy bureaus, those entrenched centers of political influence that had existed within the Navy as near-independent fiefdoms since their creation in 1842. FDR agreed at once to the first two conditions and told King that, while he couldn't change the law concerning the bureaus, he would see to it that any bureau chief who proved unable or unwilling to cooperate with King would lose his job. King's new authority was unprecedented. According to Executive Order no. 8984, he would have "supreme command of the several fleets . . . under the general direction of the Secretary of the Navy," and would be "directly responsible to the President."[9]

If King reported directly to the president, it was not clear what role the chief of naval operations (CNO) was to play in the new command structure. In King's view, his new position would make up for "the organizational deficiencies" inherent in the CNO's office, and he would naturally "fulfill some of the functions that the peacetime Chief of Naval Operations should have had under his control." The sitting CNO was Admiral Harold Stark, a "modest and self-effacing" man, according to his biographer, who would soon be overshadowed by the forceful and confident King. Like many officers who came out of the prewar Naval Academy, Stark had a nickname. During his plebe (freshman) year in the fall of 1899, an upperclassman, noting Stark's last name, asked if he was related to General John Stark. The young plebe did not know who General Stark was, and the outraged upperclassman told him rather forcefully that John Stark had led American forces at the Battle of Bennington in the Revolutionary War, during which Stark had supposedly declared, "We will win today or Betty Stark will be a widow!" Though it is uncertain that General Stark ever made such a statement, it was a piece of military lore the upperclassman thought the young plebe should know. From then on, whenever an upperclassman demanded it, Midshipman Stark had to brace up and call out in his parade-ground voice: "We will win today or Betty Stark will be a widow!" As a result, he became known to his classmates as "Betty Stark," and "Betty Stark" he remained throughout his naval career, signing his memos—even to the president—simply as "Betty." He had risen to the top of the Navy's hierarchy despite his curious nickname, as well as his gentle manner and cherubic appearance (Samuel Eliot Morison thought he "looked more like a bishop than a sailor"), but his tenure as CNO would not survive the force of King's personality. In three months, King would replace him in that job, becoming both CominCh and CNO for the duration of the war and exercising near-absolute authority over the Navy.[10]

Of course there was still the question of who would command the Pacific Fleet (or what was left of it) at Pearl Harbor. With little discussion, Roosevelt and Knox decided that the only possible choice was Chester Nimitz. Roosevelt had considered appointing Nimitz to the command back in January, but at that time Nimitz himself had suggested that he was too junior for such a post. Had he accepted, it would have been he, and not Kimmel, who was in charge at Pearl Harbor on December 7. Now, a year later, Nimitz was still relatively junior to many of the other candidates for Kimmel's job, but there was no place for such punctilio in the present crisis. Roosevelt is supposed to have exclaimed: "Tell Nimitz to get the hell out to Pearl and stay there till the war is won." King, too, thought him the right man for the job, though he was less sure that the quiet, undemonstrative Nimitz would be sufficiently aggressive in his new role. He worried that he listened to too many people and was too willing to compromise. "If only I could keep him tight on what he's supposed to do," King remarked. "Somebody gets ahold of him and I have to straighten him out." During the war, King would send scores of messages and require several meetings, all in an effort to "straighten out" Nimitz. But Pearl Harbor was nearly five thousand miles from Washington, and King had two oceans and alliance politics to worry about, which would limit his ability to micromanage Pacific strategy.[11]

In at least one respect, Nimitz was a curious choice as CinCPac, for he did not represent any of the traditional power centers within the Navy hierarchy. The U.S. Navy of 1941 was divided into clearly differentiated, and mutually jealous, warfare communities. The most visible and cohesive was composed of those who served in destroyers, cruisers, and especially battleships. For at least two generations, and certainly since the publication of Alfred Thayer Mahan's famous book *The Influence of Sea Power Upon History* (1890), governments and navies the world over had looked upon the giant steel castles of big-gun battleships as the final arbiters of naval power and, by extension, of world power. Officers whose careers were dedicated to these mighty battlewagons were members of "the Gun Club." They wore traditional double-breasted blue uniforms marked with gold stripes and black leather shoes, and in their own view, and in the view of most Americans, they were the real navy.[12]

In the 1920s, however, the first stirrings of a coming revolution in naval warfare became evident when the U.S. Navy converted the collier *Jupiter* into the country's first aircraft carrier, the USS *Langley* (CV-1). The men who signed up for pilot training—"naval aviators" in the Navy's parlance— developed a swaggering elan to match the pioneering drama of their service. In the open-air cockpits of their airplanes they wore fleece-lined leather outfits that protected them from the intense cold at high altitudes. On the ground they wore forest-green uniforms marked with black stripes, as well as brown shoes. These "brown shoe" officers conceived of themselves as elite warriors who put their lives on the line almost every day by performing inherently dangerous carrier takeoffs and landings, and they considered themselves a breed apart from the "black shoe" officers who merely drove ships. For their part, the black shoes resented the fact that because of flight pay the aviators were paid 50 percent more than they were.[13]

Nimitz belonged to neither clan, for he had spent much of his early service in submarines, starting in 1909, when the sub service was what carrier aviation became in the 1920s: a cutting-edge career that attracted ambitious and daring young officers who could rise quickly to command in an experimental service. Soon, despite his youth and his rank, Nimitz was the commanding officer of the aptly named *Plunger*, a tiny (107 ton) training submarine only sixty-four feet long and twelve feet wide. He spent World War I on the staff of Captain Samuel S. Robison, commander of U.S. Atlantic submarines, and as a member of the Board of Submarine Design. During the early 1920s, while the Navy's air arm was being created, Lieutenant Commander Nimitz was engaged in supervising the construction, and subsequently the command, of the submarine base at Pearl Harbor. As it happened, that sub base was one of the few targets the Japanese had overlooked in their strike on December 7.[14]

After World War I, Nimitz became an expert on the design and construction of diesel engines, and he supervised the engineering plant on the new-construction oiler *Maumee* (AO-2), becoming first her chief engineering officer and then her executive officer. In that capacity, he helped pioneer the practice of refueling U.S. Navy warships while they were under way, a protocol that dramatically extended the fleet's cruising range and sea-keeping capability. After a tour in command of the heavy cruiser *Augusta* in the early 1930s, he served two tours in Washington in the Bureau of Navigation (subsequently renamed the Bureau of Personnel). To some observers in the Navy, this was cause for concern. They worried that by becoming a "Washington repeater," Nimitz was spending too much time pushing paper instead of at sea. In addition, much of his time in Washington was spent working with those navy bureaus so despised by King. And his Washington

■ Admiral Chester Nimitz took over as commander in chief, Pacific (CinCPac) on the last day of 1941. Beneath a placid and stoic demeanor, Nimitz concealed both a warrior's instinct and a willingness to take bold risks. (U.S. Naval Institute)

service kept him away from the "real Navy." He did not, for example, play a role in Navy strategic planning during the 1930s, nor participate in any of the tactical fleet exercises that were an important component of peacetime service in the interwar years. On the other hand, whatever he had missed by devoting himself to the administration of BuNav, it put him in touch with, and made him known to, the nation's political leaders.[15]

When Nimitz stepped ashore at Pearl Harbor on that gloomy Christmas Day of 1941, he was met not by Kimmel but by Vice Admiral William S. Pye. Kimmel had learned on December 16 that he was going to be relieved and, appreciating that his continued presence would be awkward, had volunteered to be detached in favor of Pye, his second in command. Pye was a Naval Academy classmate of Ernie King and a half decade older than Nimitz, with forty-one years of active service, most of it in battleships. Raised in Minneapolis, he had the pugnacious physiognomy of a cop on the beat, with a bulbous nose and dark eyes crowned by shaggy eyebrows. At age 61, his hair was thin but still dark, combed straight back from a high forehead.

It was Pye who had felt compelled to order the recall of the Wake relief expedition. Kimmel had built a task force (Task Force 14) around the aircraft carrier *Saratoga* (CV-3), which had been in San Diego during the Japanese attack and returned to Pearl Harbor a week afterward on December 15. After a quick refueling, Kimmel sent her on toward Wake Island the next day under Rear Admiral Frank Jack Fletcher with an escort of three cruisers, nine destroyers, a seaplane tender, and a fleet oiler to keep them all supplied with fuel. Betty Stark gave Kimmel the authority to evacuate the garrison if necessary, but the hope was that Fletcher could reinforce the defenders of Wake by delivering supplies and a new squadron of airplanes. To distract the Japanese, Kimmel sent Vice Admiral Wilson Brown and the *Lexington* (CV-2) southward to attack the Japanese-held Marshall Islands, and Vice Admiral William F. Halsey and the *Enterprise* (CV-6) westward to support Fletcher. Critics argued subsequently that Kimmel should not have waited for the *Saratoga* before sending a relief expedition, or, alternatively, that he ought to have sent all three carriers to Wake rather than trying to distract the Japanese by sending them out on different missions.[16]

Whatever the merits of these criticisms, after Kimmel was relieved of command, the expedition became Pye's responsibility. On December 20, with the *Saratoga* task force still 725 miles from Wake, Pye learned that the Japanese had renewed their assault and, more importantly, that they had committed at least one of their carriers, and possibly two, to the attack. The two carriers were, in fact, the *Sōryū* and *Hiryū*, both of which had partici-pated in the Pearl Harbor attack. If *Saratoga* got tangled up with two (or more) of Japan's big carriers, it dramatically escalated the risk. Then, two days later, on the morning of December 22 (Hawaii time), with the *Sara-toga* task force still more than five hundred miles from its destination, Pye learned that the Japanese had secured a lodgment on the island and were overpowering the outnumbered defenders. A poignantly laconic message from the garrison's commander summed up the situation: "Issue in doubt." At about the same time, Pye received a message from Stark in Washington that read, in part, "Wake is now and will continue to be a liability." That message authorized Pye "to evacuate Wake." A note at the end read, "King concurs." But evacuation was impossible now, and Pye wired Stark to tell him so. Eager as Pye was to come to the aid of the gallant Marines on Wake Island, he was not willing to risk the *Saratoga* task force against two enemy carriers in what now looked like a lost cause, especially if Washington con-sidered Wake "a liability." Reluctantly, he issued orders for the *Saratoga* to turn around. When Fletcher got that order, he threw his hat to the deck in frustration. The pilots on the *Saratoga* who were scheduled to fly off the carrier the next day to support their fellow Marines were near mutinous, and there was angry talk about ignoring the orders and going ahead with the relief mission anyway. But discipline held; the Marines defending Wake were left to their fate.[17] *

---

* More than fifteen hundred Americans were taken prisoner by the Japanese when the island fell. Most of them (1,146) were civilian construction workers; the others included 368 Marines, 65 Navy men, and five Army soldiers. Most were transported to Japanese POW camps where they remained—those who survived—until 1945. A hundred or so of the construction workers were retained on Wake, and in 1943, when it looked like the island might be recaptured by the Americans, the survivors were lined up and shot.

The decision was a body blow to American morale. In Washington, Roosevelt was so upset he told Stark to demand an explanation from Pye. Though Stark himself had played a role in the decision, he dutifully wrote Pye that it was "essential for understanding required by higher authority that you furnish me with further information as to considerations which governed [the] retirement of two Western task forces." Pye might have written back that he did it because Stark and King had labeled Wake "a liability," but instead he wrote: "I became convinced that the general situation took precedence and required a conservation of our forces." FDR remained unsatisfied and never quite forgave Pye. Knox was furious. In a letter to Kimmel the previous January, the Navy secretary had written: "There is no such thing as fighting a safe war. . . . Prudence must be relegated to a secondary position to the bold and resolute employment of the fleet." He saw nothing bold or resolute in the decision to abandon the beleaguered Wake garrison. Nimitz, too, was disappointed that the effort to succor Wake had been recalled, but he spent no time regretting what he could not change: it was "water over the dam," he said. And he continued to hold both Pye and Fletcher in high regard. Still, it was one more bitter disappointment for a country still reeling from the shock of Pearl Harbor, and one more burden for the new commander to bear.[18]

At the Naval headquarters building, Nimitz met with the officers of Pye's (formerly Kimmel's) staff, shook their hands, and asked them to stay on to help him. Having expected a dressing down, the officers immediately brightened in response to this appeal; one recalled that Nimitz's arrival was like someone opening a window in a stuffy room. Indeed, after a careful assessment, Nimitz concluded that the terrible losses of December 7 had been less disastrous than they first appeared. Though all eight battleships had been hit, and five of them sunk, it had happened in the shallow waters of Pearl Harbor where most of them could be raised and repaired. Had the fleet gone to sea in an effort to drive off the attackers, those ships would very likely have been sunk in deep water and lost forever, and with a much greater loss of life. Instead, six of the eight battleships that were sunk or damaged on December 7 would be raised and repaired and would see action again later in the war.[19]

Moreover, while the death of the crewmen aboard these ships was unquestionably tragic, the temporary loss of the battleships themselves proved not to be all that strategically important. The very success of the Japanese attack underscored what some had been arguing for years: that battleships had been supplanted as the dominant weapon of naval warfare by aircraft carriers, and all three of America's Pacific Fleet aircraft carriers had been out of port when the Japanese struck. As already noted, the *Saratoga* was at San Diego and about to return to Pearl Harbor after a refit at the Puget Sound Navy Yard in Bremerton, Washington. The other two American carriers were also at sea on December 7. In response to a "war warning" that he received from Washington on November 27, Kimmel had sent them off the next day to ferry combat planes to the distant American outposts at Wake and Midway. Halsey and the *Enterprise*, escorted by three cruisers and nine destroyers, had ferried a dozen Marine fighter planes to Wake Island, where those planes played a major role in fighting off the initial Japanese attack, and Rear Admiral John H. Newton and the *Lexington* with a similar escort carried planes to Midway, though news of the Japanese attack led Newton to turn the *Lexington* around before he could deliver them.[20]

Kimmel had ordered Halsey to return to Pearl Harbor by December 7, but refueling at sea and an accident involving a cable that became wrapped around a propeller of the cruiser *Northampton* delayed him, and he was still several hundred miles out when he received the startling message, "Air Raid Pearl Harbor. This is no drill." Halsey's first thought was that it was a case of mistaken identity. In order not to enter port with a deck load of airplanes (which could not take off from an anchored carrier), the Americans routinely flew their airplanes into Oahu from up to a hundred miles out. Halsey had launched a number of scout planes that morning that would have been arriving at Pearl just about the time of the report; he feared that nervous gunners at Pearl had mistaken his planes for enemy aircraft. As it happened, the planes from the *Enterprise* arrived in the midst of the Japanese attack, and some of them were targeted by friendly fire. Once Halsey realized that the raid was real, he launched more planes to search for the enemy. He sent most of them southward toward a reported contact—false, as it turned out—and thus missed the retiring enemy fleet. It was just as well, for had Halsey's scout planes found the six carriers of the Japanese strike force and opened a general engagement, he would have been hopelessly overmatched, and the *Enterprise* might well have become the next victim of the day, with consequences much greater than the temporary loss of eight battleships.[21]

As a result of these circumstances, Nimitz had three large aircraft carriers he could count on to be the nucleus of his new fleet. A fourth was on the way, for the *Yorktown* (CV-5), which had been sent to the Atlantic in April along with three battleships and several light cruisers and destroyers, was now ordered to return to the Pacific. That would give Nimitz four aircraft carriers and a powerful strike force to counter future Japanese initiatives. Of course it was theoretically possible for the U.S. to bring even more warships around from the Atlantic to the Pacific, including some battleships. That was problematic, however, in light of the fact that on December 11 Hitler declared war on the United States, committing the U.S. to a two-front war with enemies in both oceans.

The onset of a two-ocean war necessitated a reconsideration of American strategic plans. For more than twenty years, the U.S. Navy had focused most of its planning, training, and war gaming on a possible war with Japan. The blueprint for that future war was officially known as Plan Orange, and the first version of it had been sketched out in 1911. Its basic outlines were simple—even simplistic. It presumed an outbreak of war triggered by a Japanese assault on the Philippines, following which the U.S. fleet would gather in Pearl Harbor and strike out across the broad Pacific for a showdown with the Japanese battle fleet somewhere in the western Pacific. Over the years the plan had been updated and modified, and several options built into it, but the basic outline remained the same.[22]

Hitler's rise to power in the 1930s had led to both ambitious rearmament programs and strategic adjustment. The Vinson-Trammel Act of 1934 began this metamorphosis, and by the time of Pearl Harbor the United States had an enormous armada under construction: eight battleships, twelve carriers, thirty-five cruisers, 196 destroyers, and more than three thousand airplanes—a force, taken together, that was larger than the entire Japanese

Navy. None of these new-construction warships, however, would be ready for deployment until very late in 1942 or early 1943. In the meantime, the Nazi conquest of France in June, 1940, and the ensuing U-boat threat to the Atlantic lifelines, dramatically changed many of the assumptions behind Plan Orange. Until then, U.S. strategists had hoped that Britain and France could hold off the Germans long enough for America to complete her rearmament. Now with France defeated and occupied, and Britain teetering on the brink of collapse, it looked possible—perhaps even likely—that Hitler might complete his conquest of Europe before the U.S. had fully rearmed. In light of those facts, in November of 1940, a few weeks after Roosevelt's reelection to a third term, and a full year before Pearl Harbor, Betty Stark wrote a lengthy memo to Secretary of the Navy Frank Knox that offered a completely new strategic blueprint.[23]

Stark's November 1940 memo was one of the most consequential documents ever submitted to the government by a naval officer. Executing Plan Orange against Japan, he wrote, "would take a long time," and as a result "we would have to accept considerable danger in the Atlantic." In fact, as Stark well knew, there was *already* "considerable danger" in the Atlantic, where U.S. destroyers were engaged in a kind of quasi-war with German submarines in an effort to keep open the line of supply from the United States to beleaguered Britain. Concerned about a British defeat, and the

■ Admiral Harold "Betty" Stark served as CNO until replaced by King in March 1942. His November 1940 "Plan Dog" memo was instrumental in reorienting American strategy from the Pacific to Europe. (U.S. Naval Institute)

dire consequences of such an event for the United States, Roosevelt repeatedly stretched the meaning of "neutral" by expanding U.S. Navy operations in the Atlantic. Stark was concerned about Britain, too, and to address those concerns, he recommended reversing twenty years of Navy planning to reorient American focus from the Pacific to the Atlantic. "The reduction of Japanese offensive power," he wrote, could be achieved "chiefly through economic blockade" while the United States devoted the bulk of its efforts to "a land offensive against the Axis powers." That would require "a major naval and military effort in the Atlantic," during which time "we would . . . be able to do little more in the Pacific than remain on a strict defensive." The great danger, of course, was that Britain might collapse in spite of American support, in which case the U.S. would find itself on the defensive in both oceans. But Stark was betting on the British to hold out.[24]

After laying out his argument, Stark presented four strategic alternatives, which he labeled A, B, C, and D. The last of them was his preferred option. Known as "Plan Dog" in Navy lingo, it asserted that in case of war with both Germany and Japan, the U.S. should remain on the defensive in the Pacific and devote its "full national offensive strength" to the defeat of Nazi Germany. "Should we be forced into a war with Japan," Stark wrote, "we should . . . definitely plan to avoid operations in the Far East or the mid-Pacific that will prevent the Navy from promptly moving to the Atlantic forces fully adequate to safeguard our interests and policies in the event of British collapse." Finally, Stark urged the initiation of "secret staff talks" with British officials.[25]

Stark's memo found a ready audience in Washington, where Roosevelt, too, was worried about a British collapse, and the staff talks that Stark had recommended took place in January 1941 in Washington. From those meetings emerged a document known as ABC-1, which outlined the strategy subsequently known as "Germany First." Specifically, it held that "since Germany is the predominant member of the Axis Powers, the Atlantic and European area is considered to be the decisive theater. The principal United States Military effort will be exerted in that theatre, and operations of United States forces in other theatres will be conducted in such a manner as to facilitate that effort." That exact language was subsequently incorporated into the

American war plan called "Rainbow 5" that was adopted in November 1941, just eighteen days before the Japanese attacked Pearl Harbor, and thirty-five days before Nimitz took command. Given these strategic realities, Nimitz knew he would not be able to count on any significant reinforcement for his Pacific command until the new-construction warships began to slide off the building way in about a year. He would have to fend off the Japanese with what he had: three (soon to be four) aircraft carriers, a dozen cruisers, a few squadrons of destroyers, and the handful of submarines that had been overlooked by the Japanese on December 7. Nimitz would also have control of Task Force 1, made up of the old battleships that survived the Pearl Harbor attack (plus the *Colorado*, which had been undergoing overhaul in Puget Sound), and three more battleships returned to the Pacific from the Atlantic. Given recent events, however, it was unclear just how much of an asset those old battleships would be.[26]*

Nimitz was eager to use the submarines right away. An old submarine hand himself, he held his change-of-command ceremony on board the submarine *Grayling* (SS-209) on the last day of the year. He did so not only because of his longtime association with submarines but also to boost the morale of the so-called silent service. Given the fact that the U.S. had gone to war against Germany in 1917 ostensibly because of Germany's conduct of unrestricted submarine warfare, it is ironic that the first operational command sent out in December 1941 was the one to "EXECUTE UNRESTRICTED SUBMARINE AND AIR WAR AGAINST JAPAN."[27]

Before the war was over, American submarines would take a terrible toll on the Japanese Navy and on her merchant fleet, and play an important role in several major surface actions as well, including Midway. But in the first year of the war, their impact was compromised by the fact that their torpedoes didn't work. The American Mark 14 torpedo was equipped with an advanced magnetic proximity detonator that was designed to run underneath the target vessel and explode when it recognized the iron hull of the

---

* In fact, these old battleships were too slow to operate with the much faster carrier and cruiser forces and needed significant modification even to fulfill their eventual role as shore bombardment vessels.

ship above it. Though no one in the Navy knew it in December 1941, the torpedoes ran eleven feet deeper than the specifications indicated, which was often too deep for the warheads to register the magnetic anomaly of a ship's hull. Even after some sub skippers changed the settings so the torpedoes didn't run so deep, the warheads often failed to detonate. Some torpedoes actually struck an enemy ship only to bounce off the hull with a perceptible metallic clang and sink. Finally, the torpedoes were so erratic that their course was unpredictable, a few of them running in a circle, targeting the sub that had fired them.

There were two explanations for these catastrophic failures. The main one was that the peacetime Bureau of Ordnance had been underfunded during the Depression years, and, since the torpedoes cost ten thousand dollars each, the Bureau forbade live-fire testing. The second explanation was that the cutting-edge magnetic warhead was classified SECRET, and, according to the official postwar history, "security . . . became such a fetish, that measures designed to protect [the magnetic warhead] from enemy eyes actually hid its defects from those who made the regulations." The result was a torpedo that often simply failed to detonate. On the very day that Nimitz arrived in Pearl Harbor, Commander Tyrell D. Jacobs, in command of the submarine *Sargo* (SS-188), fired eight torpedoes at three different ships from close range and scored no hits. He could not believe that he had missed and notified his superiors that there had to be something wrong with the torpedoes. Officers in BuOrd attributed his failure to bad shooting. Even after other skippers reported similar problems, the Bureau continued to insist that it was due to human error and not technical failure. Nimitz himself finally ordered deactivation of the magnetic proximity detonators in June of 1943, eighteen months after the war began.[28]

These were the tools that Nimitz had to hand when he assumed command of the American Pacific Fleet: a battleship fleet that rested on the bottom of Pearl Harbor, three carriers with a theoretical capacity of 264 airplanes, a handful of cruisers and destroyers, and a submarine fleet whose torpedoes did not work. The arrival of the *Yorktown* from the Atlantic would give him a fourth carrier, but because of the Allied commitment to Germany

First, as well as the industrial production schedule, he had little prospect of getting any other meaningful reinforcement anytime soon. In the weeks and months ahead he would have to decide how best to use these tools to contest Japanese domination of the Pacific, careful to preserve what he had, yet not so cautious that he conceded the Pacific to the enemy.

Throughout that period, to all outward appearances, Nimitz maintained a cool, confident demeanor that lifted the spirits of those about him. It was an act, for he was beset by unrelenting anxiety. Though he worked hard all day, at night sleep refused to come. On the day he assumed formal command as CinCPac, he wrote his wife, "I have still not reached the point where I can sleep well because there is so much going on and so much to do." He felt like he was on "a treadmill whirling around actively but not getting anywhere very fast," and even after a month, he confessed to her, "I do feel depressed a large part of the time."[29]

Meanwhile, on the other side of the Pacific, the Japanese celebrated what certainly looked like a decisive victory at Pearl Harbor, and they had already embarked on a campaign to consolidate their triumphs by establishing what they called the Greater East Asia Co-Prosperity Sphere: an empire that stretched from China to the mid-Pacific, and from Alaska to Australia. At the heart of this Japanese success was the group of six Japanese aircraft carriers that had executed the attack on Pearl Harbor, a force known as the Kidō Butai.

## 2

# The Kidō Butai

Translated literally, the Japanese term Kidō Butai means "Mobile Force," though the spirit of the term is better understood as "Attack Force," or "Strike Force." Composed of six large aircraft carriers plus two fast battleships, and screened by a dozen cruisers and destroyers, it was the most powerful concentration of naval air power in the world. The American practice was to operate carriers singly, putting each one at the center of an independent task force as Kimmel had done with the *Saratoga* for the aborted relief mission to Wake Island. That meant that an American task force could put ninety airplanes in the air at most, though sixty was more realistic. With the Kidō Butai, however, the Japanese put all their eggs into one basket, operating six heavy carriers as a single unit that, theoretically at least, could put 412 airplanes aloft at the same time. For the attack on Pearl Harbor, they had launched 350 aircraft.[1]

The man who had conceived that attack was the commander in chief of Japan's Combined Fleet, Admiral Yamamoto Isoroku. A somewhat enigmatic figure in the history of the Pacific war, Yamamoto was neither physically intimidating nor particularly aggressive. At five foot three he barely met the minimum height standard for admission to the naval academy at Eta Jima, and he possessed what one fellow officer called an "almost feminine delicacy," a characterization that was intended as a compliment. He was both keenly intelligent and fiercely ambitious, traits that contributed to his boundless self-confidence. He was also something of a maverick; one recent scholar remarked on his "pronounced individuality." While serving two tours as the Japanese naval attaché in Washington, he had taken courses at Harvard University and traveled extensively throughout the United States. He was one of a very few Japanese naval officers who supported flight training, believing strongly that aviation was key to the future of naval warfare. Subsequently, he commanded both the aircraft carrier *Akagi* (1928–29) and the First Carrier Division (1933–34). He shared at least one characteristic with Chester Nimitz: he had a quiet confidence and austerity that led others to defer to him. One associate noted that "however difficult the question, he always appeared totally unperturbed," though an American officer who knew him before the war claimed, "You could see it if something irritated him for his eyes would become hard and cold."[2]

■ Admiral Yamamoto Isoroku, shown here in his official portrait, was a maverick in the Imperial Japanese Navy who seemed to enjoy imposing his daring plans on the Army and Navy hierarchy. (U.S. Naval Institute)

In other ways, however, Yamamoto was quite different from his dour American counterpart. He was something of a showman, even a show-off, and frequently acted as if he were deliberately tempting fate. With very little encouragement, he would perform daring gymnastic feats, such as standing on his hands on a ship's railing. One of his most salient characteristics was his fondness for (perhaps even obsession with) games of chance. Though he was proficient at games of skill such as *shogi* and chess, he was infatuated with the Japanese game of *go* and American poker. (Chester Nimitz's favorite card game was cribbage.) Yamamoto would bet on almost anything and did so often, sometimes bullying subordinates into betting against him. He could play poker for hours, foregoing sleep and playing literally around the clock. That willingness to tempt fate may also have contributed to his remarkable candor. In a society in which a misspoken word might become the start of a bitter feud, he tended to speak his mind openly even when it offended powerful elements within the government. Indeed, he seemed to relish this risky high-wire act. This last quality was particularly evident during the 1930s when Yamamoto assumed great professional and personal risk by expressing opposition to the political and strategic agenda of the Japanese Army.[3]

It is impossible to understand the origins of the Pacific War without appreciating both the extraordinary influence the Army had on Japanese government policy, and the intensity of the rivalry between the Army and Navy over the direction of that policy. Because the cabinet ministers representing the armed services had to be active-duty officers, the Japanese Army or Navy could topple a government merely by withdrawing its minister. Though the Navy seldom availed itself of this gambit, the Army did—or at least threatened to do so—unless its policies were adopted. The practical result was that by the mid-1930s, the Army effectively controlled the government. Most Navy officers resented this. Yamamoto himself once incautiously referred to "those damn fools in the Army," and as a result some marked him as an obstacle to Japan's emergence as a great power.[4]

Virtually all Japanese Army officers sought to strengthen the armed forces and increase their role in national politics. There was disagreement, however, about how to bring this about. The dominant Army faction was the *Tōseiha* (Control Faction), whose members sought to work within the existing framework of government. But an extremist element known as the *Kōdōha* (Imperial Way Faction) was impatient with the slow pace of change and the perceived obstructionism of the bureaucracy. These "Spirit Warriors" sought to lead the nation to glory by championing an idealized, mythological past. While claiming to revere the emperor, they were also determined that he adopt their expansionist views. They were perfectly willing, even eager, to take unilateral action. In 1931 Japanese soldiers detonated a small explosion near the Japanese-controlled railroad in Manchuria, and the Army used that "attack" as a justification for the occupation of Manchuria. In July 1937 a brief exchange of fire between Chinese and Japanese soldiers near the Marco Polo Bridge provided a pretext for what was called "the China Incident"—in fact, a full-scale war of conquest. Many Army officers also admired the vitality and ambition of Hitler's regime in Germany and advocated a military alliance with the Third Reich. Those who opposed these views risked public criticism and disparagement—or worse, for members of the *Kōdōha* did not shrink from assassinating government ministers whom they saw as trying to thwart their aspirations. More often than not, the assassins were merely chastised rather than punished, as if extreme patriotism somehow excused their actions.

On February 26, 1936, a group of junior Army officers forced their way into the office of the minister of finance and murdered him. They also killed the lord privy seal and the inspector general of education. They invaded the home of Prime Minister Okada Keisuke, intending to assassinate him, too, though in their fervor they inadvertently killed his brother-in-law instead. Their goal, they insisted, was patriotic: to protect the emperor from ministers who did not understand the Imperial Way as Army officers did.*

This time there were consequences. After a series of trials, seventeen of the killers were executed, and other members of the *Kōdōha* were purged

---

* Imperial Navy junior officers attempted a coup of their own in May 1932 when a group of them participated in the assassination of Prime Minister Inukai Tsuyoshi. As in 1926, the long-term result was an effort to placate and appease the dissatisfied junior officers.

from the Army. Even so, the episode did not slow the Army's growing control over policy; having punished the leaders of the February 26 coup, the Army now argued that it had to be even stronger to protect the government from future coup attempts.[5]

The Imperial Army's increasing domination over government policy had disastrous consequences for Japan. Army leaders insisted on resolving the China Incident—that is, completing the conquest of China, an ambition that was jeopardized by a growing scarcity of strategic materials, especially oil. Because Japan's traditional source of oil—the United States—was increasingly unreliable, Japanese leaders convinced themselves that it was necessary to move southward to the oil-rich Dutch East Indies and British Malaya. In August 1936, the government formally adopted a document entitled "Fundamental Principles of National Policy," which established the goal of becoming "in name and in fact a stabilizing power for assuring peace in East Asia, thereby ultimately contributing to the peace and welfare of humanity." The Japanese presented this to the Americans as a kind of Japanese Monroe Doctrine, though in practice it signaled their intent to dominate East Asia and the western Pacific. To prepare for wars in two directions, both the Army and Navy were to be expanded. For the Army this meant more active divisions; for the Navy it meant formal abandonment of the Washington Naval Arms Limitation Treaty. The Imperial Japanese Navy had long resented this agreement, which restricted the Japanese to a battleship force only 60 percent as large as that of either Britain or the United States. Its abandonment now made possible the construction of a new and greatly enlarged fleet, including new battleships and aircraft carriers.[6]

The rivalry in the Army between the *Tōseiha* and the *Kōdōha* was mirrored in the Navy by competition between the so-called treaty faction and the fleet faction. Members of the latter embraced two ideas almost as articles of faith. The first was that the United States was Japan's logical, even inevitable, enemy; and the second was that because war with America was inevitable, it was essential for Japan to maintain a battle force that was at least 70 percent as large as the American battle force. Many officers believed that the 60 percent ratio imposed on them by the Washington Treaty was not only a national insult but also undermined Japan's security, and even her sovereignty. So widespread was this view among junior and middle-grade officers that some admirals feared that taking a contrary position would incite mutiny. The emperor himself worried that the Navy would "no longer be able to control its officers" and was "jeopardizing vital diplomatic issues for the sake of placating subordinate officers."[7]

Because the British and Americans did not build their own navies up to the limits imposed on them by the 1922 treaty, Japan was able to maintain her fleet at a level that was roughly 70 percent that of the United States Navy despite the treaty. It was evident, though, that if the Americans did suddenly decide to expand their Navy to the treaty limits, any serious effort to match that expansion would bankrupt Japan. Therefore, members of the fleet faction sought to overcome America's quantitative advantage by focusing on quality—that is, by building ships of such size and power that they could outrange or overwhelm American battleships. They supported the secret construction of four *Yamato*-class battleships, which, at 73,000 tons each when fully equipped, would be more than twice as big as the largest American battleship. The project was hugely expensive and commanded a disproportionate share of the national budget, but it allowed the champions of the fleet faction to argue that they had an answer to America's numerical and industrial superiority.

Yamamoto was skeptical. Speaking to a class of air cadets in 1934, he compared battleships to the expensive artwork that wealthy Japanese families displayed in their living rooms: they had no particular function, he said, except to serve as "decorations." Yamamoto's rivals in the fleet faction were infuriated. They hadn't forgotten that he had been a delegate to two naval arms limitation conferences, and his two tours as Japan's naval attaché in Washington made him suspect in their eyes. His apostasy concerning the utility of battleships was simply one more reason to distrust and even despise him.[8]

Yamamoto himself was a member of the treaty faction, which also included Navy Minister Yonai Mitsumasa. Yonai and Yamamoto held that the key overall effect of the 1922 treaty was to restrain the United States from using its overwhelming industrial superiority to outbuild the Imperial Navy, which would have placed Japan at a far more disadvantageous position than the treaty did. With the backing of the emperor, Yonai served as prime minister for six months in the first half of 1940. His efforts to promote an accommodation with the Americans were anathema to the *Kōdōha*, however, and he was the target of several assassination attempts. In July 1940, he was replaced by Prince Konoe, who was more sympathetic to the ambitions of the *Kōdōha* and the fleet faction.

The Army was suspicious of Yamamoto, too, and officially assigned a group of men to "guard" him, though their real task was to keep an eye on him. As vice minister of the Navy, Yamamoto lived in constant expectation of being murdered, and he avoided one assassination attempt only by leaving town at the right moment. Indeed, his appointment to command the Combined Fleet in 1939 was engineered by his friends in the hope that sending him to sea would save him from being killed in his bed. The appointment satisfied his enemies in the Army and the fleet faction because it got him out of Tokyo. Yamamoto was aware of the motives behind his appointment, but he did not protest. "I can turn my back on everything else," he wrote to a friend, "and devote myself entirely to naval matters."[9]

Yamamoto took up his new duties as commander in chief of the Combined Fleet on September 1, 1939, the very day Germany invaded Poland marking the beginning of the Second World War in Europe. To those pushing for closer ties with Germany, this was more evidence of the vigor and clear-sightedness of the Nazi regime, and they renewed their advocacy of an alliance with Hitler's government. It had the opposite effect on Yamamoto. Only three days after assuming command, he wrote a fellow admiral, "I shudder as I think of the problem of Japan's relations with Germany and Italy." He was convinced that an alliance with Germany meant war with the West, including the United States, and insisted that "a war between Japan and the United States would be a major calamity." His concerns fell on deaf ears. One year later, Japan signed what became known as the Tripartite Pact with Germany and Italy, and a year after that the Army's domination of the government became complete when General Tōjō Hideki became both war minister and prime minister. By then the descent into war had generated its own unstoppable momentum.[10]

Yamamoto was realistic enough to see that, whatever his own views, once Japan signed the Tripartite Pact war became inevitable, and it was his professional duty to prepare for it. As the government's statement of fundamental principles put it: "Since war with the United States may become unavoidable, sufficient preparations must be made for this eventuality." Just as American naval officers designed their war games around Plan Orange and modeled their summer exercises on imagined confrontations with the Japanese fleet, so, too, did Japanese officers—Yamamoto included—conduct their war games and fleet exercises in the assumption that the U.S. Navy was the likely enemy. As early as 1934, Lieutenant Genda Minoru, who was already emerging as one of the Imperial Navy's most original thinkers, wrote a paper at the Navy Staff College with the title "Naval Armament Essential for the Effective Prosecution of War with the United States."[11]

For Yamamoto, Genda, and other Navy planners, the question was how to structure the Navy so that it could win such a war. The traditional assumption, in Japan as well as in the United States, was that the war would culminate in a classic battleship engagement somewhere in the western Pacific. What the Japanese needed was a way to whittle down the American fleet as it moved toward this inevitable confrontation so that the smaller Japanese battle fleet could emerge victorious. To do that, Japan counted heavily on its fleet submarines and on land-based aircraft. The Japanese vastly improved their submarine capability in part by studying German World War I submarines, and they simultaneously focused on building a new generation of long-range, multiengine aircraft. According to the Japanese war plan, the American warships would be picked off one by one by submarines, or damaged by land-based aircraft operating from a web of island bases, until the opposing fleets were near parity. Massed torpedo attacks by destroyers and cruisers the night before the battle would weaken the Americans further, and in the final battle, superior Japanese fighting spirit (*Yamato damashii*) would determine the outcome.[12]

Yamamoto himself devoted much time and energy to the development of a long-range, land-based bomber. First in 1935 came the Mitsubishi G3M, which the Allies dubbed the "Nell," a big two-engine bomber that at 200 knots (230 mph) had an impressive range of over 3,500 miles, so that it could patrol widely over the central Pacific to search out American warships and damage or sink them. Then in 1939 came the G4M1, which the Allies called the "Betty." The Betty had better armament than the Nell and at 230 knots (265 mph) was slightly faster, but both planes were vulnerable, for in order to increase range, the designers sacrificed both armor and self-sealing fuel tanks. A few Japanese advocates of air power, such as Rear Admiral Inoue Shigeyoshi, believed that land-based aircraft could successfully defend Japan's island empire without the assistance of the fleet. Inoue went so far as to argue for the abolition of both battleships *and* carriers and for investing the nation's treasure exclusively in land-based bombers. Yamamoto would not go that far. He supported the development of land-based aircraft, but he also backed the production of more and bigger aircraft carriers.[13]

Organizationally, Japan's aircraft carriers were grouped into carrier divisions (CarDivs) of two carriers each. CarDiv 1 was composed of Japan's two biggest carriers, the *Kaga* and *Akagi*. Both were accidents of circumstance. The terms of the 1922 Washington Naval Arms Limitation Treaty had allocated the United States and Great Britain a maximum of 525,000 tons of battleships each, while Japan was limited to 315,000 tons. Quite apart from the perceived national humiliation of those limits, one practical problem was that Japan had several new battleships and battle cruisers under construction at the time, and their completion meant Japan would exceed the limits imposed on her by the treaty. That treaty, however, allowed both Japan and the United States to convert two of their big ships into carriers.*

Until then, carriers had been relatively small, displacing 10,000 to 12,000 tons each and carrying only enough airplanes to provide cover for the battleships. But these new carriers were constructed on top of capital-ship

---

* Initially the Japanese had planned to convert the battle cruiser *Amagi* into a carrier, but after the *Amagi* was damaged during a 1923 earthquake, the Japanese were allowed to substitute the even larger battleship *Kaga*. As shown in the next chapter, the Americans did much the same thing with two battle cruisers that they had under construction that subsequently became the carriers *Lexington* (CV-2) and *Saratoga* (CV-3).

hulls, and they were enormous. Displacing over 40,000 tons each when fully loaded, they had flight decks over 800 feet long. Together these two behemoths could carry as many as 182 airplanes. One drawback was that because of their large armored hulls, they were also relatively slow. The sleeker battle-cruiser hull of the *Akagi* allowed her to make a respectable 31 knots, but the heavy armored battleship hull of the *Kaga* kept her to a top speed of 28 knots. This compared unfavorably with the 33-knot speed of America's big carriers.[14]

The 1922 treaty also affected the size and capability of Japan's next carrier, though in a different way. Because *Kaga* and *Akagi* took up such a large percentage of Japan's available tonnage for carriers (81,000 tons), Japanese designers tried to build a carrier that displaced less than 10,000 tons in order to squeeze it in under the treaty's definition of a capital ship. It didn't work. The *Ryūjō*, laid down in 1929 and commissioned in 1933, simply could not accommodate all the necessary functions with so small a hull, and during construction her displacement crept up to 12,500 tons, though this was kept a secret at the time so that Japan would not be found in violation of the treaty.

In December of 1936, when the government formally renounced the Washington Treaty, Japan embarked on a naval expansion program that produced four new big-deck carriers in as many years: the *Sōryū* and the *Hiryū*, each of them displacing just under 20,000 tons when fully loaded and capable of carrying sixty-three airplanes each, and the *Shōkaku* and *Zuikaku*, at 32,000 tons and capable of carrying seventy-two planes each. These last two were commissioned in 1941, only four months before the attack on Pearl Harbor. By the end of 1941, the Japanese had a total of ten carriers, which were collectively capable of carrying over six hundred airplanes.*

The idea that Japan's six biggest carriers should operate as a single task group may have originated with Genda Minoru, a precocious and outspoken advocate of air power, who claimed that he got the idea while watching a

---

* Japan also had three large seaplane tenders (*Ryuho, Chitose,* and *Chiyoda*) that were converted into aircraft carriers after the Battle of Midway. See Appendix A.

U.S. Navy promotional film of all four of America's carriers steaming together. The film was merely a publicity shot for the movie-house newsreels, but Genda saw at once that deploying carriers that way for battle would allow a naval power to apply Mahanian principles of fleet concentration to air warfare. The formal proposal came from Genda's superior, Rear Admiral Ozawa Jisaburō, commander of Carrier Division 1, who proposed in 1940 that all Japanese naval air assets, both land-based and sea-based, be placed under a unified command as the First Air Fleet. Yamamoto was initially cool to the idea, and he was a bit miffed when Ozawa went over his head to propose it directly to the Navy Ministry. But after the Naval General Staff approved it in April, 1941, Yamamoto willingly implemented the new organization. Five months later, when the new *Shōkaku* and *Zuikaku* joined the fleet, he grouped all six of the big carriers into a single command—the Kidō Butai.[15]

The commander of this awesome concentration of naval air power was Vice Admiral Nagumo Chūichi. Four years younger than Yamamoto (the same age difference as between Ernie King and Chester Nimitz), Nagumo was a graduate of the Torpedo School, and for most of his career had been affiliated with the fleet faction, less because of a strong commitment to its ideology than because it was the dominant faction of the Navy leadership and therefore helpful to him professionally. That put him on the opposite

■ Vice Admiral Nagumo Chūichi commanded the six big carriers of the Fleet Striking Force—the Kidō Butai—from the attack on Pearl Harbor through the Battle of Midway. (U.S. Naval Institute)

side of most interservice arguments from Yamamoto and contributed to a strained command relationship with his boss. Moreover, unlike the austere and stoic Yamamoto, Nagumo was a worrier by nature who fretted over even small details. Occasionally he would call junior officers into his office to solicit reassurance from them that things were progressing as they should. His official photograph depicts him staring rather perplexedly into the camera lens as if he were unsure why he was there. Genda was unimpressed with him and asserted that although Nagumo "was thought to be very gallant and brave[.] actually he was very cautious." Yamamoto's chief of staff, Ugaki Matome, agreed, confiding to his diary that Nagumo was insufficiently bold to be a successful commander. "He is not fully prepared yet to advance in the face of death and gain results two or three times as great as his cost by jumping into the jaws of death." Nagumo, in short, was no gambler.[16]

If Nagumo was not prepared to "jump into the jaws of death," Yamamoto was. It was the gambler Yamamoto who conceived of, and then insisted upon, the Pearl Harbor operation. The government made the decision for war in October of 1941. While it was true enough that "those damn fools in the Army" (to repeat Yamamoto's phrase) were the initial champions of war, junior and middle-grade officers of the Imperial Navy's fleet faction proved enthusiastic partners. By 1941 opposing war within the Navy had become, in the words of one admiral, "like rowing a boat against the current . . . above Niagara Falls." To gain access to the resources of South Asia, the plan was to strike south and occupy not only the Dutch East Indies and British Malaya, including its citadel at Singapore, but also the American-held Philippines. The planners accepted the fact that this meant war with Britain, Holland, and the United States, but they were not deterred.[17]

Yamamoto insisted that since Japan was to fight the United States, it was essential to begin with a preemptive strike against the American battle fleet. "The most important thing we have to do first of all in a war with the U.S.," he wrote to the Navy Ministry in January 1941, "is to fiercely attack and destroy the U.S. main fleet at the outset of the war, so that the morale of the U.S. Navy and her people goes down to such an extent that it cannot be recovered." When members of the Naval General Staff balked at so dramatic a move, Yamamoto let it be known that unless his plan was adopted, he and his entire staff would resign. That settled the matter. Though the strategic objective was the resource base in South Asia, the war would begin with an attack on Pearl Harbor, and the instrument of that strike would be the Kidō Butai under Nagumo Chūichi.[18]

When the six carriers of the Kidō Butai departed the Kurile Islands in the far north of Japan for Pearl Harbor, their hangar decks were packed with some of the best combat aircraft in the world. Airplane development in Japan had come a long way in a short time. Though Japan had begun designing and building her own battleships as early as 1910, she did not cast off her dependence on foreign designers and begin to produce her own combat aircraft until 1932. All-metal monoplanes replaced the cloth-covered biplanes that had been the mainstay of Japanese (and American) naval air power. Though the aircraft industry in Japan was putatively private, the government asserted more and more control over production after the beginning of the China Incident in 1937.[19]

The war in China proved both a blessing and a curse for Japanese aircraft design. It gave Japanese designers and engineers a vital testing ground for their combat aircraft. However, the experience also led the Japanese to underestimate the importance of armor protection and to place undue emphasis on range and maneuverability. Most technologies are a product of the culture that spawns them. The decision to minimize the importance of armor derived from a Japanese worldview that valued attack over protection. As a result, Japanese airplanes carried heavy armament but little armor; they could fly long distances on a single tank of fuel, but those fuel tanks were not self-sealing, which meant that a single bullet could ignite an explosion. Japanese combat aircraft were lighter and more nimble and had greater combat range than their Western counterparts, but they were also much more vulnerable.

Another weakness was that even in 1941 much of the work in Japan's aircraft factories was still done piecemeal, by hand. One modern expert estimates that "half of all riveting and one-third of all sheet-metal processing in the Japanese aircraft industry was done by hand." That was due in part to the fact that Japan was still industrializing in the 1930s, but another major factor was the Japanese preference for quality over quantity. It seemed more important to them to have one hundred airplanes of the highest quality than two hundred that were merely adequate.[20]

This mindset helped make Japan's carrier airplanes among the best in the world, and this in turn contributed to the decision to go to war with the United States in the first place. It also meant that once the war began, Japan would be unable to produce replacement airplanes quickly or in large numbers. During 1941, even as Japan prepared to start a war that had already been decided upon, its aviation industry was producing only about 162 airplanes a month. By contrast, Roosevelt called for the construction of 4,000 planes a month in 1942, and by the following year U.S. plants were turning out 10,000 planes a month. Japanese industry was simply incapable of matching such productivity.* In December of 1941, however, Japan's leaders ignored this inherent weakness. Like Confederate soldiers in 1861 who believed that one Reb could whip five Yanks, they were convinced that *Yamato damashii* could overcome both numbers and industrial superiority. "You could quote them figures till you were blue in the face," one officer remembered later of the Japanese high command, "but they'd have none of it." This is what Navy Captain Ōi Atsushi meant when he wrote after the war, "The Japanese people are romantic and illogical."[21]

Japan's 1,800 frontline carrier aircraft in 1941 were divided into three types: dive-bombers, carrier attack planes (which could carry either bombs or a torpedo), and fighters. The dive-bomber was the Aichi D3A1 Type 99, nicknamed the "Val" by Allied naval intelligence.** A two-seat monoplane, with a pilot in front and a radioman/gunner in the rear seat, the Val carried one 250-kilogram (551-pound) bomb and two smaller (60 kg) bombs under

---

* During 1942, the United States built 47,836 airplanes to Japan's 8,861. Over the course of the war, the United States built more than four times as many combat airplanes as Japan: 324,750 to Japan's 76,320.

** Though the Allied code names for Japanese aircraft did not come into use until 1943, these code names will be used throughout the text for the sake of clarity.

the wings. It borrowed some design elements from Japan's new ally, having an elliptical wing like the German Heinkel and fixed landing gear like the Stuka. It proved a very reliable weapon in China against ground targets and weak opposition, but its indifferent speed of 205 knots (242 mph) would make it vulnerable to American fighters in the war to come.

More impressive, and more central to Japanese doctrine, was the Nakajima B5N2 Type 97 carrier attack plane, which the Allies dubbed the "Kate." The Kate could function as a level bomber, but it was deadliest when used as a torpedo plane. Indeed, it was very likely the best torpedo plane in the world. It had a crew of three and could handle a bomb load of over 800 kilograms (1,764 pounds), which meant that it could carry either a heavy fragmentation bomb for attacks against land targets or the new Type 91 aerial torpedo. Though the Americans had not used live torpedoes in peacetime training because of the expense, the Japanese did, and this led to improvements that paid off in wartime. The Type 91 torpedo boasted

■ The Japanese B5N2 Type 97 carrier attack plane, called the "Kate" by the allies, was the best torpedo plane in the world in 1942, especially when carrying the big Type 91 aerial torpedo, seen here. (U.S. Naval Institute)

wooden tailfins that kept it stabilized during the air drop and then broke away when it hit the water. It traveled at a speed of 42 knots (nearly 10 knots faster than American torpedoes) and had great accuracy thanks to an internal gyroscope. The one weakness of the airplane that carried this powerful weapon was that, like most other Japanese combat airplanes, the Kate was mostly unarmored, so that while it packed an impressive offensive punch, even minor damage was often fatal.[22]

The third component of the Japanese carrier triad was the Mitsubishi A6M2 Type 00 fighter. Officially the Americans named this the "Zeke," but nearly everyone called it by the name that is remembered by history: the Zero. This iconic airplane of the Pacific war came about because of Japan's desire to provide bombers in China with long-range fighter support. In the fall of 1937, the Japanese set out to build a monoplane fighter with both longer range and heavier weapons. When it debuted in 1940, the Zero was a zippy little sports car of a fighter. It had not only a longer range than any other fighter—even land-based fighters—but it could climb faster and turn sharper. Moreover, in addition to its two machine guns, it carried two 20 mm cannon in the wings, which meant that like the Kate it packed a terrific offensive punch. One problem was that these cannon fired only sixty rounds before running out, making extended combat operations difficult unless the pilots hoarded their ammunition. On some occasions, the Zeros had to land to reload after a relatively short flight. And while the Zero had an impressive maximum speed of 287 knots (330 mph), its light airframe meant that it could not dive as fast as the sturdier American fighters; American pilots learned that the best way to escape a Zero on their tail was to dive straight down. Nonetheless, Japanese pilots reveled in the acrobatic abilities of their nimble little fighter plane, and early in the war they had an unmistakable advantage over their American counterparts, especially at low altitudes. But once again their lack of armor made them vulnerable. Like so many Japanese combat planes, the Zero was all offense and no defense.[23]

It is noteworthy that the men who flew these planes off the decks of Japanese carriers were mostly enlisted men—warrant officers and petty officers—and not commissioned officers, as was common in the U.S. Navy. This is especially curious because the Japanese Navy had a higher overall percentage of officers than the U.S. Navy. Yet until 1938, the number of graduates from the Japanese naval academy at Eta Jima who chose aviation was quite small. Pilots were thought of mainly as technicians, and such technical skill was held to be only marginally relevant to the burden of command. This changed after 1938. By then most Eta Jima graduates who were physically qualified were being reserved for aviation service. When war began in late 1941, these officers were still relatively junior, and, during the war, the Imperial Japanese Navy suffered a dearth of middle-grade officers—lieutenant commanders and commanders—who had both flight training and combat experience. The few who did became squadron commanders. Most of the pilots they commanded, however, were warrant officers or petty officers.[24]

For an enlisted sailor, there were two paths to becoming a carrier pilot. One was the Pilot Trainee System, in which petty officers or seamen under the age of 24 could apply for flight training. The acceptance rate was very small. As in the production of the airplanes themselves, the selection of young men for pilot training focused on ensuring quality rather than quantity. To those who ran the programs, it seemed more important to keep out the undeserving than to encourage the marginal. The historian John Lundstrom notes that for the class of 1937, of fifteen hundred applicants, only seventy were selected for training, and only twenty-five graduated.[25]

The other source of Navy pilots was the Flight Reserve Enlisted Trainee System. In the mid-1930s the Japanese concluded that taking sailors who were already trained in surface warfare and making pilots of them wasted valuable training. As a result they began to draw aviation candidates directly from civilian life, often teenagers from the equivalent of junior high or high school. In addition to flight training, these candidates got three years of classroom education, so that their experience resembled that of students at Eta Jima, though they graduated as petty officers rather than as commissioned officers. Moreover, their numbers remained small. As in the Pilot Trainee Program, until 1938 the Japanese focused on making flight training as fierce as possible in order to wash out marginal performers. Pilots trained in small classes of only four men each. After 1941, with war looming, instructors were allowed to teach eight at a time, and by 1943 they were teaching twelve. By then, however, it was too late to make up for lost time. By then, too, many of the best instructors were either at sea operating with the carriers or had already been lost in combat. The result was that while Japan began the war with a cadre of very highly skilled and intensively trained pilots, there was no established program to add large numbers of new pilots to the fleet as the war went on. In part this was another result of the commitment to quality over quantity, and it was also the product of the Japanese assumption that the war with the United States would not last very long. That assumption led to the conclusion that it was more important to have this cadre of highly skilled pilots at the outset than to have large numbers of indifferent pilots for the long run. When the war began, the Japanese had a total of about 3,500 superbly trained and experienced naval aviators, about 90 percent of them enlisted men. (The American pool of aviators was larger, but many of them were still in training programs, and none had the combat experience of their Japanese counterparts.) The Japanese thus bet on quality triumphing over quantity, but they also gambled that the war would be a short one, for they had very little in reserve.[26]

This, then, was the Kidō Butai: the ships, the planes, and the pilots that struck at Pearl Harbor on December 7, 1941. Throughout the country, the Japanese celebrated the apparent success of that raid, though Yamamoto was disappointed that Nagumo had been content to hit and run instead of "completely destroying Pearl Harbor." Not only had the attack missed the American carriers, it had left untouched the American submarine base and especially the oil-tank farm—valuable resources that the Americans would have found it difficult to replace—though such targets were not part of Nagumo's initial assignment. Despite misgivings about him, Nagumo remained in command of the Kidō Butai because, as Ugaki put it, "the navy had no other adequate candidate."[27]

During the four months after Pearl Harbor, the Kidō Butai burnished its reputation further, as those months witnessed a dizzying string of Japanese successes that fed what historians later labeled "victory disease" in Japan, and caused lots of hand-wringing in Washington. And it was not just the Kidō Butai. Perhaps the most chilling event of this period for the

Allies was the loss of the Royal Navy battleship *Prince of Wales,* just arrived in the Far East after a lengthy high-speed cruise from the Atlantic, and her consort, the battle cruiser *Repulse,* both sunk on December 10 by land-based Japanese bombers staged out of Indochina. Though Japanese carrier bombers and torpedo planes had sunk or damaged eight U.S. battleships in Pearl Harbor, those ships had been at anchor. The sinking of the *Prince of Wales* and *Repulse* while they were alert, manned, and under way was proof that airplanes could indeed sink battleships.[28]

In the subsequent weeks and months, Japanese forces landed in the Philippines, on the Malay Peninsula, and on Borneo, Sumatra, and Java. Thailand surrendered on December 9; Hong Kong fell on Christmas Day; Manila on January 2; and, most shocking of all, the supposedly impregnable citadel at Singapore fell on February 15. The Kidō Butai attacked Darwin, Australia, on February 19. After that, the giant *Kaga* headed back to Japan for a refit after striking a submerged reef off Palau, but the other five carriers of the Kidō Butai, along with a substantial escort, steamed into the Indian Ocean. In the wake of this rampage, the Japanese conquered an island empire of more than ten thousand square miles and secured the resource base that they hoped would make them self-reliant and invulnerable. More cautious observers within the Japanese leadership might have noted that most of these dramatic naval victories had been raids—hit-and-run strikes— that the American battle fleet in Pearl Harbor had been at anchor, and that the *Prince of Wales* and *Repulse* had lacked air cover. It was hardly the time for carping, however, for the Kidō Butai and its unlikely commander had become the absolute master of the seas. In the early spring of 1942, the Japanese decision to go to war with Britain, Holland, and the United States seemed not "romantic and illogical" but shrewd—even brilliant.

# 3

# The Brown Shoe Navy

A nd what of the American carriers? Where were they during this rampage by the Kidō Butai? In January of 1942 there were three American carriers in the Pacific. Two of them were big, oversize carriers equivalent to the Japanese *Kaga* and *Akagi*—and for much the same reason. They had been laid down as battle cruisers in 1916 as part of America's buildup for possible involvement in World War I. By the time the United States entered the war in 1917, it had become clear that the most urgent need was for destroyers to protect the convoys, and the United States halted work on the big warships to concentrate on escorts. When the war ended, their big hulls lay unfinished on the building ways. American sponsorship of the 1922 Washington Naval Arms Limitation Treaty made it clear that they would never be completed as battle cruisers, and like the Japanese, the U.S. converted two of them into carriers, naming them for battles of the American Revolution: the *Lexington* (CV-2) and the *Saratoga* (CV-3). At 50,000 tons each, they were even larger than *Kaga* and *Akagi* and capable of carrying as many as ninety airplanes each.*

In addition to these two behemoths, the United States had five other carriers on the Navy List. Two of them, *Ranger* (CV-4) and *Wasp* (CV-7), were smaller ships, generally equivalent to the Japanese *Sōryū* and *Hiryū*, but three of them, *Yorktown* (CV-5), *Enterprise* (CV-6), and *Hornet* (CV-8), were all relatively new, purpose-built carriers that displaced just under 20,000 tons empty and about 25,500 tons with their embarked air group of 60 to 80 planes, which made them roughly comparable to the Japanese *Shōkaku* and *Zuikaku*.

Had all five of America's big carriers been deployed as a unit, they would have made a worthy opponent for the Kidō Butai. The United States, however, faced a two-ocean war, and consequently only one of those new carriers—the *Enterprise*—was in the Pacific. Until April 1941, the *Yorktown* had been there too, but that month Roosevelt had ordered her to the Atlantic to beef up the so-called neutrality patrols against Nazi U-boats. For its part, the *Hornet* was so new that, although she was commissioned in October, six weeks before Pearl Harbor, her final fitting-out kept her in Norfolk, Virginia, until March of 1942. In addition, both of the smaller carriers (*Ranger* and *Wasp*) were also in the Atlantic. Until the *Yorktown* returned to the Pacific and the *Hornet* was fitted out, Nimitz would have only three carriers: the *Lexington* and *Saratoga*, and the smaller but newer *Enterprise*.[1]

Nimitz kept them busy, putting each at the center of a task force that conducted nearly constant patrols north, west, and south of Hawaii. In addition to the carrier, each task force had two or three cruisers and a squadron of destroyers to provide a screen, plus a fleet oiler to keep the warships (especially the fuel-guzzling destroyers) under way. A task force of one carrier, three cruisers, and six destroyers burned up 5,800 barrels of oil every day—and more when conducting high-speed flight operations. Throughout the

---

* America's only other carrier at the time was the small converted collier *Langley* (CV-1). Thirteen steel girders supported a 523-foot-long flight deck some forty feet above her hull, giving her the appearance of a long building with a flat roof and no walls. This gave rise to her nickname, "The Old Covered Wagon." In 1937, she was converted into a seaplane tender (AV-3).

Pacific War, fought as it was over a huge expanse of ocean, it was critical for both sides to pay close attention to the fueling needs of their warships; the loss of an oiler could severely restrict the operating capabilities of an entire task force.[2]

The commanding officers of these task forces were a disparate lot, and only one of them was a brown shoe. When Congress created the Bureau of Aeronautics (BuAir) in 1921, it had mandated that all Navy flight squadrons were to be commanded by qualified pilots. In addition, a Navy board had recommended (but did not require) that only qualified aviators should command carriers. Because of that, a number of ambitious black-shoe officers, including several who were quite senior, applied for pilot training in order to have access to these new commands. Veteran pilots considered them opportunists and scornfully referred to them as "Johnny-come-latelys." Even worse, from their point of view, other senior officers who never completed pilot training at all still managed to qualify for carrier command by going through a four-week familiarization program in Pensacola, Florida, to become "naval observers." These men wore silver wings rather than gold, and though they were not certified to fly, they *were* authorized to command flight units, including carriers. Behind their backs, the pilots called them "kiwis" after the flightless New Zealand bird. Opportunism and careerism may have been factors for many, but some Johnny-come-latelys underwent a genuine conversion. One who did was William F. Halsey.[3]

Halsey graduated from the Naval Academy in 1904, three years behind King and a year ahead of Nimitz. Like most officers of his generation, he had spent most of his career as a surface warfare officer, serving aboard the battleship *Kansas* during the world-circling cruise of Teddy Roosevelt's Great White Fleet in 1907–9, and commanding destroyers during World War I. He commanded several more destroyers after the war until he was assigned to the Naval Academy in 1927 to take charge of the *Reina Mercedes*, a prize from the Spanish-American War that the Navy had turned into a training vessel for midshipmen. In that capacity, Halsey was responsible for all of the Academy's floating property, including its small seaplane squadron. Eager to learn something about this new service, he asked the squadron's young commander, Lieutenant Dewitt "Duke" Ramsey, to take him on a flight. More flights followed, some with Captain Halsey at the controls. "My whole naval career changed right then," Halsey wrote later. "I became fascinated with it. . . . Soon I was eating, drinking, and breathing aviation." Halsey was so excited by the potential of this new service that he applied for flight training at the end of his Naval Academy tour. He was hugely disappointed when he failed the eye test.[4]

After a year as a student at the Naval War College in Newport, Rhode Island, and another at the Army War College at Fort McNair in Washington, D.C., Halsey received an offer from King, then serving as chief of the Bureau of Aeronautics, to command the carrier *Saratoga* if he completed the short observer's course at Pensacola. Once he got there, however, Halsey managed to get himself transferred into the full pilot training program despite his age and his poor eyesight; he earned his gold wings as a 52-year-old grandfather. In January of 1942, he was the only vice admiral in the Navy who was a naval aviator. Officially he was commander, Aircraft Battle Force; operationally, he was the commanding officer of Task Force 8, built around the carrier *Enterprise.* Halsey did not command the ship itself—that responsibility fell to the ship's captain, George D. Murray, a career naval aviator who had earned his gold wings in 1915. Murray was responsible for the day-to-day management of the vessel and its crew. Halsey was a kind of

■ Vice Admiral William F. Halsey sports gold wings on the breast of his forest-green aviator's uniform. Note the cigarette in his right hand. (U.S. Naval Institute)

passenger on the *Enterprise*, having a suite of rooms known as flag quarters in the island amidships, and dispensing orders through a staff.

As a midshipman at the Academy, Halsey had played fullback on the football team and he possessed something of a fullback's attitude. He was direct, often blunt, occasionally profane, and utterly fearless. Some thought his facial features resembled those of a bulldog, and not only did that give him his nickname, it added to his reputation for ferocity. To balance that, he was outgoing and gregarious, a bit of a showman and, like Yamamoto, willing to speak his mind openly. Once the war began, he became a favorite of newspaper reporters, who counted on him to provide some fiery rhetoric for their columns. He seldom let them down. After Pearl Harbor, he claimed that he had always distrusted "Japs," and vowed that by the time he was through with them, the Japanese language would be spoken only in hell.[5]

The most senior of Nimitz's task-force commanders was Vice Admiral Wilson Brown, who was in charge of Task Force 11, built around the big carrier *Lexington*. Brown was three years older than Halsey or Nimitz, having graduated from the Academy in the class of 1902. Brown was, in the words of one modern scholar, "an intelligent paragon of old school formality." In the 1902 yearbook, *Lucky Bag*, his classmates described him as "modest and unassuming . . . with a sweet voice and a sweeter smile." In short, he was a dramatic contrast to Halsey in almost every way. Like Halsey, however, Brown had started out in destroyers and commanded the destroyer *Parker* in the First World War. After the war, while Halsey was still commanding destroyers, Brown occupied a series of staff positions, including a tour as naval aide to President Calvin Coolidge. When Halsey underwent flight training, Brown remained in the black-shoe community and commanded the battleship *California*, then served a tour as the superintendent of the Naval Academy, a position in which his headmasterly qualities served him well. In February of 1941, ten months before Pearl Harbor, he was promoted to vice admiral and made commanding officer of the Scouting Force. His health was suspect. Though only a few years older than Nimitz and Halsey, he looked at least a decade older. Thin and pallid, he had a slight tremor that caused his head to twitch, leading irreverent junior officers to dub him "Shaky" Brown. As events would show, he was an intelligent and thoughtful officer, but he lacked the boldness and the energetic self-confidence of Bull Halsey.[6]

The third of Nimitz's task-force commanders was Rear Admiral Herbert Fairfax Leary, who commanded the *Saratoga* group, dubbed Task Force 14. Leary was another black shoe, a 1905 classmate of Nimitz, a tall, thin, lantern-jawed man whose tenure was destined to be short. On January 11, a month after Pearl Harbor, the *Saratoga* was operating near Johnston Island five hundred miles southwest of Hawaii in seas so rough that Leary cancelled flight operations for the day. Waves broke over the bow and washed the flight deck. At 7:00 that evening, in the midst of the storm, a terrific explosion jolted the big carrier. A pilot on board said, "It felt like the whole ship had been moved about five feet." A Japanese submarine, the I-6, had slipped through the screen of cruisers and destroyers and delivered a deadly Type 95 torpedo. The blast killed six men and flooded three fire rooms. Though the Japanese submarine skipper reported to Tokyo that he had sunk a *Saratoga*-class carrier, the big flattop managed to stay afloat and steam back to Pearl Harbor under her own power, arriving on January 15. Nimitz saw that the necessary repairs could not be completed in Hawaii and two days later reluctantly ordered her back to Bremerton, Washington.[7]

That loss would have reduced Nimitz to only two carrier groups but for the return to the Pacific that same week of the USS *Yorktown*. After Pearl Harbor, *Yorktown* had been rushed into dry dock in Norfolk for a quick overhaul, and by December 16 she was en route back to the Pacific. After passing through the Panama Canal, she arrived in San Diego at the end of the month. There she joined the heavy cruiser *Louisville*, a light cruiser, and half a dozen destroyers, plus the essential oiler, to comprise Task Force 17. To command this new task force, Nimitz picked a man he knew well and who had commanded the *Saratoga* task force during the aborted relief expedition to Wake Island: Rear Admiral Frank Jack Fletcher.

Fletcher was yet another black shoe, having served in cruisers and destroyers for most of his thirty-six-year career. Graduating from the Naval Academy in 1906, one year after Nimitz and two years after Halsey, Fletcher had been a cruiser and battleship man from the start; his most recent sea service was the command of Cruiser Division 6. Called "Fletch" or "Flap Jack" while at the Academy, he had what the *Lucky Bag* called "a sunny disposition" and the habit of gesturing with his hands while talking. He was well decorated, having received a Medal of Honor as a lieutenant during the Navy's expedition to Vera Cruz in 1914 (an honor somewhat diluted by the fact that the Navy had handed out no fewer than fifty-five Medals of Honor for that expedition, passing them out, as one critic put it, "like crackerjack charms"). More important was the fact that Fletcher was well connected. He had served as naval aide to Secretary of the Navy Claude Swanson in the early 1930s and as assistant chief of the Bureau of Navigation under Nimitz in the late '30s. A biographer concedes that Fletcher's "personal connections with the decision-makers of the war set him ahead of others for important assignments." It was natural that the brown-shoe pilots on the *Yorktown* would feel an intense curiosity about their new boss.[8]

What they saw was an unremarkable man with a plain, open face, thinning dark hair, a generous nose, and dark eyes. Fletcher was neither flamboyant and outgoing like Halsey nor reserved and professorial like Wilson Brown. He was instead a straightforward, competent professional whose tight-lipped expression suggested the no-nonsense skepticism of a Midwestern farmer, which was fitting, as he had been born and reared in Iowa.

■ Though Rear Admiral Frank Jack Fletcher was a "black shoe" admiral—a surface warfare specialist—he commanded U.S. forces in both of the major carrier battles of the first six months of the Pacific war: Coral Sea and Midway. (U.S. Naval Institute)

He even smoked corncob pipes that he had shipped to him from the States a dozen at a time. Reporters seldom badgered him for interviews because he was not inclined to bloodthirsty pronouncements. Given his long service in battleships and cruisers, Fletcher would have preferred to make the heavy cruiser *Louisville* his flagship, but Nimitz wanted his task-force commanders to ride the carrier, and so in San Diego on New Year's Day, 1942 (the day after Nimitz took formal command in Pearl Harbor), the black shoe Fletcher broke his flag on USS *Yorktown*. Fletcher may have felt somewhat out of place on board the big flattop. One historian suggests that "he was the proverbial stranger in a strange land."[9]

The captain of the *Yorktown* was 52-year-old Elliott Buckmaster. Tall and handsome, Buckmaster was also quiet and reserved, even cold—though, as with Nimitz, that first impression often changed after close association. Buckmaster was a brown shoe with gold wings on his chest, but he was also a Johnny-come-lately, having passed the aviation course only five years before as a full commander. His first aviation assignment had been as executive officer (second in command) on the *Lexington*, and he had little experience as a carrier pilot. Perhaps because of this, the *Yorktown*'s executive officer, Commander Joseph "Jocko" Clark, who did have significant flight experience, was skeptical of both his commanding officer and the task-force commander. An acolyte of Ernie King, Clark thought that Fletcher and Buckmaster failed to enforce the kind of discipline he admired. That assessment, however, said more about Clark than it did about either Fletcher or Buckmaster. Clark found a lot to complain about on the *Yorktown*, writing later, "Yorktown's hopeless department heads needed a lot of King's brand of discipline." It was probably just as well that Clark did not stay long on the *Yorktown*, though when he returned to Washington after his promotion to captain, he continued to disparage the *Yorktown* and her officers, including Fletcher, and over the subsequent months his comments very likely affected King's assessment of both the ship and the task-force commander.[10]

Nimitz had hoped that the arrival of the *Yorktown* would give him four carrier groups, and the ability to begin a meaningful counterattack against the Japanese, but the loss of the *Saratoga* meant that he would have to carry on with only three: the big *Lexington* and the newer sister ships, *Enterprise* and *Yorktown*.[11]

On board those three carriers, the Americans, like the Japanese, relied on three kinds of combat airplanes. The workhorse American carrier bomber was the SBD Douglas Dauntless, a relatively new (1940) monoplane with a crew of two: a pilot in the front seat, almost always a commissioned officer, and an enlisted radioman/gunner who sat behind him and was responsible for communications as well as a .30-caliber machine gun, later increased to movable twin machine guns. Compared with the Japanese Val dive-bomber, the Dauntless was both bigger and sturdier, and its pilots referred to it affectionately as "the barge." Though the Dauntless was 25 percent heavier than the Val (thanks in part to its armor protection), it nevertheless had a slightly greater range because of its more powerful engine. It could also carry a bigger bomb load, consisting of either one 1,000-pound bomb or a 500-pound bomb plus two 100-pound bombs under the wings. The Dauntless was marginally faster than the Val, though slower than Japanese fighters. Officially, its top speed was 217 knots (250 mph), but it cruised at 130 knots (152 mph) and attained maximum speed only during an attack dive, when it might reach 250 knots (288 mph). (Its pilots joked that SBD stood for "Slow but Deadly.") The Dauntless also boasted two .50-caliber machine guns in the cowling, and on occasion it was used to augment the combat air patrol (CAP).[12]

The idea behind dive-bombing was for the pilot to approach his intended target at high altitude, say 20,000 feet, and preferably from out of the sun to avoid detection. To spot the target, the SBD had a small glass window in the floor beneath the pilot's seat, although it was rarely usable due to oil thrown off by the plane's engine. After lining up on the target as best he could, the squadron leader deployed perforated "dive brakes" on the trailing edge of his wings and went into a steep dive, around 70 degrees, with the pilots of his squadron following his lead. During the dive, the pilots felt weightless, "like you were floating," as one put it. The Dauntless did not have shoulder straps, only a seat belt, so it was "like you were hanging out on a string." Between 2,000 and 1,500 feet, the pilot released his bomb by pulling back on a bomb release lever. When he did that, it was instinctive to pull back on the control stick at the same time, and that often threw the bomb off line. To prevent this, newer SBDs were equipped with an electric trigger that allowed the pilot to release the bomb merely by pushing a button on top of the control stick. Then he pulled out of the dive, usually doing a "snap pullout" that sometimes resulted in his briefly blacking out.[13]

Dive bombing an enemy ship that was twisting and turning at 25 or 30 knots was, as one pilot recalled, "similar to dropping a marble from eye height on a scampering cockroach." It was especially difficult because often during these steep dives, the windscreen would fog up at about 8,000 feet, all but obscuring the target. One pilot said it was "like putting a white sheet in front of you and you have to bomb from memory." "Believe me," he recalled, "that's a helpless feeling when you try to dive bomb and [can] hardly see your target." All in all, it was both a physical and mental challenge to dive almost three miles straight down at nearly three hundred miles an hour with a fogged windscreen and with the target ship throwing up a wall of antiaircraft fire.[14]

It was equally challenging for the enlisted man in the back seat, whose job during the dive was to call out the readings from the altimeter, especially important when the windscreen was fogged and the pilot could not see. The backseat crewman was also the radio operator and gunner. When the pilot released the bomb and pulled out of the dive, the rear-seat gunner was pushed down into his seat with, as one recalled, "a force of one ton at eight G's," or eight times the force of gravity. Nonetheless, he had plenty to do. "Then the pilot tells you to go on the air, or switch to the homing frequency, or give hand signals to nearby crews in Morse code. All of this requires securing the guns, reaching forward, changing radio coils, and moving dials accurately and quickly." Morse-code messages were sent by hand signal in order to maintain radio silence. The radiomen/gunners smacked their palm with their fist for a dot and slapped open handed for a dash. Those in nearby planes had to watch this and translate to their pilots. It required both intense concentration and a strong stomach to perform all these tasks flawlessly.[15]

Dauntless dive-bombers made up about half of an American carrier's complement of sixty to eighty airplanes and were divided into two squadrons: one was officially a "scouting squadron" and the other a "bombing squadron." Each squadron carried a numerical designation that bound the pilots, gunners, and crew into a unit. Every American air squadron was first designated by the letter V (which simply meant that it involved heaVier-than-air aircraft). The scouting squadron bore the additional designation S and the bombing squadron B, followed by the hull number of the carrier to which it was assigned. Thus the scouting squadron on the *Lexington* (CV-2) was VS-2, and the bombing squadron was VB-2. Colloquially, these units were known as "Scouting Two" and "Bombing Two."

The men in these units developed a bond akin to the men in an infantry company, though the fact that the pilots were mostly officers and the rear-seat gunners were all enlisted men sometimes made for an awkward partnership. While in the air, the junior officer pilots depended heavily on their enlisted gunners, literally trusting them with their lives, yet aboard ship they were all but strangers. The gunners never came into the wardroom and seldom ventured into the squadron ready rooms except for "special sessions." They never played cards with the pilots or sat around with them to "shoot the shit." In the air, the relationship was fraternal and interdependent; on the ship, each man went his separate way. The gunners called the pilots "sir" or "mister," and the pilots referred to the gunners by their last names only. As one pilot put it, "Pilots were treated as one class, gunners were treated as another class." Another recalled, "We hardly ever got to talk to our gunners until we were ready to climb into the cockpits." If they accidentally ran into each other aboard ship, there might be a moment of awkwardness. One pilot recalled seeing a group of gunners reloading machine gun ammunition belts and noticed that their conversation became instantly more profane as if "they were trying to impress me with how tough they thought they were."[16]

In addition to the scouting and bombing squadrons, each American carrier also had a torpedo plane squadron (whose designation was VT), though both the planes and the torpedoes they carried were markedly inferior to their Japanese counterparts. The plane was the TBD-1 Douglas Devastator, which like the Japanese Kate could be used either as a level bomber or a torpedo plane, in which role it carried the Mark 13 torpedo, a smaller aerial version of the trouble-plagued Mark 14 used by U.S. submarines. The

Devastator had been designed and built in the 1930s for a crew of three: a pilot in front, an enlisted bombardier/navigator in the middle seat, and a radioman/gunner in the back. When carrying a torpedo, however, there was no need for a bombardier, and so the middle seat was often empty. The Devastator was state of the art when it had joined the fleet in 1937, but it was already nearing obsolescence by 1942. Heavy at 10,000 pounds, it was agonizingly slow. Officially, it had a top speed of 206 knots (237 mph), although in practice it seldom exceeded 160 knots (184 mph), and cruised at just over 100 knots (115 mph). One pilot claimed later that when carrying the 2,200-pound Mark 13 torpedo, the Devastator actually cruised at no more than 80 knots (92 mph) or "with the nose down maybe 100." When climbing, the Devastator was even slower. One pilot joked that while carrying a torpedo in a climb, the Devastator "practically backs up." Even at such slow speeds, the Devastator had a limited range of a little over 400 miles which meant, accounting for assembly time over the task force and maneuvering over the target, that it could attack only those targets within about 175 miles. That assumed that the pilot did not need to search for the target.[17]

To launch their cumbersome weapons, pilots of the Devastator torpedo plane flew to their intended target at a fairly low level, between 1,500 and 4,000 feet, then dropped even lower for the run into the target. At only 100 to 150 feet, they throttled back to near stalling speed to release their torpedo so that it did not break apart when it hit the water. The release was crucial, for if the torpedo hit the water with its nose down, it might dive too deep to have any effect; if it hit with the nose up, it could "porpoise" along the surface. Since the torpedoes ran at 33.5 knots, which was only marginally faster than the ships they targeted, it was essential for the pilot to come in fairly close before dropping his "fish." Even then he had to lead the target a little, and since the target was also maneuvering, it often took more than one pass to get a satisfactory angle on the bow. It took great concentration and a cool disregard for danger to fly a Devastator into its target, or to man the rear-seat machine gun, sitting backward and fending off swarming enemy fighters while the pilot lined up for a shot.[18]

By far the most serious problem with American torpedo bombing, however, was the simple fact that, like the Mark 14 used by American submarines,

■ A Douglas TBD Devastator from the *Enterprise* flies over Wake Island in 1942. The Devastator was both old and slow and therefore an easy target for the swift Japanese Zeros. (U.S. Naval Institute)

the warheads on the Mark 13 did not always function as advertised, and the torpedoes themselves were so delicate that when dropped at an elevation above fifty feet or at a speed greater than 110 knots they could easily be damaged upon impact with the water, meaning that they would fail to work at all. These facts were overlooked for far too long—for several reasons. One was that, as with submarine skippers, the brass at BuOrd simply refused to believe that the weapon was flawed and attributed failures to bad shooting. A few Devastator pilots contributed to this conclusion by reporting that they had scored a hit with the Mark 13 torpedo when they had not. Pilots who saw the wake of their torpedo lead right into an enemy ship understandably reported a hit, and with bombs sometimes exploding all around the target at the same time, it was easy to conclude that one of the explosions was the result of a torpedo strike. Finally, analysts in Washington who examined the damage reports of American ships in Pearl Harbor knew full well that the Japanese had great success with their aerial torpedoes, and they were simply reluctant to believe that Japanese torpedo technology was superior. Devastator pilots and their gunners would pay a high price for this unwillingness to acknowledge a technical problem.

As for American fighter planes, they were still a work in progress in early 1942. The U.S. Navy had adopted its first single-seat monoplane fighter only three years earlier. It was the Brewster F2A, named the "Buffalo," an appropriate designation given its aerodynamic performance. While an improvement over the Grumman F3F biplane that it replaced, it was small (5,000 pounds), stubby (26 feet long), and relatively slow for a fighter (260 knots, or 300 mph). After the Battle of Midway, one veteran pilot wrote in his after-action report that the Buffalo "is not a combat aeroplane. . . . Any commander that orders pilots out for combat in an F2A-3 should consider the pilot as lost before leaving the ground." Though quite a few Buffaloes remained on active service when the war began—as did a number of Grumman biplanes—a newer plane, the Grumman F4F, called the "Wildcat," replaced both models in early 1942. The F4F-3, which was the first version to reach the fleet, was longer (30 feet) and heavier (7,000 pounds) than the Buffalo, and, with a top speed of 287 knots (331 mph), much faster. Though it was still markedly inferior to the Japanese Zero in maneuverability, Navy pilots nevertheless liked the sturdy F4F-3, which had two .50-caliber machine guns in each wing.[19]

The designers were still tinkering. Within months, a newer version of the Wildcat, the F4F-4 (which the pilots called the "Dash 4") came into service. The newer version had folding wings so that more of them could be fitted into the confined spaces on the hangar deck and more could be spotted on the flight deck for an attack. Moreover, instead of four machine guns, the Dash 4 Wildcat had six. As far as the pilots were concerned, however, these changes were a mixed blessing. The folding wings meant that about 50 percent more fighters could be placed on each carrier, thus increasing the size of the VF squadrons from eighteen to twenty-seven, which was good. However, a number of pilots remained suspicious of the whole concept of folding wings. After all, if the wings could be folded up, might they not come off altogether in flight? Furthermore, the folding apparatus and the two additional machine guns added about 1,000 pounds of weight to the Wildcats, which affected their speed and especially their climbing ability. While the lighter, unarmored Zeros could climb at a rate of 3,000 feet per minute, a Dash 4 Wildcat could climb at only about 1,000 feet per minute.* American fighter pilots therefore sought to avoid engagements with Zeros at low altitudes, where the Japanese had a clear advantage, and sought instead to come in high so they could dive on their prey. These factors would play an important role in the confrontation at Midway.[20]

The two extra machine guns were even more problematical. American designers added the extra guns to allow European versions of the Wildcat (which the British called the Martlet) to compete with heavier German bombers and fighters and to increase the impact of strafing attacks against ground targets. Yet the extra firepower was overkill against the lighter, and mostly unarmored, Japanese planes. Worse, it severely restricted the length of time a Wildcat pilot could fire. The four guns in the earlier version each had a magazine of 450 rounds, but since those guns fired 700 to 750 rounds per minute, that gave the pilots only about thirty-five seconds of firepower before they expended all their ammo. In the newer Dash 4 version, despite the two extra guns, there was no increase in the size of the total magazine, and as a result pilots in an F4F-4 Wildcat could shoot for only about twenty seconds. Movie depictions of pilots boring in on a foe with guns blazing are pure fiction; the pilots had to hoard their few seconds of firepower for use only under the most ideal circumstances. Even when they fired in short two-second bursts, they risked running out of bullets. Moreover, there was no evidence that having two extra guns made the Wildcats any more lethal. As the commanding officer of VF-3, Lieutenant Commander John S. "Jimmy" Thach, put it, "The pilot who would miss with four .50-caliber guns won't be able to hit with eight. Increased firepower is not a substitute

---

* Grumman claimed that the F4F-4 could climb at a modest but respectable 1,950 feet per minute, but in combat conditions, pilots complained their Dash 4s could ascend only at about 1,000 feet per minute.

for marksmanship." Another problem with the new fighters was that the ammo belts of .50-caliber bullets, loaded into trays in the wings, shifted around violently during the high-speed maneuvers necessary in aerial combat, and as a result the guns occasionally jammed. More than once a Wildcat pilot lined up for a shot and pulled the trigger only to find that nothing happened.[21]

The fighter pilots made some adjustments on their own. In late January, Lieutenant Jim Gray urged Wade McClusky, the commander of VF-6 on the *Enterprise*, to authorize the installation of a sheet of 3/8-inch boilerplate steel behind the pilot's seat of the squadron's Wildcats. McClusky agreed. Like the Marines in Iraq sixty years later who had to "up-armor" their Humvees themselves, the pilots of VF-6 installed their own armor. Eventually, armor plate behind the pilot's seat became official and routine, but initially it was a pilot initiative. Gray soon had reason to be very pleased with his innovation.[22]

Like the scouting and torpedo squadrons, the fighting squadrons "belonged" to the carrier they rode, though circumstances could lead to their being transferred from one ship to another. Before the *Yorktown* left Norfolk to return to the Pacific, her regular fighting squadron (VF-5) had gone ashore for training and was temporarily replaced by a squadron from the USS *Ranger* (CV-4), a much smaller carrier that would remain in the Atlantic for most of the war.* The replacement was supposed to be temporary but ended up being permanent, and as a result, in addition to Scouting Five (VS-5), Bombing Five (VB-5), and Torpedo Five (VT-5), the *Yorktown* also carried eighteen Dash 3 Wildcats of VF-42 under Lieutenant Commander Oscar "Pete" Pederson, who later became the commander of all the squadrons on the *Yorktown*, or CYAG (commander, *Yorktown* Air Group). Similarly, when the *Saratoga* headed back to the West Coast for repair in January, her fighter squadron (VF-3) joined the

---

* The *Ranger* was the first U.S. Navy warship to be built from the keel up as a carrier, but her designers conceived of her as a way to provide air cover for the battle fleet rather than as an independent strike platform. As a result, she lacked both armor and internal watertight integrity. A single bomb could sink her. Thus she was kept in the Atlantic, where she subsequently provided air cover for the landings in North Africa.

*Lexington* while the *Lexington's* fighter squadron went ashore on Oahu for training. This willingness to treat air squadrons as interchangeable parts contrasted sharply with Japanese doctrine in which air squadrons were inextricably tied to their host carriers. This gave the Americans flexibility that the Japanese did not have and would pay important dividends in the battles to come.[23]

The American VF, or fighting squadrons, had a slightly different culture from the bombing or torpedo squadrons. The Wildcat was a single-seat aircraft, so there were no enlisted backseat gunners, and in the air each pilot was on his own. As one pilot put it, "The fighter pilot is a lone shark. He flies by himself, he gets angry by himself, and he talks to himself." Though all brown shoes had a kind of warrior's flair due to the inherently dangerous nature of carrier flight operations, fighter pilots had a special swagger. All but seventeen of the 138 fighter pilots in the fleet were officers. A few were lieutenants or lieutenant commanders, including some graduates of the Naval Academy at Annapolis, but most (70 percent) were lieutenants junior grade or ensigns, and most of those were products of the Naval Aviation Cadet (AVCAD) program.[24]

The AVCAD program produced pilots for all of the Navy squadrons. To enroll, a candidate had to be between 18 and 26 years old, unmarried, and a high school graduate with two years of college (later in the war the Navy began accepting candidates right out of high school). In general, they were men of action rather than contemplation. They tended to be athletes— often in several sports—and greeted one another with wisecracks and backslaps. Needless to say, given the era, they were all white. One aviation cadet who went through the program in 1941 recalled "a heavy majority of Anglo-Saxon Protestant heritage," including a statistically disproportionate number of men with blue eyes. After passing a rigorous physical, they endured a short boot camp that stressed physical training, especially swimming, as well as classroom instruction. After that, they were sent to Pensacola, Florida (the "Annapolis of the Air") for a three-month course. Some "washed out" fairly quickly; they simply couldn't handle the disorientation of air maneuvers. On the other hand, nine out of ten who survived that first phase of training completed the program. Unlike the Japanese, who sought to ensure that only the very best got through, the goal of the American program was to qualify as many pilots as possible. While Japanese instructors supervised only four student pilots at a time, American instructors each had ten students. Moreover, while a Japanese flight instructor who failed most of his students might be praised for having high standards, an American instructor who did the same would more likely be called on the carpet as an ineffective instructor.[25]

After primary flight training, aviation candidates received fourteen weeks of intermediate training, which included twenty-two hours of solo flying, usually in an open-cockpit Stearman N3N biplane, which, since it was covered in yellow fabric, was dubbed the "Yellow Peril" by the students. Advanced training included instrument flying and specialization, including acrobatics. Pilots had to learn how to do "snap rolls, loops, wingovers, the Immelmann, split-S, and falling leaf."[26]

Then, for those selected, came carrier qualifications at Opa-Locka near Miami, Florida. Mostly this consisted of field-carrier landing practice: taking off from and landing on carrier-sized outlines painted on a runway. The student pilots learned to control their aircraft while watching the landing signal officer (LSO), who stood on the deck of the faux carrier holding colorful paddles the size of tennis rackets to indicate if the pilot was coming in too high, too fast, or off line. If the approach was too high, the LSO held out his paddles in a V, bringing them down slowly as the pilot leveled out; if the plane was coming in too low, the LSO made an inverted V. If he was on track for a good landing, the LSO gave him the "cut" sign, slashing a paddle across his throat, and the pilot landed. Otherwise, the LSO gave him a "wave off" and the pilot had to go around again for another try. Mastering landing on that small a space was difficult and frustrating, as much for the LSO instructors as it was for the pilots. On one occasion, the LSO at Opa-Locka simply dropped his paddles to the ground and stood there with "a disgusted look on his face" as a rookie pilot who had ignored his signals roared past. At least once, he threw a paddle at a plane out of annoyance. Difficult as it was, however, these practice landings were much easier than landing on an actual carrier that was moving at 20 to 30 knots and heaving as much as ten or fifteen feet with the rolling sea.[27]

Finally, the pilots-to-be headed for San Diego or Norfolk for Advanced Carrier Training. Eventually every pilot-in-training had to make an arrested landing on a carrier deck. As he approached the stern of a carrier that was steaming into the wind, he had to maneuver so that a hook hanging from the plane's tail section caught one of several wires stretched across the carrier's deck; this brought the plane to a stop. Even when the new pilots successfully learned to perform this maneuver, they often did so in trainers. As a result, many new pilots who reported to the fleet in early 1942 had never made an arrested carrier landing in the type of plane they would fly in combat. After December 7, the Navy opened a number of additional training facilities and converted several vessels into practice carriers to provide more realistic training. In the first few months of the war, however, most of the American carrier pilots were relatively green.[28]

They were also relatively young. In early 1942, the fighter pilots assigned to the Navy's three Pacific aircraft carriers averaged 25.3 years of age, and the ensigns and junior-grade lieutenants averaged 23.8. The oldest fighter pilot in the fleet was 39-year-old Wade McClusky, who subsequently became the air group commander on the *Enterprise*. The youngest was Ensign Robert A. M. Dibb, a product of the AVCAD program, whom everyone called "Ram" because of his initials, and who would not turn 21 until April 1942. Dibb's debut as a fleet pilot occurred in March. Making his first carrier landing in a Wildcat, he hit the deck hard and bounced. His hook failed to catch a wire, and, still airborne, he crashed into the barrier erected across the flight deck to protect the planes parked forward. "A bright blanket of flame" shot from the nose of the plane, and Dibb jumped from the cockpit, did a shoulder roll off the wing, and landed sprawling on the deck.[29]

Dibb was not the only pilot sent to the fleet with little or no experience. Seventy percent of the fighter pilots on the American carriers had less than three years in service, and nearly a third had joined the Navy within the last year. Everything was new to them. Reporting aboard a carrier for his first sea service in December 1941, one new pilot expressed surprise that the dining area was called the "wardroom." Along with their youth and inexperience, however, they also displayed the confidence of their years, flying their trainers with joyful abandon, and often guilty of what one called "damned fool, scatter-brained flathatting." They believed they were immortal. "You understand you can be hurt or killed," one recalled after the war, "but emotionally [you think] there's not a chance in the world. Not me, anybody else but me. Not a chance in the world."[30]

Commissioned officers they might be, but in the winter of 1942, these young brown-shoe officers, and their sometimes even younger backseat gunners and radiomen, for all their daredevil courage and enthusiasm, had nowhere near the length of service, the physical and mental training, or the combat experience of their Japanese counterparts. Nevertheless, in January of 1942, the three American carrier groups, with their embarked aircraft flown by young and untested pilots, were the only offensive weapons Nimitz had to hand, and he planned to use them aggressively. The Kidō Butai was supreme in the Pacific Ocean, but there were other targets of opportunity available to the American brown shoes.

# 4

# American Counterstrike

The key question for Nimitz at the beginning of 1942 was how to employ his scarce resources. With only three carrier groups—and little else—he was in no position to seek battle with the Kidō Butai. Nor did he need to. Within a year he could expect the arrival of the first of the new-construction carriers and other warships that would give him a significant materiel superiority over the Japanese. That suggested that one possible strategy was simply to conserve his strength, hold on to Hawaii, and wait for those ships. That would have been consistent with the principle of "Germany First," the strategic concept adopted by the government just weeks before the war began. Of course that was before the Japanese had struck at Pearl Harbor, which had immediately created public pressure to strike back. Moreover, Nimitz was unwilling to concede the initiative to the Japanese. He planned to use his carriers to hit their bases in the central Pacific, striking targets of opportunity to keep them back on their heels.

His boss, Ernie King, had similar thoughts. If anything, King was more eager than Nimitz to begin a counteroffensive. He shared with Nimitz the instinct (in King's words) to "hold what you've got and hit them when you can." But unlike Nimitz, who could focus his attention and energies exclusively on the Pacific, King had to fight a global war, including the on-going Battle of the Atlantic against German U-boats. In addition, King was under pressure from America's allies, including Australian prime minister John Curtin, to maintain the communications and supply link between Hawaii and Australia. King was acutely sensitive to the fact that Japanese occupation of New Caledonia, Fiji, or Samoa in the South Pacific would sever that link, and he wanted Nimitz to focus his attention southward, writing his Pacific commander that the protection of the lifeline to Australia (see map, page 98) was second only to the defense of Hawaii itself, and not by much. He ordered Nimitz to commit both Halsey's Task Force 8 and Fletcher's new Task Force 17—two-thirds of America's carrier force in the Pacific—to protecting and screening a convoy that was carrying reinforcements from San Diego to Samoa. Only after Samoa was secure would those carrier task forces become available for offensive operations.[1]

Nimitz perforce complied, but when King also ordered him to send a squadron of patrol planes to Australia, Nimitz pushed back. He protested that the reduction of aircraft in Hawaii left it "dangerously weak," and he reminded King of the central importance of Hawaii to the Allied cause. Instead of rebuking Nimitz for his temerity, King replied that the transfer was isolated and temporary; he assured Nimitz that he fully understood the "paramount importance" of Hawaii. Over the next several months, however, there would be a subtle but steady push and pull between King and Nimitz about how, and especially where, to employ the three carrier task forces in the Pacific.[2]

By January 23 the American reinforcements had been safely landed at Samoa, and the *Enterprise* and *Yorktown* were freed up to operate against Japanese targets. Nimitz ordered Halsey to strike Japanese bases in the Marshall and Gilbert Islands. King not only approved, he urged that the strikes "be driven home" and suggested that Wilson Brown's *Lexington* force should also raid Wake Island a few days afterward. His notion was that when Halsey struck at the Marshalls, the Japanese would pull coverage away from Wake, and Brown could exploit that. Though some members of Nimitz's staff worried about sending all three carriers out simultaneously, Nimitz overruled them. For all his placid demeanor, Nimitz was perfectly willing to act boldly, taking what more conservative officers considered significant risks in order to regain the initiative. In this first American counterattack since Pearl Harbor, a robust offensive was crucial to improving morale both at home and in the fleet. As it happened, Brown's raid on Wake had to be scrubbed after a Japanese submarine sank the oiler *Neches*, which left Brown with barely enough fuel to get to Wake and back. Deciding that there was too small a margin of error, Nimitz recalled him. He was willing to act boldly, but he also knew the difference between boldness and foolishness.[3]

No one was sure how extensive, or well protected, the Japanese bases in the Marshalls were. The former German colony had been granted to the Japanese as a mandate by the League of Nations after the First World War, and since then few Westerners had been allowed to visit them, much less prepare detailed charts. For some of those islands, the most recent charts available to the Americans had been made by Charles Wilkes, who had led the first U.S. Navy exploration expedition of the Pacific in 1840. King and Nimitz assumed that behind this veil of secrecy the Japanese had built up substantial defenses in the Marshall Islands. The American raid was therefore a shot in the dark.[4]

Fletcher's *Yorktown* group made a fast run in toward the target, crossing over the international date line on January 29 and skipping at once to the 31st. Shortly before 6:00 a.m. on February 1, Fletcher turned the *Yorktown* into the wind to launch. The weather was terrible. Squalls surrounded the task force, and flashes of lightning could be seen on the western horizon in the direction of the principal target at Jaluit Atoll. The first planes spotted for launch were four Wildcat fighters that would act as combat air patrol (CAP) and protect the task force during the raid. Fletcher planned to keep the rest of his fighters aboard so he could rotate the CAP, and to act as a reserve in case of a Japanese counterattack.[5]

After the fighters were airborne, *Yorktown* launched seventeen Dauntless dive-bombers and eleven Devastator torpedo planes (armed with bombs for this mission), all of them under Commander Curtis Smiley. These planes were to strike the Japanese seaplane base at Jaluit, which was some 140 miles away. It was dawn by now, but the sky remained dark and filled with heavy clouds. The visibility was so poor that the pilots had difficulty finding one another over the task force. Smiley never did manage to gather all his planes into one group, and some of the pilots ended up flying off toward Jaluit on their own. While en route there, the Americans encountered a powerful thunderstorm with "sheet lightning and torrential rains" that reduced visibility to near zero. They pressed on nonetheless and dropped their bombs on or near the assigned target. Under these conditions it was hard to know with certainty whether they hit anything. They bombed a radio tower and strafed two small vessels in the lagoon. The advertised "seaplane base" turned out to be little more than a corrugated-tin hut. Several pilots, despairing of finding a worthy target, simply jettisoned their bombs.[6]

After that first group flew off toward Jaluit, Fletcher ordered the launch of fourteen more dive-bombers: nine for a strike on Makin, 120 miles to the south, and five more for Mili, forty miles to the north, about which virtually nothing was known. The weather was better over Makin than Jaluit, but the only targets of any value there were a minelayer and two large seaplanes, both of which were destroyed. It was all somewhat anticlimactic after the weeks of anticipation. At Mili the disappointment was even greater. It was the largest island in the Mili Atoll, and later in the war the Japanese would build an airstrip there and turn it into a major base, but in February of 1942 it was virtually unoccupied. Lacking targets worthy of their bombs, the Yorktown pilots did what they could, shooting up anything that looked worthwhile. For the most part, however, it was a wild goose chase.[7]

Then the attack planes had to go back through that appalling weather to find the task force. By then, the storm had caught up with the Yorktown. Winds gusted up to 50 knots, and the carrier pitched and rolled so wildly that Captain Buckmaster called back the circling Wildcats of the CAP. The attack pilots had to execute a landing under extremely perilous conditions while low on fuel. When Ensign Tom Ellison landed his Dauntless,

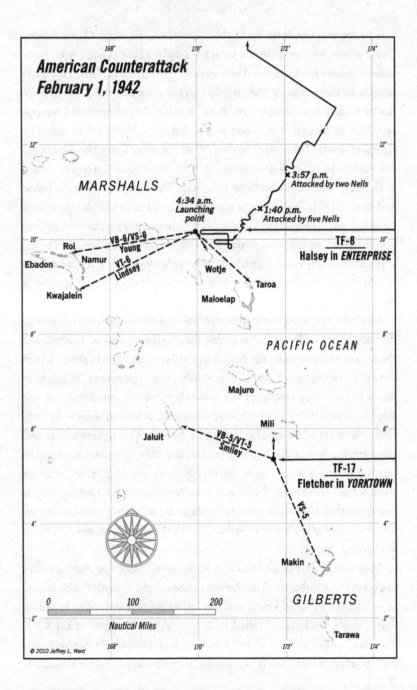

**American Counterattack**
**February 1, 1942**

MARSHALLS

168°    170°    172°    174°

12°

× 3:57 p.m.
Attacked by two Nells

4:34 a.m.
Launching
point

× 1:40 p.m.
Attacked by five Nells

10°

Roi          VB-6/VS-6
        Young                              TF-8
Namur                                Halsey in *ENTERPRISE*
Ebadon      VT-6
        Lindsey          Wotje
Kwajalein                 Taroa
                Maloelap

PACIFIC OCEAN

8°

Majuro

Mili

6°

Jaluit      VB-5/VT-5
        Smiley
                              TF-17
                        Fletcher in *YORKTOWN*

4°                                        VS-5

Makin

2°

GILBERTS

0        100        200
Nautical Miles

Tarawa

© 2010 Jeffrey L. Ward

168°    170°    172°    174°

there was not enough fuel left in his tank to taxi. Several pilots didn't make it back at all and had to ditch in the water. Fletcher ordered four destroyers to search for them, but in that storm-tossed sea not all the pilots could be recovered. After two hours, Fletcher broke radio silence to recall the destroyers, reformed his task force, and retired to the northeast. Though he had initially planned a second strike, the dearth of targets and the worsening weather convinced him to scrap it.[8]

For the fighter pilots on the *Yorktown*, the highlight of the whole raid was the downing of a big Kawanishi flying boat ("Emily") that had been hovering near the task force and reporting its position. The Wildcat pilots chased the giant four-engine plane from one patch of clouds to another, riddling it with .50-caliber bullets. When a pilot shot off its tail section, the exultant pilot radioed: "We just shot his goddamned ass off!" Nonetheless, there was no disguising the fact that overall the *Yorktown*'s initial raid had been largely unproductive.[9]

Halsey's *Enterprise* group, by contrast, had far better luck, and Halsey's natural bellicosity allowed him to take full advantage of it. The first sign that things might be going his way came the day before the strike, when a Japanese scout plane, identified on radar, flew past without spotting the task force. Ever the showman, Halsey composed a sarcastic message thanking the pilot for failing to see him, had it translated into Japanese, ran off copies on the ship's mimeo machine, and gave the copies to his pilots to drop along with their bombs. It was the wartime version of a playground taunt, and risky, too, since it could have revealed to the Japanese the effectiveness of American radar.

Nimitz had ordered Halsey to attack Japanese bases at Wotje and Maloelap in the Marshall Islands, but as Halsey moved toward the targets the skipper of the American submarine *Dolphin* reported that the defenses at the main Japanese base at Kwajalein were less extensive than previously believed, and, pressed by his eccentric and pugnacious chief of staff, Commander Miles Browning, Halsey added Kwajalein to the target list.

In the predawn darkness, twenty minutes ahead of Fletcher and some three hundred miles to the northwest, the *Enterprise* turned into the wind and increased speed to 30 knots. As on the *Yorktown*, the first planes to launch that morning were six Wildcats, to serve as CAP. Then came thirty-six Dauntless dive-bombers of VS-6 and VB-6 under Commander Howard "Brigham" Young. Their principal target was the pair of islands called Roi and Namur at the north end of Kwajalein Atoll.

The weather was better for the *Enterprise* pilots, but it was still pitch dark at 4:34 a.m. when the first planes took off. Carrier launches are dangerous under any circumstances with each plane having a full fuel tank and carrying 700 pounds of bombs, and they are particularly dangerous in the dark. To keep the *Enterprise* concealed from prowling Japanese submarines, only a few hooded lights offered a dim and ghostly illumination of the flight deck as the pilots warmed up their engines. Taking off in such circumstances was like accelerating through a tunnel into black oblivion. One recalled that it was "like being inside a black felt hat," and most of the pilots felt a "touch of vertigo" as they launched into the darkness.[10]

After takeoff, the bombers had to form up over the task force, which meant finding the other planes in the strike group as they all circled overhead in the dark. The planes, too, were blacked out except for a single white taillight. Finding their proper position in the formation was like groping blindfolded at 130 knots. Once all the Dauntless bombers were in the air, nine heavy Devastator torpedo bombers took off. Like the Devastators launched from *Yorktown*, they carried bombs rather than torpedoes. Lieutenant Commander Eugene Lindsey led this contingent, slotted for the attack on Kwajalein Island, some forty miles south of Roi-Namur and over 150 miles away. It took more than twenty minutes before the planes assembled into a formation that resembled a series of stacked Vs. Then the whole group headed off toward Kwajalein Atoll.[11]

As the attack planes flew off to the west, Halsey brought up the twelve remaining Wildcats of VF-6 from the hangar deck. Instead of keeping them so he could rotate his CAP, as Fletcher did, or sending them off as protection for the attack planes, he planned to use them offensively. Deck crews had attached 100-pound bombs under each wing, and Halsey sent the fighters off to attack the nearby islands of Wotje and Maloelap. Lieutenant Commander Wade McClusky led six Wildcats against nearby Wotje, and

Lieutenant Jim Gray led six more against Maloelap. During the launch, one of the pilots in Gray's section lost his bearings in the dark, and instead of lifting off, his plane slid sideways into the sea. The pilot was rescued, but it left Gray with only five airplanes.[12]

Like the *Yorktown* force that targeted Mili Island, McClusky's fighters found little that was worthy of their ordnance at Wotje. At Maloelap, by contrast, the five pilots of Gray's section found much more than they had bargained for. On the small island of Taroa, part of Maloelap Atoll, the Japanese had built a new concrete airfield. Constructed by prisoner labor over two years, it was large enough to host two dozen fighters and bombers, many of which were parked in rows along the apron, and several of which were at that moment taking off to defend the airstrip. There were, in fact, fifteen Japanese fighters at Taroa—older models than the vaunted Zero—and nine twin-engine bombers. To Gray it seemed like there were "thirty or forty" planes in sight.[13]

Gray's five Wildcats dropped their ordnance on the airfield and began strafing, but the attackers became targets almost at once as Japanese fighters swarmed down on them. Worse, the guns on several of the Wildcats jammed, and under such circumstances there was nothing to do but to retire as fast as possible after they had dropped their small bombs. Gray's guns did not jam, and he made three strafing runs on the airfield before he ran out of ammunition. By then there were eight Japanese fighters in the air, and Gray became the target of all of them. Bullets perforated his Wildcat's wings and fuselage and thudded into the armor plate behind his seat. After he returned to the *Enterprise*, his plane crew counted more than forty bullet holes in the plane itself, and fifteen dents in the armor plate that had been installed behind his seat only days before.[14]

While the American fighters were extricating themselves, the bombers and torpedo planes were flying westward toward Kwajalein. After about an hour, the pilots identified a line of surf marking the perimeter of the giant atoll. Like most of the atolls in the Pacific, Kwajalein was essentially a thin strip of coral reef surrounding a central lagoon. From 14,000 feet it looked like a silver necklace that had been tossed carelessly onto a blue carpet. Though the atoll was more than sixty miles long end to end, only a few pieces of dry ground were large enough to accommodate an airfield—Ebadon at the western end, Kwajalein at the eastern end, and the twin islands of

Roi and Namur at the northern tip. The dive-bombers of VB-6 and the nine Devastators of Gene Lindsey's VT-6 broke off from the attack formation and headed south for Kwajalein Island; the scout bombers of VS-6 under Young continued westward toward the larger island of Roi. The Americans had assumed that Roi was Japan's main base and expected the anchorage to be choked with shipping. Instead, when the dive-bombers arrived there at about 7:00 a.m., the sun now fully up, they found a small airfield and several support buildings, but no ships.[15]

Lieutenant Commander Halstead Hopping, the commander of Scouting Six, led the attack. Because his was the lead plane, antiaircraft fire concentrated on him. So did one of the Japanese fighters that came up behind him almost as soon as he pulled out of his dive. The fighter fired a long burst, and Hopping's plane went spinning into the sea. The other planes in his squadron pressed home their attack, dropping smaller 100-pound bombs on the buildings and parked airplanes while fending off the Japanese fighters. One bomb hit an ammunition dump, creating a satisfying explosion, but there were few targets that justified use of a 500-pound bomb. The Americans destroyed eleven planes, more than half of them on the ground. Nonetheless, they no longer expected to find anything of greater value to attack.[16]

Then they heard Commander Young's voice in their headsets—now that the bullets were flying, there was no longer any need to maintain radio silence. Young passed on a message he had received from Gene Lindsey, who reported that there were plentiful shipping targets at Kwajalein Island, forty miles to the south. One of his pilots even reported that there were "two carriers" in the lagoon. Young relayed the message to his squadron: "Targets suitable for heavy bombs at Kwajalein." The Dauntless pilots regrouped and sped southward.[17]

Halsey, too, heard the report. The *Enterprise* maintained radio silence throughout the operation—essential when operating so close to enemy territory, or indeed at any time—but he could listen in as the pilots talked to one another. When he heard Young repeat the report about the "two carriers," he launched nine more torpedo planes, armed this time with ship-killing torpedoes, under Lieutenant Lance "Lem" Massey, sending them to Kwajalein.

As Gene Lindsey had promised, the lagoon at Kwajalein was filled with Japanese shipping, including a light cruiser, several submarines, and a dozen or more freighters. There were, however, no carriers. The Japanese had no fighter cover, which meant that the American pilots could make their runs targeted only by ground fire. The first wave of bombers dropped their ordnance, shot up the shipping in the turquoise waters of the lagoon, then flew back to the *Enterprise* for more fuel and ammo. As they were returning to the carrier, they passed Massey's torpedo planes going in the other direction. Unharried by Japanese fighters, the low and slow American Devastators had time to line up on their anchored prey. There was even some competition among the pilots for the big prizes. Halsey smiled when he heard one of the pilots radio to another: "You ease off to the right; that big one is mine." In addition to wreaking havoc on Japanese shipping, one of the American bombs killed Rear Admiral Yatsushiro Sukeyoshi, an Eta Jima classmate of Yamamoto's chief of staff and the first Japanese flag officer to die in the war.[18]

Meanwhile, back at the task force, Halsey had the first group of bombers rearmed and refueled and sent them to hit the airfield on Taroa that Gray's fighters had found. Aware that the bombers parked there were the most proximate threat to his task force, he wanted to neutralize as many of them as possible. Other groups were vectored there as they became available. Lieutenant Richard Best dropped his bomb on a hangar at Taroa and then fought off several fighters, one of which clipped him in the fuel tank. The escaping vapor looked like smoke, and Best's rear-seat gunner, Aviation Radioman First Class Lee McHugh, called him on the intercom: "Mr. Best, Mr. Best, we're on fire!"

"Where? Where? Where?" Best called back.

"The right wing!"

"Dammit, McHugh, that's our gasoline leaking. Don't you ever scare me like that again."[19]

For nearly nine hours, Halsey kept the *Enterprise* maneuvering within easy range of four Japanese bases. For part of that time, Wotje Island was actually in sight; columns of smoke could be seen rising from it. Finally, after returning from yet another strike, the commander of Bombing Six, Lieutenant Commander William Hollingsworth, climbed up to the bridge and said to Halesy, "Admiral, don't you think it's about time we got the hell out of here?" A grinning Halsey agreed, and after recovering the last of its planes, Task Force 8 began its withdrawal.[20]

And just in time. Soon, five twin-engine Nell bombers appeared. There would have been nine of them, but the strikes on the Taroa airfield had destroyed two and damaged two more. Rather than wait until those last two could be repaired, the Japanese commander had sent out all the operational aircraft he had. The Nell was an older airplane, designed in the early 1930s for the war in China, and while several Nells had taken part in the sinking of HMS *Prince of Wales* in December, the aircraft was not an ideal weapon for precision bombing. Rather than trying to place one bomb directly on the target, as the dive-bombers did, Japanese doctrine called for the twin-engine bombers to pass over the ship in a tight formation and to release all their bombs simultaneously so that at least one struck the target. This time, however, the Japanese squadron commander, Lieutenant Nakai Kazuo, decided on a more direct attack. He tipped his Nell over into a shallow glide with the four other planes following his lead. At two thousand feet, they released their bombs. Explosions erupted all around the *Enterprise*, showering the flight deck with sea spray and shrapnel. Though there were no direct hits, a piece of shrapnel from a near miss mortally wounded a sailor and cut a fuel line that started a fire, though it was quickly contained.[21]

Lieutenant Nakai ordered his plane out of formation and directed it at the stern of the *Enterprise* where a dozen or more planes were parked. The Japanese would not adopt deliberate suicide as a war tactic until several years later, but Nakai's plane had been badly damaged by two of the Wildcats, and he may have concluded that he could not make it back to base. Seeing his maneuver, Aviation Machinist's Mate Third Class Bruno P. Gaido ran across the deck of the *Enterprise*, jumped into the back seat of the rearmost plane, and manned its .30-caliber guns. He fired continuously at the nose of the oncoming bomber as it flew straight toward him. The captain of the *Enterprise*, George Murray, ordered the carrier hard to starboard. Nakai—if he was still alive—was unable to match the turn. His wing sliced off the tail of the bomber from which Gaido continued to fire, and the Nell scraped forty feet of the flight deck before crashing into the sea.[22]*

There was more to come. Two hours later, as the *Enterprise* steamed northeast at 30 knots, a second attack came. The Japanese at Taroa had managed to patch up their two damaged bombers and send them out as well. These two conducted a more conventional level-bombing attack, though they, too, failed to score a hit. McClusky's Wildcat pilots went after them. Halsey grinned again when he heard Lieutenant Junior Grade James Daniels blurt out over the radio net, "Bingo! Bingo! I got one!" The second Nell, though crippled, managed to escape because the Wildcats were too low on fuel to pursue it. After this second scrape with Japanese land-based air, Halsey changed course to the northwest, using a weather front to cover his withdrawal.[23]

The *Enterprise* task force returned triumphantly to Pearl Harbor on February 5. Halsey's planes had sunk a transport and a sub chaser and damaged six other ships, including the cruiser. The raid was little more than a pinprick to the vast Japanese empire, but as Halsey noted in his after-action report it was "the first instance in history of offensive combat by U.S. carriers," and "the first offensive operation by Task Forces of the Pacific Fleet in the current war." Because of that, when the *Enterprise* task force entered Pearl Harbor, it received a hero's welcome. Ships blew their whistles as their crews lined the rails to wave their caps and cheer. Nimitz himself came on board the *Enterprise* to shake Halsey's hand.[24]

By contrast, the return of Fletcher's *Yorktown* group the next day was anticlimactic. Fletcher reported honestly that "no objectives of any real military value were known in the vicinity," and because of that, and the poor conditions, he had decided "to withdraw and refuel." It was the correct decision, but it meant that there were no whistles or waving caps for the men and the ships of Task Force 17.[25]

Gratifying as this small victory was, Admiral King remained concerned about the security of the South Pacific, and especially that tenuous

---

* Halsey noted Gaido's heroic effort and promoted him to aviation mate first class that afternoon.

communications link between Hawaii and Australia. The Japanese capture of Rabaul on New Britain Island on January 23—an operation in which four carriers of the Kidō Butai had participated—led him to press Nimitz once again to "operate a carrier group in the South Pacific." There was even a hint of sarcasm in his message, which asked Nimitz whether he was "aware of [the] serious threat to communications with Australia created by current enemy occupation of . . . Rabaul." Nimitz was indeed aware of it, but he balked at the idea of committing his mobile carrier forces to the defense of static lines of communication. It was far better, in his view, to use them offensively to disrupt the enemy's own lines of communication. In the stilted language of a naval message, he protested to his boss: "A mobile striking or covering force to remain constantly in the area [of Samoa-Fiji] seems likely to result in [the] principal employment of fleet being [the] defense [of] distant communication lines." This, he argued, would leave the initiative entirely to the Japanese. "Recommend against proposal as a guiding directive." He suggested instead that as a permanent force in the Samoan area, two cruisers and four destroyers "should be the maximum." King, too, favored the offensive, but he was under tremendous political pressure to defend American allies in the region, especially the Australians. In a compromise, he told Nimitz to send two cruisers and two destroyers to operate "continuously in Samoan area" and rotate other ships there "as you see fit."[26]

At least some of the pressure on King came from the White House. In a "fireside chat" on February 23, the president told his radio listeners, "If we lost communication with the Southwest Pacific, all of that area, including Australia and New Zealand and the Dutch Indies, would fall under Japanese domination." Were that to happen, the president warned, Japan could "extend her conquests" to the Americas, or, in the other direction, to India, "through the Indian Ocean to Africa, to the Near East, and try to join forces with Germany and Italy."* Responding to these concerns, King wrote the president that "our primary concern in the Pacific is to hold

---

\* There was another reason why the Western allies worried so much about Australia. As King wrote to FDR on March 5: "Australia—and New Zealand—are 'white men's countries' which it is essential that we shall not allow to be overrun by Japanese because of the repercussion among the non-white races of the world."

Hawaii," but that "our next care in the Pacific is to preserve Australasia." He ordered Wilson Brown's *Lexington* group into the South Pacific, effectively removing it from Nimitz's control, for a raid against the Japanese citadel at Rabaul at the northern tip of New Britain. At the same time, in order to divert Japanese attention from that raid, Halsey and Fletcher were to strike again at targets in the Central Pacific, including another attempt on Wake.[27]

The raid on Rabaul was Wilson Brown's opportunity to duplicate Halsey's success in the Marshalls. It didn't work out that way. While still several hundred miles from the target on February 20, his task force was spotted by three Japanese long-range scout planes. The *Lexington* had several Wildcat fighters of VF-3 (formerly of the *Saratoga*) aloft that day, including one piloted by the squadron's commanding officer, Lieutenant Commander John S. "Jimmy" Thach, one of the most skilled and innovative pilots in the fleet. Thach shot down the first snooper himself, and another pilot claimed a second. Despite that, Brown had to assume that the patrol planes had radioed his location, course, and speed to Rabaul. Having lost the element of surprise, and claiming an "acute fuel shortage," he decided to call off the strike, though he continued to steam in the direction of Rabaul during the daylight hours, turning around only after nightfall.[28]

The Japanese patrol planes had indeed reported the presence of the *Lexington* group to Rabaul, and at 2:00 that afternoon, Vice Admiral Gotō Eiji sent seventeen two-engine bombers to the attack. They were big Mitsubishi G4M1

■ Vice Admiral Wilson Brown commanded the *Lexington* task force during two planned raids on the Japanese base at Rabaul. Here he wears the gold aiguillette that he sported as President Roosevelts' naval aide in 1943–44. (U.S. Naval Institute)

bombers ("Bettys") that were both newer and faster than the seven Nells that had assailed Halsey in the Marshalls. The ability to employ land-based airplanes from a web of Pacific bases was a central feature of Japanese prewar defensive plans. These long-range planes could strike at American warships well before the carriers got close enough to launch their own aircraft. What the Japanese didn't anticipate was that the Americans would be able to see them coming.[29]

If the Japanese had an edge on the Americans in torpedo technology, the Americans had a huge advantage in that they had radar and the Japanese did not. Radar had made its debut in the fleet in 1937 when a prototype—looking much like a bedspring tied to the mast—had been installed on the destroyer *Leary*. A much newer and more efficient version, CXAM radar, made by RCA, was installed on the American carriers in the fall of 1940. Depending on the skill of the operator, CXAM radar could identify approaching aircraft from fifty to a hundred miles out, and surface ships fourteen to twenty miles away. The new system was idiosyncratic, however; images appeared and faded, and it was difficult, if not impossible, to determine altitude or even the number of contacts. Nonetheless, it was a huge improvement over the naked eye. Just before 4:00 p.m., the *Lexington*'s radar picked up an air contact seventy-six miles out. As it happened, the *Lexington* was about to rotate its CAP and had just launched six replacement Wildcats. The planes coming off patrol were already circling for a landing when they were ordered to stay aloft. Instead, the *Lexington* launched four more Wildcats plus eleven Dauntless bombers (without bombs), which gave them twenty-seven aircraft to contest an assault by what turned out to be seventeen Japanese bombers approaching in two waves.[30]

The first wave of nine bombers was simply overwhelmed by the Americans, which provoked cheers from the crewmen of the *Lexington*, who could see the planes falling from the sky. The Bettys were well armed, but they had no fighter support and, like most Japanese combat aircraft, were poorly armored. Jimmy Thach got one, and his squadron mates took care of the rest. Like Lieutenant Nakai, who had tried to crash his plane into Halsey's *Enterprise*, Lieutenant Nakagawa Masayoshi tried to crash his crippled bomber into the *Lexington*. When it was 2,500 yards away and closing, the guns on the *Lexington* opened up. Most of the shells exploded behind the plane, and an officer on Brown's staff who had a reputation as a crack duck hunter, yelled out "Lead him! . . . damn you, lead him!" As the *Lexington* turned away, Nakagawa's plane, riddled with bullets and with most of its crewmen likely dead, crashed into the sea.[31]

The annihilation of that first wave of bombers was gratifying, though when a second wave of eight Bettys arrived, only five recently launched Wildcats had enough fuel left to make an attack. One of them was piloted by Lieutenant Edward "Butch" O'Hare and another by his wingman, Lieutenant Junior Grade Marion Dufilho. The other three were widely separated. Dufilho's guns jammed almost at once so that O'Hare faced the challenge of fending off eight medium bombers virtually alone. The Bettys may have lacked armor, but they bristled with armament. Each plane had a machine gun in the nose, another in a blister on the top of the fuselage, two more in blisters on the sides, plus a 20 mm cannon in the tail. It took remarkable courage for one pilot to assail a formation of such planes; O'Hare had to know that as many as two dozen gunners would be aiming at him. However, unlike the Japanese, who were flying in formation, O'Hare had freedom to maneuver, and he began to pick off the Japanese bombers one by one. With only thirty to forty seconds' worth of ammunition, he attacked the starboard plane first and then worked his way through the formation. "When one would start burning, I'd haul out and wait for it to get out of the way," he said later. "Then I'd go in and get another one." He shot down three bombers and badly crippled two more, continuing his attack until he had expended all his ammunition. He was credited with five kills and became the first official U.S. Navy ace of the Pacific war.[32]*

---

* Recognizing the public relations value of O'Hare's feat, the Navy ordered him stateside, where Roosevelt awarded him the Medal of Honor, after which he was sent on a tour to sell war bonds. For that reason, he missed both the Battle of the Coral Sea and Midway.

  Few of the thousands of modern-day passengers who travel through Chicago are aware that the city's two major airports are both named to honor heroes of the Pacific War. Midway Airport is named for the battle itself, and passengers there can view a full-sized Dauntless dive bomber suspended from the ceiling of Terminal A. The larger O'Hare Airport, one of the busiest in the world, is named for Butch O'Hare.

The three surviving Japanese planes dropped their bombs over the task force, scoring no hits, and then turned to head back to base—all but one. O'Hare had shot the engine off the left wing of Lieutenant Commander Itō Takuzō's command airplane, and the big bomber spiraled out of the formation, losing altitude quickly. Like Nakagawa, Itō ordered his pilot, Warrant Officer Watanabe Chūzō, to crash into the American carrier. With only one engine, however, Watanabe could not hold his course. The *Lexington* turned hard to starboard, and the big Japanese bomber flew alongside for a few heart-stopping seconds before it splashed into the sea 1,500 yards off the port bow.[33]

Butch O'Hare's adventures for the day were not quite over. As he came in to land on the *Lexington*, low on fuel and out of ammunition, an overzealous young gunner on the carrier's port quarter opened fire on him. O'Hare saw where the fire was coming from, but coolly continued to execute his landing. After he climbed out of the cockpit, he walked slowly back to the

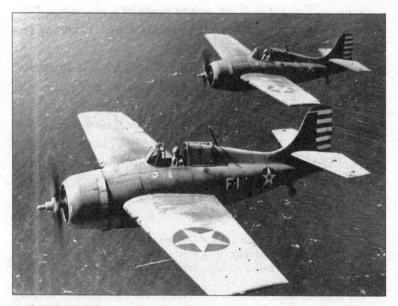

■ The F4F-3 Wildcat was the U.S. Navy's principal carrier-based fighter in the spring of 1942. In this staged photograph, two of them are being flown by two of the Navy's best fighter pilots: John S. "Jimmy" Thach flies F-1 in the foreground, and Edward "Butch" O'Hare flies F-13. (U.S. Naval Institute)

gun tub on the port quarter and, looking down at the machine gunner there, said to him: "Son, if you don't stop shooting at me when I've got my wheels down, I'm going to have to report you to the gunnery officer."[34]

When it was over, fifteen of the seventeen Japanese planes had been destroyed. The *Lexington* pilots celebrated their victory with such enthusiasm that Brown had to remind them that this was not a football game. Nonetheless, the successful defense of the task force on February 20 dramatically boosted the morale of the pilots, especially the Wildcat pilots of Jimmy Thach's VF-3. The Japanese bombers had proved remarkably vulnerable, and the Americans took to calling the Bettys "flying Zippos," after the famous cigarette lighter whose advertising slogan was that it lit up the first time, every time. The Americans lost only two Wildcats and one pilot, Ensign J. Woodrow Wilson, killed when a 20 mm shell hit his cockpit.

The air battle on February 20 had deprived Rabaul of all but three of its attack bombers (the two that managed to return and one that had been unable to make the sortie), yet it was less than a complete American victory, given that the original target had been the Japanese shipping at Rabaul. Some members of Nimitz's staff questioned Brown's decision to retire. After all, the virtual destruction of Rabaul's air arm suggested that he could have operated there with at least as much impunity as Halsey had off the Marshalls. Brown's explanation of an "acute fuel shortage" struck some as curious, since careful planning had gone into meeting the fuel needs of the task force. Nimitz gave his task-force commander the benefit of the doubt, but he was concerned when Brown reported, "Unless it is intended we return [to] Pearl, it will be necessary [to] proceed to Sydney." Neither Nimitz nor King wanted any of the American carrier groups to begin operating out of Australia for fear that once they were there, the Australian authorities would never let them go. Though he said nothing at the time, all this may have left Nimitz with nagging uncertainties about the suitability of "Shaky" Brown for aggressive carrier operations.[35]

Halsey's raid on Wake Island took place four days later. By now the *Enterprise* task force had a new numerical designation. When Halsey received his orders for the mission, he noticed that his command had been redesignated

Task Force 13, and—even worse—that it was to sail on February 13, which happened to be a Friday. Halsey insisted that both numbers be changed. He may have meant it as a joke. Nonetheless he waited until Valentine's Day before departing for Wake, doing so in command of what was now labeled Task Force 16, the designation it would carry into the Battle of Midway.[36]

On February 24, bombers from the *Enterprise* attacked Wake from the north while the heavy cruisers of Halsey's escort group—*Northampton* and *Salt Lake City* under Rear Admiral Raymond Spruance—shelled it from the south. The results were indecisive; the Americans inflicted some minor damage on the Japanese base while losing three planes. Afterward, Task Force 16 continued west all the way to Marcus Island, only a thousand miles from Tokyo, to conduct another raid. That attack, deep inside the Japanese defense perimeter, took the defenders completely by surprise. The American planes had a strong tailwind and arrived over the target before sunup. In the pitch darkness, the tracers of the Japanese ground fire looked to one pilot like "a string of oranges following me out in a gentle curve." Though the raid inflicted only minor damage, it caused considerable concern in Tokyo, and even led authorities there to order a blackout of the capital. Compared with the triumphs of the Kidō Butai throughout South Asia and on the north coast of Australia, these American counterattacks were little more than nuisance raids, but they did gain the attention of the Imperial General Staff, and, equally important, they provided America's young brown-shoe aviators with both confidence and invaluable experience.[37]

Meanwhile, King and Nimitz continued to spar over the best use of the American carrier task forces. As always, King was under pressure from several quarters. The Japanese were clearly building up their forces at Rabaul for another push southward, and this fueled his concern for the safety of the Hawaii-Australia line of communication. He was also being urged to do more to protect Australia itself. After the fall of Singapore in mid-February, the Australian Imperial Force (AIF) was recalled from the Mediterranean. Churchill wanted to use two of its divisions to defend Burma. Australia's prime minister, John Curtin, insisted that they were needed at home. Churchill begged Curtin to change his mind, arguing that the men were essential to fend off the Japanese assault on Rangoon. In response to an urgent plea from Churchill, Roosevelt promised Curtin that an American division would be sent to Australia at once. Curtin thanked FDR and accepted the offer, though he brought the Australian troops home nonetheless.[38]

All this compelled King to bolster Nimitz's southern flank, and he created a new command theater called ANZAC (Australia, New Zealand Area Command).* With the *Saratoga* in Bremerton for repairs, its former task group commander, Herbert Leary, was without a job, and after promoting him to vice admiral, King made him the ANZAC commander, with authority over the east coast of Australia, New Zealand, New Caledonia, New Hebrides, the Solomon Islands, and Fiji. King's order to Leary was to conduct "a strong and comprehensive offensive to be launched soon against exposed enemy naval forces." There was a limit to King's willingness to accommodate himself to political realities, however. When Roosevelt queried King about a request from Curtin to use an American carrier to ferry planes from California to Australia, King shot back that the carriers in the Pacific "are urgently required for offensive action as fighting carriers, and cannot logically be spared for use as ferry boats."[39]

From the start, Leary proved something of a disappointment. He set up his headquarters at Melbourne, on the Australian mainland, and when King heard about it, he immediately ordered Leary to rejoin his flagship at sea. Like Nimitz, King was concerned that forces based in Australia would become fixed there and pass beyond his effective control. Leary objected. "My considered judgment . . . is that operational command can only be exercised from Melbourne," adding, "I request reconsideration." For once, King relented and Leary remained at his headquarters at Melbourne.[40]

Not being subject to the same political pressures as King, Nimitz was perplexed by the creation of ANZAC. King had already removed Wilson

---

* This is not to be confused with the Australia–New Zealand Army Corps, also called ANZAC, which fought at Gallipoli in World War I. This new ANZAC command lasted only until April, when it was absorbed into the Southwest Pacific command under Douglas MacArthur.

Brown's *Lexington* task force from Nimitz's authority; now he declared that Leary, too, would report directly to CominCh in Washington, effectively bypassing Nimitz altogether. Nimitz wondered whether King's plan was "to gamble all upon securing Australia as a base of future operations against the enemy, and leave our Pacific Area open to attack." Rather than to act defensively, he preferred to conduct "bold operations against the enemy's flank." In fact, King agreed. "Our current tasks are not merely protective," King wrote in a message to task-force commanders, "but also offensive where practicable as [the] best way to protect is by reducing enemy offensive power ... particularly carriers." At the same time, however, he wanted some, and possibly most, of the American carrier force to be directed southward. Until New Caledonia received sufficient reinforcements to ensure its security, King suggested to Nimitz, at least one and possibly two carrier groups should operate in that area. Nimitz protested that the logistical requirements for operating two carriers so far from their base were daunting. To keep them full of fuel would require three *Cimarron*-class oilers on constant rotation, and the loss of one of those oilers would "seriously jeopardize" the task force. King acknowledged that "this depends on logistics and must be decided by CINCPAC."[41]

Nimitz found all this confusing and a bit alarming. Minutes taken at a staff meeting in February of 1942 note that King's message "did not materially clarify the command relationships." Nor was there any more illumination when Pye returned from a visit to Washington and reported to Nimitz that as far as he could tell, "no over-all plan has been adopted" for the Pacific area. Nimitz was still feeling his way in regard to his command relationship with King. To this point he had acted as a dutiful subordinate, and King had treated him accordingly. Increasingly, however, Nimitz began to believe that it was important to establish the fact that he was in command, and that he should exercise authority over the carrier task forces in his theater. When King suggested that Nimitz send major elements of his command to support the heavily pressed ABDA (American, British, Dutch, and Australian) command, Nimitz replied that his forces were too weak to supply such a reinforcement, and offered that it would be better to conduct more diversionary raids to take some of the pressure off of ABDA. The question became moot a few days later when the Japanese virtually annihilated the ABDA naval command, sinking four Allied cruisers and seven destroyers during the Battle of the Java Sea (February 27–28). At about the same time, the Japanese also sank the old *Langley*, which had been the first American carrier, though she had been converted to a seaplane tender back in 1937. These losses temporarily ended the discussion over whether Nimitz ought to support ABDA. It also made the line of communication to Australia even more tenuous.[42]

Indeed, it was evident that the Japanese were building up their forces at Rabaul for a new push southward, and to forestall that, King ordered Brown to make a second attempt to raid the shipping at Rabaul. Brown claimed that he needed a second carrier task force for such a mission. King ordered Nimitz to send him Fletcher's *Yorktown* group. Even after that, Brown hedged, reporting to King that he did not consider an attack on Rabaul "advisable." Perhaps growing impatient with Brown, King insisted.[43]

Before Brown and Fletcher could get into position, however, the tactical picture changed again, and dramatically so. The shipping that had been crowding into Rabaul Harbor left there on March 7 and appeared the next day off the north coast of New Guinea, three hundred miles to the southwest. Japanese soldiers went ashore at Lae and Salamaua to establish new outposts for their maritime empire and to protect the approaches to Rabaul. Brown at once concluded that the shipping off those two ports offered a more valuable target than Rabaul itself, and on his own he changed the objective of the raid. It was within the authority of a task-force commander to alter the target with shifting circumstances, as Halsey had done at Kwajalein, but this was the second time that Brown had been ordered to strike at Rabaul and the second time he found a reason not to do it. Moreover, instead of approaching the new target from the east, Brown decided to attack from the south, launching planes from the Gulf of Papua south of New Guinea and sending them over the Owen Stanley Mountain Range, which runs like a gigantic spine along the middle of southeastern New Guinea.[44]

Most of the planes were bombers and escorting fighters. Brown also sent off twenty-five Devastators, thirteen of them carrying the heavy Mark 13

torpedo, and the rest with bombs. The slow and heavy Devastators had difficulty getting over the mountains, and they surmounted the crest only with
the aid of a timely updraft. When the 104 American aircraft from two carriers came swooping down the verdant valleys on the north shore of New
Guinea on March 10, they found even more targets off Lae and Salamaua
than Halsey had found at Kwajalein. It was a bright, clear day, and there was
no air opposition. The Americans had a field day. Based on the testimony
of his pilots, Brown reported sinking five transports, three cruisers, a destroyer, and a minesweeper. The actual toll was less, but still impressive:
three large transports sunk plus one more severely damaged, and additional
damage to a light cruiser, several destroyers, and a large seaplane. Only one
American aircraft was lost. Indeed, the raid so savaged Japanese sealift capacity that the local Japanese commander worried about his ability to sustain his foothold in New Guinea. It was the best day of the war so far for the
brown shoes, and Roosevelt wired Churchill that it was "by all means the
best day's work we have had."[45]

The *Lexington* task force returned to Pearl Harbor on March 26. The
raid had been an unqualified success, and Nimitz recommended Brown
for the Distinguished Service Medal. Then, two days later, Nimitz tapped
Brown to head the new Amphibious Force being organized in San Diego. It was not quite a promotion, and some wondered at the time and
later whether the purpose of the appointment was to remove Brown
from the command of Task Force 11. The Pacific War historian John
Lundstrom is doubtful, insisting that Brown's "departure from carrier
command had nothing to do with any perceived impression of lack of
'aggressiveness.'" Perhaps not. But for whatever reason, both King and
Nimitz had decided that Brown's skills were better suited to other tasks.
The "Running Summary" kept at CinCPac headquarters by Navy Captain
Lynde D. McCormick noted that Brown "did not approach New Britain
at all, but went to a position south of New Guinea and sent aircraft across
the peninsula to Lae and Salamaua. . . . Even with the damage inflicted, it is
doubtful if the enemy will be greatly retarded."[46]

In that, at least, McCormick was wrong. The raid had a dramatic impact
not only on Japanese shipping but also, and more importantly, on Japanese

decision making. Vice Admiral Inoue Shigeyoshi, the Fourth Fleet commander who headed the Japanese South Seas Force, concluded that continuing the advance southward would now be impossible without carrier support. That conclusion would bring important elements of the Kidō Butai into contact with the American carriers for the first time.[47]

**5**

# Seeking the Decisive Battle

The first phase of the war had gone well for Japan—so well, in fact, that four months into it, her leaders faced the unexpected dilemma of not knowing what to do next. By March of 1942, virtually all of Japan's prewar goals had been achieved: British Malaya and its great bastion of Singapore were in Japanese hands, as were the Dutch East Indies, including the oil-rich islands of Borneo, Java, and Sumatra. Most of the Philippines, too, had fallen. Some American and Filipino soldiers still held out in Bataan, but they would surrender on April 9, after which only the tiny island of Corregidor still held out, and it was only a matter of time until it fell. Thailand had capitulated early. Rangoon, the capital of Burma, fell on March 8, and Japanese forces chased the British back toward the border with India. All this had been accomplished with a total loss to the Imperial Japanese Navy of only five destroyers, three patrol boats, seven minesweepers, seven submarines, and several transports. Not a single capital ship had been seriously damaged, much less sunk. It had been so easy that in some quarters it led to what has been dubbed "victory disease": an expectation that every new initiative would automatically result in triumph. It was not at all clear, however, what those new initiatives might be. Though the Japanese had planned the "First Phase of Operations" with close attention to detail, their notions of what might come next were vague at best.[1]

From the beginning, the Japanese had never imagined that they would be able to conquer the United States and dictate peace terms to the White House.* Rather, their goal was to demonstrate that it would be equally impossible for the Americans to conquer Japan. When the Americans launched their inevitable counterattack and attempted to fight their way westward across the Pacific, the Japanese planned to make their progress so painful that the Yankees would eventually decide that the cost of sub- duing them—in both blood and treasure—was unacceptable. Once that happened, a negotiated settlement was the only possible outcome, and in the course of those negotiations the Japanese would argue that they should be allowed to keep their Southeast Asian conquests. Their assumption that their Anglo-American opponents could be brought to the negotiating table after suffering reversals at sea was based in part on their experience in the war against Russia in 1904–5, when the Russians had accepted negotia- tions because they feared internal unrest at home more than defeat abroad. Such an assumption did not apply to the British or the Americans, how- ever, especially after Pearl Harbor.[2]

There was general agreement in Japan that to bring about the kind of stale- mate that they hoped would trigger negotiations, at some point it would be necessary to establish a defensive perimeter around her new possessions and dare the Americans to assail it. The question was, where? Initially they assumed that this defensive barrier would run from the Kuriles in the

---

* Early in 1941, Yamamoto wrote a letter to another officer who favored war with America. In that letter, Yamamoto stated that in any such war the Japanese would be compelled to seek "a capitulation at the White House, in Washington itself." After the war began, Japanese newspapers published this letter, which led the Western press to assume that this was, in fact, Yamamoto's goal. Instead, Yamamoto had written the letter as a way of suggesting that a war with the U.S. was not winnable. The next line in this letter, omitted when it was published, was: "I wonder whether the politicians of the day really have the willingness to make [the] sacrifice ... that this would entail."

northern home islands, through captured Wake Island (which the Japanese renamed Ōtorijima) in the central Pacific, then south to the Marshalls and Gilberts. But after the easy triumphs of January to March of 1942, they considered an expanded perimeter that might include Australia, Hawaii, or the Aleutians—or all three. There was also discussion about Japan's obligations to Germany under the Tripartite Pact. The Army in particular pondered both the wisdom and the timing of an attack on the Soviet Union. And finally, there was Yamamoto's determination to eliminate the threat of more American carrier raids by engineering a climactic naval battle somewhere in the central Pacific that would destroy those carriers once and for all. All of these options were contemplated by a Japanese decision-making architecture that depended less on clear lines of hierarchy and authority than on subtle and constantly shifting political and personal relationships between power centers, relationships that were frequently jealous and competitive.[3]

In theory at least, the principal decision-making body in the Imperial Japanese Navy was the Naval General Staff. Until 1933, it had been subordinate to the Navy Ministry, but a "reform" that year—in effect a coup by the fleet faction—elevated the Naval General Staff to a position of de facto superiority, giving its members responsibility for armament, education, training, personnel, and command. The head of the staff was Admiral Nagano Osami, a 61-year-old career officer who had preceded Yamamoto in command of the Combined Fleet. Nagano was a battleship-and-cruiser man, a stolid, taciturn officer who had graduated from Eta Jima in 1900 and had been a staff officer in the Russo-Japanese War. Physically, Nagano (whose nickname was "The Elephant") could hardly have been more different from the diminutive Yamamoto, but their career tracks were strikingly similar. Both men had served tours of duty in the United States and attended Harvard—in Nagano's case, Harvard Law School. Both had been members of the treaty faction before the war and participated in the 1922 Washington conference and the 1930 London conference. They had both opposed Japan's adherence to the Tripartite Pact with Germany and Italy. After that, however, Nagano adjusted his outlook. By April of 1941, when he became chief of staff, he had concluded that war had become inevitable. In light

■ Admiral Nagano Osami (nicknamed "the Elephant") headed the Naval General Staff in the spring of 1942. At a series of meetings in April, he and the rest of the staff capitulated to Yamamoto's insistence on conducting Operation MI. (U.S. Naval Institute)

of this fact, Nagano actively supported a thrust southward to occupy the Dutch East Indies and British Malaya, at least in part to prevent the Army from dominating the decision-making process.[4]

The first open split between Nagano and Yamamoto came over the wisdom of striking at Pearl Harbor. Nagano believed that it would be possible to seize the British and Dutch possessions in the South Pacific without drawing the United States into the war. He argued that the Pearl Harbor gambit was unnecessary and risky, and that it would pull resources away from the all-important strike southward. Yamamoto saw this as timidity. He opined to an associate that Nagano was "the kind of man who thinks he's a genius, even though he's not," and told another, "Nagano's a dead loss." In the end, Yamamoto got his way concerning Pearl Harbor by threatening to resign unless his plan was accepted. It was a particularly audacious piece of extortion, and Yamamoto was bold enough to tell Nagano "not to interfere too much and thus set a bad precedent in the Navy." It is unimaginable that Chester Nimitz would have made such a suggestion to Ernie King, or that he would have kept his job if he had. A bad precedent was indeed set: a fleet commander could make strategic plans on his own and force those plans onto his putative superiors by threatening to resign. In the months after Pearl Harbor, the rampage of the Kidō Butai elevated Yamamoto's prestige higher, though the admiral himself had remained aboard his flagship in Hashirajima Harbor near Hiroshima.[5]

Now in March, with most of the war's goals already achieved, Nagano and the Naval General Staff considered the next step. Their first instinct was to look southward. Nagano believed that when the Americans began their inevitable counteroffensive, they would use Australia as their base, and that could be forestalled at the outset by occupying the continent. Despite a successful raid by the Kidō Butai on the Australian naval base at Darwin in February, the Japanese Army was appalled by the notion of invading Australia. Because General Tōjō Hideki was both war minister and prime minister, the Army had a virtual veto over any plan that called for the participation of ground troops, and the Army had no interest in such an open-ended commitment. Australia was sparsely defended, as most of her soldiers had been sent to other theaters of war, but it would nonetheless take a minimum of ten divisions—some 200,000 men—to seize and hold just the northern coast, and Japan did not have ten divisions to spare, or the ships to transport and supply them.[6]

Nor was the Army interested in another proposal of the Naval General Staff: the invasion and occupation of Ceylon in the Indian Ocean. The expectation was that such a move would provoke an uprising by the restive native population of India and threaten the British Empire where its stability was most precarious. According to one member of the Naval General Staff, a principal purpose of the operation was to "carry out Indian independence." In addition, a move across the Indian Ocean toward the Persian Gulf offered the possibility of linking up with Axis forces, as well as access to the oil fields of the Middle East. Though the conquest of Ceylon would require only two divisions rather than ten, the Army was not interested. Its main concern continued to be the festering conflict in China, where four-fifths of its active divisions were concentrated. If the Army looked anywhere for new fields to conquer, it was to the north rather than the south or the west. In the late fall and early winter of 1941, as the Wehrmacht drove toward Moscow, many Japanese generals anticipated the imminent collapse of the Soviet Union, and they did not want to miss out on the spoils when that happened. They concluded that it was necessary to hold troops in readiness "to share a victory when the Germans succeed."[7]

The Army's obstructionism bred resentment not only within the Naval General Staff in Tokyo but at Combined Fleet Headquarters on board

Yamamoto's flagship, where one of his staff officers complained: "We want to invade Ceylon; we are not allowed to! We want to invade Australia; we cannot! We want to attack Hawaii; we cannot do that either! All because the Army will not agree to release the necessary forces." Yamamoto's logistics officer recalled that, "since the Army-Navy could not come up with a common agreement of effort on the second phase operations, the Navy looked more and more toward what it could do alone."[8]

Faced with the Army's refusal to support invasions, Nagano and the General Staff fell back on their plans to send the Kidō Butai on a hit-and-run raid against British bases in Ceylon. In late March, Nagumo took five carriers and their escorts westward, south of Sumatra, and into the Indian Ocean. (The *Kaga*, having struck a submerged reef, went to Sasebo, near Nagasaki, for repairs.)

Thanks to a warning from Allied intelligence, the British knew they were coming. In anticipation of the Japanese strike, Admiral Sir James Somerville mobilized his fleet, which included four old and slow battleships, but also two modern carriers—the *Indomitable* and the *Formidable*—and took up a position south of Ceylon, from where he hoped to threaten the flank of the Japanese fleet as it approached. He knew he could not slug it out toe-to-toe with the Kidō Butai; he hoped he might be able to inflict some damage with night torpedo attacks. For three days he waited. When the Kidō Butai didn't appear, he sent two heavy cruisers—*Dorsetshire* and *Cornwall*—to the naval base at Colombo on Ceylon's western coast, and withdrew the rest of the fleet to Addu Atoll in the Maldives, six hundred miles southwest of Ceylon, to refuel.

Two days later, on April 5, Easter Sunday morning, 315 planes from the Kidō Butai struck Colombo. The British commander there, Vice Admiral Sir Geoffrey Layton, had sent most of the shipping to the north to get it out of harm's way, and the two heavy cruisers sent to him by Somerville headed back for Addu Atoll. Layton also ordered out a squadron of Hawker Hurricane fighter planes—older cousins of the more famous Spitfire—plus half a dozen Fairey Swordfish biplanes armed with torpedoes for a counterattack. The Swordfish had performed well during a Royal Navy torpedo attack on the Italian naval base at Taranto the previous November, but they

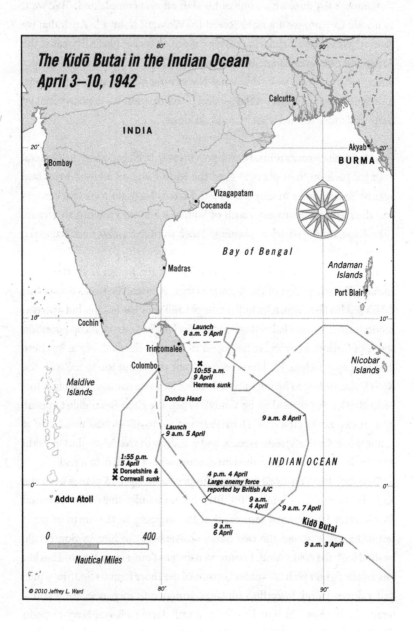

The Kidō Butai in the Indian Ocean
April 3–10, 1942

INDIA

Calcutta

Akyab

BURMA

Bombay

Vizagapatam
Cocanada

Bay of Bengal

Madras

Andaman
Islands

Port Blair

Cochin

Launch
8 a.m. 9 April

Trincomalee

Colombo

10:55 a.m.
9 April
Hermes sunk

Nicobar
Islands

Maldive
Islands

Dondra Head

Launch
9 a.m. 5 April

9 a.m. 8 April

1:55 p.m.
5 April
Dorsetshire &
Cornwall sunk

INDIAN OCEAN

4 p.m. 4 April
Large enemy force
reported by British A/C

9 a.m.
4 April

9 a.m. 7 April

Addu Atoll

9 a.m.
6 April

Kidō Butai

0                    400

9 a.m. 3 April

Nautical Miles

© 2010 Jeffrey L. Ward

were helpless against the nimble Zeros. The Hurricanes, too, got much the worst of the encounter. In barely half an hour, the British lost twenty-seven aircraft, including fifteen Hurricanes, while the Japanese lost only seven bombers. The rest of the Japanese strike force, piloted by their superbly trained enlisted pilots, flew through the intercept and attacked the naval base, dropping their bombs on ships and yard facilities. They sank three British warships and wrecked the repair shops and the rail yard (something they had neglected to do at Pearl Harbor). The Kidō Butai was never threatened. It was not as decisive a blow as the one against the Americans, but once again the Japanese had demonstrated their air superiority over the West.[9]

Worse was to come. The two heavy cruisers Layton had sent back toward Addu Atoll were en route there on April 6 when a Japanese search plane found them and radioed their location back to the Kidō Butai. Within twenty minutes, Nagumo had eighty-eight planes in the air winging their way toward the reported coordinates.[10]

The cruisers never had a chance. Like the *Prince of Wales* and *Repulse* the previous December, they had no air cover and were therefore sitting ducks. Gun crews on the cruisers threw up all the antiaircraft fire they could muster, and the ships twisted and turned in the hope of confusing the dive-bombers, but with so many planes attacking—and from different directions at that—it was hopeless. The *Dorsetshire* went down first. Hit by ten bombs and concussed by several near misses, she sank in minutes. The *Cornwall*, hit by nine bombs, followed her a few minutes later. Once again, aircraft had proved their dominance over surface warships.[11]

The Kidō Butai was not finished. Three days later, on April 9, the Japanese struck again, this time at the British naval base at Trincomalee on Ceylon's east coast. Again, the British put up all the planes they had—twenty-three altogether, including seventeen Hurricane fighters—but they were brushed aside or sent spinning toward the sea in flames by the Zeros. The British also sent nine land-based Blenheim bombers to attack the Japanese carriers. Five were shot down over the target by the patrolling Zeros; the others limped back with serious damage. None scored a hit.

As he had at Colombo, Layton sent most of his ships to sea to get them out of the way. The small aircraft carrier *Hermes*, with an escort of one destroyer, steamed southward along the coast. The Japanese found her nonetheless, and Nagumo sent ninety planes to the attack. The Val dive-bombers blanketed her with bombs, and the *Hermes* virtually disappeared under a rainstorm of hits and near misses. Within ten minutes, she and her escorting destroyer were dead in the water and sinking. After that, Somerville decided to send part of his force to Kenya on the east coast of Africa and took the rest, including the two carriers, north to Bombay, effectively surrendering the eastern Indian Ocean and the Bay of Bengal to the Japanese. "I am convinced," he wrote, "that it is not good policy to take excessive chances with the Eastern Fleet for the sake of Ceylon." Having secured Japan's southern flank, Nagumo turned the Kidō Butai back toward the Pacific.[12]

Even as the big carriers and their escorts steamed through the Straits of Malacca back into the South China Sea, the Japanese high command feuded over their next assignment. One option was to complete the isolation of Australia by seizing the islands of New Caledonia, Fiji, and Samoa—exactly what Ernie King and Franklin Roosevelt feared they would do. Even Japanese Army leaders supported these limited moves because they required fewer troops than the proposed alternatives.

Another claimant on the Kidō Butai was Vice Admiral Inoue Shigeyoshi, commander of the South Seas Force. Inoue until recently had been head of the Naval Aviation Division, and he was a ferocious advocate of air power, especially land-based air. For most of his career, he had insisted that airplanes had made much of the Navy obsolete. "The days of the battleship are gone," he had declared in 1937. "It has been replaced by the aircraft." Inoue even argued that the effectiveness of long-range land-based airplanes made carriers obsolete. If that were not sufficiently heretical, he had declared in January of 1941 that it was "impossible . . . for Japan to defeat America," and that the United States could "wipe out Japanese forces." After that bit of apostasy, he was dispatched to the South Seas command, with his headquarters on the isolated island of Truk in the Carolines. In part, his reassignment was an aspect of the reshuffling of commands in anticipation of war, but in addition, like Yamamoto, he was banished to sea duty for his unwelcome ideas and his unwillingness to keep quiet about them.[13]

It was Inoue's Fourth Fleet, with support from the Kidō Butai, that had seized Rabaul back in January. He had been shocked on February 20 when only two of the seventeen bombers he had sent out against Wilson Brown's *Lexington* task force had returned. After all, the ability of land-based aircraft to defend the perimeter of the empire was at the heart of his strategic vision and the foundation of Japan's entire defensive strategy. Inoue's shock turned to alarm after the Allied raid on Lae and Salamaua left him without enough shipping to continue the campaign. He notified both the Naval General Staff (Nagano) and Combined Fleet (Yamamoto) that before he advanced any further, he would need carrier support. He requested two carriers, but, given that the Kidō Butai was still in the Indian Ocean when he submitted this request, he declared that he would settle for the damaged *Kaga*, then undergoing repairs in Sasebo.[14]

Another demand on the Kidō Butai soon arose in connection with a plan to occupy at least some of the Aleutians, the long chain of frozen rocky islands that trailed out from Alaska across much of the North Pacific. The westernmost of those islands was within theoretical bombing range of the northernmost of Japan's home islands; the occupation of at least some of them would serve as an early-warning system in Japan's defensive perimeter and also prevent the Americans from using them to stage air raids against the homeland. Thus by the end of March, even before the Kidō Butai had returned from the Indian Ocean, Japan's naval leaders were considering two separate initiatives that would require its participation: one to break communications between Hawaii and Australia by seizing Port Moresby, the Australian base on the south coast of New Guinea, and the Solomon Islands, followed by an attack on Fiji and Samoa; and another to extend the defensive perimeter of the empire and protect Japan's northern flank by seizing the westernmost of the Aleutian Islands.[15]

Complicated as this was, it would soon get much more so, for none of this took Yamamoto into account. The apparent success of his calculated gamble at Pearl Harbor and the string of naval victories that followed had added greatly to his prestige and had given him unprecedented informal authority in crafting Japanese strategy for the "Second Operational Phase." Once the

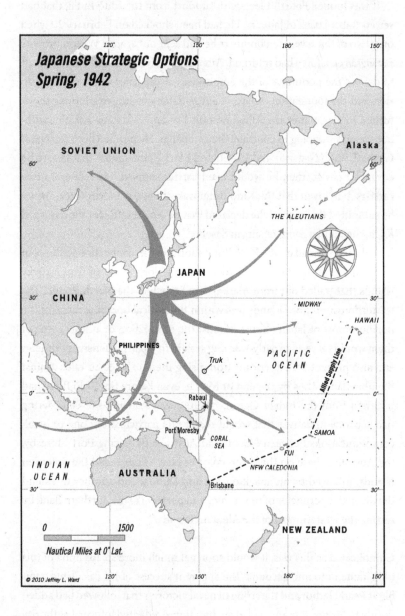

**Japanese Strategic Options
Spring, 1942**

SOVIET UNION

Alaska

THE ALEUTIANS

JAPAN

CHINA

MIDWAY

HAWAII

PHILIPPINES

Truk

PACIFIC
OCEAN

Rabaul

Port Moresby

CORAL
SEA

SAMOA

FIJI

NEW CALEDONIA

INDIAN
OCEAN

AUSTRALIA

Brisbane

Allied Supply Line

NEW ZEALAND

0        1500

Nautical Miles at 0° Lat.

© 2010 Jeffrey L. Ward

Kidō Butai returned from the Indian Ocean, Yamamoto knew exactly what he wanted to do with it, and it did not involve Australia, New Guinea, or the Aleutians. He wanted to finish the job that Nagumo had left uncompleted at Pearl Harbor.

Even before the Americans began their series of carrier-based raids on Japanese bases in the Marshall Islands and elsewhere, Yamamoto had concluded that it was essential to eliminate the danger of such raids by finding and sinking the American flattops. Though the Japanese public had celebrated Pearl Harbor as a great victory, Yamamoto himself, as noted above, had been hugely disappointed that Nagumo had not remained in the area long enough to wreck the base or to find and sink the American carriers. Nagumo had seen the American battle fleet as his most important target, and once that had been dispensed with he had broken off the raid. At the time, the young and aggressive commander of the Second Carrier Division, Rear Admiral Yamaguchi Tamon, blinkered Nagumo a signal that he had "completed preparations" for another attack, a not-so-subtle hint that there was more work to be done. But Nagumo was immune to such suggestions. Once he had recovered his airplanes, he turned the Kidō Butai around and headed for home. Had he launched a third strike, he might have destroyed the repair facilities on Oahu and especially the oil tank farm, which would have crippled the Americans far more than the loss of their battle fleet.[16]

Since then, the consequences of having missed the carriers had been vividly demonstrated by American raids on the Marshalls, Wake, Lae/Salamaua, and elsewhere. In addition, Yamamoto was haunted by the thought that so long as the American carriers roamed the Pacific, there was always a chance, however remote, that they might find a way to launch a raid against the Japanese homeland. His chief of staff confided to his diary that protecting Tokyo from air raids was "the most important thing to be borne in mind." Halsey's raid on Marcus Island, only 999 nautical miles from Tokyo, was a reminder that such a catastrophic event was not impossible. As early as January of 1941, Yamamoto had expressed the fear that "we cannot rule out the possibility that the enemy would dare to launch an attack upon our homeland to burn our capital city and other cities." He feared that the Americans might strike while the Kidō Butai was still in the

Indian Ocean, and as a precaution he ordered the establishment of a picket line of small vessels seven hundred miles off the Japanese coast, well beyond the maximum range of American carrier bombers. However, there was always a chance that one or more American carriers might sneak past those pickets and find a way to launch. Since the protection of the homeland—and especially protecting the life and safety of the emperor—was the Navy's first mission, such a possibility was unacceptable.[17]

Consequently, even before the Kidō Butai returned from its initial strike at Pearl Harbor, Yamamoto had already begun to think about ways to complete what Nagumo had left unfinished. He ordered his chief of staff, Ugaki Matome, to sketch out a plan for an invasion of Hawaii as a way of provoking a climactic sea battle that would result in the destruction of the American carriers. Ugaki spent four days in mid-January battling a terrible toothache while he outlined an operational plan to "mobilize all available strength to invade Hawaii while attempting to destroy the enemy fleet in a decisive battle." Such plans were completely unrealistic, however, because the Japanese simply did not have the resources to invade Hawaii and lacked the sealift capability to keep it supplied even if they could take it. Both the Naval General Staff and the Army made it clear that such an operation was out of the question. In spite of that, Yamamoto continued to hope that he could contrive a way to lure the American carrier force out to its destruction. He was aware that Nagano and the General Staff, and the Army, too, opposed his plan for a decisive confrontation in the central Pacific, but to Yamamoto that only made the challenge of getting his way more appealing. As strategically important as it was to get the American carriers, it was almost as important to outwit his domestic rivals within the Japanese military hierarchy.[18]

The one constant in all of these plans was the Kidō Butai. Carriers would be needed to spearhead the invasion of Fiji and Samoa, and also for the Aleutian initiative, and now Inoue was calling for at least some portion of the Kidō Butai for the assault on Port Moresby as well. Yamamoto found all these requests annoying and wrongheaded. Just as Chester Nimitz complained to Ernie King that carriers should be used offensively, not defensively, Yamamoto wanted to use his carriers to attack and destroy their

American counterparts, not to protect transports in invasion fleets. His view was that once the American carriers were out of the picture, future Japanese invasion groups could roam the western Pacific at will. To achieve this end, it would be necessary to threaten an asset so important that the Americans would feel compelled to commit most or even all of their carriers to defend it. Given Ernie King's concern for the security of Fiji and Samoa, a Japanese thrust at those islands might provoke the reaction Yamamoto sought. Yamamoto, however, did not think them important enough to ensure a decisive confrontation. He sought an objective close to the Americans' principal base at Pearl Harbor. Yamamoto continued to hope that operations in the central Pacific could somehow lead to the occupation of Hawaii, which could then be used as a bargaining chip in negotiations with the Americans. These considerations led him to examine the Hawaiian archipelago carefully. Since neither the Army nor the General Staff would support an invasion of Hawaii, he decided to target the small two-island atoll of Midway.[19]

Midway was an unlikely objective. A barren, sandy outpost in the middle of the Pacific Ocean, it was quite literally a thousand miles from anywhere: Pearl Harbor was 1,135 nautical miles in one direction, and Wake Island was 1,185 nautical miles in the other. Like every other atoll in the Pacific, Midway was essentially a circular coral reef that enclosed a small lagoon. On the southern edge of that lagoon, two small sandy islands barely broke the surface of the sea. The larger of them, appropriately named Sand Island, was less than two miles long; the other, Eastern Island, was even smaller. For hundreds of years, the chief inhabitant of those two tiny islands was the Laysan Albatross, whose odd mating dance provoked visitors to dub them "gooney birds." So remote was Midway that there is no record of its having been "discovered" until 1859, though whalers and others had certainly stopped there intermittently before that. The United States established a coaling station there after the Civil War, and two years later, in 1869, the U.S. Navy began dredging a channel between the two islands in order to provide access to the sheltered lagoon, though the project ran out of money before it could be completed.[20]

After the war with Spain in 1898, which expanded American interest in the Pacific, President Theodore Roosevelt placed Midway under the control of the Navy Department, and that same year the United States established a telegraph cable station on Sand Island, connecting it to Hawaii. The outpost was further developed in the 1930s when Pan American Airlines used it as a seaplane base for its trans-Pacific Clippers and even built a small hotel there for its passengers. In 1940, as war with Japan loomed, the Navy finally completed the ship channel into the lagoon, which made Midway a sheltered anchorage, principally for seaplanes and the occasional submarine. And in the summer of 1941, four months before Pearl Harbor, the Navy completed an airfield on Eastern Island that made it a kind of unsinkable—though also immobile—aircraft carrier.

Thus, small as it was, Midway's isolation made it an important outpost in the American defense line. Taking off from its protected lagoon, broad-winged PBY Catalina seaplanes could scour the ocean out to a thousand miles, and from that same lagoon, American submarines could initiate patrols to the very shores of Japan itself. From the new airfield on Eastern Island, bombers and fighters could guard the northern approach to Hawaii. In their communications to one another, King and Nimitz both acknowledged the importance of the "Midway-Hawaii line." Yamamoto calculated that Midway was important enough to the Americans that a threat to it would compel them to sortie from Oahu with their carriers to contest an invasion. When that happened, the Kidō Butai would pounce on them and send them to the bottom.[21]

In February, Yamamoto ordered his staff to put together an operational plan for the invasion and occupation of Midway. The Kidō Butai would approach Midway from the north (as it had the previous December) and launch a strike on its airfield, in order to destroy whatever American air assets were on the island. Meanwhile, a powerful (but not too powerful) surface force would approach Midway from the west to attract the attention of the Americans. The American carriers would presumably sortie from Pearl Harbor in response to either the bombardment of Midway or the appearance of this modest surface force, or both. When they did, a prepositioned group of Japanese submarines would inflict as much damage on them as

▓ An aerial photograph of Midway Atoll in 1942. Eastern Island, with its airfield, is in the foreground. The ship channel into the central lagoon and the channel from the lagoon to the Eastern Island dock are clearly visible. (U.S. Naval Institute)

possible as they moved toward the decisive battle. Then the Kidō Butai would steam southward to engage. The six carriers of the Kidō Butai should have little trouble with the two or three surviving American carriers, but just in case, Yamamoto himself—with several heavy battleships, including the giant *Yamato*—would back up the Kidō Butai to finish off any survivors.

Despite his early advocacy of carriers, and his criticism of depending too much on battleships, Yamamoto felt obligated to find a role in this decisive engagement for the new and expensive heavy battleships.

For all its boldness, the plan was not a complete departure from traditional Japanese strategy, for it was essentially a tactical version of the strategic plan that had been part of Japanese thinking for more than a decade: submarines and airplanes would whittle down the American striking force as it moved toward the decisive confrontation. Here was the same plan in miniature. A critical difference, however, was that this decisive engagement would take place 2,500 miles from Japanese home waters. Indeed, by targeting Midway, Yamamoto was granting to the Americans all the advantages that the Japanese had counted on in their own defense of the Pacific: shorter logistic lines, proximity to repair facilities, and land-based air cover.[22]

It is noteworthy that this plan divided Japanese naval assets into four different and independent groups. If this seemed more complicated than it needed to be, it was because Yamamoto was more concerned that the Americans would refuse to take the bait than that they might actually pose a serious threat to his armada. If he put all six carriers of the Kidō Butai *and* the battle fleet into one mighty armada, it would unquestionably dominate the Pacific, but it might also intimidate the Americans to the point that they would refuse to come out to contest it, and the opportunity to sink the American carriers would be lost. As a result, in translating Yamamoto's vision into an operational plan, the staff planners of the Combined Fleet divided up the available forces into at least four distinct groups that would sail independently.

The first of these was the so-called Midway Invasion Group, which was actually a surface force under Vice Admiral Kondō Nabutake, consisting of two battleships, five cruisers, and seven destroyers, plus the new light carrier *Zuiho*, which was capable of carrying two dozen torpedo planes and fighters. As Jonathan Parshall and Anthony Tully point out in their detailed study of Japanese operations at Midway, "Kondō was the bait." Combined Fleet planners hoped that when the Americans discovered this force approaching Midway, they would see it as powerful enough to be tempting and yet not so large as to be intimidating. That would encourage them to come out of Pearl Harbor to contest its advance.[23]

Kondō's force would screen the actual invasion force (called the "Transport Group") that would carry the five thousand naval infantry and the construction battalion that would occupy Midway and turn it into a Japanese base. Carried in twelve large transport ships escorted by a light cruiser and ten destroyers, it would also approach Midway from the west. In close support would be four heavy cruisers and two destroyers under Vice Admiral Kurita Takeo.

While Kondō and Kurita approached from the west, the Kidō Butai would approach Midway from the northwest. If Kondō's surface force did not draw out the Americans, the first strike by planes from the Kidō Butai against Midway surely would. Once again Nagumo Chūichi would command this key element of the fleet. His main purpose, as Yamamoto saw it, was the destruction of the American carrier force, but assigning him responsibility to soften up Midway for the invasion and to cover the landing also created the opportunity for confusion and uncertainty, especially with a literal-minded commander like Nagumo.

Yamamoto himself would lead what was called the "Main Body," composed of three heavy battleships, including the enormous *Yamato*, accompanied by a screen of one light cruiser and eight destroyers. This force would trail Kondō's invasion force by several hundred miles, not only to remain beyond the range of American search planes but also to enable Yamamoto to support whichever of the other two advances turned out to be the focus of the American sortie. It would be the first time in the war that the commander in chief of the Combined Fleet personally accompanied an operation. Subsequent critics cited this as a grave error, since Yamamoto would have to maintain radio silence while at sea, preventing him from exerting any active supervision over the operation. Had he remained ashore, as Chester Nimitz did, he could have listened in on the radio net and sent out orders as necessary to ensure that his command vision was fulfilled.

But passive command from a distance was unappealing to a man with Yamamoto's worldview. Though the early victories of the Japanese Navy had made him a national hero and won him many official decorations, he had not yet smelled the smoke of battle or even put himself in harm's way.

He confessed to a friend that the accolades that poured into his headquarters after the first victories left him "intolerably embarrassed." Moreover, Yamamoto may have had a political objective in mind as well. The historian Hugh Bicheno speculates that Yamamoto went to sea during the Midway campaign so that he could return to Tokyo with a decisive victory in hand and use his elevated prestige to depose Tōjō's government and open negotiations for an end to the war. Whether or not that was part of his grand strategy, Yamamoto's gambler's instinct was evident in every part of the Midway plan. Just as he had contrived the Pearl Harbor strike as a dramatic alternative to the thrust southward the previous fall, so now did he prepare a dramatic alternative to the Naval General Staff's notion of consolidating Japan's defense perimeter in the South Pacific and the Aleutians. If there was also a political element in play, that only raised the stakes for this nautical gambler.[24]

With the plan fleshed out, Yamamoto sent a representative from his staff to Tokyo on April 2 to present it to the Naval General Staff. The man he sent was Commander Watanabe Yasuji, his logistics officer and frequent *shogi* partner. Watanabe was not only a great admirer of his boss, he had also played an active role in developing the plan and therefore had a proprietary interest in its adoption. Watanabe flew to Tokyo by seaplane and reported to the two-story brick building near the Imperial Palace that housed the Naval General Staff. As he laid out the particulars, it soon became evident that the plan would monopolize virtually all the assets of the Imperial Navy and require the postponement of all other plans, including the move to Port Moresby and the seizure of Fiji-Samoa.

Both Nagano and Rear Admiral Fukudome Shigeru, head of the plans division, remained mute. It was Commander Miyo Tatsukichi, the only naval aviator in the room, who challenged Watanabe. A short, wiry man with gold fillings, he had attended both Eta Jima and the Naval Staff College with Watanabe, and the two men knew each other well. Nevertheless, their exchange grew increasingly tense. Possession of Midway, Miyo argued, would be more of a burden than an asset. Even if the invasion went flawlessly, the atoll's distance from Japan would make it extremely difficult, if not impossible, to sustain. Japan's logistical capabilities were already stretched to the breaking point, and everything needed to sustain Midway as a Japanese outpost—food, ammunition, and especially oil—would have to be shipped there across an ocean crawling with American submarines. Sufficient tankers needed to carry refined oil from Japan to Midway simply did not exist, and, if they did, how wise was it for Japan to be exporting refined oil—the dearth of which had triggered the war in the first place? Moreover, up to this point in the war, Japan had advanced from one position to another only under the umbrella of land-based air. That would not be the case with Midway. The atoll was, however, under the umbrella of American land-based air from Oahu, which would make it vulnerable to American raids and recapture. Finally, if Combined Fleet wanted a battle with the American carriers, one could be had by attacking Fiji or Samoa, the loss of which would break the American link to Australia. And a battle in the South Pacific would give Japan all the advantages that the Americans would have at Midway.[25]

Watanabe was not used to hearing such sharp and direct criticism of a plan generated by the commander in chief. He responded to Miyo by asserting that "after capture [Midway] would be supplied the same as was already being done with Wake." And he pledged "to go to Fiji and Samoa after the Battle of Midway had been won." Apparently flustered, he merely repeated the outlines of the plan that he had been entrusted to deliver. It was evident that the evidence weighed heavily against adoption of the Midway plan, but Yamamoto's influence had grown so great that it could not be dismissed outright. Fukudome, who had once been Yamamoto's chief of staff, tried to calm the heated discussion: "Come, come," he said, "don't get too excited. Since the Combined Fleet's so set on the plan, why don't we study it to see if we can't accept it?"[26]

The group met again three days later. It was clear at once that studying the details of the plan had only confirmed Miyo's doubts. He reiterated, even more strongly, its obvious defects. Unable to counter Miyo's arguments, Watanabe left the room to telephone the flagship *Yamato*. He summarized Miyo's criticisms and asked for a response. Was Yamamoto still committed to the Midway plan? He was. Watanabe returned to the room to tell the members of the General Staff that Yamamoto's mind was made up, and that "if his plan was not adopted he *might* resign."

It was Fukudome who asked the crucial question: "If the C in C's so set on it, shall we leave it to him?" No one else in the room spoke, but several nodded. Nagano capitulated once again, as he had over the Pearl Harbor raid. Miyo could only bow his head; some thought he was forcing back tears. Yamamoto had forced the Pearl Harbor raid onto the General Staff by bluff and threat. Now he was imposing the Midway plan on his skeptical and reluctant superiors. The behavior of the Naval General Staff was, as the historian H. P. Willmott has noted, "nothing less than an abject and craven shirking of responsibility."[27]

The Army's response was, in effect, a shrug. Since the plan did not call for any significant participation by the Army, its leaders seemed to say: do whatever you want so long as you don't call on us for support. But the Army did worry about Inoue's move southward to Port Moresby, for that did involve Army assets, and as a result, five days after winning his victory over the Naval General Staff, Yamamoto agreed to lend one carrier division of the Kidō Butai to Inoue for what was codenamed Operation MO—the capture of Port Moresby. For that operation, Yamamoto selected the newest and least experienced of the carrier divisions—CarDiv 5, composed of the new carriers *Shōkaku* and *Zuikaku*. Inoue had to promise that he would complete the conquest of Port Moresby swiftly, so that those carriers could rejoin the Kidō Butai in time for the Midway campaign, now codenamed Operation MI. The Fiji-Samoa operation would have to be postponed until July, though Yamamoto agreed to allow a smaller operation for the capture of Ocean and Nauru Islands (Operation RY), and another to seize the westernmost islands in the Aleutians (Operation AL). This latter effort, often referred to as a diversion for Midway, was in fact a separate initiative unrelated to the Midway Operation apart from its timing. In effect, instead of choosing between moves to the south, north, or west, the Japanese decided to undertake all three, and to do so virtually simultaneously.[28]

In addition to internal military politics, one reason for the apparent hurry was that both Yamamoto and the Naval General Staff recognized that Japan's carrier superiority in the Pacific was only temporary. The Japanese had six big carriers to the Americans' three (or perhaps four—they weren't sure where the *Wasp* was), but they knew that the Americans had no fewer than eleven big carriers under construction, all of which would become operational in 1943; the Japanese had only one under construction, the *Taihō*, which would not be available until 1944 (though they also converted several other existing ships into carriers). In short, the Japanese needed to complete their conquests and establish their defensive perimeter before the new American carriers and the flood of American airplanes began arriving in the Pacific.

The day after the Naval General Staff capitulated to Yamamoto's Midway Operation, the planes of the Kidō Butai conducted their raid on Colombo in far-off Ceylon and sank the *Dorsetshire* and *Cornwall*. Four days later they struck at Trincomalee and sank the *Hermes*. Soon they would be returning through the Straits of Malacca to the Pacific. They would need to refit and resupply, and then they would be ready for more operations. The officers and men were hoping for liberty in Hiroshima. They would be disappointed. The crews of the *Shōkaku* and *Zuikaku* would not even be allowed to reach a Japanese port. Instead, those two ships underwent a quick resupply in Formosa so they could be ready for Operation MO.

On April 16, Nagano presented the "Imperial Navy Operational Plan for Stage Two of the Great East Asia War" to Emperor Hirohito, who, in theory at least, had final approval of all operations. Plans were never presented to the emperor until all the competing elements in the military and the government had agreed; all Hirohito could do was bless a decision that had already been made. The chief of the Army General Staff was present when Admiral Nagano presented the outlines of the Midway plan. He silently acquiesced because it did not call for the allocation of any soldiers. The landings and occupation of Midway would be the responsibility of Naval Infantry—the Japanese version of Marines. The Army may have suspected that Yamamoto's plan was only the first step toward an invasion of Hawaii, which certainly would require support from the Army, but it could speak up in opposition to that move when the time came.[29]

Yamamoto had won, though it was not yet clear what the consequences of his internal victory over the Naval General Staff and the Army might be. As Commander Miyo had pointed out, the thrust into the Central Pacific was a gamble even if the Kidō Butai triumphed over the American carriers, for the logistical burden of sustaining an outpost at Midway, 2,235 nautical miles from Tokyo, was daunting, especially if the Army continued to remain on the sidelines. On April 16, the day when Nagano presented the plan to the emperor, it was hard for Army leaders to imagine a set of circumstances that would cause them to change their mind about supporting this adventure in the central Pacific.

Two days later, American bombers appeared over Tokyo.

# Pete and Jimmy

The wild card in America's carrier force was the USS *Hornet*, a sister ship of the *Yorktown* and *Enterprise* with essentially the same characteristics and capacity. Commissioned in October, six weeks before Pearl Harbor, she remained in Norfolk over the winter as she fitted out, and it was not until March of 1942 that she was ready for sea with a crew, an air group, and a commanding officer. That commanding officer was Captain Marc A. Mitscher, whose Academy nickname was "Pete." The nickname came about because Mitscher had arrived in Annapolis from Oklahoma in 1904 soon after another Oklahoma native named Pete Cade had "bilged out." Cade had been a popular mid, and his classmates were unsure that trading him for the short, skinny, and taciturn Mitscher was a good bargain. They ordered the new plebe to call out the name of the departed Cade every time an upperclassman required it. On those occasions, Mitscher would brace up and shout out: "Peter Cassius Marcellus Cade, Jr." His classmates took to calling him "Oklahoma Pete," and Pete he remained for the rest of his life.[1]

For some time it looked as if the new Pete would follow the same course as the old one at Annapolis. Mitscher got bad grades and lots of demerits. For two years, he was constantly on the brink of being kicked out. And then he was; in 1906, at the end of his second year, he was ordered to resign. In an act of defiance, he wrote out his resignation on a piece of toilet paper. In spite of that, and perhaps as a sop to the congressman who had appointed him (a friend of Mitscher's father), he was allowed to reenter the Academy, but only if he started over as a plebe. Out of either stubbornness or determination, or perhaps both, Mitscher reentered the Academy as a member of the class of 1910. Though he was repeating classes he had already taken, his grades remained poor, and his conduct worse. Nor was he especially popular. He seldom laughed or even smiled, and his natural quietness was interpreted by some as sullenness. His odd looks did not help. Short and slight, he had milk-white skin that burned easily, and white, wispy hair that was already thinning noticeably, which he combed over the top of his balding head. The 1910 *Lucky Bag* profiled him in verse:

> Pete dislikes all allusions or mirth
> On the hue of his hair or its dearth
> It gives him much pain
> When he has to explain
> That he's not an albino by birth.

He spent a lot of his time smoking and card playing, and several times came close to being expelled again. He graduated third from the bottom of his class in 1910, after six years at Annapolis.[2]

Mitscher's early career as a surface officer was as undistinguished as his record at the Academy. Despite his diminutive size, he was stubborn, argumentative, and short-tempered, and he managed to get into a surprising number of fights. Then in 1915 his career changed dramatically when as a lieutenant junior grade he was accepted into the new Bureau of Aeronautics. Mitscher decided it was an activity that was worth his time and effort—for one thing, his diminutive stature was actually an asset in an airplane's cockpit. The card-playing slacker became a hard worker and an enthusiastic devotee of aviation. Moreover, as one of the first students to show up at Pensacola in the Navy's infant flying corps, Mitscher got in on the ground floor of a new service that was soon to expand rapidly. In June of 1916, at the age of 29, Pete Mitscher became Naval Aviator Number 33.[3]

At that time, of course, there were as yet no aircraft carriers in the U.S. Navy (the *Jupiter* would not be converted into the *Langley* until 1920). For four years, Mitscher flew fabric-covered seaplanes resembling box kites from shore bases; only occasionally were they propelled off the back of cruisers. Breakdowns were frequent, and the pilots patched up their own cloth-and-string "aeroplanes" after each crash, of which there were many. One authority estimates that for every fifteen minutes of flying time, the pilots spent four hours making repairs. The newly promoted Lieutenant Mitscher described what may have been a typical day in a letter home to his wife, Frances: "We transferred ten wrecks to the yard, and repaired two.

■ Lieutenant "Pete" Mitscher at the controls of an early seaplane in Pensacola, Florida. Becoming a pilot completely changed the trajectory of Mitscher's naval career. (U.S. Naval Institute)

The other day Donohue smashed one of the remaining ten and we worked night and day to get it ready. Stone fired off with it today and smashed it again, so we now have to repair some more."[4]

To his great disgust, Mitscher did not see any action during World War I. Instead, his big break came after the war, in 1919, when he was assigned to join the Navy team that attempted the first transatlantic crossing by air. Rather than make the flight in a single hop, the plan was to fly huge seaplanes—essentially flying boats, designed by Glenn Curtiss—from the American east coast to the Azores and then on to Europe. Mitscher was a backup pilot on the NC-1 (N for Navy; C for Curtiss). Though only one of the three planes (not Mitscher's) managed to complete the trip, the exploit brought the Navy plenty of positive publicity, and Mitscher and everyone else involved received the Navy Cross.[5]

Mitscher's early involvement in naval aviation proved the making of him. In 1925, President Coolidge asked his friend Dwight Morrow to head a board to evaluate the potential of aviation for the services.* Called to testify before the Morrow Board, Mitscher declared that it was entirely inappropriate for black shoe officers to have management of pilots and airplanes. He asserted that only "experienced aviation men should have administration of the training of aviation personnel and the detail of aviation personnel." While this was entirely logical and genuinely reflected Mitscher's views, it also helped ensure that those who had managed to get into the game early would have the first claim on supervisory positions when naval aviation became a major component of the fleet.[6]

Mitscher wrote privately that it was "the great ambition of [his] life" to get on board "an aviation ship," which he finally did in 1926. A year later he was the air boss on the new Saratoga. Two years after that he was the exec on the Lexington. He was not interested in grand strategy and never attended a war college. A fellow officer described him as "a person who did not enjoy the long process of planning, of thinking too much about logistics."

---

* Dwight Morrow, a former Republican senator from Ohio, had a special interest in aviation. (His daughter Anne would later marry the famed aviator Charles Lindbergh.) It was the Morrow Board that recommended the creation of a separate Air Corps within the U.S. Army.

He just wanted to fly, and he was good at it. One problem was that his fair skin made the outdoors into a hostile environment. He burned so easily that despite wearing a specially designed long-billed baseball cap, his nose was always peeling. Eventually his sun-ravaged skin gave him the look of a withered gnome. He remained both stubborn and temperamental, though he no longer got into fistfights. He also remained taciturn, and when he did speak it was in a voice so low that others were compelled to lean in close to hear him. A fellow officer recalled that he was "very, very quiet and seldom said much," and another that "he never used five words if one would do." Despite his low voice, he disliked having to repeat things and fired a staff officer who asked him to repeat himself once too often. By 1938 Mitscher had become a Navy captain and the assistant chief of the Bureau of Aeronautics. Then in May of 1941 he was selected as the prospective commanding officer of the new-construction *Hornet*. Many of his Academy classmates were astonished.[7]

As captain of the *Hornet*, Mitscher no longer flew airplanes, and he missed it. He remained reticent, seldom telling jokes or engaging in light banter. He spent hours in his cabin chain-smoking and reading paperback detective novels. "He would go through a novel in nothing flat," a shipmate recalled. Despite that, Mitscher exuded an air of confidence and authority, especially when it came to air operations. He realized that he had a green crew—fully 75 percent of the men on board the *Hornet* were fresh from boot camp or cadet training—and he patiently tried to bring them up to the mark. The 18-year-old helmsman on the *Hornet* thought the soft-spoken skipper "gave the impression of being a kind, gentle, and highly intelligent person." But Mitscher's patience was often tested, especially when it came to air operations, and he showed occasional flashes of anger, particularly toward his young pilots. During the *Hornet's* shakedown cruise, while watching flight operations from the open bridge wing, he saw the landing signal officer wave off Ensign Roy Gee during his first approach. Gee came around again and worked his way back into the pattern, but as he made his approach the LSO waved him off again. It took Gee ten tries before the LSO finally gave him the cut sign and Gee landed safely. When he climbed out of his airplane, he was ordered to report at once to the bridge. There he was confronted by an irate Mitscher.

"Can't you fly?" Mitscher asked.

"I won't do it again, Captain," the humiliated ensign replied.

"You're damned right you won't," Mitscher told him. "You're not ever going to fly off this ship again." Mitscher ordered that Gee's name be struck from the flight roster. But if Mitscher was quick to anger, he also relented quickly. Five days later he ordered Gee restored to flight status.[8]

On the last day of January 1942, the *Hornet* was anchored off Norfolk when Captain Donald "Wu" Duncan, Ernie King's air officer, came on board. Once he was alone with Mitscher, Duncan asked him a question: "Can you put a loaded B-25 in the air on a normal deck run?" That depended, of course, on how many planes crowded the flight deck. Mitscher thought a moment. "How many B-25s?" he asked. "Fifteen," Duncan told him. Mitscher bent over the spotting board, a wooden template of the *Hornet*'s flight deck that showed where each plane was placed at any given moment. He calculated how much space a B-25 with its 67-foot wingspan would take up on the *Hornet*'s deck. Finally he answered that it could be done. "Good," Duncan replied. "I'm putting two aboard for a test launching tomorrow."[9]

The big land-based, two-engine Mitchell bombers had been named for Billy Mitchell, the interwar U.S. Army general who had been court-martialed for accusing Army and Navy leaders of "criminal negligence" for not making a greater commitment to air power. The Mitchell bombers were about the size of a Japanese Nell and, in conformance with Mitchell's vision, had been designed for coastal defense. They were too big to land on a carrier and had to be hoisted aboard the *Hornet* by crane at the Norfolk docks. On February 2 (two days after Fletcher and Halsey struck at the Marshalls in the Pacific), the *Hornet* went out into the Atlantic with two Mitchell B-25s lashed to her flight deck. At 53 feet long and with that 67-foot wingspan, the two planes looked out of place even on the broad deck of the *Hornet*. The weather was less than ideal—a light snow was falling—and the test was interrupted when one of the escort vessels reported what was believed to be the periscope of a submarine, which proved instead to be the tip of a mast on an uncharted wreck. In the end both planes took off safely and without incident, flown by young Army pilots with no previous training in carrier operations. Duncan was satisfied. He left the next day to take the news back to Washington, where several very senior officers were waiting.[10]*

From the very day of Pearl Harbor, President Roosevelt had envisioned conducting a retaliatory strike on Japan's home islands. He urged such a raid not as part of a grand strategy but to give the American public something to cheer. To conduct a carrier raid against Japan, however, would subject the Navy's scarce and valuable carriers to unacceptable danger. They would have to steam to within two hundred miles of the enemy coast and then wait there for the strike planes to return. It was simply too risky. American land-based bombers, with their greater range, could reach Japan from China. However, getting them to the airfields in China "over the hump" of the Himalayas from India would take months, and FDR was eager to strike while the pain of Pearl Harbor was still palpable. The notion that it might be possible to fly long-range, land-based bombers off a carrier deck originated with Navy captain Seth Low, Ernie King's operations officer, who thought it up while watching them lift off from airfields in Florida on which the outline of a carrier deck had been painted for practice landings. He pitched the idea to King, who told him to talk to Duncan, and soon afterward, Duncan went out to the *Hornet* to conduct the test that proved it could be done.[11]

The problem was that while B-25s might take off from the *Hornet*, they could not land there. They would have to fly off the carrier some five hundred miles out from Japan, drop their bombs, then find someplace else to land. One option was to land them at Russian airfields near Vladivostok. But Stalin, who had his hands full with the Germans, did not want to add the Japanese to his list of enemies and refused permission. The other option was China, though to make it all the way to airfields in the part of China that had not yet been overrun by the Japanese meant that the B-25s would have to be significantly modified to carry extra fuel, which would limit their bomb load. Another problem was that because the B-25s were much too

* The Army pilots were Lieutenants John Fitzgerald and James McCarthy, the first men to fly land-based bombers off a carrier deck, and they did so with no special training and very little advance notice.

large to fit on the carrier's elevators, they would have to remain on the flight deck throughout the Pacific crossing, which meant the carrier could not conduct normal air operations. In other words, the *Hornet* would be unable to defend herself. In consequence of that, a second carrier would have to be assigned to accompany her. Indeed, King even wondered if it might not require three carriers—two for the heavy bombers and one to defend the task force.[12]

Many wondered whether it was an intelligent use of rare American carriers to use most or all of them simply to conduct an air raid whose purpose was mainly to boost morale. In any event, the plan required co-operation from what in 1942 was still called the Army Air Forces, and in March of 1942 the U.S. Army and Navy were very much at odds about future strategy. It was not the kind of dysfunctional hostility that char-acterized relations between the Japanese Army and Navy but a far more subtle competition over resources and priorities. The U.S. Army continued to adhere to the Germany First strategy that had been laid down in ABC-1 and Rainbow 5 in November 1941, whereas King was already pushing hard for an early Pacific offensive. After the collapse of the ABDA coalition, the British agreed to allow the United States to assume full responsibility for the conduct of the war in the Pacific, and at a March 5 strategy meet-ing in the White House, King presented a memorandum he had prepared for the president that emphasized the importance of holding Hawaii and defending the lines of communication to Australia, but which also called for a "drive northward from the New Hebrides into the Solomons and the Bismarck archipelago," which meant attacking Rabaul. To make sure that a busy FDR didn't miss the central point of his argument, King summed it up in three bulleted items at the end: "Hold Hawaii, Support Australasia, Drive northwestward from New Hebrides."[13]

The problem was that, as King readily admitted, "Such a line of operations will be offensive rather than passive," and this ran up against the Army's de-termination to remain strictly on the defensive in the Pacific until Germany was beaten. George Marshall, the soft-spoken but strong-minded Army chief of staff, noted that the strategic principle of Germany First was still in place, and that even though an invasion of occupied Europe now seemed unlikely for 1942, it was essential to continue the buildup of forces for the invasion when it did come, presumably in 1943. Marshall was backed up by the head of the Army Air Forces, General Henry "Hap" Arnold, who had earned his nickname for his perennially cheerful expression. Despite these basic disagreements about strategy, however, when Low and Duncan went to see Arnold to propose a raid on Tokyo that combined Army bombers with Navy carriers, Arnold was immediately enthusiastic. In fact, Arnold had been thinking about how to hit back at Japan with his bombers, and only weeks before had confided in his diary, "We will have to try bomber take-offs from carriers." He told Low and Duncan to go down the hall to talk to his plans officer, Lieutenant Colonel James Doolittle.[14]

Jimmy Doolittle was already something of a national celebrity in 1942. During the 1930s he had earned a reputation within the flying community by winning virtually every speed racing trophy there was. He shared a number of personal qualities with Pete Mitscher. Born in Alameda, California, Doolittle had grown up in Nome, Alaska. Like Mitscher, he had been the smallest boy in his class at school and the object of bullying. (Even as an adult he stood only five foot four.) He was regularly involved in fights, many of which he started. He even boxed professionally as a bantamweight, mauling enough of his opponents to earn a modest reputation and some spending money. He was an indifferent student, earning mostly C's until he entered junior college, where his grades improved. He attended the California School of Mines, but he did not graduate because he enlisted in the Signal Corps when America went to war in 1917. The Army taught him to fly. He discovered that he was a natural pilot and was soon made an instructor. Like many pilots of his era (including Pete Mitscher), he was also a daredevil and was regularly grounded for dangerous stunts such as buzzing civilians or flying under bridges, wrecking several airplanes in the process.[15]

Like Mitscher, Doolittle missed seeing active service in World War I because the Army kept him stateside as an instructor. But in 1922, three years after Mitscher won the Navy Cross for participating in the world's first transatlantic flight, Doolittle won the Distinguished Flying Cross for setting a transcontinental speed record, crossing the country (with one stop) in less than twenty-four hours. A few years later he broke his own record, crossing the country (with no stops) in twelve hours. Though officially a test pilot, Doolittle was in effect a public relations exhibit for the Army, part of a team that put on flight demonstrations in order to enhance the Army's image. He was being paid to perform the kind of stunts that had got him grounded ten years earlier, and his utter fearlessness encouraged him to take personal risks. Like Yamamoto, he was willing to perform dangerous feats on a bet, and he once broke both of his ankles after falling from a second-story balcony, trying to perform a handstand on the railing while drunk. Despite the broken ankles, he flew in an air show the next day with his feet in heavy casts, strapped to the pedals. But he was more than a daredevil. The California School of Mines decided to give him academic credit for his flight time and awarded him a degree, and that allowed him to apply to graduate school. He went to MIT, where in two years he earned both a master's and a Ph.D. in aeronautical science. Doolittle left the Army and spent the 1930s as a stunt pilot for the Shell Oil Company demonstration team, earning three times the money the Army had paid him for doing essentially the same job. In the process he won a reputation as the country's fastest pilot, winning race after race and becoming nearly as well known as NASCAR drivers such as Jeff Gordon or Dale Earnhardt, Jr. became several generations later. Doolittle reentered the Army in 1940 as war loomed and by 1942 was on the staff of General Hap Arnold. His office was just down the hall from Arnold's, and he was there in February 1942 when Low and Duncan came to see him with their idea of flying B-25s off Navy carriers. He of course loved the idea.[16]

Initially, Doolittle was supposed to be the administrator of the program, coordinating the logistics from the Army side. But from the beginning he worked to ensure that he would lead the flight personally, though he had never flown a B-25. He first checked to see which B-25 squadron had the most experience, found that it was the 17th Bomb Group at Pendleton Field near Columbia, South Carolina, and ordered the planes of that squadron to fly to Eglin Field in Florida. Then he flew down to Florida himself to address the pilots and their crews. He told them he was looking for men for an important mission—volunteers only. He couldn't tell them what the mission was, he said, only that it was important, and probably dangerous. Everyone volunteered. Doolittle picked out twenty-four crews—in case of accidents or washouts—and began training.[17]

For this training, he called on the Navy at Pensacola, asking for a flight instructor who was familiar with carrier operations. The Navy sent him Lieutenant Henry Miller. Miller flew to Eglin Field with no idea why. When he presented his orders to the commanding officer there, Miller asked him why he had been summoned. Saying nothing in reply, the CO drove him over to the isolated hangar Doolittle was using as a temporary headquarters. Doolittle and Miller hit it off immediately. Both were from Alaska, both loved to fly, and both had been boxers.[18]

At Eglin Field, Miller showed the Army pilots how to lift off with only about 65 to 70 knots of airspeed. They understood the concept, though it violated everything they had learned in flight school, where the rule was to build up to about 110 knots before attempting to lift off. Taking off from a carrier would mean getting off the deck at near stalling speed and building up speed only after they were in the air. The Army pilots had to fight their instincts at every step. Nonetheless Miller soon had them lifting off within as little as 250 feet of runway.[19]

Doolittle trained with them, delighted to be flying again. He called the other pilots by their first names and joked around with them between flights. "He was very congenial," one of the other pilots recalled. The experience confirmed his determination to lead the flight personally, a notion he put to Hap Arnold. Arnold replied that he needed Doolittle in Washington to plan future operations. Doolittle protested vociferously, claiming that he had been in charge of the training, and that "the boys" deserved to have their leader with them. Eventually Arnold relented, though he told Doolittle that he would need approval from Millard F. Harmon, Arnold's chief of staff.[20]

Doolittle saluted and sprinted down the hall to Harmon's office. "Miff, I've just been to see Hap about that project I've been working on and said I wanted to lead the mission. Hap said it was okay with him if it's okay with you." Harmon replied that as long as Arnold approved, it was all right with him. As Doolittle was leaving, he heard Harmon's intercom buzz and then, after a moment, Harmon's voice. "But Hap, I just told him he could go."[21]

As the pilots trained in Florida and the *Hornet* proceeded from Norfolk to San Diego via the Panama Canal, Wu Duncan was putting together the other pieces of the puzzle. He flew to Pearl Harbor to brief Nimitz on the project. Nimitz was dubious. To him, the commitment of two carriers to what amounted to a public relations stunt was a misuse of scarce resources. The *Lexington* was in dry dock, which meant that if both the *Enterprise* and *Hornet* were sent off to Tokyo, the *Yorktown* would be the only available carrier left. On the other hand, Nimitz knew better than to get in the way of a project that emanated from Washington, especially since he suspected that he was no longer held in great favor there. To his wife, Nimitz wrote, "Am afraid he [Knox] is not so keen for me now as he was when I left," and speculated that he would be "lucky to last six months." He called Halsey into the meeting. After Duncan again explained the objective, Nimitz turned to Halsey, asking him if thought it would work. Halsey replied that it would take considerable luck. Nimitz then asked if he would be willing to take them there. He was. "Good," Nimitz responded. "It's all yours!"[22]

Halsey expressed a desire to talk to Doolittle face to face and arranged to fly to San Francisco. There he and his chief of staff Miles Browning met with Doolittle and Wu Duncan in a downtown restaurant. All four wore civilian clothes and took a table toward the back. Leaning forward and keeping their voices low, they discussed the forthcoming raid, later moving to Halsey's hotel room for greater privacy. They agreed that the carriers would try to get the bombers to within five hundred miles of Japan—four hundred if possible. If they were discovered while still within range of Midway, the B-25s would take off and fly there so that the *Hornet* could bring up its air wing to defend herself. If they were already within range of Japan—even extreme range—the bombers would take off and conduct the raid, flying back out over the Pacific afterward to ditch in the water where there was at least a chance (albeit a slight one) that an American sub might rescue them. If they were discovered in that long stretch of ocean that was out of range of both friendly fields and enemy targets, the ship's crew would simply push the bombers over the side. In any event, the *Hornet* must not be caught by enemy planes with the B-25s still lashed to her deck.[23]

Prior to that, Duncan had flown to San Diego to inform Mitscher of the mission. On this, his second visit to the *Hornet*, Duncan told Mitscher that he was going to be taking Jimmy Doolittle and fifteen Army bombers "to hit Tokyo," to which the laconic Mitscher replied, "That's fine." Soon afterward, the *Hornet* proceeded north to San Francisco Bay, tying up at the pier in Alameda on March 20. Doolittle's bombers flew cross-country from Florida to Sacramento, and then to Alameda, where they taxied from the runway right down onto the pier. There, fifteen of them were hoisted one by one onto the deck of the *Hornet*. By now, most of the pilots had figured out why they had been practicing short takeoffs.[24]

To make room for the B-25s on the flight deck, the planes of the *Hornet*'s air group had to be lowered into the hangar deck. Those with folding wings were squeezed into the available space. The crew removed the wings of the big Devastator torpedo bombers; the lighter Wildcat fighters were actually suspended from the overhead. It was the only way that the entire air group could be placed inside the hangar deck at one time.[25]

Lieutenant Miller had accompanied Doolittle's squadron out to California and was loath to say good-bye. As he and Doolittle discussed which of the crews should be used in the operation, Miller suggested that he might perform one more service by flying an extra B-25, a sixteenth, off the *Hornet* as a demonstration to the Army pilots that it could be done. He would take off one hundred miles out of San Francisco and fly back to South Carolina, then return to his duty post at Pensacola. Doolittle approved the idea immediately. Once all sixteen planes were on board, however, they seemed to fit without any difficulty. Doolittle then suggested to Mitscher that perhaps they could use all sixteen planes in the bombing mission, since there were several extra crews available. Mitscher concluded, "The advantage of having an extra plane for attack outweighed the desirability of demonstrating a proper take-off." Of course, it also meant that Miller lost his chance to fly a B-25 off a carrier.[26]

Lieutenant Miller had instructed the Army pilots about Navy protocol, and he watched with pride as they marched up the gangway of the *Hornet* one by one, saluted the flag on the fantail as well as the officer of the deck, and requested permission to come aboard. Despite that, there was a palpable coolness between the Army men and the crew of the *Hornet*. Much of it derived from the fact that the Army flyers, who had been constantly enjoined to keep quiet about their mission, were not particularly communicative. They had a "defensive aloofness," in the words of one Navy officer. They kept to themselves, messing together privately, and deflecting all of the crew's questions about them and their mission. Beyond that, however, some on the *Hornet* thought they were "undisciplined." Unlike the Navy pilots, who routinely wore neckties with their long-sleeved khaki shirts, the Army pilots wore open collars, short-sleeved shirts, and scuffed shoes. They were casual not only about their appearance but also about shipboard routine. "A briefing would be set for 8:30," one Navy pilot recalled, and "they would saunter in" around 9:00 or 9:15, and sometimes the meeting couldn't start until 9:30. Even then, "their attention span was very short, half an hour at the most." Matters improved after the *Hornet* passed under the Golden Gate Bridge and Mitscher got on the 1MC. the loudspeaker system. Though many on board had suspected what was coming, the announcement that they were off to bomb Tokyo warmed up relations between the two services. "From then on there was complete rapport," Doolittle reported.[27]

The *Hornet* and her escorts left San Francisco just after 10:00 a.m. on April 2. It was a foggy day, with visibility limited to one thousand yards, but anyone who cared to look could see the *Hornet* steaming under the Golden Gate Bridge with sixteen Army bombers strapped to her flight deck in a herringbone pattern. Most of those who thought about it, if anyone thought about it at all, probably assumed that she was on her way to deliver those planes to Hawaii or some other American outpost. The *Hornet* had an escort of one heavy and one light cruiser, four destroyers, and the essential oiler. It was designated as Task Force 16.2, because as soon as it rendezvoused with Halsey's *Enterprise* group it would become part of Task Force 16. That same day, 5,133 miles to the west, Commander Watanabe was traveling by seaplane to Tokyo to present Yamamoto's Midway plan to the Naval General Staff.[28]

Halsey was among those who watched the *Hornet* depart. He was to fly from San Francisco to Honolulu in a few days to reboard the *Enterprise* and take her out to the predetermined rendezvous point northwest of Hawaii. He almost didn't make it. Struck down by the flu, he was woozy from medication as he finally boarded the plane on April 6. Nonetheless, he arrived in time to take the *Enterprise* group out of Pearl Harbor on April 8. Four days later, the two American carrier groups were approaching the rendezvous coordinates along the international date line. Halsey informed his pilots that there was another American carrier in the vicinity to ensure that they did not bomb her. One of the pilots flying CAP that day was Lieutenant Richard Best. He spotted the approaching *Hornet*, and it seemed to him as if there was something wrong with her. Her deck was encumbered by what looked like "construction equipment . . . odd shapes, maybe tractors." As he got closer he was astonished to see that "she had two-engine bombers on board."

The now united Task Force 16 steamed westward for four more days without incident. On April 17 (Tokyo time)—the day after Nagano presented the Midway plan to Emperor Hirohito—the two carriers and four cruisers of the united Task Force 16 topped off their fuel tanks and, leaving the slower oilers and fuel-guzzling destroyers behind, began a high-speed run in toward the launch point.[29]

That night, at ten minutes past 3:00 a.m., the radar on the *Enterprise* picked up a surface contact. In these waters it could only be hostile. The task force maneuvered to avoid it, and the contact soon faded from the screen of the CXAM radar set. The radar could be temperamental, and as soon as there was enough light Halsey ordered an air search, sending out three scout bombers and eight Wildcats from the *Enterprise*. Rain squalls and wind gusts made the launch more precarious than usual, but all eleven planes got off safely. Less than an hour later, at two minutes before 6:00 a.m., Lieutenant Junior Grade Osbourne B. Wiseman flew over the *Enterprise* and dropped a beanbag onto the deck—this was how pilots sent messages back to the ship when the need to maintain radio silence was imperative. The beanbag was rushed up to the bridge, and Halsey read the attached note: "Enemy surface ship—latitude 36–04 N, Long. 153–10 E, bearing 276

■ Brigadier General James Doolittle (left) and Pete Mitscher with the Army pilots and crews on board the USS *Hornet* in April, 1942. Several American officers had medals they had been given by the Japanese government before the war, and this photo depicts them attaching those medals to the bombs to "return" them. (U.S. Naval Institute)

[degrees] true—42 miles. Believed seen by enemy." Should the observers on the contact recognize a carrier plane, they would know an American carrier was nearby. Halsey sent the cruiser *Nashville* to sink the surface craft, which proved to be the *Nitto Maru*, one of the picket boats Yamamoto had ordered out to provide early warning. It took the *Nashville* almost a full hour and nearly a thousand rounds of 6-inch ammunition to send it and another small picket boat to the bottom. By that time, radio operators on the *Enterprise* had intercepted several radio messages coming from them. A Japanese-speaking officer on board had been able to translate the unencrypted message: "Three enemy aircraft carriers sighted at our position, 650 nautical miles east of Inubo Saki at 0630." On board the *Hornet*, Mitscher turned to Doolittle and said: "They know we're here."[30]

Doolittle and Halsey had discussed this possibility during their restaurant dinner in San Francisco; both knew what to do. Halsey blinkered a message from the *Enterprise*: "Launch planes. To Col. Doolittle and his gallant command, good luck and God bless you." On board the *Hornet*, the klaxon sounded and a voice called out: "Army pilots man your planes."[31]

The seas were rough. The assistant signal officer on the *Enterprise*, Robin Lindsey, called it the "God damnest weather [he'd] ever seen." Green water broke over the bow of the *Hornet*, and everyone on deck had to wear a lifeline to avoid being swept over the side. The wind gusted up to 27 knots, and with the *Hornet* making 30 knots, the relative wind speed over the deck was 50 knots or more. Despite the choppy seas, that wind was a blessing, for it would aid in getting the 31,000-pound bombers into the air. Navy Lieutenant Edgar Osborne stood near the bow with a safety line around his waist and a checkered flag in his hand. Sea spray soaked him each time the big carrier plunged into another wave. He watched the majestic rise and fall of the *Hornet*, waving the black-and-white checkered flag over his head in a circle as a signal for Doolittle to rev his engines. Then, just as the *Hornet* reached the nadir of its plunge, Osborne slashed the flag downward. Doolittle released the brake, and his B-25 surged forward. He kept the nose wheel on the white line painted on the *Hornet*'s flight deck. If he kept it steady, his right wing tip should clear the superstructure of the ship's island by six feet. The plane raced downhill at first, and then, as the *Hornet*'s bow rose up again, his plane rose up with it and was boosted into the sky with plenty of flight deck to spare. It was exactly 8:20 a.m.[32]

Doolittle made one pass over the ship, then flew off on the coordinates he had calculated. He did not circle to wait for the rest of the planes to join him. To do so would waste precious fuel, especially since they were launching nearly a hundred miles beyond optimum range. Flying in formation used up additional fuel, since every pilot except the leader had to make constant tiny adjustments to hold his position. Instead, each plane would make its way to the target independently.[33]

The rest of the planes took off at intervals of several minutes. The second one almost didn't make it. Lieutenant Travis Hoover's plane dropped

■ Doolittle's B-25 Mitchell bomber takes off from the deck of the *Hornet* on April 18, 1942. Note the white line painted on the flight deck to help the pilots avoid hitting the ship's island superstructure. (U.S. Naval Institute)

off the end of the deck and disappeared. After a few harrowing seconds, it appeared again, struggling up into the sky. The rest of the launchings were mostly routine—as routine as launching two-engine land bombers off a carrier could be. Until the last one. The tail of the sixteenth plane extended out over the back of the *Hornet*'s fantail, and the plane had to be wrestled forward to the launching spot by the deck crew. The wind continued to gust unpredictably. One particularly severe gust caught Seaman Robert W. Wall and threw him into the left wing propeller. His arm was badly mangled and later had to be amputated. But the plane left on time.[34]

As soon as the last plane was airborne, Halsey ordered the carriers and cruisers to reverse course and steam east, away from Japan, at 25 knots while the crew turned its attention to bringing up the planes from the hangar deck so that the *Hornet* could function as a real carrier again. As

Doolittle and his bombers flew westward, Halsey and Task Force 16 sped away eastward.

The Army pilots, accustomed to navigating over land by following railroads or highways, were now flying over 650 miles of open ocean toward a target none of them had ever seen. They had practiced for the mission by flying out over the Gulf of Mexico, learning to fly by compass bearing alone. To conserve fuel, they flew at 165 knots, replenishing the tanks by hand from gas cans stored on board, saving the cans to throw over the side all at once, so that they didn't form a trail on the surface of the sea for the Japanese to follow. About a half hour into the flight, Taylor's Number Two plane caught up to Doolittle and settled in on his wing, though the rest headed for Japan independently. They flew low, about 200 feet, and passed over some small ships, mostly fishing vessels, though Doolittle thought he saw a light cruiser. Doolittle made landfall well north of Tokyo—navigating by dead reckoning was always a bit dicey. Instead of following the coast southward, as some did, he decided to fly inland and approach the target from the north. He was still flying low, the shadow of his plane jumping around on the ground as it conformed to the topography. He passed some small biplanes—perhaps army trainers—but there was no reaction from them. Other pilots recalled flying over groups of civilians who looked up and waved, assuming, not unreasonably, that these were Japanese planes on a training mission. One plane flew over a baseball field with a game in progress, and the crowd stood up to wave. The pilots waved back.[35]

Ten miles north of Tokyo, Doolittle encountered nine Japanese fighter planes flying in three tight V formations. They ignored him. At the outskirts of the city, Doolittle pulled up to 1200 feet, turned southwest, and dropped his first bomb at 1:30 p.m. (ship time). He had been flying for five hours. After dropping his four 500-pound bombs, Doolittle took his plane back down to 500 feet. There was a lot of antiaircraft fire now, though it was inaccurate; at 500 feet his plane was a difficult target. He passed over an aircraft factory where new planes were lined up in rows outside, but he had no bombs left, and he continued southwestward out over the Sea of Japan and on toward the China coast.[36]

He made landfall at dusk; soon it was full dark. He was now flying over un-known terrain with no certain objective. Doolittle pulled up to 8,000 feet to avoid running into a mountain and flew on. At 9:00 p.m., after covering 2,250 miles in thirteen hours, he was running out of gas. He got no response on the radio frequency he had been given for the Chinese airfields. He did not know that news of his mission had never made it to the Chinese. At 9:30, he or-dered his crew to prepare to jump. He ensured that they went first, and then, setting the autopilot for level flight, he followed them out into the night.[37]

He landed in a rice paddy that had recently been fertilized with human excrement. After slogging his way to solid ground, he knocked on the door of a small house where a light was showing, and tried out the phrase that the Chinese-speaking Lieutenant Stephen Jurika had taught all of them during the Pacific crossing: *Lushu hoo megwa fugi*: "I am an American." The only response he got was the dousing of the light and the bolting of the door. He walked on. The next day, after a night trying to stay warm, he encountered three Chinese soldiers. He drew them a picture of an air-plane with parachutes coming out of it. They were skeptical at first but relaxed when they found his parachute, which the unwelcoming farmer had secreted in his house. After several days, they got him to Hang Yang Airfield, and from there he, and eventually most of the others, were flown to the Nationalist Chinese headquarters at Chungking. There they were presented with presidential congratulations and notification that each of them would be awarded the Distinguished Flying Cross. Three weeks later, in a small and secret ceremony in the White House, President Roosevelt awarded Doolittle the Medal of Honor.[38]

All sixteen American bombers had successfully found their targets, hit-ting Yokohama, Nagoya, and Kobe as well as Tokyo, but none of them had landed safely on Chinese airfields. One landed in southern Russia after its skipper, Captain Edward York, discovered that he did not have enough fuel to make it to China.* The rest crash-landed somewhere in China or along

---

* Very likely, Captain York's plane burned fuel faster than the others because the me-chanics at McClellan Field near Sacramento, unaware that the carburetors on the Mitch-ell bombers had been specially recalibrated for fuel economy, reset them to normal.

the Chinese coast. Of the eighty Doolittle raiders (five men per plane), seventy-three eventually made it back to the United States—though it took a while for some of them. Two died when their plane crashed, and another was killed bailing out. Eight were captured by the Japanese. Of those, three were executed, one died in prison, and the others survived the war in a POW camp. The crew of Captain York's plane was interned in Russia. Just over a year later, those five escaped from the Soviet Union into Iran and eventually made it back to the States.

For their part, the Japanese made light of the Doolittle raid, punning on his name to claim that his handful of bombers had done little to hurt the great empire, which was true enough. The American pilots had hit an oil tank farm, a steel mill, and power plants; one bomb slightly damaged a brand-new carrier—the *Ryūhō*—still in the shipyard. But they also hit several schools and an army hospital. Naturally, Japanese newspapers declared that the bombers had targeted schools and hospitals to "kill helpless children," the usual wartime propaganda. Despite their defiant pronouncements, however, the Japanese high command was humiliated; the ability of the Imperial Army and Navy to protect the life of the emperor had been called into question. The Doolittle raid did not trigger the Midway expedition—that decision had already been made. It did, however, remove any doubts the Army had about backing the operation. According to Watanabe, "With the Doolittle raid the Japanese Army changed its strategy and not only agreed to the Midway plan of the Navy but agreed to furnish the troops to occupy the island."[39]

In the United States, news of the raid was received jubilantly. Americans thought of it as payback for Pearl Harbor. One might note that the Americans had lost all sixteen bombers, one more plane than the Japanese had lost in the American air victory off Rabaul on February 20. Still, there had been so little good news in the war so far that the Doolittle raid inspired both celebration and speculation about how those planes had managed to cross the Pacific. Though the Japanese learned from the captives that the bombers had been launched from a carrier, that fact remained an official secret for more than a year, and when asked where the planes had taken off, Roosevelt answered puckishly that they had flown from "Shangri-La," the mythical and mystical city of James Hilton's popular novel *Lost Horizon*. In homage to that, one of the new *Essex*-class carriers then under construction would be christened *Shangri-La*.

Halsey's Task Force 16 arrived back in Pearl Harbor on April 25. Mitscher had hoped to grant liberty to the crew of the *Hornet*; its men had been at sea almost continuously since leaving Norfolk. But with only four American carriers in the Pacific, there was no time for that. The men of the *Hornet* and *Enterprise*, as well as their escorts, had to forego leave in Hawaii, just as the men of the *Shōkaku* and *Zuikaku* had to forego leave in Japan. The Japanese sailors on their two carriers were bound on a special mission. And thanks to a handful of men working secretly in the basement of the Fourteenth Naval District headquarters building in Pearl Harbor, the Americans knew what that mission was.

# 7

# The Code Breakers

In addition to the men who drove the ships, flew the planes, or manned the guns—and those who some months later waded ashore carrying M-1 rifles—there were others whose contributions to victory in the Pacific were of an entirely different sort. Among the most consequential were those whose job it was to intercept, decrypt, and analyze Japanese radio traffic. In a windowless basement room at Pearl Harbor officially dubbed the Combat Intelligence Unit and which those working there called "the dungeon," more than two dozen men toiled around the clock in an effort to glean useful intelligence out of the Japanese radio messages that were plucked out of the ether every day by the radio receiver at He'eia on Oahu's north shore. It was the most secret organization in the U.S. Navy. Some of these men (called the "on-the-roof gang," or "roofers" in the workplace vernacular) wore headsets and transcribed the blizzard of dots and dashes into

number groups or Japanese kana characters.* Others sought to find pat-
terns in those characters by running primitive IBM card-sorting machines
that spewed out millions of punch cards each day. Still others sat at desks
or tables and worked through tall stacks of intercepts, looking for repeated
codes or phrases that might provide a hint about Japanese movements or
intentions. It was an eclectic team of idiosyncratic individuals that collectively played one of the most important roles in the Pacific War, and particularly in the Battle of Midway.[1]

As far back as World War I, the United States had been successful at breaking the Japanese diplomatic code. In the 1920s, a clandestine organization
headed by Herbert Yardley and rather dramatically dubbed "the Black
Chamber" devoted itself to breaking the diplomatic codes of several nations, including Japan. Their success had allowed the Americans to take a
hard line at the 1921–22 Naval Arms Limitation Conference in Washington, where they had proposed that 10:10:6 ratio in battleship tonnage for
the United States, Great Britain, and Japan. Though the Japanese were holding out for a 10:10:7 ratio, the American chief negotiator—the secretary
of state and future Supreme Court chief justice Charles Evans Hughes—
knew from reading intercepted Japanese secret messages that Tokyo would
accept the 10:10:6 formula rather than let the talks fail.

Six years later, when the State Department was preparing for the London Naval Conference, Yardley sent President Hoover's new secretary
of state, Henry Stimson, a batch of decrypted messages that revealed
Japan's negotiating strategy. Instead of praising Yardley, Stimson was
horrified. He was said to have remarked that "gentlemen do not read
other gentlemen's mail." Whether or not he actually made this statement, he shut down the Black Chamber and ended, temporarily, efforts
to read Japanese diplomatic messages. Yardley, who apparently could not

---

* The "on-the-roof gang" got its name from the fact that the men were trained on the
roof of the Navy Department Building in Washington on which the radio intercept
tower was located. Because the building had not been designed for such use, the
trainees had to climb a ladder to get there.

resist claiming public credit, got even with Stimson a few years later by exposing the operation he had led in a series of magazine articles, and then by publishing a memoir, *The American Black Chamber* (1931), in which he revealed the once highly secret operation. For their part, the Japanese complained that the Americans had been cheating and resolved to improve their codes.[2]

The U.S. Navy was less fastidious than the State Department; efforts to break the Japanese Navy's operational code continued uninterrupted. This quite separate effort began in 1924, when the communications intelligence organization was established on the top floor of the Navy Department building in Washington under the Code and Signals Section. Placed under the director of Naval Communications, this office was designated as OP-20-G. For almost twenty years, OP-20-G was the private fiefdom of the gifted and eccentric Commander Laurance F. Safford, a lugubrious, bespectacled 1916 Annapolis graduate with darting eyes and disheveled hair who looked, one coworker said, as if "he had been scratching his head in perplexity."[3] It was Safford who established the unit's two satellite stations, one in Manila in 1932 called Station Cast, and Station Hypo in Hawaii in 1936.* It was also Safford who recruited the first team of analysts who became key players in the wartime code-breaking effort.**

One of those whom Safford recruited was Ensign Joseph J. Rochefort, who had enlisted in the Navy in the last days of World War I and earned a commission after briefly attending Stevens Institute. Rochefort was a tall,

---

* The term Hypo (the British phonetic code for the letter H) derived not from its location in Hawaii or Honolulu but from the radio tower at He'eia. Hypo was later redesignated as the Fleet Radio Unit, Pacific (FRUPAC). Station Cast was named for Cavite Navy Yard in Manila and later moved to Corregidor when the Japanese overran Manila. Eventually it relocated to Melbourne, Australia, where it was renamed Belconnen, and later Fleet Radio Unit, Melbourne (FRUMEL).

** In the interest of accuracy, not to mention fairness, it is important to note that one of the prime movers of this early organization was Agnes "Miss Aggie" Driscoll, who began working in the Code and Signal Station when Safford did in 1924. She held the rank of chief yeoman (the highest then available to women), though she all but invented the science of cryptanalysis and trained most of the men who later played such a crucial role in American code breaking.

■ Joe Rochefort, seen here as a captain in a postwar photograph, was a key figure in the American code-breaking apparatus before and during the Battle of Midway. (U.S. Naval Institute)

thin, and soft-spoken man whose ready smile disguised a fierce intensity. He had not set out to be a code breaker, and never requested the duty. Nevertheless, in 1924 his former commanding officer on the fleet oiler *Cuyama*, Commander Chester Jersey, when asked to nominate someone for the Code and Signals Section, recalled that Ensign Rochefort had been particularly good at crossword puzzles. He sent in Rochefort's name, and in 1925 Ensign Rochefort became Safford's number two man. Four years later, the Navy sent Rochefort to Japan for a three-year tour, ostensibly as an attaché but really to study Japanese language and culture.[4]

Both Safford and Rochefort proved adept at the tedious and exacting work of code breaking, but they could not remain continuously in the job. Because the Navy expected its officers to serve at sea if they expected to be promoted, the two men adopted the practice of filling in for one another: Rochefort took over OP-20-G when Safford went to sea, and Safford resumed command when it was Rochefort's turn to deploy. In June of 1941, with war looming, Safford sent Rochefort, by now a full commander, out to Hawaii to take over as the head of the Combat Intelligence Unit (CIU), colloquially known as Station Hypo. There, Rochefort had particular responsibility for breaking what was called the "Japanese admirals' code." Station Cast in Manila remained focused on trying to decrypt the Japanese Navy's operational code.[5]

As it happened, the Japanese made little use of the admirals' code, and for several months—including the critical month before Pearl Harbor—Rochefort and his team spent a lot of time chasing down blind alleys. Since they did not have access to the intelligence gathered from either the

Japanese diplomatic code (known as "Purple") or the operational codes, Rochefort could not share information gathered from those sources with his boss, Admiral Kimmel.[6]

Instead, Rochefort and his team relied heavily on traffic analysis, that is, an examination of the external character of the messages rather than of their content. The analysts noted the call sign, the message classification, its level of importance or precedence, the frequency of transmission, its length, and the location of the transmitter to draw conclusions about what the message might mean in terms of Japanese naval movements. If, for example, the volume of message traffic suddenly surged, it could mean that a fleet was getting under way. Of course, since fleets at sea often maintained radio silence, the *absence* of radio traffic might be equally significant. When messages to or from the Kidō Butai suddenly stopped, that could be as important as a sudden flurry of messages, or even more important. In addition, it was occasionally possible for a veteran operator at He'eia to determine the identity of the sender of a particular message by recognizing the characteristic tempo or cadence (called a "fist") of his Morse-code transmissions. If the sender was known to work at a specific base or ship, it provided the Americans with one more piece of intelligence. Traffic analysis had limitations, however. On one occasion, when radio traffic showed that several destroyers usually associated with a particular Japanese carrier were in the Marshalls, Rochefort assumed the carrier was there, too. He was wrong. His rare error was an example of how the analysts had to apply intuition to determine the utility of the intercepts.[7]

None of this, of course, helped the Americans predict the attack on Pearl Harbor, and after December 7 it seemed to many that a housecleaning was in order. Just as Kimmel was shoved aside in Hawaii, Safford was replaced at OP-20-G by Captain John R. Redman. A member of the Naval Academy class of 1919 who had graduated early for service in World War I, Redman had excelled in athletics. A standout on the football and lacrosse teams, he was also captain of the wrestling team, a sport in which he competed at the 1920 Olympic Games in Antwerp, finishing fourth as a light heavyweight and just missing an Olympic medal. Redman had a strong personality and long service as a communications officer in cruisers and battleships, but

■ Captain John Redman, seen here as a rear admiral in a postwar photograph, headed up the intelligence office in Washington (OP-20-G) and was often suspicious of Rochefort's analysis. (U.S. Naval Institute)

no real experience or expertise in code breaking. In fact, his prime qualification for his new job may have been that his older brother, Rear Admiral Joseph R. Redman, was the director of Naval Communications.

Captain Redman's appointment not only shelved the experienced Safford, it introduced a new tension into the cryptanalytic community. Redman did not know Rochefort or any of the veteran cryptanalysts personally. Perhaps because Rochefort was Safford's appointee (and not an Academy graduate), Redman was loath to take Hypo's assessments at face value. Much later, Rochefort recalled, "As long as Safford was in Washington, I just about knew what to expect. . . . It worked very nicely on a personal basis. It was when other people became involved in it as part of the expansion that we began to have trouble." In effect, Redman did not trust Rochefort's judgment enough to be receptive when Rochefort used his intuition to fill in the many blanks in decrypted naval messages. Fortunately, Rochefort found a more sympathetic audience for his assessments in Chester Nimitz. Though Rochefort was under the administrative command of the 14th Naval District and reported officially to Redman in Washington, his mission made him invaluable to CinCPac, and in the end it was Rochefort's relationship with Nimitz, not the one with Redman, that proved crucial.[8]

Besides Safford's dismissal, another change was wrought by the onset of war. On December 17, Rochefort finally received authorization to drop the unprofitable pursuit of the Japanese admirals' code and join in the common effort to crack the Japanese Navy's far more widely used operational code, often referred to as the "five-number code." Nimitz wanted him to pay particular attention to the "deployment of enemy carrier strike forces." Soon the team in the dungeon began to squeeze bits and pieces of intelligence out of the messages.[9]

Back in the 1920s, when the Americans first began to pay serious attention to the Japanese naval code, they dubbed it JN-1 (Japanese naval code, version one). Over the years, the Japanese regularly changed their codes, and every time they did so, the American code breakers had to start over again. In June of 1939, the Japanese adopted a new and more complicated system. Since it was the twenty-fifth version of the code, it was dubbed JN-25. Then on December 1, 1940, the Japanese modified that code yet again, and this new variant was labeled JN-25b. It resisted the code breakers right up to the day of Pearl Harbor. When Rochefort's team received authorization to turn their efforts to this code, they attacked it with a vengeance.[10]

The JN-25b code consisted of 40,000 to 45,000 five-digit number groups, such that the messages that went out over the air waves looked something like this:

   48933      19947      62145      02943      20382      16380

Some of the number groups were dummies, or fillers, added to confuse the code breakers. In addition to that, however, before sending a message, the Japanese enciphered the code again by using a cipher tablet. The encoder selected a five-digit number from this tablet and added it to the first number group in the message; the next cipher number was added to the second number group, and so on throughout the message. An indicator buried in the message itself revealed the exact location—page number, column, and line—where the cipher number additives could be found in the secondary tablet. Thus the code group for "east" might be 10236, but it would be encrypted again by adding another five-digit number from the cipher tablet. If the encoder added the number 45038, the word "east" became 55264. (Note that in adding the two numbers, there was no carrying: although adding 8 and 6 yields the number 14, only the second digit was used in the product.) To decrypt the message, the recipient needed the initial code book, the secondary code tablet, and the indicator, showing how to subtract the second from the first. The puzzle, in short, was extraordinarily complicated, which is why the Japanese remained confident that their radio messages were secure. In May 1941, when Japanese officials conducted a review of their message security, they concluded: "We need not worry about our code messages."[11]

Breaking through these layers of secrecy was tedious. It was helpful that the Japanese ensured that all of the original number groups were divisible by three. The reason for this was to let the recipient know he had subtracted the correct cipher—if the final code number was not divisible by three, he had probably made a subtraction error. Of course, this also allowed the code breakers to know if they were on the right track.

In addition, the volume of message traffic in JN-25 ballooned after the war began, giving the analysts more opportunities to divine the structure of the code. And finally, for a few weeks the Japanese sent messages in both the JN-25 code and the new JN-25b code because some commands had not yet received the new codebooks. This allowed the Americans to compare the messages. Station Cast identified two messages—one that was encrypted and another that was sent out in plain language—that appeared to be identical. It was the Rosetta Stone of naval messages, and it allowed the Americans to verify several of their guesses. Despite that, there were few such "aha!" moments at Station Hypo, and lots of tedious and often unrewarding analysis—plus some educated guesswork.

Because there was a shortage of personnel at Hypo, men frequently worked twelve-hour shifts, or longer. Only about 60 percent of all the messages that were intercepted could be subjected to analysis at all because there were so many messages—five hundred to a thousand every day—and breaking them took time. Of those that were analyzed, fewer than half yielded any useful information, and within those only small fragments, perhaps 10–15 percent, might be rendered comprehensible. Often the code breakers at Hypo could determine the sender and the recipient, and perhaps one or two other phrases. Here, for example, is an actual decrypt from May 5, 1942:

"KAGA and (blank) (blank) less (blank) and (blank) will depart Bungo Channel (blank) May 4th and arrive (blank) (blank)."

It was Rochefort's job to fill in those blanks. To say, then, that the Americans were "reading" the Japanese message traffic is an exaggeration. After much hard work, they might in the end be able to decipher a tiny fraction of it, and they had to rely on their experience, informed guesswork, and intuition to determine what it might mean and how to take advantage of it.[12]

Rochefort and his team worked long hours and with great intensity. Unable to tell whether it was night or day in their windowless quarters, they ignored the clock and often worked all night. It was routine for many of them to work twenty hours or more per day. Even the "roofers" worked watch and watch: twelve hours on, twelve hours off. One member of the Hypo team, Lieutenant Jasper Holmes, later wrote, "Had I not witnessed it, I never would have believed that any group of men was capable of such sustained mental effort under such constant pressure for such a length of time."[13]

Because air conditioners were needed to protect the IBM machinery, it was cold in the Dungeon. Ensign Donald Showers recalled later that "it was cold as hell down there." To ward off the chill, Rochefort often wore a maroon-colored corduroy smoking jacket over his uniform. To protect his feet from the hard concrete floor, he wore slippers. This has led some to conclude that he was highly eccentric. In the 1976 film *Midway*, Hal Holbrook portrayed him as a kind of cheerful goofball. In fact, Rochefort, by now a full commander, was a serious-minded and entirely professional naval officer. Asked about the smoking jacket after the war, he replied simply, "It was a practical matter, and I was just cold." He often slept on a cot in the Dungeon instead of heading back to his lonely quarters. (His family had been evacuated back to California.) In part, his intensity derived from the nagging sense of guilt—that if only he had had access to the JN-25 intelligence before December 7, he might have been able to predict the raid.[14]

At his desk, Rochefort laid out the pieces of message traffic that he or someone else on his team had been able to decrypt. "You see a whole lot of letters and a whole lot of numerals, perhaps in the thousands or millions," Rochefort recalled after the war, "and you know that there is a system in there, and there's a little key to the system that's something real simple, and you just keep after it until you finally solve it." Another team member recalled, "We went over the papers one by one, we went through the whole compilation of traffic analysis, how each command, or unit, became associated with others." Eventually, by matching number to number, phrase to phrase, and unit to unit, Rochefort could begin to assemble a bigger picture. One officer likened it to being able to visualize the overall pattern of "a Virginia reel or square dance."[15]

For several weeks after Pearl Harbor, Rochefort and Hypo confined themselves to providing raw data about fleet movements and communications activity, the result, perhaps, of their intense disappointment that they had failed to predict the raid. Then in January, 1942, Rochefort noted that several of the messages he and his team were working on contained the

■ Lieutenant Commander Edwin Layton was Chester Nimitz's intelligence officer. Layton briefed his boss every morning at five minutes to eight, passing along whatever information the Hypo team had managed to cull from the airwaves. (U.S. Naval Institute)

code group that he believed stood for *koryaku butai* (invasion force), and that some of those same messages also contained the letters "RR," which he believed stood for Rabaul. (In the Japanese system, all geographic locations were assigned a two- or three-letter code.) Based on that, and the overall pattern of message traffic, Rochefort predicted that the Japanese would invade Rabaul in the third week of January. When the Japanese went ashore there on January 23, it seemed proof of Rochefort's ability to produce substantial intelligence out of a few scraps of radio traffic, and it helped lay the groundwork for a partnership of trust that soon emerged between Hypo and CinCPac—that is, between Rochefort and Nimitz.[16]

The man who acted as the liaison in that partnership was Edwin Layton, a 39-year-old lieutenant commander with dark curly hair, thick glasses, and prominent ears. He looked more like a high school math teacher than a naval officer. After graduating from Annapolis in 1924, Ensign Layton had been assigned to escort a group of visiting Japanese naval officers around San Francisco, and he was surprised to discover that they all spoke perfectly colloquial American English. He wondered how many American naval officers spoke Japanese, and when he learned that the answer was none, he wrote to the Navy Department, deploring this fact and volunteering to become the first. At the time, Navy regulations stipulated that in the entire U.S. Navy, only two officers at a time could be assigned to language studies, and, in any case, no one could apply for it until he had completed five years of sea service. Five years later, after serving aboard the battleships *West Virginia* and *Pennsylvania*, Layton applied again. This time he was accepted. While crossing the Pacific en route to Tokyo for his new assignment as a Japanese-language officer, he met another young officer bound on the same mission. It was Joe Rochefort.[17]

While in Japan, Layton and Rochefort studied not only the language but also the culture. After the few hours of formal classroom study, they went out into the streets to strike up conversations. "I was most interested in why [the] Japanese do certain things they way they do," Layton recalled, "why they think the way they do—why they approach a problem the way they do." What both men learned was that in Japanese culture, as well as in their language, "there is more nuance than directness." Even if the words were clearly understood, they might not reveal the true meaning of any given statement.[18]

Layton went back to sea in 1939 as the commanding officer of the destroyer-minesweeper USS *Boggs*, but in February of 1941 he was assigned to Kimmel's staff as his intelligence officer. After Nimitz took over as CinCPac, he told Layton, "I want you to be the Admiral Nagumo on my staff, where your every thought, every instinct, will be that of Admiral Nagumo's; you are to see the war, their operations, their arms, from the Japanese viewpoint and keep me advised about what you (as a Japanese) are thinking." Of course it was not Nagumo that Layton should have been channeling, but Yamamoto. Nagumo, as we have seen, was merely a link in the chain, and not a particularly imaginative one. Yamamoto was the prime mover. Still, Layton got the idea. It was his job not only to monitor whatever fragments of information Rochefort's hard-working team was able to glean from the Japanese message traffic but also to draw conclusions about what they meant as well. Soon a regular routine evolved in which Rochefort talked to Layton, often several times a day, on a secure phone line, summarizing what he had found and what he thought it meant, and then Layton would go see Nimitz.[19]

Layton briefed Nimitz every morning at precisely five minutes to eight. If a message came in that suggested a special urgency, Rochefort would call Layton or send a messenger to his office. If it was something of particular significance, Layton would go to fleet headquarters early or, more rarely, show up in the middle of the day. When that happened, Nimitz would interrupt whatever he was doing to see him. In effect, Rochefort was the cryptanalytic scientist doing the lab work in the Dungeon; Layton was the spokesman whose job it was to convince Nimitz to trust Rochefort's conclusions. In Australia, the head of Station Cast, Lieutenant Rudolph Fabian, provided similar intelligence briefings for Admiral Leary and General Douglas MacArthur, yet without the kind of mutual trust and confidence that emerged in Hawaii.[20]

One problem in the command relationship was that technically Rochefort did not work for Nimitz but for the Commandant of the 14th Naval District, and he reported to Redman in Washington, where a new office called Combat Intelligence (OP-20-GI) was supposed to collect the data and do the analysis. Layton, who was on Nimitz's staff, was not in this chain of command. But because Rochefort and Layton were such good friends, based on their years together in Japan, there was a strong sense of partnership to their efforts. Then, too, Rochefort believed that he was uniquely placed to provide both the raw data as well as conclusions about what it meant. "I felt that I had the knowledge and experience of being able to estimate and form a judgment on what [the] traffic actually meant," he said later. "I was in a better position to say what they meant than anyone else." As a result, the Layton-Rochefort partnership effectively bypassed Washington and took intelligence estimates directly to the theater commander, a practice that Redman increasingly deplored and resented.[21]

The unrelenting work schedule yielded results. In February the team at Hypo achieved a kind of breakthrough, and soon they were filling in many more blanks in the Japanese message traffic. By April, they were often able to intercept, decrypt, and translate Japanese messages within hours of the original transmission. On April 5, three days before Halsey and the *Enterprise* left Pearl Harbor to join the *Hornet* en route to Tokyo, Rochefort was working on an operational message that had been sent from Combined Fleet headquarters at Hashirajima. It was addressed to the aircraft carrier *Kaga*, still undergoing repairs at Sasebo. One number group in the message stood out. Rochefort had already determined the code for "invasion group," and now he saw that code used in close association with the letters "MO." Rochefort suspected at once that it referred to Port Moresby. The Japanese had used a variety of other geographical designators for Moresby, including RZ, RZQ, and RZP, and all of these had appeared with increasing frequency in messages from Inoue's Fourth Fleet. Now, with this new intercept, Rochefort concluded that the Japanese were planning an invasion that would involve the *Kaga* and at least one other carrier, initially misidentified as the *Ryūkaku*, though it subsequently proved to be the small carrier *Shōhō*.[22]

Rochefort called Layton on the secure phone and told him that he had "a hot one," and that he was sending the raw decrypt over by messenger. "It looks like something is going to happen," Rochefort told him, "that the man with the blue eyes will want to know about." When the courier arrived, the many blanks in the message left its meaning ambiguous to a nonexpert. Though it was clear enough to Rochefort, anyone not versed in reading such messages would conclude that it was hardly a smoking gun. Over the next several days, however, more clues arrived. All that week, the men of Station Hypo focused on the growing pile of evidence that the Japanese were about to launch an offensive through the Coral Sea to Port Moresby. Holmes recalled that "the chart desk was strewn with charts of New Britain, New Guinea, and the Solomon Islands." After the British station in Colombo, Ceylon, intercepted a message that referred to special orders for Carrier Division 5—the *Shōkaku* and *Zuikaku*—Rochefort's team studied the traffic for any reference to those two carriers. "Each incoming message was quickly scanned for references to [Inoue's] Fourth Fleet or Carrier Division 5," Holmes recalled. "We lived and breathed and schemed in the atmosphere of the Coral Sea."[23]

It paid off. By midmonth, the stream of messages indicated quite a bit about both the target and the time frame, though it was less clear which units would participate. The Japanese were evidently planning a major operation in the South Pacific. There were references to at least four carriers, two cruiser divisions, and a destroyer squadron, plus various land-based units. Altogether nearly three hundred surface units appeared in the message traffic—the largest assembly of warships in the war to date. In this regard, it was unclear what Nimitz could do about it. By now both the *Enterprise* and *Hornet* were beyond recall, more than halfway to Tokyo with Doolittle's bombers. That left only the *Yorktown*, still in the South Pacific after the Lae-Salamaua raid, though in serious need of a refit and resupply, and the *Lexington*, which was in Pearl Harbor having her big eight-inch guns removed and replaced by antiaircraft guns. With the departure of Vice Admiral Wilson Brown for San Diego, the *Lexington* task force was now under the command of Rear Admiral Aubrey "Jake" Fitch, a short, broad-shouldered brown-shoe officer who had earned his gold wings in 1930. Even assuming that Fitch's *Lexington* group could get to the Coral Sea in time to join the *Yorktown*, the two American carriers might prove insufficient to interfere with the thrust, given the size of the

Japanese commitment. At an April 18 staff meeting, the general agreement at headquarters was that "CinCPac will probably be unable to send enough force to be *sure* of stopping the Jap offensive."[24]

The next day, Doolittle's bombers completed their mission over Japan's cities, and Halsey's two carriers began steaming back toward Pearl, though it would take them a week to get there. Layton briefed Nimitz on April 22 that Rochefort's intercepts offered clear "evidence of a powerful concentration in the Truk area," and he suggested that "this will be the force which will make the long expected attack to the Southwest." Jasper Holmes urged Rochefort to tell Nimitz that he should order Halsey not to return to Pearl at all but to refuel at sea and steam directly south to the Coral Sea. Rochefort reminded the enthusiastic Holmes that it was not the place of Navy lieutenants, or commanders for that matter, to tell four-star admirals what they should do. Their job was to provide the information that would allow the admiral to make his own decisions.[25]

Nimitz did not order Halsey to steam southward; the logistic realities made such a decision impossible. Nonetheless, he did trust Rochefort's analysis and, despite the odds, was determined to commit his other two carriers to confront the Japanese offensive. He notified King that it was his "strong conviction" that the Japanese thrust toward Port Moresby "should be opposed by [a] force containing not less than two carriers."[26]

The message triggered alarms in Washington. Redman remained distrustful of Rochefort and the assessments of Hypo. Station Cast, by now removed to Melbourne, Australia, and referred to as Belconnen, reported the Japanese objective as "RO," not "MO," and suggested that the target might be the Aleutian Islands rather than Port Moresby. If Rochefort were mistaken, Nimitz would be sending his last two carriers in the wrong direction. Though Rochefort was able to demonstrate that Belconnen had incorrectly decrypted the code, Redman remained skeptical. In fact, he was more than a little annoyed that Rochefort had bypassed him by taking his analysis directly to Nimitz. Redman wanted all intelligence intercepts to be sent to OP-20-GI in Washington, interpreted there, and then disseminated out to the fleet commanders. Rochefort should confine himself to purely tactical matters while

Washington dealt with the broader strategic questions. Redman couldn't complain about this to Nimitz. He did, however, express his doubts to King.[27]

With Nimitz urging instant action and Redman expressing skepticism, King took the unusual step of writing directly to Rochefort to ask for "Station Hypo's estimate of . . . future Japanese intentions." In effect, King wanted Rochefort to defend and justify his assessment.

Rochefort wired back his response only six hours later (with a copy to Nimitz) in a concise report that made four main points:

1. The Kidō Butai was in the process of withdrawing from the Indian Ocean, and its next effort would be in the Pacific.

2. The Japanese did not plan to invade Australia.

3. A new plan of operations involving some, but not all, of the Kidō Butai was preparing to strike southward from Rabaul through the Coral Sea toward Port Moresby.

4. There were hints of another, even larger operation that would take place after Port Moresby, though its scope and objective were not yet clear.

The summary was remarkable for both its candor and its accuracy, and it convinced King that Rochefort knew what he was talking about. King even suggested that the American force in the Coral Sea might be bolstered by sending several American battleships there—the rehabilitated survivors of the Pearl Harbor attack.[28]

Nimitz, too, accepted Rochefort's conclusions, but he was skeptical that sending battleships to the Coral Sea offered any kind of solution. He thought the battleships too slow, too vulnerable, too difficult to keep full of fuel, and in any case unlikely to affect the balance of power in the South Pacific. Nimitz ordered them back to the West Coast, mainly to get them out of the way. Instead, he would pit his two carriers against the three (or possibly four) carriers that the Japanese committed to the operation. He was willing to accept the odds because of, in his words, "the superiority of our personnel in resourcefulness and initiative, and of the undoubted superiority of much of our equipment." It was still remotely possible that Halsey could get to the Coral Sea in time, but even if he couldn't, Nimitz was determined to oppose the Japanese thrust anyway. He ordered Fletcher to head for Noumea to restock the *Yorktown's* near-empty larder and equip the Wildcat fighters with new self-sealing fuel-tank liners. Meanwhile, Fitch's *Lexington* task force would steam from Pearl Harbor for the Coral Sea. The two carrier groups would rendezvous on May 1, at which time they would constitute "a single force under [the] command [of] Rear Admiral Fletcher."[29]

That, too, worried King, who remembered that it was Fletcher who had commanded the failed relief expedition to Wake, and that Fletcher had accomplished little during the raid in the Marshalls in early February. Just a month earlier, King had seen a copy of a message Fletcher had sent to Nimitz informing him that he was "en route [to] Noumea . . . for provisions." Without consulting Nimitz, King shot back: "Your [message] not understood if it means you are retiring from enemy vicinity in order to provision." The pugnacious King declared that the men should live off hardtack and beans as long as they could still fight. In fact, the crew of the *Yorktown* had already been eating emergency rations—mostly beans and canned spinach—for several weeks. When there were only five steaks left on board, Captain Buckmaster had raffled them off, drawing the winners' names from a hat. King was unimpressed; during those same weeks, after all, the *Yorktown* had not struck a blow. Now he worried that Fletcher would not be sufficiently aggressive commanding a two-carrier task force in the Coral Sea. To discuss it, King asked Nimitz to meet him in San Francisco, and Nimitz flew there on April 24.[30]

At their meeting, Nimitz summarized his plan to concentrate all four American carriers in the Coral Sea, though he acknowledged that since Halsey could not get there until May 13 at the earliest, it meant that Fletcher's two carriers would very likely have to take on at least three, and perhaps as many as five, Japanese flattops. King again raised the idea of sending some old battleships there; Nimitz gently deflected the suggestion. They also discussed Fletcher's command temperament. Both men expressed "uneasiness as to Fletcher's operations," but short of flying Halsey down there to take over Fletcher's task force, which would be awkward in the extreme, there seemed to be no alternative. King reminded Nimitz that April 29 was the emperor's birthday and suggested that the Japanese might have some special operation planned to coincide with that date. Nimitz acknowledged that, but based on Rochefort's analysis he remained convinced that the operation would not begin until May 3. Nimitz flew back to Pearl on April 28 not knowing King's final decision. When he arrived, he was gratified to find that King had approved his plans. Halsey would return to Pearl, resupply his task force, and then take it south to join Fletcher as soon as possible. If Halsey did not get there in time, however, which seemed likely, Fletcher would simply have to do the best he could.[31]

The very day that Nimitz flew to San Francisco, Rochefort's team broke another message from Admiral Inoue himself. As usual, there were many elements of the message that could not be read, but it contained call signs for "the MO fleet" and "the MO attack force," as well as "the MO occupation force." Another message contained code groupings for the *Shōkaku* and *Zuikaku* as well as other ships. Rochefort was able to tell Layton, who then told Nimitz, that a Japanese invasion force with at least one carrier and possibly more was planning to enter the Coral Sea around the eastern end of Papua/New Guinea on or about the third of May, and that another task force that included the *Shōkaku* and *Zuikaku* would provide cover for the operation. Rochefort reported that X-Day, the day scheduled for the landing at Port Moresby, was May 10.[32]

Halsey's Task Force 16 left Pearl on April 30.* It had taken five days to resupply his two big flattops and their escorts not only with oil but also with ammunition, beef, and beans (and presumably canned spinach). That same day (May 1st west of the International Date Line), the *Shōkaku* and *Zuikaku* left their base at Truk in the Caroline Islands almost due north of

---

* That same day, the Japanese changed their code system for geographical designators. They often did this just prior to a new operation to ensure secrecy. This time, however, their decision backfired, since the change helped confirm the imminent attack, and the message contained both the old and new designators, which allowed the code breakers to update their dictionary of designators.

Rabaul. Since they had to travel less than a third of the distance that Halsey did to reach the Coral Sea, it was now certain that Halsey would not get there in time. For better or worse, the defense of Port Moresby would depend entirely on the *Lexington* and the *Yorktown*, their very names evoking the alpha and the omega of the American Revolution, with both of them under the tactical command of Rear Admiral Frank Jack Fletcher.[33]

# The Battle of the Coral Sea

The Coral Sea is one of the world's most beautiful bodies of water. Named for the coral reefs that guard Australia's northeast coast, it is bounded by Australia on the south, New Guinea on the west, the Solomon Islands on the north, and the New Hebrides on the east. On May 1, 1942, the same day that Halsey's Task Force 16 left Pearl Harbor, Jake Fitch and the *Lexington* task force joined Frank Jack Fletcher's *Yorktown* force four hundred miles southeast of Guadalcanal Island. The two task forces operated independently for six days, but when they were formally amalgamated into a single unit on May 6, it put Fitch in an awkward position. So long as the *Lexington* operated separately, he commanded the task force. Once it became part of Task Force 17 under Fletcher, he had no job at all. He didn't even command the *Lexington* itself—that was the job of Captain Frederick C. Sherman. Instead, Fitch was, in effect, a passenger on the *Lexington*—a high-ranking passenger to be sure, but a passenger nonetheless. Fletcher resolved the situation by designating Fitch, a 1906 Annapolis classmate and a close friend, as the tactical air officer for both carriers. Fletcher retained operational control of the combined task force, but the brown shoe Fitch would assume tactical responsibility for air operations. It was a creative and diplomatic way to resolve an awkward command problem and to take advantage of Fitch's experience and expertise.[1]

That same May 1st, fifteen hundred miles to the northwest in the Japanese-controlled Caroline Islands, the *Shōkaku* and *Zuikaku* and their escorts got under way from the spacious lagoon at Truk and steamed southward toward the Coral Sea to cover Operation MO. The commander of this Japanese force was Vice Admiral Takagi Takeo, who, like Chester Nimitz, was an old submarine man. Despite his seniority, Takagi had no experience in air operations and used a heavy cruiser as his flagship. Consequently, he delegated control of carrier operations to his close friend Rear Admiral Hara Chūichi who commanded Carrier Division (CarDiv) 5. Hara was a big man (his nickname was "King Kong"), but that did not impress the judgmental and diminutive (five foot two, 120 pounds) Genda Minoru, who believed that while Hara "looked tough," "he did not have the tiger's heart." Though the *Shōkaku* ("Soaring Crane") and *Zuikaku* ("Happy Crane") were the newest of Japan's big carriers, their pilots were also the least experienced, and despite performing well at Pearl Harbor and in the Indian Ocean, they had yet to earn the full respect of the veterans in CarDivs 1 and 2. This independent operation was a chance for both Hara and the pilots of CarDiv 5 to prove themselves.[2]

Also on that busy May 1st, eighteen hundred miles further north, a group of senior officers met on board the Combined Fleet flagship *Yamato*, anchored in Hashirajima Harbor near Hiroshima, to participate in a war game for the attack on Midway. The officers who bowed to Yamamoto as they prepared to game out the battle plan were confident that in a few days the Port Moresby operation would be complete, CarDiv 5 could be reunited with the Kidō Butai, and they could turn their attention to bigger things.[3]

Fletcher's orders from Nimitz were specific as to his objective but discretionary as to his movements. "Your task," Nimitz wrote him, was to "assist in checking further advance by [the] enemy . . . by seizing favorable opportunities to destroy ships, shipping, and aircraft." Nimitz did not tell him how to accomplish this; he left the tactical decisions to his subordinate.[4]

Fletcher already knew more about the Japanese movements than they did about his. He knew that they planned to conduct an operation in the Solomons to enhance their search capabilities over the Coral Sea. He knew, too, that around May 3 or 4 the Port Moresby invasion force would be moving south around the eastern tip of New Guinea through the Louisiade Archipelago and that it would be screened by a surface force that included at least one carrier (at that point assumed to be the mythical *Ryūkaku*, but in fact the light carrier *Shōhō*). Finally, he knew that the two big carriers of CarDiv 5 were somehow part of the operation, though their position and course were more of a mystery. Fletcher was fairly confident that the Japanese did not know his whereabouts, or even that he was in the Coral Sea, and he planned to keep it that way by maintaining radio silence and waiting until the analysts at Hypo, or one or another of the Allied search planes, could tell him where the Japanese were. All of this gave Fletcher an indisputable advantage, though none of it guaranteed success.[5]

One problem that Fletcher had was logistical. As Nimitz had reminded King, the Coral Sea was 3,500 miles from Pearl Harbor and at least 600 miles from the nearest source of fuel oil. It was imperative that Fletcher keep his two-carrier task force fueled up and ready, and to do that he would depend heavily on his big fleet oilers—*Tippecanoe* and *Neosho*. Fletcher's biographer notes that he "constantly worried about uncertain logistics," and that worry would remain an important feature of Fletcher's decision making in the battles to come.[6]

Inoue did not expect American naval forces to interfere with Operation MO. Given his confidence in the power of land-based bombers, he thought the greatest threat to the Port Moresby invasion force was from aircraft on the Australian mainland. To neutralize that threat, he wanted the big carriers of CarDiv 5 to conduct raids against the Allied bases at Townsville and Cookstown on the Australian north coast. To accomplish this, Takagi was not to approach the Coral Sea from the north—the most direct route—but to steam around the Solomon Islands and enter the Coral Sea from the east, to stay beyond the range of Allied search planes from Australia. In military terms, he was planning a flank attack—or, in football terms, an end run. Hara was dubious about the mission. Worried about taking his carriers too close to the barrier reefs, he succeeded in getting Yamamoto to cancel the raids. His new assignment was to cover the approach of the Port Moresby invasion force and deal with any Allied surface units in the Coral Sea that might turn up. If an American carrier were in the Coral Sea, Takagi and Hara were to make it their primary mission. Given that Takagi and Hara did not know that both *Lexington* and *Yorktown* were already in the Coral Sea, or that they had 141 planes to the 124 on the two Japanese carriers, there was more reason than they knew to be concerned.[7]

At the last minute, Takagi and Hara got saddled with an extra job. Since they were already going that way, Inoue ordered Hara to ferry nine Zero fighters from Truk to Rabaul. Though it seemed unimportant at the time, this added requirement would prove crucial. Hara intended to fly the Zeros off his decks as he passed within 250 miles of Rabaul, but the weather worsened as he headed south, and when he sent them off on May 2 they were unable to fight their way through the storms and had to return to the carriers. Hara tried again the next day, with no better results. Indeed, this time one of the fighters had to ditch in the water while trying to return to the carrier. Consequently, the whole force lingered another day near Rabaul before the eight remaining planes could be delivered and CarDiv 5 could continue on its mission. That put Takagi and Hara forty-eight hours behind schedule, which meant they would not enter the Coral Sea until May 5.[8]

Meanwhile, the newly arrived *Lexington* and her escorts refueled from the oiler *Tippecanoe*. This process was still under way on the evening of May 3 when Fletcher learned that Allied planes from Australia had spotted five or six big ships in the Solomon Islands. He deduced from their position that the target of this expeditionary force was the commodious anchorage at Tulagi, and believing that, in his words, "this is just the kind of report we have been waiting two months to receive," he left the *Lexington* group behind to complete refueling and headed north with the *Yorktown*.[9]

Steaming all night at high speed, Fletcher put the *Yorktown* in position for a dawn strike against the shipping gathered off Tulagi on Florida Island, located on the other side of Guadalcanal. Early on the morning of May 4, the *Yorktown* launched forty attack planes: twenty-eight bombers and twelve torpedo planes. Because he did not expect the Japanese at Tulagi to have much air cover, and because he wanted to ensure protection of the *Yorktown*, Fletcher kept all eighteen of his Wildcat fighters with the task force. This might have been disastrous had CarDiv 5 been on schedule, but since it was not, the only air opposition the Americans encountered consisted of a handful of float planes.[10]

The eager pilots from the *Yorktown* swooped down on the roadstead in the harbor off Tulagi and saw what looked to them like a rich target. They reported seeing a nest of three cruisers, several destroyers, and a seaplane tender, plus a lot of cargo and transport ships. Their eagerness distorted their vision. The "three cruisers" were actually an armed minelayer (the *Okinoshima*) and two destroyers. American planes expended thirteen 1,000-pound bombs and eleven torpedoes on the *Okinoshima* and still failed to sink her. The American attacks were piecemeal and uncoordinated in part because Captain Buckmaster wanted the air group commander, Oscar "Pete" Pederson, to stay on board the *Yorktown* as fighter director, and no other officer had been appointed to command the strike group in his absence. In three separate strikes that lasted all morning and into the afternoon, the Americans dropped seventy-six 1,000-pound bombs on the shipping near Tulagi and made only eleven hits. The relative inexperience of the pilots was one reason for this disappointing total; another was that when the Dauntless bombers dove from altitude, the windscreens on many of them fogged up and made accurate bombing difficult. Total losses for the Japanese were one destroyer (the *Kikuzuki*), three minesweepers, and four seaplanes. By the end of the day it was evident that the strike had fallen short of the staggering blow that Fletcher had anticipated, though it did provide valuable experience for the *Yorktown* pilots, a kind of warm-up for the main event.[11]

The *Yorktown* rejoined the *Lexington* the next day, and while the *Yorktown* refueled from the *Neosho*, Jake Fitch flew over to the flagship in the back seat of a dive-bomber in order to talk with Fletcher face-to-face. When his plane landed on the *Yorktown*'s flight deck, a member of the deck crew assumed that the man in the back seat was the plane's enlisted gunner and greeted him with a jibe: "Well, chief," he said, "you guys kinda missed out on some fun yesterday." Fitch grinned and replied, "Yes son, I guess we did." By then Fitch's two stars were exposed and the poor deck hand was rendered speechless.[12]

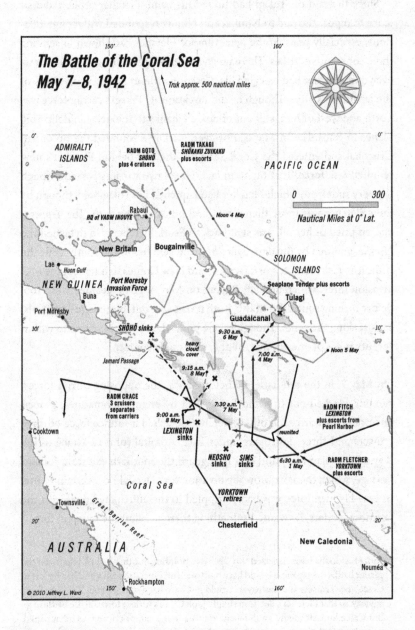

**The Battle of the Coral Sea**
**May 7–8, 1942**

Truk approx. 500 nautical miles

ADMIRALTY ISLANDS

RADM GOTO
*SHŌHŌ*
plus 4 cruisers

RADM TAKAGI
*SHŌKAKU ZUIKAKU*
plus escorts

PACIFIC OCEAN

Rabaul

HQ of VADM INOUYE

Noon 4 May

0    300

Nautical Miles at 0° Lat.

New Britain

Bougainville

SOLOMON ISLANDS

Lae    Huon Gulf

NEW GUINEA

Port Moresby
Invasion Force

Seaplane Tender plus escorts

Buna

Tulagi

Port Moresby

Guadalcanal

SHŌHŌ sinks

9:30 a.m.
6 May

Noon 5 May

heavy
cloud
cover

Jamard Passage

7:00 a.m.
4 May

9:15 a.m.
8 May

RADM CRACE
3 cruisers
separates
from carriers

9:00 a.m.
8 May

7:30 a.m.
7 May

RADM FITCH
*LEXINGTON*
plus escorts from
Pearl Harbor

Cooktown

*LEXINGTON*
sinks

reunited

6:30 a.m.
1 May

RADM FLETCHER
*YORKTOWN*
plus escorts

*NEOSHO*
sinks

*SIMS*
sinks

Coral Sea

*YORKTOWN*
retires

Townsville

Great Barrier Reef

Chesterfield

New Caledonia

AUSTRALIA

Nouméa

© 2010 Jeffrey L. Ward

Rockhampton

Since the raid on Tulagi had tipped his hand, Fletcher broke radio silence to report the raid to Nimitz, and Nimitz responded with congratulations, especially praising the perseverance Fletcher had shown in sending three consecutive strikes. There was no disguising the meager results, however, and Fletcher had revealed his presence without having spotted any of the Japanese carriers. Though he did not know it, Takagi's carrier force was north and west of him, still out of range (thanks to the delay in delivering planes to Rabaul). On May 5, however, CarDiv 5 rounded the tip of San Cristobal and entered the Coral Sea from the east behind Fletcher's now reunited task force. That night, in fact, Hara's two carriers passed through the very spot from which Fletcher had launched his Tulagi raid, though by then Fletcher was more than a hundred miles to the south. The *Tippecanoe*, emptied of her oil, was sent back to Pearl. Fletcher also detached the *Neosho*, guarded by the destroyer *Sims*, and sent her to the south while the American task force steamed west toward New Guinea to intercept the MO invasion force, which had left Rabaul on May 4. Hara steamed west, too, before turning south. On May 6, both forces sent out long-range air patrols, each seeking the other. Though at one point the two forces came to within seventy miles of one another, neither side made contact.[13]

On May 7, in the full darkness before dawn, the opposing carrier forces, running blacked-out to avoid being seen by enemy submarines, groped uncertainly toward each other. Fletcher detached a surface force of three cruisers and three destroyers under Rear Admiral John G. Crace of the Royal Australian Navy and sent it to guard the southern exit from Jomard Passage, which the Port Moresby invasion force was almost certain to use. In case his own force was badly crippled in the anticipated duel with the Japanese carriers, he wanted something there to blunt the invasion force.*

---

* Some historians have criticized this decision, pointing out that had Fletcher won the carrier battle, the Japanese would have had to call off Operation MO, and had he lost it, Crace's few cruisers and destroyers would not have been strong enough to stop them anyway, so that Fletcher's decision simply took Crace's surface force off the battle map. But Crace himself sought an independent role in the campaign, and, as it happened, he had a completely unforeseen role to play.

It was a bit of a risk, for Crace's detached surface force would be without air cover, but Fletcher did not want to separate his two carriers with the Japanese so near, and he could not be in both places at the same time.

The most important job now was to find those enemy carriers. To do that, Fletcher ordered search planes out a half hour before dawn. Based on a decrypted Japanese message forwarded to him by Nimitz, Fletcher believed that the Japanese would be approaching from the north, and he sent ten search planes fanning out in that direction. However, Rochefort's analysts had confused the invasion force with the covering force; Hara's carriers were actually some 210 miles to the *east* of him. Both American carriers also launched Wildcats as CAP, and Dauntless bombers for anti torpedo plane control; after that, Fletcher could only wait.[14]

Hara also sent out predawn patrols, but he sent them mostly to the south. With the Americans searching northward and the Japanese searching southward, neither carrier force spotted the other—though pilots from both sides soon found other targets.

Lieutenant John L. Nielsen, flying a Dauntless dive-bomber from the *Yorktown*, was searching amid the islands off the eastern tip of New Guinea when he spotted an Aichi E-13A "Jake" float boat—a "snooper" in the parlance of carrier operations. Fearing that it would alert the Japanese to the presence of an American carrier plane, if given time to send a contact report, he determined to shoot it down before it could transmit. With both planes firing, Neilsen chased it down out of the clouds and finished it off at low level. "He couldn't have been 20 feet off the water when I hit him," Neilsen recalled, "and he went down and under like a rock."

About 15 minutes later, near the island of Misima in the Louisiade archipelago, his back-seat gunner, Walter Straub, spotted the wakes of surface ships below. Nielsen looked them over carefully before telling Straub to call in the report of "two cruisers and four destroyers," giving their bearing and range from Point Zed.* Straub used the code table to

---

* Point Zed was a predetermined location that could be used as a reference point in radio transmissions so that the radio reports did not give away the location of the American task force.

transcribe the message, but when he tried to send it he found that their plane's antenna was gone, apparently shot away by the Japanese float plane. Only the short-range radio was operating. Nielsen flew back toward the task force to close the range while Straub repeatedly broadcast the sighting report until finally, at 8:15, he got a "Roger" from the *Yorktown*. What he did not know was that the code table Straub had used was misaligned, and instead of reporting two cruisers and four destroyers the message that arrived on board the flagship was that he had spotted *two carriers and four cruisers*.[15]

The report triggered a burst of excitement on board the *Yorktown*. Both Fletcher and Fitch knew that whoever got in the first blow had a tremendous advantage, and here was a chance to get a jump on the Japanese. The problem was that the range was too great. The reported sighting was 225 miles to the north—much too far for the torpedo planes or fighters, and a stretch for the dive-bombers. Fletcher therefore put the task force on a northerly course to close the range, and launched the first attack plane at 9:26. Just before the pilots climbed into their planes, Fletcher came out onto the bridge wing of the *Yorktown* with a bullhorn in his hand to tell them: "Get that goddamn carrier!"[16] By 10:15, Task Force 17 had ninety-three planes in the air heading toward the contact sent in by Lieutenant Nielsen.

Then, disaster. Neilsen's returning scout plane reached the task force soon afterward and, flying low over the *Yorktown*, Straub dropped a beanbag onto the deck with an attached note that confirmed the location of the Japanese force. When the note reached the flag bridge, however, Fletcher was horrified to read that it reported the sighting of two *cruisers* and four *destroyers*. When Nielsen reported to him after landing, Fletcher asked him, "What about the carriers?" Neilsen looked back at him and asked, "What carriers?" It is possible to imagine the blood draining from Fletcher's face upon hearing that response. He had just sent his full strike force off to attack a relatively unimportant group of surface ships; the Japanese carriers were still out there somewhere. He thought briefly about recalling the strike, but if enemy carrier planes were headed his way, which was at least possible, given that a number of Japanese scout planes had been spotted nearby, he did not want to be caught in the middle of recovering airplanes. One witness later claimed that Fletcher told Neilsen, "Young man, do you know what you have done? You have just cost the United States two carriers."[17]

Maybe not. Soon after that exchange, and with a humiliated Neilsen still standing on the flag bridge, an officer rushed in to tell Fletcher that a land-based Army bomber from Australia was reporting a Japanese carrier and twenty or more other ships only thirty miles away from the sighting that Neilson had sent in. This was no sure thing, for Army pilots were notoriously unreliable in identifying ship types; anything from a cargo vessel to a light cruiser might be reported as a carrier. Still, if this *was* a carrier, it was a more important target than the two cruisers that Neilsen had found. Fletcher decided that given the circumstances he had no choice but to break radio silence and vector the whole attack group toward the new sighting, which he did at 10:53, sending the message in the clear. His decision was made easier by the fact that it was likely that Takagi and Hara already knew where Task Force 17 was. But if they didn't before, they would now.[18]

As it happened, a Japanese snooper had reported Fletcher's location at 8:20 that morning. The report came too late, however. Like the Americans, Takagi and Hara had already shot their bolt, having sent their attack planes toward an inaccurate sighting. An hour earlier at 7:22, Hara had received a report from another of his scouts who spotted the huge silhouette of the loitering oiler *Neosho* below him, along with its escorting destroyer, and reported them as a carrier and a cruiser. An excited Hara ordered a full strike of seventy-eight planes from both of his carriers. The Japanese dive-bombers and torpedo planes flew southward to the reported coordinates for the American "carrier," only to find the *Neosho* and *Sims*. After conducting a search for better targets—a search that used up more valuable time—they settled for blasting these two hapless victims, sinking the *Sims* with three bombs, and hitting the *Neosho* with seven, damaging her so badly that she stayed afloat only because of the reserve buoyancy of her partially empty oil tanks.

While the loss of the tanker would inhibit Fletcher's movements some-what, it was not the death blow Hara had hoped for.* Worse, while his strike planes were thus engaged, Takagi and Hara got a report of another enemy surface force composed of battleships and cruisers near the exit from Jomard Passage. This, of course, was Crace's cruiser-destroyer force. Hara assumed that these "battleships" were operating with the American carrier and that it must be there, too. Because of the range, he would have to steam westward for several hours to get close enough to launch another attack, and in the meantime he still had to recover the planes he had sent after the *Neosho*.[19]

While the Japanese strike force flew southward toward the *Neosho* and *Sims*, the air group from *Yorktown* and *Lexington* flew northward toward the reported location of the Japanese carrier. At 11:00 a.m., the pilots spotted the MO screening force under Rear Admiral Gotō Arimoto that included the carrier *Shōhō*. The *Shōhō* was a new carrier, having been converted from the sub tender *Tsurugisaki* only months before, and she was significantly smaller than the big carriers of the Kidō Butai, carrying only about twenty airplanes. When the American strike force arrived, the *Shōhō*'s escorts maneuvered to separate themselves from one another. Un-like American doctrine, which called for the escorts to close in on the car-rier to provide additional antiaircraft fire, Japanese doctrine was to spread out so the carrier would have plenty of room for evasive maneuver.

By arrangement, the *Lexington* dive-bombers of Bill Ault's Scouting Two attacked first. The *Shōhō* maneuvered radically, completing a full circle to port and managing to avoid all the bombs from Ault's squadron. The *Shōhō* then turned into the wind and launched three more fighters to join the four she had flying CAP, but it was her last hurrah. At 11:15 the *Lexington*'s tor-pedo planes split into two groups for an "anvil attack," dropping down to

---

* Sixty-eight members of the crew of the *Neosho* abandoned ship into four life rafts. The rest (123 men) stayed on board and were subsequently rescued by the destroyer USS *Henley*. Most of those who went into the life rafts did not survive. On May 16, the USS *Helm* found one of the rafts with two life jackets in it but no men. After the rescue operation, the *Henley* sank the *Neosho* with torpedoes and shellfire.

fifty feet above the water and slowing to under 100 knots to make their run. At the same time, 16,000 feet above, the dive-bombers of Lieutenant Commander Weldon Hamilton's Bombing Two pushed over, opening their dive brakes and flying down at a steep 70-degree angle before releasing their 1,000-pound bombs at about 2,500 feet. For once, everything worked the way it had been drawn up in the training manuals. The windscreens did not fog up and the bombing was unusually accurate. Hamilton laid his own 1,000-pound bomb squarely in the middle of the *Shōhō*'s flight deck, and this was followed by several other hits by his squadron mates.[20]

Only minutes later, the *Yorktown* dive-bombers had their turn. The commander of Scouting Five, Lieutenant Commander William Burch, later claimed, "It was the best attack I ever made in my life." "I never saw such beautiful bombing," another rhapsodized. Even the American fighters held their own against the few Zeros. Wildcat pilot Lieutenant Junior Grade Walter Haas recalled, "We'd push over, single out a plane, and come down with all the speed we could build up in eight or ten thousand feet. We'd make a quick pass and find ourselves in a melee of twisting, dog-fighting planes." Using these tactics, Haas got the war's first confirmed kill of a Japanese Zero by an American Wildcat. By the time the *Yorktown*'s torpedo planes arrived, the *Shōhō* was mortally wounded and burning fiercely. They pumped ten more torpedoes into her anyway.[21]

Altogether, *Lexington* pilots claimed five bomb hits and nine torpedo hits, and *Yorktown* pilots claimed fourteen bomb hits and ten torpedo hits. Even allowing for exaggeration, the *Shōhō* had been smothered by bombs and torpedoes, and she all but disappeared under a blizzard of exploding ordnance. With black smoke pouring out of her, she continued to steam at high speed until she literally drove herself under the surface. "She went straight ahead," recalled Burch, "sinking as she went, and was under the waves seven minutes after our first bomb hit her." Out of a crew of 736, only 204 survived. Lieutenant Commander Robert Dixon, commanding the *Lexington*'s scouting squadron, continued to circle the area to watch the *Shōhō*'s death plunge. At 11:35, he went on the radio to send a prearranged message back to the task force: "Scratch one flattop."[22]

The flight back to the task force was jubilant. There was some concern that the task force might run out of fuel on the long flight home, but they all made it. Only three Dauntless bombers had been lost in the attack. When Lieutenant Commander Joe Taylor, who commanded the *Yorktown*'s torpedo squadron, touched down on the flight deck at about 1:00 p.m., Dixie Kiefer, the ship's executive officer, ran up to him and lifted him off the deck in a big bear hug. Taylor and Bill Burch, the skipper of Scouting Five, hurried up to the flag bridge to give their report.

"Well, Joe, what did you see?" Fletcher asked.

"I'll show you in a minute," Taylor answered mysteriously.

"Come now," Fletcher replied, "this is no time for joking."

"I'm not joking," Taylor told him. "We took pictures."

Soon Taylor's back seat gunner came running up with the still wet images he had printed at the ship's photo lab. When Fletcher and Buckmaster looked

■ The Japanese light carrier *Shōhō* on fire and sinking in the Battle of the Coral Sea on May 7, 1942. (U.S. Naval Institute)

at the photos of the burning and sinking *Shōhō*, Taylor remembered, "they jumped up and down like a couple of old grads in the grandstand when a last minute touchdown saved the day."[23]

Fletcher gave some thought to ordering a second strike aimed at the other ships in the invasion fleet, but launching a strike after 2:00 in the afternoon meant that the attack planes would have to return in the dark. Besides, the remaining Japanese carriers were still out there somewhere and had not been located. Finally, given the activity of several Japanese "snoopers" in the last few hours, there was a good chance that Task Force 17 could soon expect an attack of its own. He decided to retire southward and await more information. That decision did not sit well with Lieutenant Forrest Biard, one of Rochefort's Hypo analysts, who had been placed on board the *Yorktown* as a Japanese linguist, to intercept and translate messages sent in the clear. Biard worked in a small radio shack adjacent to Fletcher's command post at flag plot, where he listened to the Japanese radio traffic and reported directly to Fletcher. The easygoing Fletcher and the intense and abrasive Biard did not get along well. Though Biard insisted passionately that the Japanese carriers were off to the east and within range, he could not provide a bearing or a distance, and he failed to convince Fletcher to launch.[24]

At 5:47 p.m., the radar on the *Yorktown* picked up a number of bogeys, and the Americans scrambled more fighters to join the CAP already circling above the task force. Altogether, the two carriers were able to put thirty fighters in the air to meet an incoming attack by twenty-seven bombers and fighters. In fact, the attackers had no idea that the American carriers were there. Despite the snoopers, the *Yorktown* and *Lexington* remained hidden under heavy cloud cover. Instead, Hara had sent this late-afternoon strike toward the reported position of those "battleships" off the Jomard Passage, which Takagi believed also included a carrier. Crace's cruisers had been the recipients of an attack by land-based Japanese bombers that afternoon; now Hara's carrier planes sought to find them as well. The Japanese bombers were flying low amid the clouds and in the growing darkness and not expecting to find carrier-based fighters in their flight path. When the American Wildcats came screaming down on them from 5,000 feet, they were thrown into confusion. One excited Japanese pilot reported, "Enemy

fighters have completely destroyed the attack group." This was an exaggeration, but the Americans did shoot down seven planes and damaged two
others. The rest fled.[25]

Or at least they tried to. As dusk turned to full dark around 6:30 p.m.,
the *Lexington* and *Yorktown* were recovering the fighters that had driven off
this ill-fated sortie when several unidentified planes flew past the *Yorktown*
with their running lights on and began flashing messages in code. It was
not a code that anyone on the *Yorktown* recognized. Then the planes swung
around and entered the landing pattern, as if preparing to come aboard. By
now it was evident that these were hostile planes whose pilots had mistaken
the *Yorktown* for one of their own. A few of the American escorts opened
fire, and then the *Yorktown*'s own antiaircraft guns joined in, sending a curtain of ordnance into the group of circling planes, both friendly and hostile.
When that happened, Ted Sherman recalled, "aircraft disappeared into the
darkness like a flock of birds flushed by hunters." Twenty-three-year-old
Ensign Richard Wright was startled to see tracers from his own ship fly past
the cockpit of his Wildcat fighter. He insisted that "some of those tracers
came between my face and the instrument panel," and he shouted into his
transmitter, "What are you shooting at me for?" As the Japanese planes fled,
so did the American pilots, including Wright. One of them, Ensign John D.
Baker, was subsequently unable to find his way back again in the dark. Pete
Pederson, the *Yorktown*'s air group commander acting as fighter control director, watched Baker's blip on radar and radioed him a course to follow to
get back, but Baker never answered and was never seen again. When Pederson could not raise him on the radio, he wept.[26]

That Japanese planes would mistake the *Yorktown* for one of their own
carriers suggested that their flattops might not be far off. Those manning
the radar on the *Yorktown* watched as the blips representing the surviving
Japanese planes retired eastward. A few of them began to circle only about
thirty miles away before disappearing off the screen, as if they were landing. That led some to surmise that the Japanese carriers might be very close
indeed. It was too dark now for an air mission, but Fletcher toyed with the
idea of sending his cruisers and destroyers for a night surface attack. The
problem was that the location of the Japanese carriers was only speculative,

and if it were incorrect, dawn would find his surface ships well off to the east—sitting ducks for a Japanese air strike. Then, too, a high-speed run to the east would use up a lot of fuel, an important consideration now with the *Neosho* smashed and no other tanker expected until May 13. Once again, Fletcher decided to wait for more information. Despite subsequent criticism, it was the correct decision, for in fact the Japanese planes had *not* been landing; they were lost. Many never did find their host carrier. Of the twenty-seven planes Hara had sent out, only eighteen managed to return to their own ships, which were, in fact, more than a hundred miles northeast of Task Force 17.[27]

On the whole, May 7 had been a good day for the American pilots. They had sunk the *Shōhō* in a textbook attack and shot down a total of nineteen planes while losing only three bombers and three fighters of their own. For his part, Admiral Hara was devastated. He felt that he had been unlucky in not finding the Americans first. He was so frustrated that, as he said later, he "felt like quitting the navy." The Americans were as elated as Hara was despondent. As Bill Burch put it, "Despite the pounding we had given them on former occasions, we all felt that this, our first opportunity to try our punch against a major unit of the enemy fleet, was our compensation for the years of training and the weary months of steaming over trackless tropic seas." It was, however, only the prologue.[28]

The next day, the opposing carrier forces finally found one another. As they had the day before, both sides sent out pre-dawn air searches. The first sighting of the day came from Lieutenant Junior Grade Joseph Smith flying a Dauntless from the *Yorktown*. He reported sighting "Two carriers, two battleships." Then, before he could complete the report, his radio cut out. Nevertheless, Fletcher knew what sector Smith had been searching, and at 9:08 he turned tactical command over to Fitch, who ordered a full strike by seventy-five airplanes. The location of the target was confirmed a half hour later by Bob Dixon, who had sent the "Scratch one flattop" report the day before, and who was searching the sector next to Smith's. He flew over to Smith's area and was able to complete the report: "Two carriers, two battleships, four heavy cruisers, several destroyers, 170 miles to the northwest."

The actual distance was closer to two hundred miles, but luckily for the Americans, Hara was steaming toward them as fast as he could go. He, too, had received a sighting report from his patrol planes, and at 9:15, he sent sixty-nine planes to attack Fletcher. En route to the target, flying at 17,500 feet, Bill Burch looked down and saw the Japanese attack force below him headed in the other direction.[29]

The *Yorktown* dive-bombers arrived over the Japanese carrier force at 10:32. Hara's two carriers were about eight miles apart, one ahead of the other, steaming at high speed almost due south toward the American task force. The lead carrier (*Zuikaku*) was about to enter a cloud, but the trailing carrier (*Shōkaku*) was in the open. The dive-bomber pilots were eager to strike, but they waited for the slower torpedo planes to arrive so that they could conduct the kind of coordinated attack that had proved so successful the day before. While they waited, they could see Japanese fighters taking off from the *Shōkaku* and begin climbing up from sea level. It was agonizing to watch, Johnny Neilsen remembered. "We sat up there 20 minutes waiting for those torpedo planes, watching the Zeros climbing up toward us." Worse, all that time, the lead carrier was getting closer to the protective cover of the weather front.[30]

Finally, around 11:00, the torpedo planes arrived. Burch waved his arm and waggled his ailerons as a signal, and peeled over into a dive. The Japanese Zeros circled and waited, making side runs at the bombers as they flew past. Burch and the other bombers had been almost directly above the *Shōkaku*, and they dove nearly vertically, their planes corkscrewing as they plunged downward. As Burch passed through a thermal layer at about 8,000 feet, his windscreen fogged up so badly he couldn't see at all. He tried sticking his head out of the cockpit; though at 250 knots that was impossible. Meanwhile, the carrier turned and twisted so that, instead of making a bombing run along her length, he had to attack from abeam, which gave him a much narrower target. As a result, the *Yorktown* bombers made only two hits. One of them was by Lieutenant John J. Powers, who had sworn before he left the *Yorktown* that morning that he was going to lay his bomb on the flight deck of a Jap carrier. Powers kept his Dauntless in a full dive until he was barely five hundred feet from the target before releasing his bomb. His plane was destroyed by the ensuing blast. He was subsequently awarded a posthumous Medal of Honor.[31]

Meanwhile Joe Taylor's Devastators dropped down to fifty feet for their torpedo attack. The Wildcat fighters drove off the first assault by six Zeros, but this time there were more Zeros than Wildcats. Their fire was so heavy that Taylor thought the bullets striking his plane "sounded like rain on the roof." As a result, most of the torpedo bombers dropped their fish from too great a distance. Though the pilots reported making four hits, this was wishful thinking. One problem was that because the American torpedoes ran at only 33.5 knots; the 34-knot *Shōkaku* could simply outrun them.[32]

The *Lexington* strike force, arriving later, had even less luck. By now the *Zuikaku* had made it under the cover of the weather front and only the *Shōkaku* was visible. Moreover, amid the thickening weather there was a lot of confusion, and most of the *Lexington*'s bombers never found a target at all. Those that did encountered a sky full of Japanese fighters and cloud bursts from antiaircraft fire. "It was an incredible scramble," one pilot recalled. "People yelling over the radio, mixed up, and you never knew who the hell was on top of whom." In the end, only four bombers from the *Lexington* dove on the *Shōkaku*, and only one got a hit. The American pilots reported a total of six hits, but the *Shōkaku* was actually hit only three times, though all three were by 1,000-pound bombs, which damaged her deck so badly that she could no longer launch or recover airplanes. After that, Takagi decided to send her northward, out of the fight. Hara directed the planes from the *Shōkaku* that were still airborne to land on the *Zuikaku*, which had escaped entirely.[33]

Meanwhile, 150 miles to the south, Hara's planes were hitting Task Force 17. By now, the cloud cover no longer protected the American carriers, and both of them were clearly visible in the bright sunshine. Thanks to radar, the Americans had spotted the incoming bogeys at 68 miles, and they braced for the attack. All available fighters, seventeen of them (the rest had gone with the attack force), were put in the air, bolstered by twenty-three Dauntless bombers (without bombs). On board the carriers, watertight doors were secured, gasoline was purged from the fuel lines, and fire hoses and first aid kits were made ready.[34]

The Japanese used a coordinated attack with torpedo planes coming in from both sides in an "anvil" attack while their bombers prepared to dive out of the sun. Ted Sherman, skipper of the *Lexington*, wrote admiringly that their attack was "beautifully coordinated." Soon, the water around both carriers was filled with erupting geysers from near misses and the tracks of swiftly running torpedoes. The two carriers maneuvered radically in an attempt to avoid the torpedoes. The *Lexington*, however, was not a nimble ship. According to Sherman, "it took 30 to 40 seconds just to put the rudder hard over. When she did start to turn, she moved majestically and ponderously." Despite that, she seemed for a time to lead a charmed life. On one occasion, a torpedo ran alongside on the port beam while another streaked past the starboard beam, both missing. Two more ran directly under her without exploding. But the *Lexington*'s luck could not last forever. Within minutes, she was struck by two bombs and two torpedoes. Several fires broke out, and the ship gradually took on a 7-degree list.[35]

The *Yorktown* also received attention from the attackers. She was repeatedly shaken by several near misses, including one explosion that was so violent it lifted the stern of the big carrier clear out of the water so that her four brass propellers could be seen spinning in the air. She also took one direct bomb hit amidships, fifteen feet from the ship's island. That bomb penetrated the flight deck and exploded deep inside the ship. The "main steam lines vibrated excessively for a few seconds then steadied." The lights blinked and went out, and three of the ship's nine boilers had to be secured. Buckmaster called down to the engine room to ask what speed the engines could produce under these circumstances. The engineer told him he could generate steam for 24 knots. Buckmaster wondered if they should back off from that to avoid overtaxing the remaining boilers. "Hell no!" was the answer. "We'll make it."[36]

Back in Hawaii, Nimitz was kept appraised of the action by Rochefort and the "roofers" at Hypo who listened in on the radio traffic, both friendly and hostile. The Japanese pilots were reporting the destruction of one carrier and serious damage to another. Soon afterward, Fletcher reported damage to both American carriers, but also that they both continued to operate.[37]

Then, as quickly as it started, it was over. The attack had lasted about half an hour—from 11:13 to 11:40. On the *Yorktown*, Buckmaster allowed some members of the crew to go down to the mess deck to get something to eat. When they got there, they found that the ship's surgeons had used the mess tables to lay out some of the fifty-five men who had been killed in the attack. Yeoman Second Class Sam Laser remembered, "They hadn't been covered yet, and many of them had horrible wounds—blood streaming from their eyes, missing limbs, and so on. We had to walk past all that to get to the chow line, and the only thing they had was crackers and salmon. For five years after that I couldn't eat salmon."[38]

▪ This photograph captures the moment at 12:47 p.m. on May 8, 1942, when an internal explosion on the *Lexington* triggered the sequence of events that led to her destruction. (U.S. Naval Institute)

Over on the *Lexington*, Sherman corrected the ship's list with counter-flooding, and by 12:30 both carriers were recovering the planes returning from the strike against the *Shōkaku*. Then at 12:47 p.m., there was a huge internal explosion deep inside the *Lexington*. The big carrier had linear gas tanks that went from the bottom of the ship up several decks, and they had been ruptured by a number of near misses. Gas fumes had accumulated, and a spark from an electric generator ignited a massive explosion. It was so powerful that the huge forward elevator platform flew into the air and crashed down onto the flight deck "with a great bang" on top of an airplane. The explosion also started a number of fires that the damage-control teams struggled to contain. An hour later came a second explosion that destroyed the *Lexington*'s ventilation system. Sherman had to order the engine rooms evacuated before the men there were asphyxiated. At 2:50 p.m., he blinkered a message to Fletcher on the *Yorktown*: "This ship needs help." Destroyers came alongside to help fight the raging fires, but it was a losing battle. The *Lexington* had no power, and the fires were burning out of control. At 4:00 there was a third blast. The out-of-control fires were cooking off the stored ammunition. As the big torpedoes exploded, one officer thought that it "sounded like a freight train rumbling up the hangar deck." Fitch leaned over the rail of the flag bridge and told Sherman that he had better "get the boys off the ship."[39]

Discipline held. Sherman recalled that as the crew came topside and prepared to go over the side, "some of them lined up their shoes in orderly fashion on the deck before they left, as if they expected to return." Most of the crew was saved—more than 2,700 men. Sherman made sure he was the last one off, and by nightfall, as one witness recalled, "the whole sky was lit up red with that ship burning from stem to stern." That night, Fletcher sent the destroyer *Phelps* to sink her with torpedoes. It took five of them. As the *Lexington* sank, there was one more "tremendous explosion" underwater as she broke apart.[40]

Again, Fletcher considered another strike. Though the *Yorktown* now trailed a fifty-mile long oil slick behind her, she could still make 25 knots, more than enough to launch and recover aircraft. The problem was that although most of his attack planes had returned, they were, in the words of one pilot, "all shot to hell," and of questionable utility. Fletcher decided instead to retire southward, and Fitch agreed.[41]

Takagi and Hara also considered a second strike. But they had only nine bombers and torpedo planes left, and the *Zuikaku* was running low on fuel. Admiral Inoue had ordered Gotō's invasion force to turn around and head north soon after the *Shōhō* went down, and now he sent the same order to Takagi and Hara. For his part, Hara was glad to get it. He admitted later in a private conversation with Yamamoto's chief of staff that the battle with the Americans had broken his confidence. Consequently, while Fletcher and the *Yorktown* retired to the south, Hara and the *Zuikaku* steamed north. That afternoon, about the time that Sherman ordered the crew of the *Lexington* to abandon ship, Inoue postponed Operation MO indefinitely.[42]

There was one more tense moment for the Americans on May 9, when Lieutenant Junior Grade Frederic Faulkner reported sighting undamaged Japanese carriers only 170 miles away. Fletcher rang up 28 knots and sent Bob Dixon with four dive-bombers (of the sixteen he had left) to try to pinpoint their location. Dixon returned, having spotted nothing but coral reefs. Fletcher began to suspect that what Faulkner had seen was a series of small islands. He called Faulkner to the flag bridge and spread out a chart of the area.

"Here's a chart that shows a chain of small islands at the identical spot at which you made your contact," he told Faulkner. "Do you think you could have made a mistake?" A chastened Faulkner replied that he might have been wrong. Fletcher expressed no anger. He merely replied, "That's all I wanted to know." He reduced speed to 15 knots to conserve fuel and headed for Noumea in New Caledonia.[43]

In the Battle of the Coral Sea—the first engagement in history between opposing carrier forces—the Japanese inflicted more damage on the Americans than the Americans did on the Japanese. The United States lost its largest carrier (*Lexington*), a fleet oiler (*Neosho*), and the destroyer *Sims*, and suffered damage to the *Yorktown*; the Japanese lost only the small carrier *Shōhō* and suffered significant but not mortal damage to the *Shōkaku*. On the other hand, Japanese airplane losses were heavier. The Americans lost 81 planes while the Japanese had lost 105. Moreover, while the Americans recovered all but a few of their pilots, the Japanese did not. Many of their best frontline pilots had been killed, a loss they could ill afford. When Hara sent the twenty-seven-plane attack toward the American "battleships" on the afternoon of May 7, he had handpicked his best pilots for the mission because of the difficult conditions. Nine of them had failed to return.

In spite of that, the Japanese were generally pleased with the outcome. They believed that they had sunk *both* of the American carriers. Newspapers in Japan trumpeted the Battle of the Coral Sea as a major victory. When the pilots of Carrier Division 1 heard the results of the battle, they mocked the surviving pilots of CarDiv 5 good naturedly by declaring that if the "sons of the concubine" could win a victory over the American carriers, imagine what the "sons of legal wives" would do. Within the Japanese high command, however, there was disappointment. Yamamoto was furious that Inoue had called off the action without ensuring the destruction of the American carriers. His chief of staff confided to his diary that "a dream of great success has been shattered."[44]

In post-battle evaluations, the Americans, too, had a mixed response to the battle. The loss of the *Lexington* was a major blow. On the other hand, the Japanese invasion force had been turned back. Fletcher had fulfilled the strategic objective assigned him by Nimitz "to assist in checking further advance by [the] enemy . . . by seizing favorable opportunities to destroy ships, shipping, and aircraft." As it happened, the Japanese never did take Port Moresby, and the complex timetable of their several interdependent operations was irredeemably wrecked. The damage to the *Shōkaku*, though not fatal, was enough to convince the Japanese to keep her out of the forthcoming Midway operation. Though the *Zuikaku* was not damaged at all, the loss of so many of her planes and pilots led to a decision to keep her out as well. At the time, it hardly seemed to matter. With the loss of two American carriers, the Japanese believed that the odds had actually improved.

Over time, the assessment of historians has been that the Battle of the Coral Sea was a tactical victory for the Japanese but a strategic victory for the Americans.

There was one more way in which the Americans benefited from this confrontation. Before the battle, Japan's experienced pilots had given them a great tactical advantage. Now, with the loss of so many of those pilots, and with the experience gained by the Americans, that advantage had diminished.

# The Eve of Battle

On the same day that Fletcher and Fitch effected their rendezvous in the Coral Sea, a score of Japanese admirals lined up in their barges alongside the massive hull of the Combined Fleet flagship *Yamato* in Hashirajima Harbor near Hiroshima. They came aboard one by one, glittering in their dress uniforms, each of them trailed by a gaggle of earnest young staff officers. They saluted the quarterdeck smartly and made their way forward to the mess area, which had been cleared of all furniture, and where the crew had assembled a huge square wooden table. Around the perimeter of that table were all the senior officers who would execute Operation MI. There were so many admirals that little room remained for "mere captains," who, during the lunch breaks, had to eat standing up on the open deck. Yamamoto's chief of staff, Rear Admiral Ugaki Matome was the host, responsible for ensuring that all went smoothly during the "table maneuvers" that would take place over the next four days.[1]

The purpose of such war games was to fine-tune operational plans by exposing any weaknesses, so that the planners and operators could make whatever adjustments were necessary. A senior Japanese officer was assigned to command the enemy force (the "Red Force"), while another commanded the Japanese ("Blue") Force.* Tokens representing ships and fleets were moved across the huge table with long poles similar to those employed by a croupier at a Las Vegas roulette or craps table. When the forces came into contact, a roll of the dice determined battle damage, giving the exercise the element of chance. On board *Yamato*, however, the players and observers seemed disinclined to expose any defects of the plan. Most were veterans of the astonishingly successful campaigns of the first six months of war, and their attitude was, as one put it, "This is a necessary drill, but don't worry, we'll take care of anything that comes along." Nagumo Chūichi, who would command the force that would execute it, should have been asking the toughest questions. Instead, aware that he was not in favor at Combined Fleet headquarters, he remained mostly mute throughout the exercises. Rather than try to expose flaws in the plan, most of the participants seemed determined to demonstrate that the plan had no flaws at all.[2]

No one was guiltier of this than Ugaki himself, who was not only the official host, but the chief judge. At least twice during the games, Ugaki intervened to change the outcome. On one occasion, the Japanese officer commanding the Red (American) Force sent his carriers to sea ahead of the predicted moment and positioned them on the flank of the approaching Kidō Butai. Ugaki ruled that such a move by the Americans was so improbable that it could not be allowed. The Red Force commander protested, according to one witness, with "tears in his eyes." He was less concerned about not being allowed to employ this gambit during the war games than he was about the planners ignoring "the chance of American task forces appearing in the seas near Midway." Like nearly every other senior Japanese naval officer—the Red Force commander notwithstanding—Ugaki simply did not believe that the Americans had the kind of fighting spirit necessary to attempt such a bold maneuver. This was especially curious in light of

---

* It is interesting that for war-gaming purposes, both the Americans and the Japanese made their own forces "Blue" and the enemy "Red," though in a bow to the defunct Plan Orange, Americans most often referred to the Japanese as "Orange."

the fact that the entire Japanese plan was premised on the assumption that when the Americans learned of the Japanese threat to Midway, they would sortie with their carriers to try to stop it. No one seemed to notice that these assumptions were contradictory. The official "Estimate of the Situation" decreed: "Although the enemy lacks the will to fight, it is likely that he will counterattack if our occupation operations progress satisfactorily." No one offered an explanation as to why an enemy who lacked the "will to fight" would "counterattack" during a successful Japanese operation.[3]

An even more egregious example of this kind of wishful thinking—or denial—was evidenced later when the same Red Force commander launched an air attack on the Kidō Butai. The table judge rolled the dice to see what damage had been inflicted. The result was dismaying: the dice decreed that the Americans had scored nine hits and sunk both the *Kaga* and the flagship *Akagi*. Once again Ugaki intervened. Such an outcome was impossible, he declared. He ruled that the Red Force had scored only three hits, and that the *Akagi* had not been sunk—merely damaged. The *Kaga* was taken off the gaming table, though Ugaki later allowed it to be returned in order to participate in the invasion and occupation of Fiji and New Caledonia.[4]

After two days of war gaming, the brass on board the *Yamato* learned that while they were thus engaged, the Americans—the real Americans, not the Red Fleet at the gaming table—had conducted a carrier attack on Tulagi in the Solomon Islands. This, of course, was Fletcher's raid on May 4. If nothing else, it proved that the Americans had at least one carrier in the Coral Sea, some 3,500 miles from Pearl Harbor, where, it was assumed, the American carriers would be passively waiting. The news did not interrupt the games, however, or in any way alter Japanese assumptions, nor did the fact that several of the Japanese units scheduled to take part in Operation MI were not in a condition to do so. These were mere distractions to a high command determined to remain on schedule. That night, Ugaki wrote in his diary, "Although some forces haven't enough time to make ready, we have decided to carry it out as originally planned."[5]

Toward the end of the games, Yamamoto himself interjected a question that implied that he, at least, was willing to consider that it was possible not everything would go exactly according to plan. What would happen, he asked, if American carriers suddenly showed up in an unexpected place while the Kidō Butai was engaged in operations against Midway? Here was an opportunity for a genuine discussion about contingency planning. Instead, Genda Minoru, the resident strategic genius, replied with a boast: "*Gaishu Isshoku.*" Literally this means "One touch of the armored gauntlet"; idiomatically, it connotes an easy victory. Perhaps unwilling to dampen the mood of confidence and high morale, Yamamoto did not openly chastise Genda for his dismissive attitude. But the question continued to bother him. Two years earlier, before the war, he had told a group of schoolchildren, "It is a mistake to regard the Americans as luxury-loving and weak. I can tell you Americans are full of the spirit of justice, fight, and adventure." He did not say anything of the sort now. Nonetheless, he ordered Nagumo to keep half of his bombers and torpedo planes armed and ready at all times.[6]

In general, the table exercises for Operation MI held on board *Yamato* from May 1 to May 5 were all but useless. The most knowledgeable scholars of the Japanese side of the action at Midway describe it as "four days of scripted silliness."[7]

The day after the games ended, Combined Fleet issued the official orders for the invasion of Midway. The timing implied that the table maneuvers had exposed no weaknesses and demonstrated the certain success of the operation. That same day, the ships of Japanese Battleship Divisions 1 and 2 engaged in a routine training mission off the coast. At the seventh salvo from the *Hyūga*, the flagship of BatDiv 2, the breechblock on the left gun in turret number 5 blew off, killing every man in the gun crew. The canopy of the turret flew high into the air and landed on the port side, killing a half dozen sailors. Flames ignited more charges and penetrated to the shell magazine. But for the quick flooding of the magazine, the entire ship might have exploded. It was not a happy augury for the forthcoming operation.[8]

News of the Battle of the Coral Sea arrived at Hashirajima almost as soon as the table maneuvers ended. Inoue reported that Hara's pilots had inflicted severe damage to a "Saratoga type" carrier and "another of the Yorktown type," both of which, he reported, were very likely destroyed—very likely, but not definitely. The news triggered official celebrations throughout Japan. Yamamoto and those in his immediate circle joined in the celebrations, though privately they were disappointed and angered that Inoue had not followed up on his victory. Instead of pursuing the defeated enemy, he had called off the invasion of Port Moresby and sent Hara's carriers northward. As a result, the fate of the two American carriers was not known for sure. "Their sinking was not confirmed," Ugaki confided to his diary, "but is considered certain." If true, it would mean that the American carrier force in the Pacific had just been reduced by half, achieving 50 percent of the objective for which the Midway plan had been crafted.[9]

Gratifying as this news was, Yamamoto was disgusted that Inoue had apparently been intimidated by the sinking of the Shōhō and the damage to the Shōkaku. Inoue also continued to worry—unnecessarily in Yamamoto's view—about those Allied air bases in Australia. Yamamoto's eager young staff officers were equally outraged by Inoue's timidity. They recalled Inoue's apostasy concerning the importance of aircraft carriers, and suspected him of lacking a true warrior's instinct. Partly in response to pressure from them, Yamamoto authorized Ugaki to send a message to Inoue's chief of staff, demanding to know "the reason for issuing such an order [to retire] when further advance and attack were needed." This revealed, yet again, the ability of junior officers to intimidate their seniors into bellicose behavior. Yamamoto remained unsure just how many U.S. carriers—if any—had been sunk, and how many were left. "God only knows what is true," Ugaki wrote in his diary. "I regret that I don't know myself."[10]

A week later, on May 17, the Shōkaku limped into port at Kure. She could not moor at her regular buoy because of the battle damage that was still visible on her deck, and simply dropped anchor among the fleet. Yamamoto went on board the same day and conducted an inspection of the damage. It was worse than he thought, and this may have muted his anger at Inoue for not pursuing the enemy more aggressively. He thought the Shōkaku "was very lucky to have gotten off lightly with such damage," and fairly quickly concluded that she could not be repaired in time to take part in Operation MI.[11]

Much more consequential was the assessment that the *Zuikaku*, too, would have to be withheld from the coming operation. Though entirely undamaged, she had lost so many of her planes and pilots that she was deemed not battleworthy. The historians Jonathan Parshall and Anthony Tully have conducted a careful analysis of the number of airplanes that were available to the *Zuikaku*. She came into port at Kure with all of the planes—from both carriers—that had survived the battle. Relatively few were fully operational attack planes—merely nine bombers and six torpedo planes—through there were twenty-four Zero fighters. In addition, however, there were eight bombers, four torpedo planes, and one more fighter that were only lightly damaged and could have been repaired in time to take part in Operation MI. That would have given the *Zuikaku* a total of fifty-six airplanes, which was only seven short of her normal complement.

An alternative would have been to assign air squadrons from other carriers to the *Zuikaku*, though that violated not only Japanese doctrine but also their sense of propriety. It would be like sending eight baseball players out on the field, dressed in mismatched uniforms. Parshall and Tully conclude that "*Zuikaku* could have been made available if her presence had been considered vital." But it was not, and that reflected Japanese overconfidence as well as their assumption that the Americans had lost two carriers in the Coral Sea, so that as a result the superiority of the Kidō Butai over the Americans had actually been increased even without CarDiv5.[12]

There was another consequence of the Battle of the Coral Sea that should have given the Japanese, and Yamamoto in particular, pause. Although the Americans had failed to sink either of the big Japanese carriers, their dive-bomber pilots had put three 1,000-pound bombs onto the flight deck of the *Shōkaku*—the newest and fastest of Japan's carriers. This alone should have diminished the smugness within the Combined Fleet staff that the Kidō Butai was so vastly superior to its opponent that the outcome of a confrontation was a foregone conclusion—that all it would take to eliminate the American carriers was "one touch of the armored gauntlet."[13]

In Hawaii, Rochefort's operatives in Hypo had followed events in the Coral Sea with intense interest, but they continued to monitor other radio traffic as well. On May 7 (the day American pilots sank the *Shōhō*), they intercepted a message that revealed Japanese plans to hold an "aviation conference" in which all four carriers of CarDiv 1 and 2 would participate. The next day (the day the *Lexington* went down), another message associated those four carriers with two battleships of BatDiv 3 and the cruisers of CruDiv 8. On May 10, Layton briefed Nimitz that "forces in Jap waters involving 1 or 2 CarDivs, a BatDiv, and Light Forces are preparing for operations" that were likely to begin on or about the end of May.[14]

Rochefort was convinced that the target of this new offensive was Midway. The formation of a new enemy fleet, the dramatic increase in radio traffic, and the buildup of forces in Saipan all pointed to an offensive in the central Pacific. The clincher was the frequent use of the geographic designator "AF" in the message traffic. Anyone at all involved in traffic analysis knew that in the Japanese two-letter geographical designator system, "A" stood for an American possession (Hawaii, for example, was "AH"). Moreover, it was clear that "AF" had an airfield and that it was near Hawaii. In March, a Japanese seaplane reporting weather conditions near Midway had reported back to its base that it was passing AF. To Rochefort there was no other possible conclusion: AF meant Midway. In May, a circulated list of "known area designators" included AF as Midway. Rochefort's number two man, Lieutenant Thomas H. Dyer, recalled that "there was little doubt in the minds of FRUPAC [HYPO] that AF was Midway."[15]

In Washington, however, doubts remained that Midway could be the target. Redman in OP-20-G continued to suspect Rochefort's analysis; he worried that the Japanese might be preparing another attack on Port Moresby, or, even more worrisome, an assault on New Caledonia or Fiji. Long-range Japanese plans did indeed include an attack on Fiji and New Caledonia, but only after the capture of Midway. Rochefort found Redmond's suggestions wrongheaded and annoying. Even a quarter of a century later, the memory of it still angered him. "There was no other line of reason," he insisted in a 1969 interview, "just none at all." He knew that Redman had little expertise in code breaking and attributed his skepticism to the not-invented-here syndrome. In an obvious reference to Redman, Rochefort recalled, "We were quite impatient that people could not accept our reasoning."[16]

On May 15, Layton's morning brief to Nimitz concluded that "there can no longer be any doubt that the enemy is preparing for an offensive against U.S. Territory. It is known that an attempt will be made to occupy MIDWAY and points in the ALEUTIANS." That same afternoon, however, Nimitz received a message from King in which the CominCh and CNO declared it was "probable" that the next enemy thrust would be aimed at "Northeast Australia, or New Caledonia and Fiji," and in which King suggested that the apparent interest in Midway was intended "to divert our forces away from SoPac." He even suggested that the planes and air crews from the lost *Lexington* and the crippled *Yorktown* should be sent to airfields in Australia and Hawaii as a defensive force.[17]

Nimitz found King's advice less than helpful. A week before, perhaps in response to Nimitz's transfer of air units to Midway, King had sent him a note reminding him that theater commanders were not authorized to "permanently transfer units" within their command area "without authority from War or Navy Department." At the bottom of that message, Nimitz had scrawled: "In spite of unity of command." It was as close as he came to open rebellion. Now, in response to King's latest suggestion that Midway might be a mere diversion, Nimitz was tactful. "There may well be three separate and possibly simultaneous enemy offensives," he wrote back, but they included "a major landing attack against Midway for which it is believed the enemy's main striking force will be employed." Since he lacked sufficient strength to oppose all three operations at once, Nimitz thought it logical to deploy the available American carrier assets to defend the most important of them—at Midway. Moreover, he preferred to keep the *Yorktown* operational and use the orphaned squadrons from the *Lexington* and *Saratoga* to fill out her complement of planes and pilots. Nimitz was willing to push back against King because he was confident that Rochefort and Layton knew what they were talking about. The Running Summary at CinCPac headquarters for May 16 read, in part, "Unless the enemy is using radio deception on a grand scale, we have a fairly good idea of his intentions."[18]

King capitulated, writing Nimitz, "I generally agree with you." Even now, however, he urged Nimitz to keep an eye on New Caledonia and Fiji and to be prepared to shift forces there if necessary. Though Nimitz did not expect it would be necessary, he promised that he would do so. "Will watch situation carefully," he pledged, "and return Halsey to Southwest if imminent concentration is indicated." He ordered Halsey to return at once to Pearl Harbor and to avoid being sighted by the enemy as he did so—his sense of urgency reflected in a follow-up message to Halsey to "expedite" his return. As King had anticipated, the removal of U.S. carriers from the southwest Pacific had implications for the Anglo-American alliance. When an alarmed British first sea lord queried King about why the carriers were being withdrawn, King risked a security breach by telling him that the "imminence of enemy attacks on Midway and Alaska" made it necessary.[19]

King had come around to the belief that Midway was the enemy target. Nonetheless, given the size and strength of the Japanese offensive, he advised Nimitz to be responsibly cautious in responding to it. "Our appropriate strategy," he wrote to Nimitz, "is to . . . employ strong attrition tactics, and not repeat *not* allow our forces to accept such decisive action as would be likely to incur heavy losses in our carriers and Cruisers." He even proposed sending the *Yorktown* back to Bremerton for repairs "in order to avoid exposure to attack."[20]

But "decisive action" was exactly what Nimitz had in mind. He expected Halsey to reach Pearl on about May 25; the *Yorktown* was to arrive three days later. If *Yorktown* could be patched up in less than four days, he planned to send her out again, to join Halsey's two carriers in a battle with the Kidō Butai. He had been willing to pit two American carriers against three or four enemy carriers in the Coral Sea. Now he was willing to send out two or three American carriers against four Japanese flattops. For all his cool manner and calm demeanor, Nimitz was eager to confront the Japanese. Unlike Yamamoto, he was no gambler, nor did he ignore inconvenient facts. His was the calculating mind of a man who reviewed all the available information, weighed the odds carefully, and planned accordingly.[21]

As he saw it, three American carriers, plus the airstrip on Midway Island, gave him four airplane platforms—the same as the Japanese; and if the airfield on Eastern Island at Midway could not maneuver, neither could it be sunk. Indeed, Nimitz greatly increased the number of planes on Midway. By the end of the month, it would house well over one hundred planes—patrol planes, scout bombers, torpedo planes, Marine fighters, and twenty-three U.S. Army bombers, including nineteen B-17 Flying Fortresses—more planes than on any carrier. To be sure, many of them were not frontline combat units, and few of their pilots had been trained in antiship tactics. Nonetheless, at the very least Midway seemed able to defend itself and would likely contribute to the attack on the Japanese carriers.[22]

Finally, and decisively, the Americans knew what was coming, where it was coming from, and more or less when it was coming. Nimitz believed he held a strong hand. He expected to win.

Though King now accepted that Midway was the object of the Japanese movement, Nimitz still encountered resistance from Washington, and in particular from Redman in OP-20-G and Richmond Kelly Turner, the head of the War Plans Division, both of whom continued to worry that the real Japanese target might be New Caledonia or Fiji. Rochefort was annoyed by this, and was tempted to tell them so. Instead, he sought to find a way to convince the skeptics, telling Jasper Holmes that they needed to do something that would "prove to the world that AF is Midway." Holmes, whose background was in engineering, immediately thought of the large salt-water evaporators that supplied fresh drinking water to the Midway garrison. This led to a gambit that has subsequently become famous in the lore surrounding the Battle of Midway. On May 19, Rochefort asked that a message be delivered to Midway by submarine cable, ordering them to send a radio message to Pearl Harbor—in the clear—stating that their salt-water evaporator had broken down and that they were running short of fresh water. Sure enough, two days after this bogus report hit the airwaves, an intercepted Japanese message reported that "AF" was short of drinking water.* Rochefort did not wave this evidence in the face of the skeptics. In fact, he did not even report the message when it came in, allowing the stations in Melbourne and Washington to discover and report it on their own.[23]

---

* An interesting postscript to this gambit is that the message did affect Japanese logistical planning for the invasion of Midway. One of the *marus* (transport ships) in the invasion force was assigned to carry two new salt-water evaporators to replace the "broken" one on Midway after occupation.

Nimitz scheduled a staff meeting for the morning of May 25 to make final plans. Halsey's Task Force 16 was due in that day, and Nimitz needed to be sure that everyone understood the timetable for the turnaround and redeployment. Nimitz invited Army General Delos C. Emmons, commander of the Hawaiian Department, and General Robert C. Richardson, a personal friend of General George C. Marshall, who represented the War Department. Nimitz wanted them to hear the latest intelligence report from Rochefort himself. It was the first time Rochefort had been invited to brief the high brass personally. The admiral and generals assembled at the appointed hour, but Rochefort was not there.

Rochefort was late because he and his team were cobbling together information from a dozen messages, all of them dated May 20, that collectively provided a much clearer view of the Japanese plan.* Though these messages had been intercepted four days earlier, they had been consigned to what was colloquially called the "crap traffic" bin because they were badly garbled and therefore less likely to reveal any useful intelligence. Layton noted in his private journal that Hypo analysts were "unable to do much with" the messages "due [to the] necessity [of] keeping up with current traffic," which was exceptionally high, and that "only [a] garbled copy [was] available." Nevertheless, as the cryptanalysts began to strip away the secondary cipher groups on one of those messages, the five-number code for "attack" appeared in close association with the geographical designator "AF." This provoked a burst of excitement, and both Hypo and Belconnen got to work on it in earnest. As it happened, the Melbourne version and the Hypo version were garbled in different places, which meant that with both versions in hand, more of the message could be recovered.[24]

---

* There has been a lot of confusion about the character of these decrypts. In his postwar oral history, Rochefort described it as a single op order in twelve parts, which is often how it is described. However, the list of raw decrypts shows that the information was retrieved from a dozen different messages, all dated May 20, each of which dealt with a different aspect of the plan. No single comprehensive operational order dated May 20 has been found. It is very likely, therefore, that Rochefort, in making his presentation to Nimitz on May 25, simply conflated these several messages into one. For a longer discussion of this, see Appendix E.

Moreover, this message was accompanied by others. One noted the departure of two battleships and a cruiser division from Kure; another referred to a "main body" and a screen; a third referred to a rendezvous of this force with "the Striking Force" of CarDivs 1 and 2. One contained a reference to "AF and AO occupation forces." The cryptanalysts at both Hypo and Belconnen worked furiously to break as many of these messages as they could, and the two units traded insights and information. Piece by piece, what emerged was, in Layton's words, "a detailed report of Japanese forces to be used at Midway." The time for Rochefort's meeting with Nimitz came and went, but Rochefort was determined to take this new key intelligence with him. When he showed up at Nimitz's headquarters a half hour late, he apologized and handed Nimitz a sheaf of papers, saying he hoped "this would explain everything."[25]

It did. The new decrypts not only confirmed that Midway was the target, they offered important details about the Japanese plan of attack. They did not reveal the complete order of battle—the Americans still did not know that Yamamoto himself planned to be at sea with the *Yamato*, for example—but there was enough about the Kidō Butai that Rochefort could tell Nimitz with some confidence that the enemy would have four carriers, and that those carriers would approach Midway from the northwest. Rochefort himself declared later that the intercepts contained "the strength of the attack and the composition of the attack forces," and even "such things as where the Japanese carriers would be when they launched their planes," though that last claim was slightly in error; all the messages revealed for sure was that the carriers would approach Midway from the northwest. Despite subsequent mythology about this intelligence breakthrough, it was not quite like having a copy of the enemy's plans. Still, the information was detailed enough that some wondered if it might be a trick. Rochefort was convinced that it was genuine and stood his ground before probing questions from the flag and general officers. "I could not understand why there should be any doubt," he later insisted.[26]

To all outward appearances, Nimitz remained impassive. When, years later, Rochefort was asked to describe the admiral's reaction, all he could recall were those cool blue eyes looking at him. Nimitz did ask Rochefort whether he was certain about the number of enemy carriers. If the Kidō Butai consisted of all six carriers of the original Pearl Harbor strike force, the American carriers would be outnumbered two to one (or if the *Yorktown* could not be patched up in time, three to one). Rochefort predicted confidently that there would be only four enemy carriers. All of the message traffic referred only to Carrier Divisions 1 and 2, not to Carrier Division 5. Moreover, Rochefort knew that the *Shōkaku* had arrived in Japanese home waters some days before and an intercepted message sent on May 22 appeared to be the "arrival" message of the *Zuikaku*.

One missing piece of essential information was the date. To find it, Lieutenant Commanders Wesley Wright and Joe Finnegan stayed up all night in the Dungeon, trying to crack the various layers of encipherment in the messages. At 5:30 the next morning (May 26), Wright reported to Rochefort that the evidence suggested that the attack would begin at dawn on June 4 Tokyo time, June 3 Hawaii time. At the time they made that analysis they were correct, though that very afternoon the Japanese high command postponed the attack date from June 3 to June 4.[27]

Later that day, Nimitz asked his staff to outline the strengths and weaknesses of both sides in the forthcoming collision. The Japanese advantages were obvious: they would have more carriers and the gunfire support of two battleships; their fighters were superior; and their attack airplanes had a longer range. On the other hand, they were operating at a daunting distance from their base, and even moderate damage to their carriers might therefore prove fatal. The American advantage was their knowledge of Japanese plans. The wild cards were whether or not the *Yorktown* would be available, and the "uncertain" value of the Army bombers on Midway. Nimitz concluded that "we cannot afford to slug it out with the probably superior approaching Japanese forces." As King had suggested, the best approach would be to "reduce his forces by attrition." To do that would require what Nimitz called "the principle of calculated risk." As he had said in response to an earlier event, "Timidness won't win this war, neither will foolish recklessness." Much would depend, therefore, on the ability of the officer in tactical command, Vice Admiral William F. Halsey, to know the difference.[28]

As Nimitz soon learned, however, there was one more wild card in the deck.

———————

Halsey's two big carriers entered Pearl Harbor that afternoon (May 26). On board the flagship *Enterprise*, a haggard-looking Halsey prepared to go ashore. For weeks he had been suffering from a severe form of dermatitis that was aggravated by exposure to the sun. It was so painful that he could not leave his cabin in the daytime. In consequence Halsey had not slept in days, and he had lost more than twenty pounds. His ravaged skin hung on his frame like an old coat, and the ship's doctor told him in no uncertain terms that he had to go to the hospital. Despite that, he was determined to call on Nimitz first. When he showed up at CinCPac headquarters, Nimitz was horrified by his appearance and ordered him at once to report to the hospital. Before he went, however, Nimitz asked him who should assume command of Task Force 16 in his absence. Halsey had anticipated the question and had an answer ready: Raymond Spruance.[29]

Fifty-five-year-old Rear Admiral Raymond A. Spruance (he would turn 56 on July 3) was a 1907 Academy graduate* who had served in cruisers and destroyers for his entire career, and currently commanded the cruiser escort of Task Force 16. At 5 feet 9 1/2 inches and 140 pounds, he had a slender, almost skeletal frame and a thin face. He was calm in his demeanor and courtly in his manners, reminding one interviewer of "a soft-spoken university professor." His chief of staff noted later, "There were some who thought he had no sense of humor. He actually had a very keen one, but it was recognized only by those who knew him well and could spot a slight twinkle of the eye." Spruance and Halsey were close friends. It was a curious friendship; Halsey was outgoing and affable, colorful, and emotional, while Spruance was cool, reserved, and disciplined. Halsey tended to shoot from the hip, and Spruance was "serene and methodical." As the historian

———

* The Naval Academy class of 1907, which was particularly large, was commissioned in three sections to smooth the entrance of so many new officers into the fleet. With his high class standing, Spruance graduated with the first group on September 12, 1906, even though he was a member of the class of 1907.

■ Rear Admiral Raymond A. Spruance commanded the cruiser escorts of Halsey's Task Force 16. Just days before the Battle of Midway, he was charged with overall command of Task Force 16, including its two carriers. (U.S. Naval Institute)

John Lundstrom aptly puts it, Halsey and Spruance were "fire and ice." Yet in spite of those differences, or perhaps because of them, they had been close for years. They had seen duty together, and their families were also close. In some ways they complemented each other: Halsey admired Spruance's ascetic intellectualism, and Spruance admired Halsey's cheerful bonhomie. One great advantage in making Spruance the stand-in commander, was that he was already familiar with the personnel in Task Force 16.[30]

The problem was that Spruance was a black shoe. Unlike Halsey, he had never earned his gold wings—or even the silver wings of a "naval observer." Like Frank Jack Fletcher, he was a dedicated surface-warfare officer. Moreover, he was junior to Fletcher, which meant that Fletcher would be the officer in tactical command of the combined carrier group—assuming that the *Yorktown* could participate at all. Spruance's selection to command Task Force 16 meant that the fate of America's crippled and dwindling carrier force would be in the hands of two black-shoe admirals. Although Nimitz did not know Spruance personally, he admired his record and had already formally requested Spruance as his new chief of staff. Moreover, Spruance's partnership with Halsey in all the operations of Task Force 16 since the raid on the Marshalls had prepared him to move into the command position. For his part, Halsey was so sure of his recommendation that he had prepared a letter, which he now handed to Nimitz. In it, Halsey praised his subordinate's "outstanding ability" as well as his "excellent judgment and quiet courage." He concluded: "I consider him fully and superbly qualified to take command of a force comprising mixed types [of ships] and to conduct protracted independent operations in the combat theater in war time."[31]

Nimitz approved Halsey's proposal on the spot. Halsey turned to his flag lieutenant, William H. Ashford. "Go back to the *Enterprise* and tell Ray Spruance he's to take the task force out, using my staff. Tell him to shift his flag to the *Enterprise*." Then Halsey went resignedly to the base hospital to begin what would stretch into two months of sick leave.[32]

The next afternoon (May 27) the *Yorktown*, still trailing a ten-mile-long oil slick, appeared off the entrance to Pearl Harbor, one day ahead of schedule. At dawn the next morning, she crept cautiously into Drydock Number One, where special blocks had been set up to receive her. Ordinarily, safety concerns would have required her to spend a day purging her stored aviation fuel, but Nimitz was in a hurry; he issued a special order voiding the rule. When the massive gates of the drydock were closed and the water pumped out, the giant *Yorktown* settled onto the blocks, and gradually her damaged hull was exposed.[33]

Among those who inspected it was Nimitz. Wearing big hip boots over his khaki slacks, he sloshed through the foot or more of water in the bottom of the not-quite-dry drydock as he looked over the damage. Fletcher had radioed ahead that while the *Yorktown* had lost her radar and refrigeration system, her main power plant was still operating, the airplane elevators were working, and the bomb hole in the flight deck had been patched. The real concern was the *Yorktown*'s hull. The several near misses in the Coral Sea had opened seams in the skin of her hull from frames 100 to 130 and ruptured the fuel-oil compartments, which were still leaking. Jake Fitch had estimated that it would take ninety days in a shipyard to repair the hull. Nimitz didn't have ninety days. Even before the *Yorktown* arrived, he had sent the yard superintendent and a team of specialists out to her to make a preliminary study. They radioed back that she might be patched

■ The USS *Yorktown* (CV-5) undergoing repairs in the massive drydock at Pearl Harbor on May 28, 1942. Though some thought those repairs would require three months or more, Nimitz insisted that she be patched up in three days. (U.S. Naval Institute)

up in time, but that it would take a supreme effort. Now, as he looked over the ship, Nimitz turned to the members of the inspection party. "We must have this back in three days." There was an awkward moment of silence, and a few men exchanged glances, but there was only one possible response: "Yes, sir."[34]

Nimitz authorized shore liberty for the *Yorktown*'s crew, partly as a reward for their long cruise and partly to get them out of the way of the yard workers. Soon, some fourteen hundred fabricators, shipfitters, and welders were swarming over the big carrier. They went to work with a purpose and intensity that suggested every minute counted, which it did. Whereas Yamamoto assumed that the loss of the *Shōkaku* and *Zuikaku* only narrowed the Kidō Butai's margin of superiority, Nimitz knew that if the Americans were to have any chance against the oncoming juggernaut, they would need all three of their carriers.

The work continued around the clock. Though Honolulu was still blacked out for fear of enemy air raids, the dockyard at Pearl Harbor was lit up by giant floodlights and acetylene torches that burned through the night. The demand for electricity became so great that some districts in Honolulu endured power outages so that the yard could get all the power it needed. Pushed to make quick fixes rather than permanent repairs, the men did not bother with blueprints or plans. They cut plywood templates on board to match the gaping holes, sent the templates ashore to be duplicated in steel, then welded or bolted the patches into place. Deep inside the ship, work parties shored up sagging bulkheads instead of replacing them.[35]

When Fletcher met with Nimitz in his Pearl Harbor headquarters, he thought the normally placid Nimitz seemed uncharacteristically tense. Nimitz asked how he felt, and Fletcher acknowledged that he was "pretty tired." After all, he had just completed a 101-day deployment, fought a major battle, and ridden the crippled *Yorktown* back across 3,500 miles of ocean. Fletcher thought he and the crew of the *Yorktown* had earned a respite; he had even stopped for a quick drink en route to Nimitz's headquarters. Nimitz agreed that Fletcher and his crew would ordinarily be entitled to a long refit on the West Coast. But these were not ordinary times. "We have to fix you up right away and send you out to Midway." He explained what he knew of the Japanese plan. The *Yorktown*'s air group, depleted by the Battle of the Coral Sea, would be brought up to full strength with squadrons from the *Saratoga*.* The *Yorktown* would be repaired and refloated by the next day (May 29) and go to sea again the day after that.[36]

There was more, of course. Nimitz revealed that Halsey would be unable to participate in the forthcoming engagement because of his skin

---

* The *Yorktown* retained most of Wally Short's bombing squadron (VB-5) though it was redesignated as VS-5 in order to make room for Max Leslie's VB-3 from *Saratoga*. *Yorktown*'s fighter squadron, originally VF-42 from *Ranger*, supplied some pilots but was merged into VF-3 under Jimmy Thach; the squadron was also assigned the newer Dash 4 Wildcats. The torpedo squadron (VT-3 under Lem Massey) also expected replacement planes, hoping to get the newer and faster Grumman Avengers, though the strictness of the timetable meant that the pilots of VT-3 flew out to the *Yorktown* in the older and slower Devastators.

condition, and that Spruance would take over Task Force 16. Then, to Fletcher's growing perplexity, Nimitz began to ask him pointed questions about various aspects of his command tenure in *Yorktown*. The roots of this awkward interrogation reached back to Ernie King's suspicions about Fletcher's timidity. King remained disappointed that Fletcher had not attacked the shipping at Rabaul. His disappointment had sharpened into anger when he had read Fletcher's March 29 message informing Nimitz that he was retiring to Noumea to refuel; King had dashed off an angry and almost insulting blast to Fletcher that his message was "not understood." Indeed, King seemed ready to write off Fletcher as an operational commander, and a few days after sending that missive he had proposed that Fletcher be moved into a shore billet as the acting commander of the South Pacific. Nor had the Battle of the Coral Sea eased King's doubts. King acknowledged to his British counterpart that "we had rather the better of it" in the Coral Sea, but after reading the battle reports, he wrote to Nimitz (with a copy to Fletcher) that while he was "not familiar with all the circumstances," he had "a feeling that destroyers might have been used in the night attacks" on May 7. Now, before Nimitz handed Fletcher the command of all of America's remaining carriers in what was shaping up to be the decisive battle of the Pacific War, King wanted Nimitz to interrogate Fletcher sharply to determine his suitability for such an important job.[37]

The conversation was as embarrassing for Nimitz as it was for Fletcher, and the discussion became increasingly stilted. Finally, Fletcher said he would have to consult his log to respond in detail, and Nimitz, probably relieved, said that that was reasonable and they moved on to other topics. That night, after a second meeting that included Ray Spruance, Fletcher stayed up late to compose a typed thirteen-page single-spaced letter that began, "My dear Admiral Nimitz," in which he explained all his command decisions in detail, especially in the Coral Sea. He had not attacked Rabaul, he wrote, because he did not have timely intelligence about suitable targets and it would have revealed his presence to the enemy. He did not order a destroyer night attack on May 7 because the location of the enemy carriers was uncertain. The airplane seen on the radar scope circling only thirty miles away was very likely a lost friendly. "All things considered," he wrote, "the best plan seemed to be to keep our force concentrated and prepare for battle with enemy carriers next morning."[38]

Nimitz forwarded Fletcher's letter to King, along with one of his own ("Dear King"), in which he wrote that he had "finally had an opportunity to discuss with Fletcher . . . his operations in the Coral Sea area, and to clear up what appeared to be lack of aggressive tactics of his force." As far as Nimitz was concerned, "these matters have been cleared up to my entire satisfaction, and I hope, to yours." Fletcher, Nimitz wrote, "is an excellent, seagoing, fighting naval officer and I wish to retain him as task force commander." Fletcher had passed the test, though if King had been grading it instead of Nimitz, the outcome might have been different.[39]

Nimitz ended his letter by quoting King's own words back to him. In the days before Pearl Harbor, when King had commanded the Atlantic Fleet, he had frequently reminded his subordinates that despite shortages, "we will do the best we can with what we have." King had used it so frequently that it had become the semiofficial slogan of the Atlantic Fleet. Now Nimitz used that phrase to close his letter of May 29: "We are actively preparing to greet our expected visitors with the kind of reception they deserve," he wrote, "and *we will do the best we can with what we have.*" In this context, though, it had a double meaning. It meant not only that they would make do with the ships and equipment they had—Halsey's two carriers (though without Halsey), and a patched-up *Yorktown* carrying planes and pilots from the *Saratoga*—it also clearly meant that they would make do with the commander that was available.[40]

Nimitz gave Fletcher his orders later that same day. Though Fletcher would command the entire American carrier force, Nimitz wanted him to keep the *Yorktown* group separate from Task Force 16. Spruance's two carriers were to launch the first strike while Fletcher held the *Yorktown*'s air group back as a reserve until all of the Japanese carriers had been definitely located. Nimitz also reiterated "the principle of calculated risk," and, using King's language, he cautioned Fletcher not to "accept such decisive action as would be likely to incur heavy losses in our carriers and cruisers." If defeat seemed likely, he was to break off the engagement and retire. After all, as Commander Miyo had repeatedly but fruitlessly pointed out at the conference in Tokyo at which Watanabe had pitched Yamamoto's original plan, Midway was too far from Tokyo to make its occupation by Japan sustainable. Even if the Japanese took it now, the Americans could always get it back later.[41]

Early the next morning (May 29), Drydock Number One was reflooded, the Yorktown floated off her blocks, and the gates were opened. The big flattop backed gingerly out into the main harbor and over to a loading dock, where she began to take on board the fuel, ammunition, and provisions she would need over the next several days. By then, Spruance was already at sea. Elements of Task Force 16 had begun to leave Pearl Harbor on the morning of May 28. The destroyers had gone out first and set up a screen. Then the cruisers followed, one at a time, at five-minute intervals. Finally, the two carriers departed. They were naked of airplanes—the planes and their crews were still at Kaneohe Air Station and Ewa Field and would fly out to the carriers only after the task force was well out to sea.[42]

As the work on the Yorktown progressed, an ensign named Jack Crawford, only six months out of the Naval Academy and fresh from radar school at MIT, reported his arrival in Pearl Harbor. He had orders to report to the Yorktown for duty and was eager to get aboard his first ship. The personnel officer at Pearl told him that there was no rush, since the Yorktown was likely to be in drydock for several months, but the young ensign was in a hurry. Told he would need the signature of the chief of staff to effect the transfer, Crawford went to the captain's house and knocked on his door. The Filipino steward who answered told him that the captain was watching a movie. With the impatience of youth, Ensign Crawford told him to get the captain out of the movie; he needed a signature. The obviously irritated captain signed the orders, but he warned Crawford that his attitude did not bode well for his future career. "Son," he told him, "you're headed for trouble." He was more right than either of them knew. Crawford went aboard the Yorktown at ten o'clock that night.[43]

The next day, Nimitz came aboard and talked to Fletcher and Buckmaster. He had no more instructions; he merely wished them "good luck and good hunting." Soon afterward, the Yorktown was under way. Once in open water she joined the ships of her escort for the cruise northward to a rendezvous with Spruance's Task Force 16 at a predetermined point 1,400 miles north of Oahu and 325 miles north of Midway that had optimistically been designated as "Point Luck." There, the American carriers would be on the flank of the Kidō Butai as it approached. Ironically, it was very near the spot where the Japanese commander of the Red Team during the shipboard War Games at Hashirajima had put them, and where Rear Admiral Ugaki Matome had insisted they could never be.[44]

## 10

# Opening Act

The battle opened not in the central Pacific but among the fog-enshrouded islands of the Aleutian archipelago some two thousand miles to the north. Part of the price that Yamamoto had to pay for getting the Navy General Staff to accept Operation MI was his agreement to continue with Operation AL—the occupation of several small islands in the western Aleutians. Though at the time the Americans assumed that this was a diversion for the Midway campaign, it was a stand-alone operation with quite limited goals: the occupation of the islands of Attu and Kiska in the western island chain in order to expand the empire's defensive perimeter. To prevent the Americans from interfering with these landings, the Japanese planned to neutralize the American base at Dutch Harbor on the island of Unalaska, some four hundred miles east of Attu and Kiska. The overall operation was under Vice Admiral Hosogaya Moshirō, who commanded the Japanese Fifth Fleet, and the force assigned to strike Dutch Harbor consisted of two carriers and their supports under the command of Rear Admiral Kakuta Kakuji. One of the two carriers was the *Ryūjō*, which carried only thirty-seven planes. The other was the 24,000-ton *Jun'yō*, which carried fifty-three planes. Combined with two heavy cruisers and a destroyer screen, they comprised the Second Striking Force—a kind of mini Kidō Butai.

Though the entire Japanese operational plan for June of 1942 was characterized by a dispersal of force, the decision to send two carriers to the Aleutians seems particularly profligate. In fact, however, neither could have been used to reinforce the Midway-bound Kidō Butai. The *Ryūjō* was simply too small, and the *Jun'yō*, which had originally been laid down as a passenger liner and converted into a carrier only recently, had a top speed of only 24 knots, which meant she could not keep up with the Kidō Butai; even the plodding *Kaga* could sustain 28 knots. On the other hand, the fighters and bombers on the decks of those two carriers might have played an important—even a decisive—role in the Battle of Midway had some or all of them been transferred to the *Zuikaku*. This was not done mainly because the Japanese did not believe the *Zuikaku* was needed, but also because the pilots in the *Jun'yō's* air wing were relative novices with little if any battle experience. Because of that, though the *Jun'yō* nominally carried fifty-three aircraft, Kakuta could count on only about thirty-three of those for combat operations.[1]

The Americans had long been aware of Alaska's vulnerability. The tail end of the Aleutian archipelago at Attu was only 650 miles from the northernmost of the Japanese Kurile Islands. The Japanese had a small base on Paramushiro in the Kuriles, but until 1937 the Americans had virtually no military presence in Alaska. That year, the Navy began construction of a seaplane base at Sitka, and soon afterward another at Dutch Harbor, though that was still some 1,400 air miles from Paramushiro. By 1942, these two American bases hosted two destroyers, three Coast Guard cutters, and a handful of long-range PBY Catalinas, all under the command of Navy Captain Leslie E. Gehres. The Army had twenty bombers plus forty pursuit planes under the command of Brigadier General William O. Butler.

In January 1942, Roosevelt had asked King about "operational readiness in the Alaskan area." At the time King dismissed the idea of a Japanese assault there because "a landing in Alaska would be a costly undertaking,

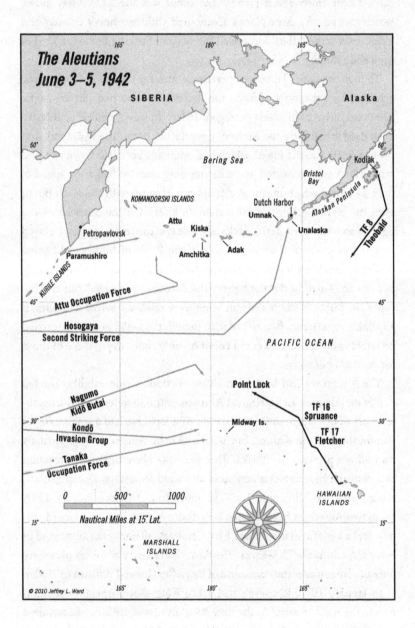

The Aleutians
June 3–5, 1942

SIBERIA

Alaska

Bering Sea

Kodiak

Bristol
Bay

KOMANDORSKI ISLANDS

Dutch Harbor

Umnak

Attu

Kiska

Adak

Unalaska

Alaskan Peninsula

TF 8
Theobald

Petropavlovsk

Amchitka

Paramushiro

KURILE ISLANDS

Attu Occupation Force

Hosogaya
Second Striking Force

PACIFIC OCEAN

Point Luck

TF 16
Spruance

Nagumo
Kidō Butai

Midway Is.

TF 17
Fletcher

Kondō
Invasion Group

Tanaka
Occupation Force

HAWAIIAN
ISLANDS

0      500      1000

Nautical Miles at 15° Lat.

MARSHALL
ISLANDS

© 2010 Jeffrey L. Ward

unproductive of immediate results, and would expose the occupying forces to strong counter attack." Despite King's skepticism, however, the United States did begin to build up its Alaskan forces, largely in response to Alaska's governor, Ernest Gruening, who complained to FDR's secretary of the interior, Harold Ickes, that "Alaska is far from prepared for eventualities." What Gruening wanted was money—for airfields, planes, and equipment. And he got it. Ickes recognized that Gruening's request was as much political as strategic, and he sent it on to the president, who approved the construction of a new 5,000-foot airstrip on the island of Umnak, just west of Dutch Harbor.[2]

For his part, Nimitz knew (thanks to the code breakers) that the Japanese planned to attack the Aleutians at the same time as they closed on Midway. He was not willing to weaken his carrier task force to defend those distant islands, nor was he willing to let them go by default. He appointed newly promoted Rear Admiral Robert A. "Fuzzy Theobald, a stocky 1907 Annapolis classmate of Ray Spruance, to command a surface force of five cruisers (two heavy cruisers and three light cruisers) plus four destroyers as Task Force 8, and gave him orders to defend the archipelago and "inflict maximum attrition" on the enemy attackers.[3]

Without carriers, Theobald knew he had to depend on General Butler and the Army for his air support. In theory, at least, Theobald had command authority over Butler's bombers, for in April Marshall and King had agreed that "when a state of fleet-opposed invasion is declared, unity of command is vested in the Navy." The problem was that neither service had any practical experience with joint operations, and there was no clear chain of command or channel of communications that allowed the two services to work together efficiently. As there was no Department of Defense or Joint Chiefs of Staff at the time, the two services were entirely separate. Though Nimitz asked King to "inform Army that surface force will be almost completely dependent on them for air cover," King could not order it. The only person with simultaneous command authority over both the Army and the Navy was the president himself. As a result, there was confusion and missed opportunity on the American side, though, as it turned out, this was matched by confusion and missed opportunity on the Japanese side, too.[4]

■ Rear Admiral Robert A. "Fuzzy" Theobald
commanded the cruiser-destroyer force dubbed
Task Force 8 that Nimitz assembled to defend
the Aleutian Islands. (U.S. Naval Institute)

Theobald and his task force reached Kodiak Island, some five hundred
miles east of Dutch Harbor, on May 27—the same day that the crippled
*Yorktown* appeared off Pearl Harbor. He met with General Butler at his
headquarters and explained his plan to inflict "maximum attrition" on the
approaching enemy, in conformance with Nimitz's directive. Theobald's
surface force could not close with Kakuta's carriers unless the Americans
first gained command of the air. The Navy Catalinas were ideal for scouting,
but they were flimsy and vulnerable and relatively useless in an attack, especially against carriers. Theobald could not even plan a night destroyer attack, because at that latitude in early June there was hardly any night. Butler
would have to bring his Army bombers to the forward airstrip at Cold Bay
and the new field at Umnak, where they would wait for a sighting report
from the Catalinas and then attack. If their attacks sufficiently weakened
the carriers, Theobald could then close with his cruiser force and finish
them off with gunfire.[5]

Butler was less than enthusiastic about this plan. He objected to con-
centrating his air forces at Cold Bay and Umnak, more than five hundred
miles to the west, instead of at Kodiak, where they could protect the city
of Anchorage. Those western bases lacked support facilities and protective
revetments; Butler worried that his planes would be sitting ducks. The conversation was courteous enough, but Butler stubbornly resisted the idea of

staging his bombers that far west. Theobald considered asserting his newly established prerogatives as joint commander and simply ordering Butler to do it, but feared that if he did so it would "create an initial schism between the Army and the Navy that [would] adversely affect all [their] operations from then on." So he tried to reason with Butler, pointing out the advantages of acting offensively rather than defensively. He reminded Butler that his own surface ships "could accomplish little until the enemy aircraft carriers were definitely accounted for" and reminded him of Nimitz's orders to inflict "maximum attrition" on the enemy. By the end of their five-hour conference, Theobald thought he had convinced Butler, and on June 1 he returned to his flagship, *Nashville*, and led his task force back to sea, taking up a position four hundred miles to the south. There his ships were cocooned in a seasonal fog so thick that, as one officer on the *Nashville* recalled, "for three days we never saw the ship ahead of us."[6]

Kakuta launched his first strike against Dutch Harbor early on the morning of June 3 (Alaska time). He sent off partial strikes from both of his carriers, but the inexperienced pilots from the *Jun'yō* got lost in the thick weather and turned back, and as a result only nine bombers from *Ryūjō*, plus three fighters, made it through to the target. The *Ryūjō*'s planes inflicted moderate damage, hitting the radio station, the oil tank farm, and an Army barracks, killing twenty-five Americans at the cost of two of their own planes.[7]*

Now was the time for the American Army counterstrike against the carriers. Navy search planes found Kakuta's carriers a mere 165 miles away and radioed their coordinates; one of the snoopers even managed to drop a few bombs, though none struck an enemy ship. Theobald expected that the Army bombers would now sortie. Instead, the Army pilots insisted that "they had to await an order from General Butler," who had apparently had second thoughts since agreeing to Theobald's arrangements. He told another Navy officer that he doubted the Army planes could even defend

---

* After the raid, one Japanese Zero pilot attempted to land his crippled plane on a nearby island. His wheels stuck in the spongy tundra, and the abrupt landing broke his neck. The plane, however, was barely damaged, and five weeks later it was recovered by Americans and sent back to the States, where it was repaired and flight-tested. That helped American aircraft designers assess its strengths and weaknesses.

their own airfields, much less damage the enemy. He therefore radioed Theobald from Kodiak, "Unless otherwise directed by you [I] will not advance bombing squadrons from Kodiak to Cold Bay Area." Since Theobald was observing radio silence, he could not respond to this astonishing message. Instead, he sent the destroyer *Humphreys* racing back to Kodiak with a written order.[8]

Thus prodded, Butler released his bombers, though this did not result in an immediate strike. While en route to the target, the first group of Army planes received a radio report that the Catalinas had temporarily lost contact with the enemy. Rather than continue on in the expectation that contact could be reestablished—which it was—they turned around and returned to base. When a second group of bombers flew out toward the coordinates, the Army pilots fanned out to attack individually rather than attempt a coordinated strike. Most bombed from high altitude, some releasing their bombs blindly from above the stratus cloud layer, simply guessing at the enemy's position "by calculation"—essentially by dead reckoning. As Theobald noted later, "such an attack could not be sure of hitting Kiska Island," much less an enemy warship.[9]

A few of the bombers had been equipped with ship-killing torpedoes, but the Army pilots, inexperienced with such weapons, released them, too, from high altitude, all but ensuring that they would break apart upon striking the water. (One Army pilot claimed that he landed his torpedo square on the deck of a carrier, though that proved false.) Some pilots failed to locate the enemy at all and returned to base still carrying their heavy torpedoes. To avoid landing with such volatile cargo, they jettisoned them on the rocks offshore. Unaware that the torpedo warheads became armed only after the torpedo ran for a prescribed distance in the water, they reported them as "duds" because they didn't explode. Theobald was willing to forgive their ignorance of torpedo ordnance but regretted the loss of the torpedoes themselves, since they were scarce and expensive. By the end of the day, the Navy had lost six PBY Catalinas; the Army had lost two bombers and two P-40 pursuit planes. The Japanese lost four scout planes—shot down by Army P-40s operating from the field on Umnak—yet suffered no damage to their strike force. Having conducted the required attack on Dutch Harbor, Kakuta turned west to cover the landings on Attu and Kiska. The ever-present fog delayed those landings, and he decided to send a second strike against Dutch Harbor on June 4. This time his planes destroyed several oil tanks and a few more buildings, though they again failed to knock out the base.[10]

Theobald was so disgusted with the performance of the Army bombers that he decided to return personally to Kodiak in his flagship to talk again with Butler. He arrived there on the morning of June 5 and immediately went to see a somewhat chagrinned Butler, who was aware of how little his bombers had accomplished. Theobald formally requested that Butler allow the pilots to strike without waiting for permission and suggested that they make concentrated and coordinated attacks rather than isolated high-altitude bombings. He left that same afternoon, believing, or at least hoping, that the problems had been resolved. Nonetheless, Butler's planes never did manage to strike the Japanese fleet. Indeed, so feeble was the American attack on Kakuta's carrier force that the Japanese commander may have been unaware that he had been under attack at all. As one senior naval officer reported to King regarding the Army bombers: "Either they were too slow in taking off, or the weather was too bad, or the distance was too great, or they couldn't find the enemy." In the conditions that prevailed off the Aleutian archipelago, some of this was not altogether surprising. Still, the Navy was inclined to attribute it, in part at least, to Army timidity.[11]

Kakuta, too, was disappointed with the effect of his air attacks on Dutch Harbor. Far more distressing, however, was the radio message he received the afternoon of June 5 from Yamamoto. For the commander in chief to break radio silence at all was astonishing enough; the message he sent was even more so. Hosogaya and Kakuta were to break off their attacks in the Aleutians, cancel the landings, send the transports back to Japan, and close in on the Kidō Butai near Midway. Four hours later, Yamamoto reversed himself and cancelled those orders, telling his northern force commanders to complete their mission after all. But clearly, something had gone very wrong with the Kidō Butai.[12]

In fact, nearly everything had gone wrong, starting with the fact that the Japanese had failed to determine whether the American carriers they hoped to lure out to their destruction were even present in Pearl Harbor. They did have a plan to find out. Nearly three months earlier, well before the fateful conference in Tokyo at which Nagano and Fukudome had capitulated to Yamamoto's blackmail and approved the Midway plan, the Japanese had conducted a long-range reconnaissance of Pearl Harbor using two giant Kawanishi flying boats. These remarkable four-engine seaplanes, called "Emilys" by the Allies, were 92 feet long (30 feet longer than the American Catalinas) and had an astonishing range of over 4,500 miles, which meant that, theoretically at least, they could fly from the Marshall Islands to Pearl Harbor and back without stopping. Such a flight would leave no margin for error, however, and so Commander Miyo (who a month later would strenuously oppose Yamamoto's Midway plan) suggested that their range could be extended even further by refueling them at sea from submarines. This notion hinted at using them to bomb American cities along the continental West Coast. More immediately, it provoked discussions about a second attack on Pearl Harbor, a scheme that was code-named Operation K.[13]

Americans were very much aware of the possibility of long-range air strikes by seaplanes refueled at sea. Three months before Pearl Harbor, Hypo analyst Jasper Holmes, writing under the pen name "Alec Hudson," had published a story in the *Saturday Evening Post* about American seaplanes refueled by submarines striking enemy bases three thousand miles away. In Holmes's fictional tale, "twelve big bombers" attacked an enemy base "with machinelike precision," wrecking an invasion convoy. Edwin Layton later speculated that Holmes's story might have given the Japanese the idea for Operation K, but in fact the Japanese had begun experimenting with a seaplane-submarine partnership as early as 1939. After the war began, the Japanese planned to conduct a whole series of seaplane raids against Pearl Harbor—to keep track of the comings and goings of American warships, as well as to keep the Americans on edge and off balance by bombing them periodically. In the end, however, this dual objective undermined Japanese ambitions, for it focused American attention on the program and therefore compromised it.[14]

The first (and, as it turned out, only) seaplane attack on Pearl Harbor occurred in the first week of March 1942, before Yamamoto even submitted

▨ The long range of the big four-engine Kawanishi H8K Type 2 seaplanes, called "Emilys" by the Allies, encouraged Japanese planners to consider long-range raids against American bases. (U.S. Naval Institute)

his Midway plan to the Naval General Staff. Two Kawanishis, each of them armed with four 500-pound bombs, took off from Wotje Island in the Marshalls on March 2 and in thirteen and a half hours flew 1,605 miles to an unoccupied atoll called French Frigate Shoals, halfway between Pearl Harbor and Midway. There they refueled from two prepositioned submarines, then flew on to Oahu, another 560 miles to the southeast, arriving just past midnight on the morning of March 4. By then the weather had thickened, and visibility over the American naval base was virtually zero. The pilot of the lead plane, Lieutenant Hashizume Hisao, could see a slight glow through the cloud layer, but not much else. Thinking that he had glimpsed the outline of Ford Island in Pearl Harbor through a gap in the clouds, he dropped his bombs. His consort did the same. Then both planes headed back for the Marshall Islands, another two thousand miles and fifteen nonstop hours away.

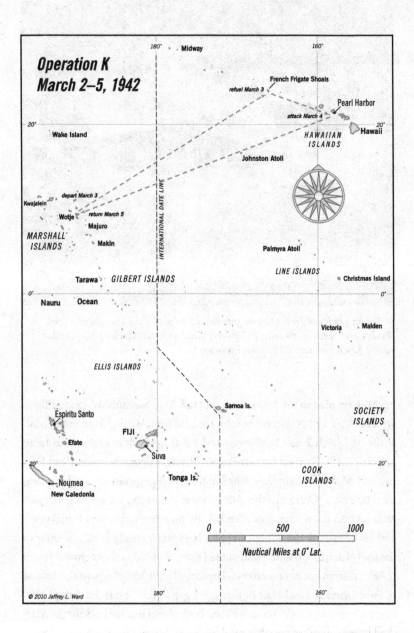

**Operation K**
**March 2–5, 1942**

Midway

160°

French Frigate Shoals

refuel March 3

Pearl Harbor

attack March 4

20°

Wake Island

*HAWAIIAN ISLANDS*

20°

Hawaii

Johnston Atoll

depart March 3

Kwajalein

Wotje    return March 5

Majuro

*MARSHALL ISLANDS*

Makin

INTERNATIONAL DATE LINE

Palmyra Atoll

*LINE ISLANDS*

Christmas Island

Tarawa    *GILBERT ISLANDS*

0°

0°

Nauru    Ocean

Victoria    Malden

*ELLIS ISLANDS*

Espiritu Santo

FIJI

Samoa Is.

*SOCIETY ISLANDS*

Efate

Suva

20°

*COOK ISLANDS*

20°

Noumea

New Caledonia

Tonga Is.

0          500          1000

*Nautical Miles at 0° Lat.*

© 2010 Jeffrey L. Ward

180°

160°

For all the effort and expended fuel, the raid did no damage whatever. Hashizume's four bombs fell on the forested slopes of Mount Tantalus behind Honolulu, and the four from the other plane fell into the water near the entrance to Pearl Harbor. Moreover, the heavy cloud cover meant that Hashizume could not report with much certainty about what ships were or were not in the harbor, though he claimed to have seen at least one carrier.[15]

The most important consequence of this raid was that it drew Nimitz's attention to the threat. Nimitz asked Layton how the Japanese had managed to drop four bombs on Oahu (the four that fell into the harbor had disappeared altogether, and no one was even aware of them until after the war). Layton was fairly sure that they had done it with seaplanes refueled from submarines, and he told Nimitz about Jasper Holmes's story in the *Saturday Evening Post*. Layton also speculated that the Japanese had used French Frigate Shoals to refuel. As a result, Nimitz stationed an American seaplane at French Frigate Shoals, sending the USS *Ballard*, a destroyer recently converted to a seaplane tender, there in late March.[16]

For a variety of reasons, the Japanese did not continue their planned series of raids on Hawaii, but when Yamamoto sought reassurance that the American carriers were still in Pearl Harbor on the eve of the Battle of Midway, his staff suggested a reprise of Operation K. Again Hypo was able to alert Nimitz to the Japanese plan. On May 10, Layton informed Nimitz about an intercepted message that referred to the "K campaign" involving both aircraft and submarines, and three days later he reported that "the K campaign [was] underway."[17]

The Japanese committed six submarines to the project: two filled with aviation fuel, two as radio beacons, one as a plane guard, and one as a command boat. The first of them, the I-123 commanded by Lieutenant Commander Ueno Toshitake, arrived at French Frigate Shoals on May 26. When Ueno approached the atoll and peered into the lagoon through his periscope, he saw a U.S. Navy warship anchored there. When the two fuel-laden submarines showed up the next day, the American warship was still there. In fact, another converted seaplane tender, the

*Thornton*, had joined her. The submarines were in no position to challenge them—the Type KRS submarine had been designed as a minelayer and did not have torpedoes or torpedo tubes. A surface attack would be suicidal, since each of the American surface ships boasted four 4-inch guns. Besides, the whole point of Operation K was stealth. The Japanese could only hope that the Americans would simply go away. Ueno radioed the circumstances back to his superior in the Marshalls and received orders to wait one more day. On May 31, several Catalina PBYs landed in the lagoon to join the tenders. Informed of this, Vice Admiral Tsukahara Nishizo cancelled Operation K. There would be no reconnaissance of Pearl Harbor before the Battle of Midway; the Japanese would simply have to trust that the American carriers were still there. Of course, the day before that, on May 30, the *Yorktown* had left Pearl Harbor to join Task Force 16 at Point Luck.[18]

The second thing that went wrong that week was that the Japanese were tardy in establishing the submarine cordons that were supposed to track the American carriers as they left Pearl Harbor in response to an attack on Midway. Seven submarines, constituting Cordon A, were to occupy a north-south line west of Pearl Harbor. Six more would constitute Cordon B north and east of French Frigate Shoals. Another six would occupy a line near Midway. The subs were to report the carriers' movements and then inflict whatever damage they could as a prologue to the main event. All three cordons were to be established by June 2. They got a late start out of Japan, however, and also lingered a day in Kwajalein, so that they were late in arriving. In addition, several subs were delayed by their involvement with the aborted Operation K. As a result of all this, only one sub made it into position by June 2; the others did not arrive until June 4. By then, the American carriers were nearly a thousand miles to the north. Watanabe Yosuji, Yamamoto's loyal logistics officer, blamed the submarine commander Captain Kuroshima Kameto. Watanabe insisted that Kuroshima was simply not energetic in pursuit of his duties. Whatever the merits of that assertion, Yamamoto and Nagumo steamed eastward unaware that the American carriers—their principal quarry—had already flown the coop.[19]

On June 2, Yamamoto's battleships and Nagumo's carriers, fighting their way eastward through rough seas, were blanketed by a fog so thick that the ships had to use searchlights to find one another in the formation. On the one hand this was a stroke of luck, for it hid them from the prying eyes of American long-range search planes from Midway. On the other it also prevented Nagumo from sending out search planes of his own, and it was stressful for the entire formation to execute the required zigzag course (to confuse American submarines) while maneuvering through a fog. A witness on board *Akagi* recalled seeing Nagumo and members of his staff on the bridge staring "silently at the impenetrable curtain surrounding the ship, . . . each face tense with anxiety." Nagumo may indeed have been anxious. He had heard nothing from the submarines other than one report from I-168 off Midway, which relayed the information that, although the Americans were conducting intensive air search operations, the only vessel in sight was a picket submarine off Sand Island. Nagumo had to assume that no news was good news.[20]

In fact, of course, the Americans were very much on the alert. On May 29, Nimitz had designated Navy Commander Logan C. Ramsey as the operational air coordinator for the airplanes at Midway, and Ramsey dramatically stepped up both the frequency and the range of the air search patrols. There had been some discussion within the American high command about Ramsey's authority to send Army B-17 Flying Fortress bombers on such missions. Just as Theobald and Butler quarreled over their respective roles in defending Alaska, Army and Navy leaders at Midway squabbled over whose job it was to search for enemy warships. The Army insisted that the B-17s should be reserved for combat missions. The Navy's position was that (in the words of one admiral) it was "criminal waste and stupid folly" not to take advantage of their two-thousand-mile range for air search missions. The discussion made it back to Washington, where George Marshall decided in favor of the Navy. As a result, the Americans were able to use not only the Navy PBY sea planes but also the heavy B-17 Army bombers in their air search pattern.[21]

The work was tedious. Every morning before dawn, the PBYs took off one by one at five-minute intervals from Midway's protected lagoon while the B-17s took off from the airstrip on Eastern Island. They flew for seven or eight hundred miles out on their assigned vectors, then flew back again along a different axis to cover more area. After ten to twelve hours in the air, the crews landed, secured their planes, ate, slept, and then got up the next morning before dawn to do it all again. They flew mostly at low altitude—around 1,000 feet. That narrowed their search area, but the visibility was better and they were less likely to make mistakes in identification.[22]

The first sighting report came in at 9:00 a.m. on June 3 from Ensign Charles R. Eaton, piloting a PBY about five hundred miles west of Midway. Eaton reported seeing "two Japanese cargo vessels" that fired on him with antiaircraft fire. Back in Midway, Captain Simard concluded, correctly, that these were only minesweepers patrolling ahead of the main body. Only minutes later, another report from a different search plane electrified the listeners at Midway, at Pearl Harbor, and out at Point Luck where Fletcher, Spruance, and the American carriers lay in wait.[23]

The report came from Ensign Jewell Reid, flying another PBY out of Midway. Near the end of his plotted search area, some seven hundred miles west of Midway, he saw some tiny specks on the horizon. At first he thought it was dirt on the windscreen. His copilot snatched up the binoculars and stared out the windscreen. Reid postponed his turn for home and maintained his course. As the range closed, he saw that they were indeed ships— many ships. At 9:05 he sent the message: "Sighted main body."[24]

Back at Midway, Ramsey ordered Reid to amplify his report. Already near the edge of his plane's maximum range, Reid dived toward the water, stayed low, and completed a wide circle out to the north. At about 9:30, he eased his plane up to about 800 feet and peered southward. At 9:35 he sent in a more complete report: "Six large vessels in column." Again Ramsey asked for clarification: What kind of ships? What course? What speed? To get that information, Reid headed back to low altitude and maneuvered around behind the formation. He reasoned that the lookouts on the Japanese ships, which still lacked radar, would more likely be searching forward than aft. With the sun behind him, he crept back up to 800 feet to have another look. Finally he was able

■ Ensign Jewell "Jack" Reid (perched on the wheel strut) and his PBY crew were the first to make a visual sighting of the approaching Japanese force on June 3. (U.S. Naval Institute)

to deliver the information that Simard, Nimitz, and Fletcher needed: "Eleven ships, course 090 [due east] speed 19 [knots]." The formation included "one small carrier, one seaplane tender, two battleships, several cruisers, several destroyers." He also requested instructions. By now, he was well past his optimum turnaround time for fuel use, and an entire Japanese fleet was between him and his base. His crew was therefore much relieved when the radio crackled out permission for him to return to Midway.[25]

At Pearl Harbor, Nimitz was engaged in conversation with Layton when Arthur Benedict, who had just gotten off watch at Hypo, came running in waving a piece of paper. It was a copy of Reid's sighting report. Nimitz had maintained his usual placid public demeanor through the past several days, though he confessed privately in a letter to his wife that his days were full of "anxious waiting." Based on the initial Hypo intercepts, he had expected the enemy to begin the attack on June 3, and the absence of any sighting reports had been worrisome. Now, as he read Ensign Reid's report, his weathered face broke into a broad grin. This must be Kondō's "Invasion Force," the "bait" that was supposed to lure the American carriers to their doom. Its composition was exactly what Rochefort had predicted, and it was almost exactly where Rochefort had said it would be. Nimitz handed the report to Layton. "This ought to make your heart warm."[26]

Nimitz knew, however, that this was not the "main body," as Reid had reported it. Technically, the "main body" was Yamamoto's battleship force, which the Americans still did not know about, though the real target—the key piece in the entire puzzle—was the enemy's carrier force, the Kidō Butai, and so far there was no word as to its whereabouts. Aware of that, Nimitz decided to forward Reid's report to Fletcher even though he was certain that Fletcher's own communications team had monitored it. He did so because forwarding the message allowed him to add his own comment at the end. "That is not, repeat not, the enemy striking force," Nimitz wrote. "That is the landing force. The striking force will hit from the northwest at daylight tomorrow." Nimitz did not want to micromanage his operational commanders, but neither did he want them to go off half-cocked. At Point Luck, Fletcher was still well beyond striking range of this target, and the subtext of Nimitz's forwarded message was unmistakable: Wait. Be patient.[27]

Kondō's force was, however, a perfectly appropriate target for the Army's heavy bombers on Midway. If Fletcher's position at Point Luck was still a secret, the location of Midway was never a secret, so launching an air strike from the atoll gave nothing away. As soon as word could be sent to the airfield, nine Army B-17s under the command of Colonel Walter Sweeny took off from Eastern Island and headed west to strike the first blow. It took them most of four hours to find the Japanese, and when they did it was not Kondō's "Invasion Force" but the nearby "Transport Group" under Rear Admiral Tanaka Raizō, consisting of one light cruiser, ten destroyers, and thirteen transport ships filled with the 5,000 men of the landing force. Tanaka had outrun his air cover, and as a result all he could do now was try evasive maneuvers while his destroyers threw up as much antiaircraft fire as they could muster.*

The big American bombers dropped their ordnance from 10,000 feet. Each B-17 carried four 600-pound bombs—thus a total of nearly eleven tons of bombs fell among the ships of Tanaka's command. The Japanese ships maneuvered radically under the rain of ordnance, most of which exploded when it hit the water. The flash of the explosions, the enormous geysers of water they generated, and the black smoke from the Japanese ships as they twisted and turned in the roiling water all looked pretty spectacular from 10,000 feet. Making accurate damage assessments is difficult in the best of circumstances, and especially so for Army pilots untrained in antiship operations. The returning pilots did the best they could. They reported five hits, one probable hit, and four near misses against two battleships and two large transports. Sweeny reported that one transport was on fire and that a battleship was on fire and sinking. Based on that report, American submarines were vectored toward the site to finish off the damaged battleship.[28]

In fact, there were no battleships in Tanaka's group, only a light cruiser and several destroyers, and none of them had suffered any damage. Despite all the sound and fury, no ship had been hit; no one, on either side, had been injured.

Nevertheless, the apparent success of the raid inspired Rear Admiral Patrick N. L. Bellinger, commander of PBY Patrol Wing Two, to attack as well. Bellinger was a career aviator who had sent the famous radio report that had informed the world of the Japanese attack back in December: "Air Raid, Pearl Harbor—This is no drill." Now, eager to retaliate, he devised a way to use his PBYs to strike at the foe in a night torpedo attack. He had four of his

---

* There is some uncertainty concerning the identification of Kondō's and Tanaka's units. Some students of the battle assume that Sweeny's B-17s struck at the same force that Reid had reported that morning. However, the makeup of each force, as well as the Japanese battle reports, suggest that while Reid saw Kondō's "Invasion Force," which included two battleships (*Kongo* and *Hiei*) as well as four heavy cruisers ("Six large vessels in column"), Sweeny's B-17s actually struck at the "Transport Force" guarded by one light cruiser and ten destroyers.

Catalinas modified to carry the heavy Mark 13 torpedo, and he called for volunteers to fly them out to attack the enemy. As Gordon Prange remarked forty years later, this was an idea "straight out of a comic strip," but it illustrated the American willingness and ability to improvise.[29]

More important, it worked. Despite the darkness and the range, the four Catalinas, led by Lieutenant William L. Richards, actually found Tanaka's "Transport Group." At about 1:00 a.m. Richards saw "what appeared to be [an] endless line of Japanese ships" silhouetted against a bright full moon. He told his crew, "Drop that damn thing and let's get the hell out of here." They did, and even scored a hit—the first of the battle—on the small tanker *Akebono Maru*. The Japanese antiaircraft guns opened up, and, in the words of one witness, "it was like the fourth of July with tracers coming through the plane." The PBYs escaped without significant damage, though the pilots had trouble staying awake during the long flight back to Midway. "One of us would fly the plane," a crewmember recalled, "and the other would whack him in the face to keep him awake." Their torpedo strike had killed eleven men and wounded thirteen more, though the damage to the tanker was limited. One Japanese officer concluded that the torpedo's warhead had failed to detonate (not unusual with the Mark 13 torpedo), for the *Akebono Maru* stayed afloat and even managed to maintain her place in the convoy.[30]

These air attacks on Tanaka proved that the Americans now knew of the approach of the Japanese. Since there seemed little reason to maintain radio silence any longer, Kondō reported the attacks to Yamamoto. The commander in chief, however, did not pass the information on to Nagumo. For one thing, Yamamoto was maintaining radio silence so that the Americans would not be aware of him. Moreover, he very likely assumed that Nagumo was paying attention and had heard the report himself. As it happened, Nagumo had not, and he remained unaware that the Americans were alerted, or that they had already dispatched two air strikes to contest the approach of the transport force. Even had he known, it is not clear it would have made any difference. After all, the American air attacks had proved fruitless. The various elements of the Japanese armada remained essentially unharmed, and they continued to close in on Midway in accordance with the operational timetable drafted by Combined Fleet back in April. At noon on June

3, the Kidō Butai, still enshrouded by the convenient weather front, altered its course from east to southeast and increased speed to 26 knots to close on its predetermined launching point for a dawn strike the next morning. For their part, the American carriers at Point Luck moved westward at an easy fourteen knots in anticipation of an imminent sighting by the patrol planes from Midway. The real battle was yet to be joined.[31]

The American forces at Point Luck operated two hours ahead of the clocks on Midway. The ships of the Kidō Butai were still on Tokyo time, their clocks twenty-one hours ahead. Nevertheless, as all the clocks moved toward midnight on the ships on both sides that cleaved the waters of the Pacific Ocean, officers and enlisted men prepared for the changing of the watch: in the engine room, in the radio shack, on the topside lookout, and on the bridge. It was a ritual that had taken place a hundred thousand times before, and would a hundred thousand times again. By tradition, the man coming to assume the watch arrives early. On the bridge, he familiarizes himself with the ship's course and speed and all other pieces of pertinent information. When he feels he has a firm grasp of the circumstances, he salutes the officer of the deck and pronounces the words that make him responsible for the ship over the next four hours: "I relieve you, sir." His watch will last until 4:00 that morning when another officer will appear to take his place, but for now, at this moment, he is driving the ship. The night slips silently past. With the ship blacked out and all but invisible, it seems to exist in a world of its own. Of course, it is actually part of a complex pattern that stretches over half of the central Pacific, with more than 150 ships—carriers, battleships, cruisers, destroyers, transports, supply vessels, and submarines—each moving at its own speed toward its destiny.

In military time, 2400 became 0001 as a new day began. To the Japanese, operating on Tokyo time, it was now June 5, but for the Americans, it was now officially June 4, 1942.

# Nagumo's Dilemma
## (4:00 a.m. to 8:30 a.m.)

I t was still full dark at 4:00 a.m. (local time) on June 4 when a bugle on Nagumo's flagship *Akagi* called the crew to battle stations.* The fog had dissipated, though there was a low cloud cover over the Kidō Butai, and the seas were choppy. It was not ideal flying weather, but better than it had been for days. Was this a good omen? The strike force for the air attack on Midway was scheduled to begin launching a half hour later, at 4:30, in order to be over the target just after dawn. The air crews and maintenance crews had been at work since 2:45, servicing the Aichi Type 99 dive-bombers (Vals) and Nakajima Type 97 carrier attack planes (Kates). For this mission, instead of a torpedo, the Kates would each carry an 800 kg (1,760-pound) bomb. The planes had been manhandled onto the elevators and lifted up to

---

* To avoid confusion, all times used in the text will reflect the local time in the area of the Battle of Midway, which was two hours earlier than the time kept on board U.S. ships. The Japanese maintained Tokyo time on their ships, which was twenty-one hours ahead of Midway time.

the flight deck; some were already being warmed up by the flight crews, and the roar of engines could be heard throughout the ship as the men assumed their battle stations. The carriers turned away from each other to open the box-shaped formation, so that all four carriers could launch simultaneously without the planes getting into one another's way.[1]

Altogether, Nagumo had some 225 combat aircraft on his four carriers, plus two more for reconnaissance. The four carriers also had twenty-one additional Zeros among them, earmarked to become the garrison squadron for Midway after it was occupied. Not all of those fighters could be used to augment the strike force or even to defend the Kidō Butai, since only about half of their pilots were carrier qualified. Still, adding those twenty-one Zeros gave Nagumo a theoretical total of 248 airplanes—a hundred fewer than he had used to attack Pearl Harbor back in December, but Midway was a less imposing target. Nor could Nagumo send all of those planes to strike Midway at once, for not only was it essential to keep back a number of fighters as CAP to protect the task force, there was Yamamoto's requirement that Nagumo retain half of his attack planes—and his best pilots—for a strike against American surface forces, just in case. These factors contributed to Nagumo's decision to send a strike force of 108 airplanes, thirty-six of each type—dive-bombers, torpedo planes, and fighters—for the attack on Midway.[2]

The first to take off that morning were eleven Zero fighters that would fly CAP over the task force. Immediately afterward, the strike force began to launch from all four carriers at once. There were no catapults on Japanese carriers, and the planes needed at least 27 knots of relative wind speed over the deck in order to launch. With the ships of the Kidō Butai steaming into the wind and the engines of the airplanes roaring, the air operations officer gave a signal to the flight-deck officer to launch. Crewmen pulled the chocks out from under the wheels, and the first plane surged toward the bow. The lightweight Zeros needed the shortest takeoff space and could get airborne in as little as 230 feet; the bombers, and especially the bigger Kate attack planes, needed more. Soon the planes were launching quickly, roaring past the tiny island amidships and lifting off every fifteen to twenty seconds, while members of the deck crew cheered and waved their caps.

■ Lieutenant Tomonaga Joichi led the Japanese morning attack on Midway Atoll on June 4. He was a last-minute replacement for Commander Fuchida Mitsuo, who suffered an attack of appendicitis. (U.S. Naval Institute)

Rather than send full deck loads from two of the four carriers, Japanese doctrine called for partial strikes from each of them. The carriers of CarDiv 1 (*Akagi* and *Kaga*) each contributed eighteen Val dive-bombers, keeping their torpedo planes in reserve on the hangar deck; the carriers of CarDiv 2 (*Hiryū* and *Sōryū*) sent up eighteen Kate attack planes, keeping their dive-bombers on board. Each carrier also contributed nine Zeros to protect the attack force and to strafe the Midway airfield. The combined strike force of seventy-two attack planes and thirty-six fighters was led by Lieutenant Tomonaga Joichi, the handsome, baby-faced air commander on the *Hiryū*. Tomonaga was a veteran of the war in China but was participating in his first mission against the Americans. He was a last-minute replacement for Fuchida Mitsuo, the air commander on the *Akagi* and the man who had led the attack on Pearl Harbor. During the Pacific transit, Fuchida had suffered a severe attack of appendicitis. He begged the doctor to postpone the surgery so that he could take part in the battle, but the doctor had insisted on operating immediately, and on the morning of June 4, Fuchida was still recovering. He managed to struggle into his uniform and report to the bridge in time to see the planes depart. The planes circled over the Kidō Butai until all of them joined the formation, and then, with the eastern sky turning from full dark to a pinkish gray, they flew off toward the southeast.[3]

No sooner had the last plane lifted off than the loudspeaker on the *Akagi* blared out an order to "prepare second attack wave." On the brightly lit hangar decks, workers began to arm the next cadre of planes with ship-killing ordnance. On the *Akagi* and *Kaga*, the big Kate torpedo bombers were armed with the seventeen-foot-long Type 91 torpedoes. Brought up from the magazine by elevators, the big torpedoes were placed onto hand trucks and manhandled across the crowded hangar deck to each plane. Then they had to be jacked up manually and attached to special brackets under each plane. On the *Hiryū* and *Sōryū*, the dive-bombers were armed with 551-pound armor-piercing bombs. Thus armed and fueled, the planes remained on the hangar decks. That way, Nagumo's carriers could keep their flight decks clear for the rotating CAP and for the return of the strike force. By 5:00 a.m., with the rim of the rising sun appearing over the eastern horizon, the second wave of fighters, bombers, and torpedo planes was poised

■ The Aichi E13A "Jake" floatplane, carried on the stern of Japanese battleships and heavy cruisers, was used primarily for reconnaissance. The delayed launch of one of these planes on June 4 played a key role in the ensuing battle. (U.S. Naval Institute)

and ready in the hangars, awaiting news of any American surface forces that might be in the area.[4]

The Japanese conducted an air search that morning, though for a strike force operating deep in enemy waters, the search was somewhat slapdash. Perhaps because the op plan confidently proclaimed that the American carriers would remain in Pearl Harbor until after the strike on Midway, this dawn air search was largely pro forma. The Japanese often used their Kate attack planes (minus the torpedo) for search missions. This time Nagumo intended to rely primarily on the floatplanes from his escort ships. The Aichi E13A "Jakes," which boasted huge pontoons nearly as large as the fuselage, had a longer range than combat aircraft (nearly 1,300 miles) and were specifically designed for the reconnaissance mission. Though Nagumo did send two Kates to search what he considered the most important quadrant—due south, the direction from which the American carriers would come, if they came at all—he relied on five floatplanes, carried on the sterns of his battleships and cruisers for the rest—a total of seven search planes altogether. (By comparison, not quite a month before, on May 7 in the Coral Sea, Fletcher had launched ten search planes, and Hara twelve; they had still failed to find each other.) Nagumo's rather cavalier search betrayed his assumption that things would proceed pretty much as scripted.[5]

One way to envision the search that Nagumo ordered that morning is to imagine the Kidō Butai as at the center of a clock face, with each hour of the clock comprising a sector of the search. Because the ships of the Kidō Butai had come from the northwest (about 10:30 on our imaginary clock), and because other units of the Imperial Japanese Navy were behind them, there was no reason to search in that direction. The air search, therefore, would cover the quadrants *east* of the Kidō Butai from roughly 1:00 o'clock (almost due north) to 6:00 o'clock (due south). Each search plane would fly three hundred miles out along its prescribed path, fly sixty miles counterclockwise, then fly back again. As noted above, Nagumo assigned the two Kates to the most important quadrants—at 5:00 and 6:00 o'clock; he assigned the shorter-ranged float plane from the battleship *Haruna* to the least likely quadrant—to the north at 1:00 o'clock. The other quadrants,

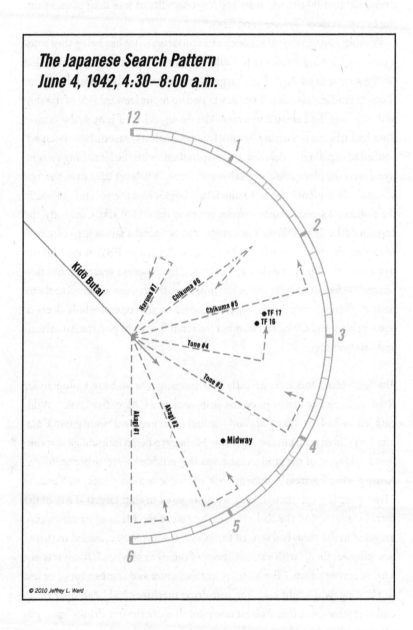

The Japanese Search Pattern
June 4, 1942, 4:30–8:00 a.m.

12
1
2
3
4
5
6

Kidō Butai

Haruna #7
Chikuma #6
Chikuma #5
● TF 17
● TF 16
Tone #4
Tone #3
Akagi #1
Akagi #2
● Midway

© 2010 Jeffrey L. Ward

from 2:00 to 4:00 o'clock, were the responsibility of four float planes from the heavy cruisers *Chikuma* and *Tone*.[6]

Piloting a floatplane off the back of a cruiser was a lot like being shot from a cannon. Lacking a runway to build up speed, the planes were propelled off the ship with an explosive charge. Upon returning, they used their pontoons to land in the water, then they taxied up to the leeward side of the ship and were winched aboard by crane. On the morning of June 4, the cruiser *Tone* had trouble launching her floatplanes. Various reasons have been advanced to explain it—delayed orders, problems with the launching system, trouble on the plane itself, or perhaps all three. Whatever the cause, the first of *Tone's* float planes did not launch until 4:45, and the second (officially the number 4 search plane) did not get away until 5:00 a.m. Curiously, the captain of the *Tone*, Okada Tametsugu, did not send a message to Nagumo reporting this tardy launch. And unlike the American PBYs from Midway that conducted their searches at 1,000 feet, the Japanese search planes flew near 5,000 feet in order to cover the broad swath of ocean assigned to them. At that altitude, even moderate cloud cover might conceal whole fleets of enemy ships, and *Chikuma's* number 5 aircraft flew right past the Americans and saw nothing.

The Americans, too, were up early that morning. On Midway, Commander Ramsey, in charge of air ops on the atoll, sent up a CAP of five Dash 3 Wildcats (all he had) at 4:00 a.m., and the first of an eventual twenty-two Catalina PBYs lifted off from the lagoon at Midway to begin long-range searches north and west of the atoll. As soon as the Wildcats were airborne, fifteen Army Flying Fortress bombers took off for a second attack on Tanaka's "Transport Group," though they were prepared to shift targets if any of the patrol planes found the Kidō Butai. The rest of the Midway air crews congregated in the mess hall to wait for news. "It was pretty crowded in there," one pilot recalled, "with various crews of different services." There was not a lot of conversation. "The atmosphere was quiet and somber, more or less foreboding, you might say." The soft-drink machines had been opened up and everything was free. At least one pilot thought the free drinks "gave you a 'last meal' feeling."[7]

Meanwhile, 320 miles northwest of Midway, Fletcher also launched early that day, sending up a CAP of six Wildcats at 4:20, followed by ten Dauntless dive-bombers for a "security search" to cover the area north of him out to a hundred miles. He knew the Catalinas were patrolling out of Midway, and he relied on them to report any contacts to the west where, according to Hypo, the Kidō Butai would be found. He sent these ten Dauntlesses to the north, to ensure that the Japanese did not attempt an end run as they had in the Coral Sea. Spruance did not send up a CAP that morning because the two carriers of Task Force 16 were already loaded and cocked—the decks of both carriers spotted with the strike force intended for the Kidō Butai when it was discovered. Had Spruance launched fighters for CAP, he would not have been able to recover them without sending the attack planes below, thereby delaying the eventual launch. Fletcher's need to steam into the wind to launch both the Wildcats for CAP and the Dauntlesses for the search drew him away toward the east, and soon Spruance's two carriers were beyond sight.[8]

At 5:34 the Americans at Midway received a report from Lieutenant Howard P. Ady, piloting a PBY northwest of Midway. The first words of his report sent a jolt through the listeners: "Enemy Carrier bearing 320 [degrees], distance 180 [miles]." At 180 miles from Midway, this target was within easy range of the American bombers on Eastern Island. The pilots in the mess hall scrambled for their equipment anticipating an immediate order to attack. Before any of them could man their planes, however, another PBY pilot, Lieutenant William A. Chase, called in to report: "Many planes headed Midway." Obviously, the Japanese carriers had already launched, and Midway would soon be the target of a bombing attack. The radar station picked up Tomonaga's strike force ninety miles out. Captain Simard and Marine Corps Colonel Ira Kimes scrambled all the available fighters they had to contest them. Between 6:00 and 6:30, the Eastern Island airfield was a frenzy of activity, with planes taking off every few seconds. Simard and Kimes sent all their available bombers out toward the reported position of the Japanese carriers and all their available fighters out to intercept Tomonaga.[9]

The attack planes from Midway comprised an eclectic collection that included four Army medium bombers (armed with torpedoes), six Navy torpedo planes, and thirty Marine Corps dive-bombers of two different types. Kimes wanted all the planes to fly in a single formation and to attack together, but the three services had never practiced a coordinated assault against an enemy task force and did not even have a doctrine for doing so. Moreover, the four types of airplanes all flew at different speeds. In the end, therefore, the American attack on the Kidō Butai turned into a kind of free-for-all, with each group attacking on its own, employing whatever tactics seemed appropriate at the time. If the cavalier Japanese air search that morning reflected a cultural preference for combat, the haphazard American bombing strike betrayed the American tradition of service independence. Finally, because the Americans sent all of their available fighters out to challenge Tomonaga's incoming attack force, this mixed bag of bombers and torpedo planes not only attacked piecemeal, it did so without any fighter cover. Perhaps the best that could be said of this effort was that at least the planes were not sitting passively on the runway when Tomonaga's bombers arrived. By 6:45 the only planes left on Midway were the few that were undergoing repair or maintenance.[10]

While the American bombers flew off to find the reported enemy carriers, the fighters of Midway's Marine Fighter Squadron (VMF-221), commanded by Major Floyd Parks, were vectored toward the incoming attackers. Parks was short and stocky, with dull red hair (his nickname was "Red") and "lots of energy." Twenty-one of the twenty-six Marine pilots, including Parks, flew the old and slow Brewster Buffaloes, and one of those had to turn back because of engine trouble. Five others flew the newer Dash 3 Wildcats.* They climbed to 16,000 feet and headed off to meet Tomonaga's strike force. Forty miles out, they spotted the Japanese two thousand feet below them in a series of stacked V formations, with the Zero fighters on top. Marine Captain John F. Carey, leading a section

---

* All five operable Wildcats on Midway were launched as CAP at 4:00 a.m., but Ramsey recalled them once all of the long-range search planes had departed. Two of the pilots did not hear the recall order and continued to circle. They finally landed at 6:15, just as all the other fighters and attack planes on Midway were being launched. Quickly refueled, they sped north to join their squadron mates.

of three Wildcats, radioed, "Tally ho! Hawks at Angels twelve supported by fighters," and dove to the attack. Parks and the others attacked as well. For a few precious seconds the Marines had a tactical advantage, since the Zero pilots had been looking downward and were surprised when American fighters dove on them from above. Carey flew directly at the lead plane in the enemy bomber formation. A bullet punched a hole in Carey's windshield, missing his head by inches, but he held his course and fired a long burst at the lead Japanese bomber, which caught fire and fell out of the formation. Carey's wingman, Second Lieutenant Clayton Canfield, targeted the third bomber in the formation, and it, too, caught fire and fell away. Soon enough, however, the swarming Zeros overwhelmed the Americans. As one pilot put it, "After the first coordinated attacks the thing degenerated into a rat race." Parks was one of the first to be hit. He successfully bailed out of his burning aircraft, but a Zero fighter strafed his chute as he descended and then strafed him again in the water. His body was later found on the rocks near Midway.[11]

One of the rear-seat gunners of a Kate peppered the right side of Carey's airplane, and bullets smashed both of his legs. Carey executed a power dive almost straight down—the only chance he had to escape the swift Zeros—and managed to pull out just at wave height. Unable to perform combat maneuvers—indeed, barely able to maneuver at all—he nursed his crippled plane back to Midway, where he executed a controlled crash landing on the runway. Canfield also managed to get back to the airfield. His landing gear collapsed when his plane touched the runway, but he extricated himself from the wreck and rolled into a nearby slit trench to avoid the Japanese bombs that were already falling.[12]

Carey and Canfield were among the lucky ones. Though the Marine pilots claimed six kills that morning, the slow and clumsy Brewsters were easy pickings for the nimble Zeros. Of the twenty-five Marines who flew out to challenge Tomonaga's strike force, fourteen were killed, and four more wounded—a loss rate of over 70 percent. Even those who survived did not come back unscathed. Second Lieutenant Charles Kunz had the disquieting experience of having Japanese bullets graze his scalp twice, one on each side of his head. That night, after treating him, the surgeon prescribed several "stiff shots" so that Kunz could get to sleep. As Carey reported afterward, "The 'Zero' fighters out-maneuvered, out-performed, and out climbed the Brewsters and Grummans in every respect."[13]

Ady's 5:34 sighting report did not reach the American carriers until 6:03, when it was relayed from Pearl Harbor. Officers on all three carriers bent over the chart tables and made a quick calculation. The reported location of the enemy carriers put them just over 200 miles southwest of their own position. Since the Wildcat fighters and Devastator torpedo bombers had an effective combat radius of about 175 miles, they were not quite within range. In his conversations with Nimitz, Fletcher had agreed that his best hope was to hit the Kidō Butai first, and hit it hard. It was understood that the two carriers of Task Force 16 under Spruance were to strike first, while Fletcher held his air group in reserve. But before Fletcher gave Spruance the "go" order, two factors stayed his hand. The first was that Ady's report indicated the presence of only two carriers. Thanks to Rochefort and Hypo, Fletcher knew that the Japanese were almost certain to have at least four, and possibly five. Where were the others? If Fletcher unleashed Spruance's two air groups at once, they might catch the two enemy flattops early and sink them; they might also miss the rest of the Kidō Butai. Not quite a month before, in the Coral Sea, Fletcher had sent ninety-three planes to savage the Shōhō while Hara's two big carriers remained undiscovered and unscathed until the next day. He did not want a repeat performance now. In fact, all four Japanese carriers were there and Ady had simply not seen them, but there was no way for Fletcher to know that.

The second factor was the timing. When Fletcher heard Chase's report of "Many planes headed Midway," he knew that an enemy carrier (or carriers) had launched a strike against the atoll. What he did not know was how many was "many." Was it a deck load from one or two carriers, or an entire strike force from the combined Kidō Butai? More to the point, the news that the enemy had launched gave Fletcher a kind of timetable for their operations. He knew that it would take the Japanese planes about three hours—that is, until around 8:30 or so—to complete their mission over Midway and return to the Kidō Butai. Ideally, the best time to hit them would be when they were in the midst of recovering planes that were low on fuel and needing to land. Then, too, if Fletcher waited until that critical moment, it would give the Catalinas more time to find the rest of the Kidō Butai. If he could wait an hour, perhaps two, before launching, he might catch Nagumo's force unready and vulnerable. On the other hand, Fletcher knew that his greatest advantage was that the Japanese still had no idea where the American carriers were, and he wanted to launch his attack before they found out. A Japanese snooper might discover them at any moment, and the element of surprise would be lost.[14]

That last concern proved decisive. At 6:07 Fletcher used the short-range TBS (talk between ships) radio to order Spruance: "Proceed southwesterly and attack enemy carriers when definitely located. I will follow as soon as planes recovered." While Spruance attacked, Fletcher would hold the *Yorktown*'s planes in reserve, pending "receipt of information on additional enemy carriers." In the meantime, Fletcher could recover the planes returning from the morning search. As the *Yorktown* continued northeast on the point option recovery course, Spruance headed southwest toward the enemy. Eventually the two task forces ended up some twenty miles apart.[15]

Over on the *Enterprise*, Spruance was ready. Ever since the first sighting report, Captain Miles Browning, the volatile and self-confident chief of staff he had inherited from Halsey, had been eager to attack. Browning was something of an eccentric in the aviation community. Tall and ruggedly handsome, and with the same kind of bad-boy allure that made Ernie King attractive to women, Browning was a temperamental loner on shipboard. An excellent pilot and an imaginative tactician, he was also cocky and dismissive, characteristics that did not endear him to subordinates. Lieutenant Richard "Dick" Best, who commanded the bombing squadron on the *Enterprise*, found Browning intolerable. "He was a bully," Best recalled after the war. "I despised him." The ebullient Halsey, however, got along very well with Browning and had recommended him for his promotion to captain. For his part, Spruance thought Browning was "smart and quick," and he knew that Halsey trusted him. Moreover, because Spruance was not an aviator, he was bound to rely heavily on Browning for tactical advice. Six days earlier, soon after Task Force 16 had left Pearl Harbor for Point Luck,

■ Captain Miles Browning, Halsey's brash and confident chief of staff, also served as Spruance's chief of staff during the Battle of Midway. (U.S. Naval Institute)

Spruance had called a meeting in his cabin to which he invited the air group commander and the four squadron commanders. Almost at once, Browning took charge of the meeting, outlining the plan to ambush four Japanese carriers north of Midway, even naming the four carriers that would be involved. He did not tell the pilots where the information came from—that was still classified—and the information was so detailed that some of the pilots were skeptical. Best thought it sounded "phony." He asked Browning, "Suppose they don't attack Midway, suppose they keep going east and hit Pearl Harbor again?" Browning looked at him with narrowed eyes for a long minute, then replied, "Well, we just hope they don't."[16]

Upon receipt of Fletcher's order, Spruance told Browning "to launch everything they had at the earliest possible moment." In accordance with the predetermined battle plan, he would hold back only a small CAP and send everything else—seventy-one dive-bombers, twenty-nine torpedo planes, and twenty Wildcats—to hit the Japanese first.[17]

One practical problem remained. Task Force 16 had closed the range to the Kidō Butai slightly in the past half hour, but the enemy carriers were still at the extreme limit of the American torpedo bombers and fighters. Moreover, the wind that day was very light—only about five knots—and it was coming out of the east. In order to launch, the *Hornet* and *Enterprise* would have to turn into the wind, *away* from the target, and build up speed to at least 25 knots. It would take at least half an hour, and probably more, to launch those 120 airplanes, which would add back all the miles the Americans had gained since the first sighting. At Browning's suggestion, Spruance decided to continue steaming southwest, toward the target, for another 45 minutes before launching at about 7:00 a.m. It would still be a long flight to the target. Nonetheless, this later launch was likely to allow the attack planes sufficient time over the target to get the job done and get back safely.[18]

Meanwhile, Tomonaga's strike force from the Kidō Butai was hammering Midway. The Japanese pilots had expected to catch the tiny atoll by surprise. The ambush by VMF-221 had disabused them of that expectation, and they were also disconcerted to encounter extremely heavy ground fire. They were greatly disappointed to find the airfield on Eastern Island nearly bare of airplanes. Nevertheless, their attack was ferocious—and effective. The sixty-six bombers that survived the intercept dropped a total of just over thirty-eight tons of explosive ordnance on the two tiny islands that made up Midway Atoll. They took out the power plant, the Eastern Island command post, the mess hall, and the post office; they wrecked the aircraft servicing area, cut the water lines, destroyed the seaplane hangar, and damaged the barracks. One bomb hit a rearming pit and set off eight more 100-pound bombs and 10,000 rounds of .50-caliber ammunition. Another set fire to the oil storage tanks, from which great clouds of black smoke roiled the sky. By the time the raid was over, the entire atoll appeared to be severely damaged. Nonetheless, the Japanese had missed the main aviation fuel supply, the runways were only superficially damaged, and only eleven Americans had been killed and eighteen wounded.[19]

Tomonaga was among the first to drop his bomb. Then he circled the target to assess the damage by his strike force. Before he had left the Kidō Butai, he had been given several code messages designed to apprise Nagumo of the results of the raid. Several Japanese pilots broke radio silence during the attack to announce their success: "Hangar and runways have been hit," reported one; "Great results obtained," asserted another. Of course, because Simard had launched almost everything that would fly, few American planes were on the ground when the Japanese struck. As a result, at 7:00 a.m., Tomonaga radioed a code phrase back to the Kidō Butai. "There is need for a second attack."[20]

The message reached Nagumo on the bridge of the *Akagi* at 7:05. It could hardly have surprised him. From the beginning, he had suspected that a single strike with half his force would not be sufficient to soften up Midway for the planned amphibious landing. Though Yamamoto's principal goal was to get the American carriers, the plan also charged Nagumo with wrecking Midway's defenses to prepare the way for invasion. As he considered Tomonaga's report, however, Nagumo had other concerns, for at that moment the Kidō Butai itself was under attack. These were not the planes from *Hornet* and *Enterprise*—those planes were just then taking off 175 miles to the east. Instead, it was the first contingent of the diverse collection of bombers and torpedo planes that Simard had launched from Midway an hour before.

The first to arrive were six brand-new TBF Avenger torpedo bombers. Designed as a replacement for the slow and aging Devastators, the Avengers were bigger, had a greater range, and were much faster. When the *Hornet* had left Norfolk back in March, half of her VT pilots had remained behind to take delivery of the new Grumman-built aircraft. When the twenty-one new planes were delivered, the pilots flew them across the country in stages to San Francisco, where they were loaded aboard the transport *Hammondsport* for the trip out to Hawaii. The Avengers arrived there on May 29, one day after the *Hornet* left for Point Luck. Eager to get at least some of them into the fight, Nimitz ordered the air crews at Pearl to stay up all night in order to attach belly tanks to six of them so they could fly the 1,100 miles out to Midway. They made the eight-hour flight from Oahu to Midway on

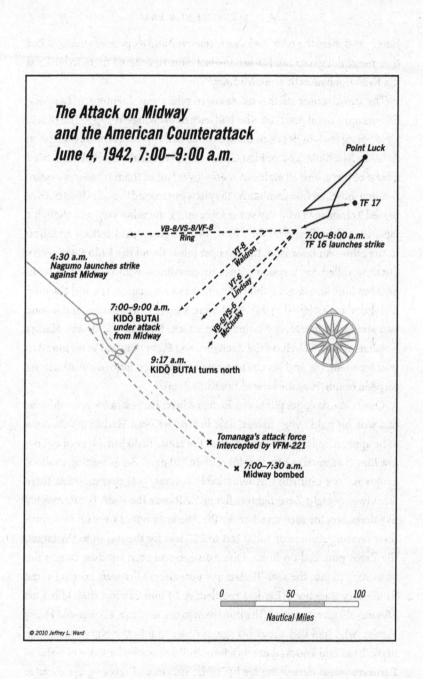

**The Attack on Midway
and the American Counterattack
June 4, 1942, 7:00–9:00 a.m.**

Point Luck

• TF 17

VB-8/VS-8/VF-8
Ring

VT-8
Waldron

VT-6
Lindsay

VB-6/VS-6
McClusky

7:00–8:00 a.m.
TF 16 launches strike

4:30 a.m.
Nagumo launches strike
against Midway

7:00–9:00 a.m.
KIDŌ BUTAI
under attack
from Midway

9:17 a.m.
KIDŌ BUTAI turns north

✕ Tomanaga's attack force
intercepted by VFM-221

✕ 7:00–7:30 a.m.
Midway bombed

0    50    100

Nautical Miles

© 2010 Jeffrey L. Ward

June 1, and there the belly tanks were removed and torpedoes attached. But they never did get to the *Hornet.* Instead, Simard ordered them to strike at the Kidō Butai directly from Midway.[21]

The most senior of the six Avenger pilots was Lieutenant Langdon Fieberling, a naval reservist who had earned his wings in 1937. The others were young ensigns between the ages of 22 and 25, and a rare enlisted pilot, Aviation Machinist's Mate First Class Darrel Woodside. Each plane carried a crew of three, and all eighteen men—over half of them teenagers—were heading into their first combat. As they flew out toward the coordinates, they passed Tomonaga's Midway strike force going the other way, and though a Japanese fighter flew over for a look, neither group paid serious attention to the other. An hour later, the Avenger pilots found the Kidō Butai. Navy doctrine called for torpedo planes to coordinate with dive-bombers, in order to limit the target's ability to effect evasive maneuvers. But the only dive-bombers assigned to this attack were Marine Corps planes, and no one had arranged for a Navy-Marine joint attack. Besides, the slower Marine bombers were well behind the Avengers, and Fieberling was in no mood to wait for them. He and his squadron mates began an immediate attack: six torpedo bombers against the entire Kidō Butai.[22]

One of the Avenger pilots was Ensign Albert Earnest, a 25-year-old who had won his gold wings sixteen days before the Pearl Harbor attack. Now as he approached the awesome sight of the entire Kidō Butai spread out below him, it seemed to him that there were "20 or 30 Zeros waiting to shoot us down." His estimate was remarkably accurate—at that moment there were twenty-eight Zero fighters flying CAP over the Kidō Butai, roughly five defenders for each attacker. As the Avengers nosed over to drop from their cruising altitude of 4,000 feet to 200 feet for the run-in to the target, the Zeros pounced on them. One Avenger, and then another, caught fire and dropped into the sea. "Bullets and anti-aircraft fire were coming at me from every direction," Earnest recalled. A 20 mm cannon shell killed his 18-year-old turret gunner. The third man in the airplane, 17-year-old Harry Ferrier, who had lied about his age in order to join the Navy, was struck in the head and knocked unconscious. Bullets punched a score of holes in Earnest's plane, destroying his hydraulic system and severing the elevator cables. The control stick went dead in his hand. Shrapnel from a 20 mm shell shattered his instrument panel, and his plane dived toward the water. Struggling to keep his plane in the air, Earnest dropped his torpedo in the general direction of a cruiser, hoping the loss of weight would allow him to remain airborne. The drop seemed to have no effect, however, and the plane continued to dive toward the water out of control. Earnest braced for a crash landing and, just before impact, reflexively reached down to adjust the four-inch wheel that controlled the trim tabs, something he routinely did before landing. When he did so, the nose of his plane came up, and the Avenger gained a bit of altitude. Zeros continued to make runs at him, and it was all Earnest could do to hold his plane in a more or less straight course. He felt like "a tin duck in a shooting gallery" as the Zeros made repeated runs at him. Relying on the trim tabs to remain airborne, he kept low and flew southward. "A couple of Zeros swooped in to finish me off," he recalled, "but I was so close to the water, they couldn't make a real good run at me."[23]

Eventually the Zeros gave up the chase. Earnest still had to make it back to Midway with a plane that could barely fly. Badly wounded, with blood running from a neck wound, and all of his instruments out—even the compass—he used the angle of the sun to estimate which direction was south. He called his two gunners on the plane's intercom, but got no

◼ Ensign Albert Earnest piloted one of the new Grumman TBF Avenger torpedo bombers from Midway in the first attack on the Kido Butai on the morning of June 4. He and his enlisted radioman, Harry Ferrier, also seen here, were the only survivors of the mission. (U.S. Naval Institute)

response. He nursed the Avenger up to 3,000 feet and flew on. He did not know whether or not his torpedo had successfully dropped. After some time, Harry Ferrier regained consciousness and called him up on the intercom to report that he was still alive. Eventually, Earnest spotted a tall column of black smoke from the burning oil tanks on Midway. Ignoring a wave off from the airfield controller who didn't think the crippled plane would survive a landing, he touched down on the runway on one wheel, his plane doing a ground loop before coming to a stop on the apron. Only later did he learn that he and young Harry Ferrier were the only survivors of the Avengers strike, and that none of the American torpedoes had struck an enemy ship.[24]

One reason the Zeros did not pursue Earnest's crippled plane was that they had another target to deal with. Only seconds behind the Avengers were four Army medium bombers under Captain James Collins, Jr. The two-engine B-26 Marauders had been specially modified to carry torpedoes, which meant that they, too, approached the Kidō Butai at low altitude, around 200 feet. Collins flew through the swarming Zeros and the exploding flak to drop his torpedo, and as his plane passed over the *Akagi* his nose gunner strafed the big carrier, killing two of its crewmen. First Lieutenant James Muri followed Collins in. He heard "the shells coming into the side of the fuselage and near the turret." Muri's turret gunner, Corporal Frank Melo, saw "beads of sweat" on Muri's forehead. Muri had a cigarette in his mouth, but he had bitten it in two, and "it hung by a slender strip of paper" as he focused on making the attack run. Like Collins, he came in very low to drop his torpedo, passing so low over the *Akagi* that Nagumo and his staff on the small bridge reflexively ducked. The other two planes in the formation were less lucky. Both of them, riddled with cannon shells and machine gun bullets, crashed into the sea. The two surviving planes, each with more than half their crew wounded, headed for home. Muri's ground crew later counted more than five hundred bullet holes in his plane.[25]

If this was the best the Americans could do, Nagumo had to feel fairly sanguine. To be sure, it had been a scary moment when that big two-engine American bomber seemed headed for his command bridge, but in the end the Americans had failed to inflict any damage on the Kidō Butai beyond the two men killed when Collins strafed the *Akagi*. The Zeros had shot down seven of the ten American airplanes and sent the other three limping home. Nagumo had already decided to send a second strike against Midway, but this attack by planes from that island base may have played a role in his decision about how to execute that second strike. According to Yamamoto's oral instructions, he was supposed to keep half his airplane strength, and half of his pilots, on hand in case any American surface ships appeared. Strict adherence to those orders, however, now meant that he would have to wait to recover Tomonaga's attack force, strike them below to the hangar deck to be refueled and rearmed, and then send them back up to the flight deck for launch, while half his planes sat idle and his best pilots cooled their heels in the ready room. Surely Yamamoto did not expect Nagumo to keep half his planes unused throughout the battle? That would be like asking him to fight with one hand tied behind his back. As Nagumo's chief of staff wrote after the war, it was "intolerable" to expect a frontline commander to keep half his strength idle "for an enemy force which might not be in the area after all." It would be far more efficient to use the planes that were now on the hangar deck for the second strike, then recover Tomonaga's planes and arm them with antiship ordnance in the unlikely event that any American surface ships appeared. At 7:15, therefore, as the few surviving American planes retreated over the horizon, Nagumo ordered that the planes on the hangar decks of his four carriers be rearmed with fragmentation bombs for a second strike against Midway.[26]

The changeover in armament was a major task, especially for the carriers of CarDiv 1, where the Kate torpedo planes were armed with the big 1,870-pound Type 91 antiship torpedoes. Because there were a limited number of hand trucks on each carrier, the crews could rearm only six planes at a time. The carts had to be positioned under the planes; then, after the arming device had been removed, the torpedoes had to be gingerly lowered by hand crank down onto the carts. Because the ammunition handlers were busy bringing up the heavy bombs that would replace those torpedoes, the torpedoes themselves were not returned to the magazine. Instead, they were pushed over to the bulkhead and lifted by hand onto holding racks. Even after the torpedo was removed, the crew still had to remove the mounting brackets that kept the torpedo attached to the plane and replace them with mounting brackets for the 800-kilogram (1,760-pound) fragmentation bombs, which also had to be maneuvered under the planes by hand cart and then cranked up into place.[27]

This labor-intensive process had been under way for at least half an hour when Nagumo received a radio message from Petty Officer First Class Amari Yoji, piloting search plane number 4 from the cruiser *Tone*. This was the plane that had been delayed that morning and had left a half hour behind schedule. Now Amari sent a stunning report, one that was entirely unexpected: "Sight what appears to be ten enemy surface units, in position bearing ten degrees [almost due north], distant 240 miles from Midway." The fact that the one plane that had been delayed by half an hour that morning was the very one assigned to search the quadrant where the American carriers lay in wait is one of the events that has led some students of the battle to dub the subsequent American victory a "miracle," for it is hard to resist the notion that this was the moment when Providence put its finger on the scale of History. The Japanese thought so, too. After the war, Fuchida Mitsuo wrote in his memoir, "The delay in launching *Tone*'s planes sowed a seed which bore fatal fruit for the Japanese in the ensuing naval action." And yet, an analysis of the morning's events suggests that, if anything, that delay was a stroke of good luck for the Japanese.[28]

Amari's orders that morning had been to fly three hundred miles nearly due east (100 degrees), then turn north for sixty miles before returning. After his late start, however, he was eager to get back on schedule, so rather than flying the prescribed three hundred miles, he instead turned north at about 6:45 when he was only 220 miles out and in doing so found Spruance's Task Force 16 (see map, p. 223). Had he left on time and flown his assigned course, he very likely would not have sighted the Americans until he began his return leg sometime after 8:00. Consequently, the delay in launching Amari's float plane that morning may have hastened the moment when Nagumo learned of the presence of American surface ships northeast of him.[29]

Exactly when Nagumo got that report has been disputed. Although Amari sent it at 7:28, he sent it to *Tone*, his host ship, where it was decrypted in the radio room, rushed up to the bridge, and then blinkered over to the flagship. In his after-action report, Nagumo wrote that he got the message at "about 0500" (8:00 a.m. local time). In that same report, Nagumo also wrote, "The delay in the delivery of message from Tone's #4 plane greatly affected our subsequent attack preparations." Most evidence, however, puts the information in Nagumo's hands by 7:45. First of all, there is the ambiguity of that "about 0500." More significantly, the Japanese radio message log indicates that Nagumo received the message at 7:45, and it logged Nagumo's reply to Amari at 7:47, a time confirmed by Hypo, which intercepted and recorded the reply.* Almost certainly, Nagumo received Amari's message at about 7:45, and even though Amari did not say so, Nagumo had to suspect that there might be an American carrier operating with those "ten enemy surface units," for there would be little reason for an American task force to be operating north of Midway without a carrier. Nagumo's chief of staff, Rear Admiral Kusaka Ryūnosuke, recalled thinking, "There couldn't be an enemy force without carriers in the area reported and there must be carriers somewhere." Finally, given the coordinates that Amari had sent, Nagumo also knew this target was just over two hundred miles away from his own carriers, already within striking distance because of the longer range of the Japanese attack planes.[30]

In response to this stunning information, Nagumo consulted with his staff, especially with Kusaka and Commander Genda Minoru. It was a bit awkward to hold a strategy conference in a crowded public space; Nagumo would doubtless have preferred to retreat somewhere more private for the conversation. But the pressure of the moment did not allow that. While

---

* In his book *Midway Inquest*, Dallas Isom makes a strong case that Nagumo did not receive this information until 8:00 a.m. He argues that the 7:45 time given in the radio traffic log was reconstructed from memory because the original radio traffic log went down with the *Akagi*. Isom also asserts that the time noted on the Hypo intercept log was added after the war based on the reconstructed (and inaccurate) Japanese log. The timing was important, Isom argues, because if Nagumo did not receive the message until 8:00, it meant that the rearming had been going on for forty-five minutes instead of half an hour, and as a result it took longer to reverse the process. It is an interesting and plausible argument, but also highly speculative, and the preponderance of noncircumstantial evidence puts the message in Nagumo's hands by 7:45.

they discussed this new information, Nagumo suspended the change-over of armament down on the hangar deck and ordered the thirty-six Val bombers on the *Hiryū* and *Sōryū* "to prepare to carry out attacks on enemy fleet units." Before he sent them off, however, he needed to know more about those American ships. Nagumo had not been at the Battle of the Coral Sea. Nonetheless, he was certainly aware of Hara's disastrous blunder in sending a full air strike against what turned out to be an oiler and a destroyer. Before he completely restructured his attack plan, Nagumo wanted to know what kind of American ships were out there two hundred miles away, and in particular if they included any aircraft carriers. He therefore ordered Amari to "ascertain [ship] types" and to "maintain contact." For a few precious and irrecoverable minutes, the entire Japanese strike force was frozen in suspension while Nagumo waited for the answer.[31]

It came in at 8:09: "Enemy ships are five cruisers and five destroyers." That seemed curious, to say the least, for—again—it made little sense that such a force should be operating at that location without a carrier. Still, cruisers and destroyers could be dealt with later, and even if an enemy carrier were with them, Nagumo knew that the Americans could not launch an attack against him from such a distance due to the limited range of the American torpedo planes and fighters. He did not need to scramble his reserve planes for an immediate strike, and this was just as well, for just at that moment, the Kidō Butai came under renewed air attack from Midway, and his carriers needed to keep their flight decks clear in order to launch and recover Zero fighters. Indeed, over the next twenty minutes, the Japanese launched two dozen more Zeros to defend the Kidō Butai. By 8:30 they had a total of thirty-six fighters aloft. Since Tomonaga had taken thirty-six fighters with him to hit Midway, Nagumo had now launched very nearly every fighter he had.[32]

They had plenty of work to do. First, came sixteen Marine Corps Dauntless dive-bombers, under the command of Major Lofton Henderson. Aware that his rookie pilots, virtually all of them on their first combat mission, had little or no training in dive-bombing techniques, Henderson felt compelled to order a glide-bombing attack. The 30-degree approach to the target made the Dauntlesses easy prey for the Zeros, which started by attacking the lead plane and then working their way methodically back through the formation. Henderson's plane was one of the first to go down. The survivors at the rear of the formation determinedly carried on through the blitz of bullets and 20 mm cannon fire to drop their bombs, some waiting (so they reported later) until they were a mere five hundred feet from the target. Their bombs bracketed the *Hiryū*, sending up great geysers of water, and afterward they reported three hits and several near misses. In spite of their reckless courage, however, none of their bombs struck home.[33]

Though Henderson's attack, like its predecessors, had been futile, it greatly alarmed Admiral Yamaguchi Tamon. The commander of CarDiv 2 wondered if the appearance of carrier-type airplanes meant that an American carrier was nearby. If so, where was it? Though the Japanese had suffered no damage in this attack, their sense that everything was under control began to slip.

Even as the Marines were completing their ill-fated attack, fifteen Army B-17 Flying Fortress bombers appeared three miles above them at 20,000 feet. These were the planes that had been sent out from Midway before dawn to attack Tanaka's transport force; they had been redirected to the Kidō Butai after Ady's sighting report. Though the B-17s were unmolested by the Zeros, precision bombing from 20,000 feet was impossible. Sticks of 600-pound bombs exploded in rows all around the big enemy carriers, but none of them actually struck a ship. Despite that, the returning pilots again reported that they had made several hits and that they had left three aircraft carriers burning.

The B-17s were unmolested, but the Marine Dauntless pilots were savaged by the Japanese CAP, and the survivors had a difficult time getting back to Midway. With Henderson killed and the formation scattered, each pilot was on his own. Many stayed low and skimmed the surface; others sought to hide in the cloud cover. None escaped unscathed. Captain Richard Blain nursed his Dauntless for twenty miles before his fuel pump went out. Then the engine stopped altogether. It recaught momentarily, then went out again. He crash-landed in the sea, and he and his rear-seat gunner, Sergeant Robert Underwood, scrambled into their tiny life raft. Finding that it had a hole in it, they put an ersatz makeshift patch on it and spent much of the next two days bailing. After two days and two nights, they were rescued by a PBY. In the end, only eight of the sixteen planes that set out from Midway made it back. On one of them, maintenance crews found 179 bullet holes; on another they counted 219.[34]

The Americans were not done yet. After the Dauntlesses departed, a dozen antiquated Marine Corps SB2U Vindicators made a run at the Japanese carriers. These aged canvas-covered monoplanes were even older than the Brewster Buffaloes and literally held together by adhesive tape. The pilots derisively referred to them as "Wind Indicators" since the tag ends of the tape fluttered in such a way as to indicate the wind direction. Many of the pilots had never flown one before. They came out of the cloud cover over a Japanese battleship, and immediately came under attack by the Zeros, which convinced Major Benjamin Norris, who commanded the group, to target the battleship rather than take the time to look for the carriers. Three of his planes were shot down almost at once. It would have been worse except that by now many of the Zeros had expended their 20 mm cannon ammunition and had only their lighter 7.7 mm machine guns. Two more Vindicators were hit by bursts of antiair fire from the battleship. The shell explosions buffeted the flimsy planes so violently that, as one pilot recalled, "it was practically impossible to hold the ship in a true dive." Nevertheless, they grimly persisted and dropped their ordnance. Once again, none of them scored a hit.[35]

Thus it was that between 7:55 and 8:35 that morning, the Kidō Butai endured three separate attacks by more than forty American aircraft from Midway. The Americans had hurled themselves on the Kidō Butai in a series of uncoordinated attacks, heedless of danger and profligate with their lives, but none of them managed to land any of their ordnance on target. Eighteen of the attackers were shot down, and most of the rest were so badly damaged that they were of questionable further use. Only the high-flying B-17s had been spared.

There were, however, two important consequences of these attacks that greatly affected the subsequent course of the battle. First, because the big Japanese torpedoes and fragmentation bombs could not be moved about on the hangar decks of the carriers while they maneuvered radically under air attack, the American onslaught slowed the transfer of armament for most of that forty-minute period. And second, because Nagumo felt compelled to commit virtually all of his remaining Zero fighters to the defense of the Kidō Butai, he would have to recover, rearm, and refuel those fighters before they could be used to accompany his bombers and torpedo planes in an attack on the American warships.

In the midst of these attacks, at about 8:20, Nagumo received an up-date from Amari. Apparently the clouds had parted enough to give him a better look at the ships below him, and he now reported: "Enemy force [is] accompanied by what appears to be an aircraft carrier to the rear of the others." Though Nagumo had suspected as much, this was nevertheless critical news. Kusaka later asserted that though he knew it was likely, he was still "shocked" by the report, describing it as "a bolt from the blue." Here was not only a worthy target but also the primary objective of the whole mission. This was the moment to launch those ship-killing attack planes Nagumo had been hoarding on the hangar decks. The problem was that by now Tomonaga's strike force was returning from Midway and needed to land. In addition, the Zeros that had fended off the American air attacks from Midway were low on both fuel and ammunition and also needed to land. Nagumo had used all four carriers to launch the planes of his Midway attack force; he would need all four decks to recover them. He could not re-cover planes and launch at the same time. He seemed to have two choices: order the returning strike force and his own Zero fighters to circle the task force (and risk having them run out of fuel as they did so) while he brought up the reserve planes for an attack on the American surface forces—an at-tack that would have to go with little or no fighter cover—or recover his CAP and Tomonaga's planes, rearm and refuel them, and dispatch a fully coordinated strike.[36]

On *Hiryū*, Rear Admiral Yamaguchi Tamon, the commander of CarDiv 2, had also received Amari's updated report. He was bold enough to offer Nagumo some unsolicited advice by blinker signal: "Consider it advisable to launch attack force immediately." Back in December, Yamaguchi had been the one who had blinkered Nagumo that he was ready to launch an-other strike at Pearl Harbor. Nagumo hadn't taken the hint then, and he was disinclined to accept Yamaguchi's impertinent advice now. It was not just a matter of pique, however, for launching "immediately" was not really an option. Yamaguchi's dive-bombers on *Sōryū* and *Hiryū*, which were armed with the smaller 551-pound bombs, were ready (or nearly ready) to go, but the big torpedo-carrying Kates of CarDiv 1 were not, and even after they were armed, they would have to be brought up from the hangar deck and spotted for launch. That would take half an hour at least, and likely longer, and by then Tomonaga's returning planes might well run out of gas.[37]

Of course, Nagumo could order a partial strike by Yamaguchi's thirty-six Val dive-bombers, and that may have been what Yamaguchi had in mind. The difficulty was that those bombers would have to proceed not only without the cooperation of the torpedo bombers but also with little fighter protection. An attack by only thirty-six dive-bombers (less than a quarter of his available force) without any coordinating torpedo planes or fighter cover would violate Japanese doctrine to strike the enemy with full strength in a combined and coordinated attack. Moreover, Nagumo had just watched the Americans hurl their odd collection of bombers and torpedo planes at him without fighter protection, and not only had they failed, they had been all but obliterated. As Kusaka put it later, "I witnessed [how] enemy planes without fighter cover were almost annihilated. . . . I wanted most earnestly to provide them [our bombers] with fighters by all means." Nagumo made his decision: He would recover his CAP and Tomonaga's returning planes, and then prepare his entire strike force for an all-out death blow against the American flattop.[38]

By the time Nagumo made that decision, it was 8:35. The planes from the *Hornet* and *Enterprise* had been in the air for more than half an hour.

# The Flight to Nowhere
## (7:00 a.m. to 11:20 a.m.)

At 7:00 a.m., about the time that Tomonaga was informing Nagumo that Midway needed a second strike, and while the Kidō Butai was fending off the first of the American bomber attacks from Midway, the two carriers of Spruance's Task Force 16 were turning into the wind to launch. Mounting a coordinated attack by air groups from two different carriers was unusual—indeed nearly unprecedented—for the Americans, who continued to conceive of their carriers as independent units. While U.S. Navy doctrine called for the air squadrons from each carrier to cooperate, there was no established doctrine about how planes from multiple carriers might operate together in an integrated formation as the Japanese did routinely. Back in March, when planes from the *Lexington* and *Yorktown* had attacked Lae and Salamaua on New Guinea, and again in May when they attacked the *Shōkaku* and *Zuikaku* in the Coral Sea, the air groups from the two American carriers had flown to the targets separately, each under its own commander. Though Spruance and Browning had visions of a single, combined strike by planes from both *Hornet* and *Enterprise*, in the end each of the air groups flew to the target independently, and this meant that much of the responsibility for the conduct of the attack fell to the captains of those two carriers and to their respective air group commanders.

This was especially true in the case of the *Hornet*, the only American carrier that did not have a flag officer on board, though Pete Mitscher had been selected for Rear Admiral (and some members of his staff already referred to him as "Admiral Mitscher"). Mitscher had logged as many air miles as any other American officer afloat, and he may have been a bit miffed that Spruance had designated George Murray, captain of the *Enterprise*, as the tactical air officer for the combined task force. Murray was slightly senior as a pilot (he was Naval Aviator #22 and Mitscher was #33), but Mitscher was senior to Murray in rank. Spruance likely made this decision because Murray had more combat experience and was on the *Enterprise* and therefore closer to hand. In the end, Murray would have little influence over the *Hornet*'s attack against the Japanese carriers that day, an attack that would be orchestrated and managed by Mitscher and the *Hornet*'s air group commander, Stanhope C. Ring.

To all outward appearances, Mitscher and Ring were complete opposites. Mitscher, as we have seen, was short, slight, sun-ravaged, and bald; Ring was tall and movie-star handsome, with a full head of hair. Ring, as the expression went, wore the uniform well; one junior officer thought he

▪ Stanhope C. Ring, shown here as a rear admiral in a 1954 photograph, was the commander of the *Hornet* air group (CHAG) in the Battle of Midway. (U.S. Naval Institute)

was "the picture of the ideal naval officer." The two men were also different in background and temperament. At the Naval Academy, where Mitscher had been a poor student and a discipline problem, Ring had graduated in the top 25 percent of his class and had few demerits. Ring was urbane and sophisticated, and a strong believer in protocol and discipline. As a sailor on the *Enterprise* put it, Ring "belonged to the starchy, do-it-by-the-book side of the Navy."[1]

Ring's Nordic good looks and polished manners very likely played a role in securing him a number of plum staff jobs during his career. After a tour on the *Lexington*, he became the aide to Rear Admiral William Moffett, and after that he served as the naval aide to President Herbert Hoover. Following tours on the *Langley* and *Saratoga*, Ring worked in the Bureau of Aeronautics, and then as the U.S. naval attaché in London, where he was the American observer on the staff of Admiral Sir James Somerville (whose fleet was subsequently decimated by the Kido Butai in the Indian Ocean). Somerville had liked him and, at the end of Ring's tour in October 1941, recommended him for the Order of the British Empire. For his part, Ring was so taken with the British way of doing things that he began carrying a swagger stick, a habit that led many to mock him behind his back. Promoted to the rank of full commander, he was assigned as the *Hornet's* air group commander, or CHAG, an unfortunate acronym that was pronounced "sea hag."[2]

Ring was generally well liked by his superiors, including Mitscher, but not by the young pilots in his charge. Even forty years later, they seethed with resentment. The main reason for this was that Ring led by authority rather than by example. He was quick to assert his rank, as, for instance, when he grounded several pilots because they failed to stand up when he entered the wardroom. During the brief stopover at Pearl Harbor before heading out to Point Luck, the pilots on *Enterprise* and *Yorktown* had been granted shore leave. Ring decreed that the *Hornet* pilots had to remain at Ewa Airfield on continuous alert. One pilot recalled that "there was much grumbling and a near 'mutiny' against the CHAG" as a result of that decision. A few pilots risked court martial by "expressing their opinion of CHAG to his face."[3]

Ring's strictness might have been tolerable but for the fact that he himself was an indifferent pilot. When the *Hornet* was first put in commission, he insisted on being the first to land a plane on her deck. Ensign Troy Guillory was in the rear seat of Ring's SBC-4 scout biplane, and he remembered that Ring made his approach too high and too fast. Guillory heard "this little tweet, tweet, tweet, tweet" alarm and thought to himself that they were signaling the crash signal for somebody. In fact, it was for them. The plane hit the deck hard and much too fast, failed to catch a wire, and struck the crash barrier. It damaged the plane's landing gear and broke the support wires on the wings. No one was hurt, but it was a bad omen for the first arrested landing on a new ship, and a poor augury for Ring's credibility as CHAG. A week later, when a camera crew came on board *Hornet* to film carrier operations, Ring insisted on being the one photographed. As his plane accelerated down the flight deck, he turned his head to the camera and affected a pose, to the disgust of the pilots who witnessed it. Nor were Ring's navigational skills up to par. On one occasion, he got lost while leading a training exercise in the Gulf of Mexico and had to turn the mission over to the executive officer of the scouting squadron, Gus Widhelm, to find the ship. As a result of these and other incidents, the pilots in the *Hornet*'s mostly inexperienced air group had limited confidence in Ring as a pilot or a navigator. At Midway, the extent of their confidence would be sorely tested.[4]

No aspect of the Battle of Midway is more controversial or enigmatic than the role of the *Hornet* air group under Stanhope Ring on June 4. Four squadrons took off from the *Hornet* that morning, but only one managed to find the Kidō Butai—and that one did so only because its squadron commander flagrantly disobeyed Ring's direct orders. The rest of the air group—two squadrons of bombers and all of the fighters that were committed to the strike—forty-four planes altogether—failed to see the enemy at all. Worse, in trying to get back to the *Hornet*, thirteen of those planes ran out of gas and had to ditch in the ocean, subjecting the pilots to hours or days of terrible suffering and, in two cases, death. That flight has become known in the lore of the Battle of Midway as "the flight to nowhere." In effect, despite Nimitz's furious efforts to ensure that the Americans would have three carriers at Midway to confront the Kidō Butai, only two of them succeeded in attacking the enemy that morning.

Reconstructing how this came about is difficult. For one thing, Mitscher and Ring never wrote or spoke candidly about it. Mitscher's official report not only avoids the key issues, it is manifestly incorrect in several elements. Ring either never wrote a report or Mitscher failed to forward it, for it has not surfaced in the seventy years since the battle. In addition, none of the reports of the four squadron commanders survive, if indeed they were ever written. Submitting an after-action report following a mission was mandatory under Navy regulations. Nevertheless, other than Mitscher's flawed report, the only contemporary evidence of what happened to the *Hornet*'s air group that morning comes from the oral testimony of the survivors, much of it written decades afterward and some of it contradictory. Telling the story of the *Hornet*'s air group on the morning of June 4 therefore remains a daunting task.

Breakfast call for the pilots on the *Hornet* sounded at 3:30 that morning. Few of them had slept much anyway, and, knowing they would have a busy day, they headed down to the officer's mess for "a hurried breakfast." Some opted for a "one-eyed sandwich," a slice of toast holed out to accommodate a fried egg, though others merely grabbed a mug of coffee and went directly to the ready room, their leather helmets and goggles close to hand, to wait for the call to man their planes. Many were understandably nervous; none of them had any combat experience, including the squadron commanders. Unlike the pilots on the other American carriers who had participated in the raids on the Marshalls, Wake, or New Guinea, or fought in the Coral Sea, those on the *Hornet*, including Ring, were facing their first combat mission. The *Hornet* had gone to sea only in March. The pilots had conducted air operations during the shakedown cruise, but new pilots had to make eight carrier landings to become carrier-qualified, and many had not yet met that standard by the time the *Hornet* passed through the Panama Canal on her way to the Pacific. In San Diego, the dive-bombing squadrons got new planes, so that even those who had qualified had yet to make an arrested landing in the plane they would fly in combat. Some had qualified off San Diego before the *Hornet* headed up to Alameda. From March 20 to April 18, however, the *Hornet*'s deck was encumbered by the sixteen B-25 bombers that she had carried into the western Pacific for the Doolittle raid. Flight operations had resumed immediately afterward, but even with that, the *Hornet* pilots had a total of only about six weeks of on-board training. Many had still not completed the initial training syllabus. In short, they were rookies, and the Battle of Midway would be their trial by fire.[5]

In the four ready rooms (one for each squadron), time passed slowly. There was much less of the usual banter; a few pilots tried their hand at reciting or inventing bawdy limericks, but for the most part it was quiet. One recalled, "The boys were getting fidgety." A few tried to read; several napped. Most kept one eye on the teleprinter that projected the sighting reports onto a 3-foot-by-3-foot screen. Not long after 6:00, they read Lieutenant Chase's report of "many planes headed Midway," and soon afterward Lieutenant Ady's report of two enemy carriers 180 miles from Midway. The pilots copied the coordinates onto their plotting boards. The squadron commanders in particular focused on this data, for it would be their job to lead their pilots to the target. They wrote down the enemy position relative to Midway, the reported course and speed, plotted the *Hornet*'s own course and speed, then entered the usual variables: wind speed on the surface and at various altitudes, plus magnetic compass variation. Applying all these elements, each worked out for himself the navigational solution for a course from the *Hornet* to the reported enemy position.[6]

The only squadron commander who did not do so was the CO of the fighting squadron (VF-8), Lieutenant Commander Samuel G. "Pat" Mitchell. Given that the job of the fighters was to escort and protect the attack squadrons, Mitchell felt that he did not need to compute an independent course; he would necessarily conform to whatever course they chose. Mitchell himself had very little time as a fighter pilot—no more, in fact, than the young pilots he led—and it was a bit unusual that he had never served as a squadron executive officer before taking over as skipper of Fighting Eight. A 1927 Naval Academy graduate, he had spent most of his career piloting seaplanes and flying boats. He had worked for Pete Mitscher at the Bureau of Aeronautics, and when Mitscher got command of the *Hornet*, he brought Mitchell along.[7]

Thanks to the folding wings on the new Dash-4 Wildcats, there was room for twenty-seven fighter planes on board the *Hornet*, but since many of their pilots were inexperienced, and because some needed to stay behind to protect the task force, only ten would be committed to the strike. Mitchell's main concern that day was which element of the strike force he would protect. The dive-bombers would fly at 20,000 feet, and the torpedo planes at 1,500 feet. Those ten Wildcats could therefore protect one group or the other, but not both—unless they split into two sections. Pat Mitchell felt that the old torpedo planes had first call on his fighters. Not only were the Devastators significantly slower, their heavy and ungainly torpedoes required them to approach the target at no more than 100 feet and to hold a steady course while they lined up on the target. All this made them sitting ducks for the Zeros that would be flying CAP. The American dive-bombers by contrast, came in high and dove on the target at nearly 250 knots. Moreover, the Dauntless dive-bombers carried twin .50-caliber machine guns and were better equipped to defend themselves. They were often used (without a bomb load) as additional fighters to protect the task force. In Mitchell's view, these circumstances dictated that his fighters should go with the torpedo planes.[8]

Certainly that was the view of the skipper of the torpedo squadron, Lieutenant Commander John C. Waldron. Waldron was a twenty-year Navy veteran from South Dakota who at age 41 was nearly twice as old as some of his pilots. Born at a time when the West was still wild, he had grown up on a hardscrabble farm in Canada and then on an Indian reservation near Pierre, South Dakota. He was proud of being one-eighth Sioux, a heritage affirmed by his facial features, dark eyes, and prominent chin. At the Academy, his nickname was "Redskin," and a few of his fellow officers on the *Hornet* referred to him simply as "the Indian." Waldron claimed that this heritage gave him a kind of sixth sense about coming events. He had a reputation as a skilled pilot and an enthusiastic reveler. He worked and played hard. As one person who knew him put it, "He had his parties when he had his parties, and when he got aboard ship it was business." He was

∎ Lieutenant Commander John C. Waldron, who some nicknamed "the Indian," commanded Torpedo Squadron Eight on the *Hornet* on June 4. (U.S. Naval Institute)

a demanding taskmaster. Aware that his mostly rookie pilots had yet to complete all the training considered necessary before combat, he maintained a tough regimen of both classroom study and physical training. One pilot described it as "work, work, and more work." His was the only squadron where the pilots reported for calisthenics every morning. Pilots in the other squadrons thought this was amusing and offered taunting suggestions during the exercises. That did not deter Waldron, who thought war no joke. To a nephew who was about to enter pilot training, Waldron wrote a letter advising him to "take this business seriously. It is a serious business and it is not a sport."[9]

At a meeting of officers four days earlier, on May 31, Waldron had taken the opportunity to argue that his torpedo squadron had a greater need for fighter protection than the bombers. Pat Mitchell had supported him, but Pete Mitscher shook his head. Not only were there more than twice as many bombers (34) as torpedo planes (15), but Mitscher knew that the great weakness of the Wildcats—especially the new Dash-4 version on the *Hornet*—was their indifferent climbing ability. The light and nimble Zeros could climb at nearly three times the rate of the Wildcats, and the best chance the American fighters had in dealing with their Japanese counterparts—maybe the only chance—was to dive on them from above. To Mitscher, this meant the fighters had to come in high. This would allow them to protect the dive-bombers and the torpedo planes too, because when the Zeros attacked the lumbering Devastators, the Wildcats could come screaming down on them from altitude. Of course, one option was to split the difference and send some fighters with each group, as Fletcher had done in the Coral Sea. The outcome there had been disappointing, however, for there had not been enough fighters to protect either group fully, and the bombers had suffered far more than the Devastators from the Zeros. The Wildcats had experienced their best success when they dove on the Zeros during the attack on the *Shōhō*. Whether or not Mitscher was aware of this, he chose *not* to divide Mitchell's fighters into two sections and declared that all ten Wildcats would go with the dive-bombers. The torpedo planes, at least at the outset, would be on their own. Mitchell and especially Waldron were unhappy with the decision. They were overruled.[10]

There were two false alarms that morning when the teleprinter in the ready rooms clicked out orders for the pilots to man their planes, provoking a quick scramble for equipment and plotting boards, until in the same message a correction appeared: "Do not man planes until directed." Apparently, when Mitscher heard Fletcher's 6:07 order to Spruance to attack, he anticipated an immediate launch order. Instead, as we have seen, Spruance decided to wait until 7:00 in order to close the range. Mitscher had to order his pilots to stand down. During that hiatus, at about 6:30 Mitscher called Ring and the four squadron leaders to the bridge for final instructions. There, Waldron tried once again to convince Mitscher to send the fighters with his torpedo planes, and once again Mitchell supported him. Mitchell later recalled that he went up to the bridge that morning expressly to "recommended to Captain Mitscher that we [the fighters] go in with protection for the torpedo planes alone." But it was Waldron who was so persistent that he verged on insubordination. If Mitscher would not send all ten fighters with his squadron, Waldron argued, he could at least send some of them. When that plea failed, he begged Mitscher to send just one fighter. (It is possible to imagine the emotional Waldron holding up a single finger and demanding "one, just one" fighter.) If Mitscher didn't want to commit a fighter pilot, Waldron argued, he could have one of his own pilots fly a Wildcat, though none of them had ever been up in one before.

254 ■ THE BATTLE OF MIDWAY

This was an absurd argument, and by now Mitscher was surely becoming annoyed. He was not the type to negotiate with junior officers. The answer was still no. Mitchell recalled Mitscher telling him to "go out and stay with the bombers." The planes were already warming up on the flight deck and there was no room for another discussion of alternatives. It was time to go. The squadron commanders wished each other good luck and good hunting and went down to man their airplanes.[11]

A more critical issue than deciding the role of the fighter planes was the launch sequence and the departure plan used on the *Hornet* that day. At 6:38, Mitscher finally got orders from Spruance to launch aircraft at 7:00 a.m., and those orders specified that the air groups were to "use deferred departure." Instead of having the planes head off toward the target as they launched and effecting a rendezvous en route, the first of them would circle the task force until all the planes in the strike group were in the air; then they would assemble into one grand formation and fly to the target together. The intent of a deferred departure was to ensure unity, attack discipline, and a coordinated strike against the enemy. Almost certainly this order came from Miles Browning, for it is highly unlikely that the black shoe Spruance would have dictated to the brown shoes the type of departure they should use.[12]

With the order to man their planes, the pilots wished each other good luck, quit their ready rooms, and hurried up the ladders to the flight deck. There they met briefly with their back seat gunners, went over the mission and recognition charts, and gave their planes a quick inspection before climbing into the cockpits. It was habit, and perhaps superstition, that led them to kick the tires. For most of them, this would be the first time they had ever taken off from a carrier while carrying a live bomb. One recalled that as he sat in his plane waiting for the signal to start engines, he "got the same feeling of apprehension and butterflies in the stomach" that he used to get "at the start of competition in high school."[13]

The ten Wildcat fighters went first—they needed the shortest runway to get airborne. The air officer watching from the ship's island gave the go order to the officer on the flight deck who was designated as Fly One. That individual waved his take-off wand in a circle as the pilot revved his engines to full power. When the pilot gave a thumbs-up sign to show that he was ready, Fly One dropped into a crouch and pointed toward the bow. The pilot released his brakes and the plane roared forward. The process was repeated with the next plane. Once all ten Wildcats were in the air and began their climb to their assigned cruising altitude of 20,000 feet, the fifteen Dauntless dive-bombers of VS-8, each of them armed with a 500-pound bomb, began to take off. Next came the CHAG, Stanhope Ring, whose plane also carried a 500-pound bomb, and following him were the eighteen bombers of VB-8, which carried 1,000-pound bombs. The big Devastator torpedo planes of Waldron's VT-8, each with a 2,200-pound Mark 13 torpedo, needed the longest deck run to get aloft, and because of that they were spotted at the back. Only six of them fit on the crowded flight deck, so the other nine had to be brought up from the hangar deck afterward and launched separately. This launch sequence meant that the Wildcats, which had the shortest range, were in the air first, burning up fuel while they circled and waited, and the Devastators, which were the slowest, launched last and were therefore certain to lag behind the rest of the formation.

Once all the fighters and bombers were in the air, they began jockeying into formation. Ring mandated a double V-shaped "parade" formation with himself at the point and the two bombing squadrons on either side of him. Mitchell's ten fighters flew above and slightly behind them. Assembling this large formation took longer than it should have. Ensign Ben Tappan, piloting a Dauntless in Walt Rodee's Scouting Eight, felt that "they were doing too much fiddle faddling around . . . waiting to get permission to go."[14]

Even after they were finally assembled into formation, they had to continue their climb up to 20,000 feet. That climb to altitude took more time—and a lot of gas. While a Dash-4 Wildcat consumed 42 gallons of fuel per hour in level flight, it could burn up as much as 300 gallons per hour in a vertical climb (five gallons a minute). The fact that they had launched first and then had to climb up to 20,000 feet meant that some of the Wildcats used up a significant percentage of their 144-gallon fuel capacity even before the air group headed out for the target. Then, in order to maintain their position above the bombers, which flew at 130 knots, the

Wildcats, which cruised at 150 knots, had to serpentine back and forth in a series of lazy S curves to avoid overrunning the bombers flying below them, and that, too, wasted fuel. The bombers also used up extra gas in an effort to maintain the precise formation of the air group. One pilot recalled, "We flew parade formation and the throttle was in use constantly to maintain position."[15]

While the fighters and bombers climbed to altitude, the pilots in Waldron's torpedo squadron formed up nearly three miles below them, at 1,500 feet. By the time all fifty-nine planes of the *Hornet's* strike group were in the air, with the bombers and fighters at 20,000 feet and the torpedo planes at 1,500 feet, it was nearly eight o'clock. The launch had taken most of an hour. By contrast, earlier that morning the Kidō Butai had launched 108 planes in just over seven minutes, though they had used four carrier decks to do it. Nevertheless, the *Hornet* air group was at last aloft, formed up, and on its way.

But in what direction?

Without doubt, the most puzzling aspect of the "flight to nowhere" is the course flown by the *Hornet* air group when it did finally set out. A week after the battle, Mitscher submitted an after-action report in which he wrote, "The objective, enemy carriers, was calculated to be 155 miles distant, bearing 239° T[rue] from this Task Force." Based on that, students of the battle long assumed that Ring led the *Hornet's* bombers and fighters on a course of 239 degrees—that is, to the southwest. This was also the course indicated on the battle map that Mitscher submitted with his report (shown in gray on the map opposite). According to that report, Ring's air group missed finding the Kidō Butai that morning because Nagumo reversed course and turned north, and Ring consequently flew south of him. Nonetheless, most other evidence indicates that the *Hornet's* air group did *not* fly southwesterly at 239 degrees but instead flew almost due west at 265 degrees; it missed the Kidō Butai because that course led the air group eighty to a hundred miles *north* of the target. In addition, the distance to the target may have been very near 155 miles at 7:00 a.m. when the *Hornet* turned into the wind to launch, but because the *Hornet* steamed away from the target at 25 knots for

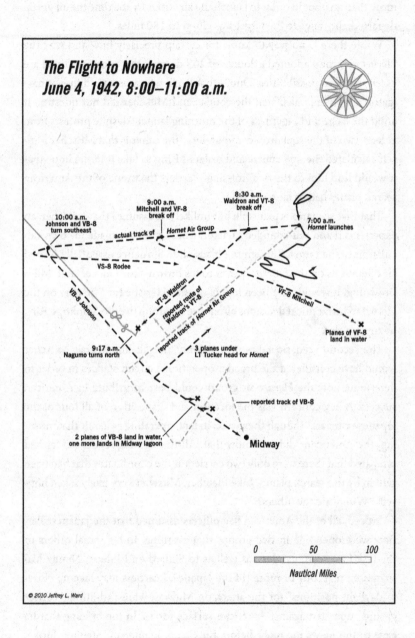

**The Flight to Nowhere**
**June 4, 1942, 8:00–11:00 a.m.**

9:00 a.m.
Mitchell and VF-8
break off

8:30 a.m.
Waldron and VT-8
break off

10:00 a.m.
Johnson and VB-8
turn southeast

7:00 a.m.
*Hornet* launches

actual track of *Hornet* Air Group

VS-8 Rodee

VT-8 Waldron

reported route of
Waldron's VT-8

VF-8 Mitchell

VB-8 Johnson

reported track of *Hornet* Air Group

Planes of VF-8
land in water

9:17 a.m.
Nagumo turns north

3 planes under
LT Tucker head for *Hornet*

reported track of VB-8

2 planes of VB-8 land in water,
one more lands in Midway lagoon

**Midway**

0        50        100

*Nautical Miles*

© 2010 Jeffrey L. Ward

more than an hour in order to launch the air strike, by the time the air group departed, the range to the target was closer to 180 miles.[16]

While there is no way to know for certain precisely how and why the *Hornet* air group adopted a course of 265 degrees that morning, there are essentially two possibilities. One is that Ring, who was an indifferent navigator, simply miscalculated the course, and Mitscher did not question it amid the haste and eagerness of the morning launch, despite protests from at least two of the squadron commanders. The other is that Mitscher himself calculated the 265 course and ordered Ring to take it in the hope that it would lead him to the two "missing" carriers that none of the American search planes had so far reported.

That first scenario is plausible but unlikely. It assumes that Mitscher, an experienced and self-confident aviator, would not have made his own calculation to the target. Though the black shoe Spruance essentially turned air operations on the *Enterprise* over to his brown-shoe chief of staff, Miles Browning, it would have been highly uncharacteristic for Mitscher on the *Hornet* to turn critical decisions about the air group over to Stanhope Ring or anyone else.

The second scenario takes into account the likelihood that Mitscher would have considered the broader operational circumstances in order to determine how the *Hornet* air group could best contribute to American success. A key concern was the location and disposition of all four of the Japanese carriers. Though they were, in fact, operating as a unit that morning, the Americans did not know that. All the sighting reports so far had indicated that there were only two carriers at the coordinates that had been sent in by the search planes. Like Fletcher, Mitscher very likely asked himself, "Where are the others?"[17]

Indeed, all of the American flag officers assumed that the Japanese carriers were operating in two groups that morning. In his initial orders to the task-force commanders, as well as to Simard on Midway, Nimitz had suggested that "one or more [of the Japanese] carriers may take up close-in daylight positions" for the attack on Midway, while "additional carrier groups" operated against American surface forces. In the briefing that he gave to the pilots the night before the battle, Lieutenant Stephen Jurika,

Mitscher's intelligence officer, announced that "there were at least two carriers, two battleships, several cruisers and about five destroyers in the attack
force which would attempt to take Midway. *The support force some distance
behind contained the rest of their forces*" (emphasis added). And at 6:48 on
the morning of the battle, just before the *Hornet* began launching, Fletcher
sent a message to Spruance by TBS (a message which Mitscher no doubt
monitored) to remind him that "two carriers [are] unaccounted for." All of
that may have encouraged Mitscher to send his air group to the west rather
than the southwest in the expectation of finding that second enemy carrier
group. In the only comment Ring ever made about the course he flew that
day, he wrote: "Departure from Hornet was taken on predetermined inter-
ception course, Group Commander leading." Predetermined by whom he
does not say.[18]

If this is indeed what happened, it is curious that neither Mitscher nor
Ring shared the object of the mission with the squadron commanders,
and because of that Waldron became even more frustrated and unsatisfied.
He knew that a course of 265 degrees would not lead them to the carriers
that had been reported and plotted by all the squadron commanders. As
he made his way down to the flight deck, he pulled aside his squadron's
navigator, Ensign George Gay, and told him that he thought the assigned
course was wrong. If necessary, he told Gay, he would fly his own course

■ Rear Admiral (Select) Pete Mitscher
observes flight operations from the bridge
wing of the USS *Hornet*. (U.S. Naval Institute)

to the target. "Don't think I'm lost," Waldron said. "Just track me so that if anything happens to me the boys can count on you to bring them back."[19]

────────────

Over the next hour, the *Hornet* was fully occupied in launching aircraft, and the pilots were busy jockeying into formation. By 7:55 a.m. the entire air group was in the air, and Ring led it westward on a course of 265 degrees. The radar operator on the *Hornet* tracked them as they flew westward until they disappeared off the scope. The pilots flew under radio silence, yet only about fifteen minutes into this flight, Ring's radio crackled to life and he heard Waldron's voice: "You're going the wrong direction for the Japanese carrier force." Ring was furious that Waldron had broken radio silence, and equally furious to be challenged like this on an open radio net, in effect in front of the entire command. "I'm leading this flight," he snapped back. "You fly with us right here." Waldron was not intimidated. "I know where the damned Jap fleet is," he insisted. Ring was adamant, as well as angry: "You fly on us. I'm leading this formation; you fly on us." There was a brief silence, and then one more broadcast from Waldron: "Well, the hell with you. I know where they are and I'm going to them." Three miles below, Waldron banked his plane off to the left, heading southwest, and his entire squadron, most of whom had probably heard the radio exchange, went with him. It was just past 8:30. At about that moment, Nagumo was making his decision to recover the Midway strike force before launching his attack against the Americans.[20]

Stanhope Ring—perhaps with clenched teeth—flew on with the forty-four bombers and fighters. Below them, nothing was visible save patchy clouds and open ocean. By now the fuel gauges on some of the Wildcats were nearing the halfway mark. Ensign Ben Tappan kept one eye on his gas indicator as he flew. He remembered thinking they'd never make it back. He wasn't the only one. Ensign John E. McInerny was also unsettled. He looked over to his wingman, Ensign Johnny Magda, and made an open-handed shrug, as if to ask, "What's going on?" Magda shook his head, which McInerny interpreted as, "I don't know either." They flew on.[21]

A half hour later, with his fuel gauge now well below the halfway mark, McInerny broke formation, climbed up to Pat Mitchell's lead Wildcat, and settled in next to him. When Mitchell looked over, McInerny gesticulated forcefully toward his gas gauge. Mitchell simply shook his head. McInerny went back into his position on Madga's wing, but he continued to stew. After a few more minutes, he tried it again. This time Mitchell reacted angrily, waving him back into position and pointing to him (in Mitchell's words) "as a warning."[22]

If Mitchell was angry, so was McInerny. He went back to his position in the formation. Getting Magda's attention, he mouthed, "Come with me." He then banked out of the formation and began to fly a reciprocal course back toward the *Hornet*. He was essentially abandoning the formation and his commanding officer, and even as he did it he assumed that he would be court-martialed for it. Magda went with him. One by one, so did all the other Wildcat pilots of VF-8. Abandoned by his squadron, Pat Mitchell turned too. He insisted later that he did it on his own. "I broke off," he claimed in 1981, "when I saw . . . that it would be foolish to go any farther." In fact, Mitchell had lost control of his command and had to hurry back to the front of his mutinous squadron to remain a part of it. All ten fighters now headed back toward the *Hornet*, leaving the thirty-four bombers on their own. It was around nine o'clock.[23]

It is not certain that Ring was even aware of the moment when his fighter cover left him. The Wildcats were flying above and behind him, and no one had broken radio silence. Even a few of the fighter pilots were unaware of it. Focused on keeping their position in the formation, some made the slow turn to the left without realizing they were doing it until they noticed that instead of the sun being at their backs, it was now in their faces.

Abandoned by both the torpedo bombers and the fighter escort, Ring and the thirty-four dive-bombers continued to fly westward. At about 9:20, a few of the bomber pilots, or rather their radiomen, overheard a call from Waldron: "Stanhope from Johnny One." If he heard it, Ring did not reply. Waldron tried again: "Stanhope from Johnny One." Again there was no response. But there was more from Waldron, including, "Watch those fighters!" and then later, "Attack immediately!" After that, there was this: "My two wing men are going in the water." Then nothing. To those who heard it, it was now evident that Waldron had been correct about the bearing to the target, and that he had found the enemy—and they had found him.[24]

Lieutenant Commander Robert "Ruff" Johnson, the commander of VB-8, may or may not have heard Waldron's broadcasts. Johnson was a popular squadron commander with a "genial disposition." One of his classmates said of him: "To know him is to like him." Johnson's greatest concern now was that the planes of his squadron were running out of fuel. Though his pilots flew the longer-range Dauntless dive-bomber, they had each been armed with a 1,000-pound bomb, which cut into their fuel efficiency. Now after flying over two hundred miles, well beyond the presumed intercept point, he concluded that they had missed the target. He worried that his pilots would not be able to make it back to the carrier. He decided to fly south toward Midway, partly to see if he could find the Japanese carriers, and partly in the hope of making it to the landing field on Eastern Island. He signaled to his wingman and turned southward. His squadron followed. Ring went on the radio to order the bombers to stay with him, but only his assigned wingman, Ensign Clayton Fisher, did so. The other sixteen planes of VB-8 went with Johnson to the southeast. Now Ring led a strike force composed only of the fifteen dive-bombers of Walt Rodee's scouting squadron, plus Fisher.[25]

Ring and what was left of his command continued to fly westward. Soon even the scout bombers, loaded with the lighter 500-pound bombs, were beginning to run low on fuel. Rodee and his squadron had stuck with Ring for 225 miles. Now, past ten o'clock, having been in the air for most of three hours, Rodee, too, turned his squadron around. Every other plane in the formation followed him. In his only postbattle writing on this event, Ring claimed that he "attempted to rally the departing aircraft of VB-8 and VF-8 in order to lead them back to *Hornet*, but I could not catch them." As a result, he headed for the *Hornet* (in his words) "proceeding singly at 20,000 feet." In other words, he flew back to the *Hornet* completely alone. One can only imagine his emotional state.[26]

Since neither Browning nor Mitscher had established a point option for the recovery, Ring and the others were dependent on the *Hornet*'s YE-ZB homing system. Using a dedicated YE transmitter, the ship sent out a single Morse-code letter to various quadrants—a different letter for each 30-degree arc of the compass. Pilots who received the signal in their ZB receivers could then determine a course back to the ship. Ring got a reading on his ZB receiver, but it was the signal from *Enterprise*, not *Hornet*. As a result, Ring relied on "dead reckoning" to find the carrier, and he flew— unerringly for once—back to the task force. His was the first plane to land on the *Hornet's* deck at 11:18 a.m., after four hours in the air. Not noticing that Ring's plane still carried its 500-pound bomb, the *Hornet's* crew assumed he was returning from a successful strike and cheered when he climbed out of the cockpit. Ring did not acknowledge the cheers and went straight to his stateroom without reporting to the bridge. Not until Walt Rodee landed a few minutes later and climbed up to the bridge to report did Mitscher find out what had happened.

The mission was not yet over for everyone. Ruff Johnson's heavily laden bombers flew to the southeast until it was obvious they had missed the enemy, and then Johnson turned them northeast hoping to get back to the *Hornet*. Shortly before 10:00, they encountered an American PBY, which blinkered them a course to Eastern Island. At about the same time, the squadron exec, Lieutenant Alfred B. Tucker, picked up the YE homing signal from the *Hornet*. At this point, the squadron broke up: Johnson with fourteen planes flew on to Midway; Tucker and his section of three planes turned northeast to try to find the task force. Of Johnson's fourteen planes, two ran out of fuel en route and had to ditch; a third plane ran out of gas just as it approached the airfield and ditched in the Midway lagoon. The rest encountered "friendly" AA fire as they attempted to land at Midway, though it stopped once they were recognized. The eleven surviving planes were refueled, rearmed (they had jettisoned their 1,000-pound bombs), and eventually sent back to the *Hornet*. Tucker's three-plane section also found the *Hornet*, so that in the end only three bombers were lost on the mission. None, however, had dropped a bomb on the enemy.

The Wildcat pilots were less fortunate. Mitchell did not pick up the *Hornet's* YE homing signal, though several other Wildcat pilots did. Mitchell therefore turned the lead over to Lieutenant Stan Ruehlow, who led the loose formation of fighters eastward at a comfortable 150 knots. The fighters dropped gradually from 20,000 feet down to 8,000 feet, not only to conserve fuel but also because below 8,000 feet they did not need their oxygen canisters, which were also running low. Unfortunately, at low level the ZB receivers were less efficient, and the fighters flew past the *Hornet* without spotting it. As they continued eastward, their engines began to cough and sputter, and then one by one they stopped altogether, the propellers windmilling in silence as the planes ran out of fuel. The heavy Wildcats were poor gliders, and it required some skill to bring them down onto the water for a controlled crash landing. Each man sent out a perfunctory Mayday message and then focused his attention on all the things he had to do once the plane hit the sea: throw open the cockpit cover, unbuckle his seat belt, grab his canteen, climb out onto the wing, manipulate the hatch cover to release the small life raft and inflate it along with his "Mae West" (life preserver), and then clamber into the raft—all before the plane sank.[27]

Most of them grouped up for company. When McInerny's plane went down, his wingman, Johnny Magda, still had power, though his gas gauge showed empty. Magda calculated his chances of finding the task force at zero and decided he was better off sticking with his wingman, so he ditched in the water alongside Mac. Mitchell, too, went down near two other pilots, Dick Gray and Stan Ruehlow. It was fortunate for him that he did, for Mitchell couldn't get his life raft out of its compartment and ended up as the third man sharing two tiny one-man rafts. Over the next four days, they rotated, taking turns in the water. That was particularly dicey during the several shark attacks. The sharks were especially aggressive on the third night, pushing and bumping the rafts; once a shark's fin cut the fabric on one of the rafts and it began losing air, though the men were able to patch it. There was also only one set of emergency rations, and the three pilots allowed themselves only one sip of water each day. "We watched each other take this drink," Mitchell recalled. Small fish swam near the rafts occasionally, and Dick Gray was able to grab one with his bare hands and eat it raw. The sun was merciless, and all of them suffered severe sunburn. The rafts were slowly losing air. Soon instead of sitting, they had to straddle them with their feet dangling in the water. Mitchell got blisters on his head from sunburn, as well as swollen feet from constant immersion in the water.[28]

Eleven PBY Catalinas from Midway were committed to the search for the downed pilots. Eight of the ten fighter pilots were rescued on June 8 and 9. After Lieutenant Junior Grade Frank Fisler's PBY touched down in the water to rescue Johnny Talbot, Ensign Jerry Crawford helped Talbot into the plane. Talbot's face and hands were completely covered with huge blisters from sunburn, and the blisters themselves were encrusted with salt. Crawford knew Talbot well but did not recognize the man in the raft. Talbot eventually recovered, as did the others. The downed bomber pilots were rescued as well, though two of the fighter pilots were never found, and of course all ten of the fighter planes were lost.[29]

———

On board the *Hornet*, Pete Mitscher was no doubt horrified to learn from Walt Rodee what had happened. In its first mission against the enemy, the *Hornet*'s air group had literally fallen apart. First the torpedo planes, then the fighters, and finally the bombers had all abandoned their commanding officer, who had returned alone. None of the torpedo planes or fighters had returned at all, and by noon, after five hours, Mitscher had to know they never would. Of the fifty-nine planes that had launched from the *Hornet* that morning, only twenty had come back. Eleven more bombers of VB-8 would eventually fly in from Midway, but for all those losses in both men and machines, not one bomb had been dropped on the Japanese.

Neither Mitscher nor anyone else on the *Hornet* yet knew what had happened to Waldron's torpedo squadron.

# Attack of the Torpedo Squadrons
## (8:30 a.m. to 10:20 a.m.)

I f the story behind Stanhope Ring's flight remains something of an enigma, the story of the attack on the Kidō Butai by John Waldron's Torpedo Squadron Eight is one of the best-known episodes of the Battle of Midway. Waldron's command was virtually wiped out in its bold but utterly futile attack, and after it was over only one man was left alive to tell the tale. As a result, the episode carries with it some of the aura of the Battle of Little Bighorn, with "the Indian," John Waldron, in the unlikely role of George Custer and Nagumo Chūichi in the even more unlikely role of Chief Sitting Bull. By deciding to abandon Ring and fly his own course to the Kidō Butai, Waldron almost certainly expected to be court-martialed afterward, but he was willing to face that fate in order to strike a blow against the enemy. Had he lived, he might very well have been brought up on charges; his disobedience was too overt and too public to be ignored. But since he was martyred in the sacrificial loss of his entire squadron during what turned out to be an American victory, he was instead awarded a posthumous Navy Cross.

In addition to Torpedo Eight, two other American torpedo squadrons attacked the Kidō Butai that morning—those from the *Enterprise* and *Yorktown*. They fared little better. The attacks by Torpedo Six (from *Enterprise*) and Torpedo Three (from *Yorktown*) were equally heroic and equally tragic. For years it has been assumed that this terrible slaughter was redeemed by the fact that the sacrifice of these planes and pilots brought the Japanese fighter cover down to their level and thereby cleared the path for the American dive-bombers. That turns out to be true, but it was not the full measure of their contribution.

At around 8:30, when Waldron and his fifteen planes flew away from Ring's air group, they flew toward the southwest. Earlier that morning Waldron had calculated a course of 240 degrees to the enemy target, which was simply an extrapolation of the enemy's course based on Lieutenant Ady's initial report. Since taking off from the *Hornet* at 7:55 that morning (his plane was the last one to lift off), Waldron and his squadron had flown a westward course below Ring for twenty minutes or so before making the turn southward. As a result, the relative-motion problem had changed. Now Waldron

■ The pilots of Torpedo Squadron Eight pose on the deck of the USS *Hornet*. George Gay, the only survivor of the attack on June 4, is kneeling in the center of the front row. (U.S. Naval Institute)

had to fly a few degrees more to the south to make up for his westward reach. He took the lead, heading southwest on a course of 234 degrees.[1]

The planes of Torpedo Eight flew in two sections, with Waldron leading the first section of eight, flying in four two-plane groups, and Lieutenant James C. Owens leading the second section of seven planes. Owens led the squadron's second section because when the *Hornet* had departed Norfolk back in March, the squadron's executive officer, Harold Larsen, had stayed behind to accept delivery of the new TBF Avengers. Now Larsen was at Pearl Harbor, frustrated by the fact that not only had he arrived in Hawaii too late to board the *Hornet* in time for its sortie, he had not been chosen to be one of the six Avenger pilots to fly out to Midway. Consequently he did not participate in the attack on the Kidō Butai that morning, though his nonselection probably saved his life. Now Owens, who had been the backup quarterback on the USC football team before the war, flew in his place. Unlike Larsen, who was the squadron's enforcer and therefore unpopular, Owens had a quiet confidence that the other pilots appreciated and admired.[2]

The weather was good and "visibility was excellent," with only a few broken clouds at 1,500 feet and light winds of no more than eight knots. Though Waldron was sure he was at last going in the right direction, he had no clear idea of the precise location of the enemy (despite his frequent assertion that he had a sixth sense about such things). After about a half hour, therefore, he ordered his eight-plane section to fan out in a scouting line. His rookie pilots did so, but soon they were spread out so wide that Waldron had to signal them to close back in. Just as he did so, he saw black smoke on the horizon to his right. He turned toward it and soon saw that it came from ships—many ships. George Gay, flying "tail end Charlie" as the squadron's navigator, saw them too. The first ship he recognized was a large carrier, then two more, then another, and then more ships "all over the damned ocean." Waldron had found the Kidō Butai. He tried to call the sighting into Ring—"Stanhope from Johnny One . . . Stanhope from Johnny One." Despite getting no response, he left his radio on, very likely in the hope that someone would pick up the radio chatter and use it to locate the target.[3]

On the flag bridge of the *Akagi*, Nagumo already knew that yet another group of American planes was headed his way. Petty Officer Amari, still hovering in the vicinity of Task Force 16 in *Tone*'s number 4 scout plane, had spotted torpedo bombers en route and reported their approach. For Nagumo, it was unwelcome news. The last of the surviving American planes from Midway had only recently departed, and his carriers were busy recovering Tomonaga's force returning from Midway and striking those planes down to the hangar deck to be rearmed and refueled. No doubt, Nagumo hoped for a period of relative quiet to complete that process. After the last of Tomonaga's planes landed, at 9:17, Nagumo ordered the Kidō Butai to turn to the northeast to close the range to the American carrier group.* One minute later, Nagumo's big cruisers *Tone* and *Chikuma* spouted plumes of black smoke in order to alert the flagship to the approach of Waldron's squadron. Here was yet another attack by the so far inept but obviously determined Americans. The *Kaga* launched six more fighters to join the eighteen that were already in the air, and twenty-four Zeros headed out to intercept Waldron's fifteen plodding Devastators.[4]

Waldron had no good options. He could not attack according to doctrine, for there were no dive-bombers for him to cooperate with. He could not circle and wait for them, because even if the bombers responded to his call and found the Kidō Butai, by then the Zeros would have shot down all his planes—unless the Devastators ran out of fuel first. There was really only one option. Waldron went on the radio and announced: "We will go in. We won't turn back. Former strategy [of a coordinated attack] cannot be used. We will attack. Good luck." Back in formation now, the pilots of the fifteen torpedo planes closed in tighter and began to drop down to attack level. At their cruising speed of 110 knots, the run-in to the drop site must have seemed like an eternity. The four big carriers turned away from them, toward the west, to present a narrower target and to compel the attackers

---

* The fact that Nagumo made his turn at 9:17 is more evidence that Ring did not miss the Kidō Butai because it turned northward during his flight as stated in Mitscher's report. If Ring and his air group had flown a course of 240, he would very likely have found the Kidō Butai *before* Nagumo's turn northward, as Waldron did. See appendix F.

to fly a longer distance to get an angle on the bow. Waldron had picked out the southernmost carrier as the initial target. After the formation turned, however, he shifted to another carrier that was slightly closer. Though at least one pilot believed it was the *Kaga*, it was in fact the *Sōryū*. Long before the Americans got within range of either ship, at about eight miles out, the Zeros were on them.[5]

The Zeros attacked from above and behind, starting with the lead plane and working their way back in the formation. "Zeros were coming in from all angles and both sides at once," Gay recalled. "They would come in from abeam, pass each other just over our heads, and turn around to make another attack." Some, after making one pass, performed an acrobatic vertical loop to come in behind the next plane in the formation. "Watch those fighters!" Waldron barked out over the open radio, perhaps intending the remark for his backseat radioman/gunner, Horace Dobbs. Dobbs and the other gunners swiveled their twin .30-caliber machine guns and fired at the Zeros as they flashed past. Instead of jinking and sliding to try to throw off the enemy fighters, Waldron and the other Devastator pilots held a steady course to achieve a good torpedo drop and to provide their gunners with a stable firing platform. Waldron called his gunner on the intercom to ask, "How am I doing, Dobbs?" Because Waldron still had his radio on, the question was heard throughout the squadron, and by at least one radioman in Ring's air group eighty miles to the north.[6]

Boring in from above, the Zero pilots used their machine-gun tracers, which one pilot described as "thin whips of light," to get the range. Then they fired their 20 mm cannon for the kill. The sturdy Devastators could absorb a lot of machine-gun fire, but the cannon shells were fatal. One Devastator went down, then another. The American rear-seat gunners were firing, too, and Waldron thought he saw a Zero crash into the sea as well. "See that splash?" Waldron called out. "I'd give a million to know who done that!" But there were too many Zeros, and they were too fast for the backseat gunners. One by one, the skilled Japanese pilots sent the slow and level-flying torpedo bombers spinning into the sea. "My two wing men are going in the water," Waldron reported to no one in particular. It was his last broadcast. Hit by several cannon shells, his plane "burst into flames." George Gay saw it dive for the sea, and he reported later that he saw Waldron throw back the canopy and stand up in the cockpit, putting one leg out onto the wing just as his plane "hit the water and disappeared."[7]

Those few Devastators that were left continued on to the target. At one of their training sessions the week before, Waldron had passed out a mimeographed sheet he had typed up himself. It is quoted here in its entirety:

> Just a word to let you know I feel we are all ready. We have had a very short time to train, and we have worked under the most severe difficulties. But we have truly done the best humanly possible. I actually believe that under these conditions we are the best in the world. My greatest hope is that we encounter a favorable tactical situation, but if we don't and worst comes to worst, I want each of us to do his utmost to destroy our enemies. If there is only one plane left to make the final run-in, I want that man to go in and get a hit. May God be with us all. Good luck, happy landings, and give 'em hell.[8]

Now worst had indeed come to worst and the skipper was gone, but true to his spirit the remaining Devastators continued on, lining up on the *Sōryū*, which now made a radical turn to starboard to throw off the attackers. It seemed unlikely, however, that any of the American planes would get close enough to drop what Waldron had always called "the pickle."

Gay was the last in line and so far had been spared, but now he too came under attack. On his intercom he heard his gunner, Robert K. "Bob" Huntington, call out, "They got me," and, glancing back, saw Huntington slumped in his seat. No longer needing to maintain a steady firing platform for Huntington, Gay began to jink and slide all over the place. He also went to full throttle ("balls to the wall," as he put it), as fast as the lumbering Devastator could go. It wasn't fast enough. Bullets thudded into the armor plate of his cockpit seat, others clanked into the plane's fuselage; one hit him in the left arm. It seemed to him that "there were at least thirty Zeros" in the air, and only three Devastators still flying.[9]

Soon there was only one. Gay flew on alone, and decided that the time had come to drop his "pickle." He "punched the torpedo release button," but nothing happened. The Japanese bullets had wrecked his electrical system. So he shifted hands on the control stick and reached for the manual release. When he pulled it, the cable came out in his hands. The torpedo may have dropped—or not; he didn't know. In any case, it was time to get out of there. He flew low over the *Sōryū's* deck and banked left out over the stern. The Zeros had pulled off him when he entered the envelope of the ship's antiaircraft fire, but now they were back—and he was the only target. A 20 mm cannon shell punched though his engine and set it on fire. Gay cut the fuel switch to prevent an explosion and prepared to ditch. As he glided down for a water landing, his right wing touched first, and his plane ground looped on the surface. Shaken but still conscious, Gay unstrapped his shoulder harness and prepared to get out as the cockpit filled with water. He struggled with the canopy and feared the heavy plane would take him down before he could extricate himself. Finally able to scramble out, he checked on Huntington, but he appeared to be dead, and in any case Gay couldn't get him out of his harness. Gay swam away from the plane before it sucked him down.[10]

Before they had taken off that morning, Huntington had suggested putting the plane's life raft in the empty middle seat just in case. Now, as Gay flailed in the water, trying not to swallow too much of it, that raft and the seat cushion floated past him. He grabbed both of them. He threw off his goggles, fearing that the glass lenses would reflect in the bright morning sun and attract the attention of the circling Zeros, and decided not to inflate the raft until later since its bright orange color would also draw their attention. He pulled the seat cushion over his head and treaded water as the Zeros continued to circle for a few minutes, then left.[11]

On board the *Akagi*, Nagumo could feel pleased that yet another American air attack had been shattered—indeed, annihilated—and once again with no damage to his own force. On the other hand, Nagumo had to suspect that these fifteen torpedo bombers had come from a carrier, which meant that the American carriers were now within range and knew where he was. There was no time for detailed consideration of that, however, for no sooner had the Zeros splashed the last plane of this group than another group showed up, this one flying in from the south. If nothing else, these Americans were persistent.

The new attack came from the torpedo squadron on the *Enterprise* (VT-6), led by 37-year-old Lieutenant Commander Eugene Lindsey, a thin-faced 1927 Naval Academy classmate of Pat Mitchell. Lindsey was a natural pilot who found flying a lot like gymnastics or diving, sports at which he had excelled at the Academy. That morning, however, there had been some doubt about whether or not he could fly at all. Six days earlier, in the flight out to the *Enterprise* after it left Pearl Harbor, Lindsey had come in too low and his left wing had clipped the big carrier's stern ramp. His plane skidded across the deck and went over the side. Lindsey and his two crewmen were picked up by the destroyer *Monaghan*, which was acting as plane guard that day. The two crewmen were fine, but Lindsey was badly injured and confined

■ The planes of Gene Lindsey's Torpedo Six on the flight deck of the *Enterprise* on the morning of June 4. Only four of the planes seen here returned from the strike. (U.S. Navy)

to sick bay; for a while the doctors feared that he had broken his back. On June 4 he was still in some pain, and his face was so swollen he couldn't put on his goggles. When the air group commander, Wade McClusky, sat down at breakfast that morning, he was shocked when Gene Lindsey sat down next to him. McClusky asked him if could fly, and Lindsey answered, "This is what I have been trained to do."[12]

Like Waldron's torpedo squadron from *Hornet*, Lindsey's group was the last to take off from its host carrier that morning, and, like Waldron's, it was the first of its air group to attack the Kidō Butai. The circumstances, however, were very different. While Waldron had deliberately abandoned his air group commander, Lindsey had been left behind by his.

As on the *Hornet*, there were a few false starts on the *Enterprise* that morning as pilots were sent running to their aircraft more than once only to be recalled again a few minutes later. Wade McClusky remembered Spruance and Browning having a "heated discussion" about when to launch. Finally, at 7:00, Spruance gave the go order, and planes began to lift off a few minutes later. Browning mandated a deferred departure for the *Enterprise* air group as he had for the *Hornet*, but it didn't work out that way. The eight Wildcats of the morning CAP began launching at 7:05. The Dauntless dive-bombers of Earl Gallaher's VS-6 and Dick Best's VB-6 were already spotted for takeoff, but as they warmed up, four of them developed engine problems and had to be struck below. This entailed manhandling them up to the forward elevator and lowering them down to the hangar deck.[13]

There were other delays. Ordinarily, the deck crew would have begun bringing up the planes of the second deck load via the rear elevator while the last of the dive-bombers were launching forward. But the bombers of Best's VB-6, each lugging a 1,000-pound bomb, needed a full deck run to get aloft, so the crew did not start bringing up the fighters and torpedo bombers for the second deck load until after the last of the dive-bombers was aloft. It took twenty minutes to bring up the ten Wildcats of VF-6 (via the forward elevator) and Gene Lindsey's fourteen Devastators (via the rear elevator). The Wildcats launched without mishap, but then one of the torpedo bombers had engine trouble, and though it was eventually fixed, that, too, took time.[14]

By 7:45, Spruance had run out of patience. Five minutes earlier, Gil Slonim, his radio intelligence officer, had reported that he had picked up a contact report from a Japanese snooper—almost certainly Petty Officer Amari in the *Tone*'s number 4 scout plane. Soon, the enemy would know where they were. Time was running out. Sensitive to the fact that he was not a naval aviator, Spruance had so far declined to interfere in the management of air operations. Nonetheless, deciding that enough was enough, he ordered that McClusky be sent a message by flashing light to "proceed on mission assigned." It was the right decision. Had McClusky and the thirty-two other dive-bombers of VS-6 and VB-6 continued to circle and wait for the torpedo planes, they very likely would not have had enough fuel left to conduct a search at the end of their flight, a search that eventually proved decisive.[15]

Of course, that decision also meant that McClusky's dive-bombers headed off to the southwest while Lindsey's big torpedo planes were still on the flight deck. By the time Lindsey got his fourteen planes into the air and headed off to find the Japanese, the dive-bombers were beyond sight, and Lindsey set his own course.

When McClusky's dive-bombers flew off to the southwest on a course of 231 degrees, the Wildcats did not go with them; unlike Mitscher, Browning wanted the fighters to stay on top of the Devastators. The CO of VF-6, James S. Gray, was only six years out of the Naval Academy and, at age 27, the youngest of the squadron commanders. He recalled Browning telling him that his fighters should "go to high altitude so they could come down to the torpedo planes' defense if they gave a signal." Gray went to see Lindsey's second in command, Lieutenant Arthur Ely, and the two of them agreed that if the torpedo bombers needed support, Lindsey or Ely would simply radio, "Come on down, Jim," and Gray would dive from altitude to assail the attacking Zeros.[16]

Because of the delay in launching the torpedo bombers, however, Gray's Wildcats were halfway up to 22,000 feet by the time Lindsey's squadron of fourteen planes got airborne. As with Mitchell's squadron, that climb to altitude used up a lot of gas, a fact that would play an important role later. Now, however, looking down from about two miles above, with patchy cloud cover in between, Gray had an imperfect view of what was going on with the task force. He saw a torpedo squadron below him, lost it for a while under the overcast, then found it again, and followed it, weaving back and forth so as not to overrun it as he continued to climb. What he did not know was that he had picked up not Gene Lindsey's VT-6 but John Waldron's VT-8.[17]

The whole time that Torpedo Squadron Eight was being annihilated by the Japanese Zeros, American fighter cover was nearby and available. Four miles above Waldron and a few miles to the northeast, Gray's squadron of ten Wildcats circled slowly overhead waiting for a call from below. Gray saw the fifteen torpedo planes enter a cloudbank ten miles out from the carrier force and assumed that there was no call for help because the torpedo bombers were using the clouds to conceal their approach. Besides, he was also waiting for the arrival of McClusky's dive-bombing group. Though Waldron left his radio on throughout the subsequent fight, and his various calls were picked up not only by the planes in his own squadron but also by at least some of those in Ring's group eighty miles away, neither Gray nor anyone else in his fighter squadron heard anything. As Gray wrote in his after-action report, "Prearranged distress signal from torpedo planes was not given." Gray was convinced that it was not a radio problem. "Our radios were working perfectly on this flight," he wrote in 1963. "There wasn't one peep from any of them [Waldron's planes] during their run in." Of course Waldron knew nothing about a prearranged signal because Gray and Waldron were from different carriers, which also meant that they were using different radio frequencies. As a result, Gray and his fighters circled uselessly above the Kidō Butai for most of an hour (9:10 to 10:05) while the Japanese methodically shot down all of Waldron's planes.[18]

Meanwhile, Gene Lindsey's group of torpedo bombers was approaching the target from the south. Lindsey might have missed the Kidō Butai altogether, because he had selected a course that took him just to the south of it. (Wade McClusky, as it turned out, took a course even further south.) What turned Lindsey toward the target was the black smoke that *Tone* and *Chikuma* had generated to signal Nagumo that they had spotted Waldron's planes. Thus, indirectly, Waldron did manage to lead other squadrons to the

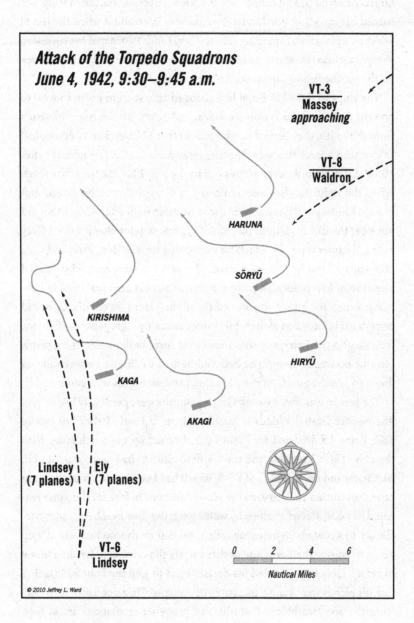

**Attack of the Torpedo Squadrons**
**June 4, 1942, 9:30–9:45 a.m.**

VT-3
**Massey**
*approaching*

VT-8
**Waldron**

HARUNA

SŌRYŪ

KIRISHIMA

HIRYŪ

KAGA

AKAGI

Lindsey
(7 planes)

Ely
(7 planes)

VT-6
**Lindsey**

0   2   4   6

*Nautical Miles*

© 2010 Jeffrey L. Ward

target. At about 9:30, Lindsey saw the smoke over his starboard wing and turned his squadron northward. Ten minutes later, about when the last of Waldron's planes was spinning into the sea, Lindsey ordered his squadron to separate into two seven-plane sections in order to conduct an anvil attack on the southernmost Japanese carrier, the *Kaga*.[19]

The ships of the Kidō Butai had changed course from north to west to present their sterns to Waldron's attack, and now with Lindsey's approach from the south, they turned north again so that Lindsey, like Waldron, had to overtake a force that was steaming away from him. A few minutes after 10:00, Lindsey took seven planes out to the left; Ely took the other seven off to the right. Lindsey also radioed Jim Gray to "come on down," but though Lindsey and Gray *were* on the same radio frequency, Gray either did not hear the call or did not respond. One fellow pilot characterized Gray as "a L'il Abner type," by which he meant that he was "big, dark, and . . . a little square." But he was no coward. This was the same man who had led a section of five Wildcats against a Japanese airfield on Taroa back in February. When the guns had jammed on all the planes except his, Gray had completed his mission alone while under attack by eight Japanese fighters, returning to the *Enterprise* with more than forty bullet holes in his plane. On this occasion, though, he believed he had to choose between diving down to join the attack on the Kidō Butai and saving his own command.[20]

The reason was fuel. By now, Gray's Wildcats were perilously low on gas. The heavier Dash 4 Wildcats, issued to them in Pearl Harbor just before Task Force 16 departed for Point Luck, burned up gas much faster than the older Dash 3 models, and the climb to altitude had used up a lot of it. McInerny and the Wildcats of VF-8, which had launched at about the same time, had turned back toward the *Hornet* an hour before for the same reason. Gray had stayed at altitude, waiting for the dive-bombers under Mc-Clusky to show up. When they didn't, he had to choose between diving down to engage the Zeros and perhaps strafe the carriers or heading home to refuel. Gray later justified his decision not to join the fight by insisting that his planes were simply incapable of doing so. "In a dogfight," he wrote, "throttles are 'two blocked' at full, and propeller revolutions are at high R.P.M. Under this kind of demand, gasoline disappears as though there is a hole in the tank. We simply were now without that capability." Years later, Gray explained his dilemma to a group of Midway veterans. "If I went down to mix it up," he said, "all of us would have landed [in the water] out of gas, I had enough gas to get home, nothing more. So I elected to go home and refuel." He sent two messages back to the task force, one a sighting report describing the target as including two carriers, two battleships, and eight destroyers, thus perpetuating the notion that the Japanese might be operating in two carrier groups, and another, a few minutes later, announcing that he was "returning to the ship due to the lack of gas."[21]*

While Gray led his fighters back toward the *Enterprise*, Lindsey's Devastator pilots, like Waldron's, flew low and slow toward the Kidō Butai without fighter cover. The pilots of Torpedo Six, however, had three advantages that Waldron's men did not. The first was that Lindsey's pilots were mostly experienced veterans, having participated in several previous missions. They also benefited from the fact that when they flew in from the south, the Japanese Zeros were a dozen miles away, north and east of the Kidō Butai, finishing off the last of Waldron's planes, and it took them several crucial minutes to hurry back southward to fend off this new attack. Most important of all, however, was that many of the Zero pilots had used up much of their 20 mm cannon shells in smashing Waldron's squadron. Each Zero carried only sixty rounds of this heavy ammunition, and once it was gone, they had only their light (7.7 mm) machine guns.

The arriving Zeros found Ely's section first. Using the tactics that had worked so well against Waldron, they scissored back and forth over the Americans, making side runs in pairs. One of the surviving American pilots recalled that the Zeros attacked "from overhead and rear," but that the attacks "were not pressed home in face of free gun fire" from the American

---

* Gray's second report, sent at 10:00 a.m., caused a moment of consternation on board the *Enterprise*. John Lundstrom notes that both Spruance and Browning initially thought the report had come from McClusky, and they were appalled that he might be returning to the task force without attacking. McClusky sent in his own sighting report at 10:02, but it is not clear that it was received at the task force. In any case, responding to one or the other of these reports, at 10:08 Miles Browning grabbed the handset and hollered: "McClusky, attack! Attack immediately!"

backseat gunners. Nevertheless, one by one, the American torpedo planes began smoking and headed for the water. One exploded spectacularly when a 20 mm cannon shell detonated its torpedo. Soon, only two of Ely's seven planes were still aloft. Those two got close enough to drop their torpedoes, and despite heavy damage they turned and headed for home. The Zeros let them go and turned on Lindsey's section. By now, few of the Zeros had any 20 mm cannon shells left, and they had to rely on their machine guns. The American Devastators were struck again and again, and four of them, including Lindsey's, succumbed, but the American gunners were firing too and claimed at least one Zero. The three Devastators that survived this onslaught successfully launched their torpedoes. For all that effort and sacrifice, however, none of the American torpedoes found its mark. By 10:15, the five planes that had survived the strike, all of them shot through with dozens of 7.7 mm rounds, headed back for the *Enterprise*.[22]

Four of them made it; one of them was so riddled with bullet holes that the air crews simply pushed it over the side the next day. A fifth plane, that of Machinist Albert W. Winchell, an enlisted pilot, and his backseat gunner, Aviation Radioman Third Class Douglas M. Cossett, didn't get back at all. Their engine began to labor and vibrate, and Winchell realized he was losing power. He elected to land in the water. The two men scrambled into their little raft. Like Mitchell and the fighter pilots of VF-8, they battled sharks, sunburn, dehydration, and starvation while waiting to be found. For the first few days, whenever a distant plane flew past without sighting them, Winchell would shake his fist and say, "All right you bastards, see if I buy you a drink at the O Club." Soon it wasn't funny any more. After twelve days, they saw a submarine and signaled frantically until they saw that it was Japanese. Then they stopped waving and sat quietly in their raft, waiting to see what the sub would do. It came near and stopped. Members of its crew came out on deck to look at them for a few moments, then, apparently deciding that the Americans were not valuable enough to capture, and not worth shooting, they went below. The sub turned and moved away. After seventeen days of surviving on rainwater and an albatross that they had managed to catch and eat raw, they were picked up on June 21 by a PBY that had spotted their orange raft.[23]

Once again, Nagumo's Zeros had fought off a determined and coura-
geous attack by American torpedo bombers, and once again the Americans
had scored no hits. Nagumo may have been more relieved than exultant.
He still had to rotate his CAP, refuel and resupply the Zeros with 20 mm
ammunition, and complete the rearming of his strike force. But instead of a
respite, there came another attack by yet another American torpedo squadron. This time it was twelve Devastators from the *Yorktown* under Lieutenant Commander Lance "Lem" Massey.

After ordering Spruance to attack at 6:07 that morning, Fletcher had continued steaming eastward with the *Yorktown* task force until he recovered
the ten planes of the morning search. He had hoped that by then the patrolling PBYs might have found the two missing carriers of the Kidō Butai,
but there was still no word beyond Ady's initial sighting of "two carriers
and two battleships." Nimitz had received a number of combat reports from
the Midway planes that had attacked the Kidō Butai; none of them had indicated that there were more than two enemy carriers at the target location, and, as a result, the information that all four Japanese carriers were
operating together never reached the task force commanders. Even now, as
Fletcher steamed toward the known target to close the range, he anticipated
that at any moment a new sighting report would locate those two missing
carriers. His course brought him to within 160 miles of the estimated position of the "two carriers and two battleships" of the initial sighting, and by
8:30, he decided he could wait no longer. He would hold back Wally Short's
scouting squadron (VS-5, formerly VB-5) in case a late report located the
missing flattops, but he would send his other bombing squadron, Max Leslie's VB-3, and all the torpedo planes, plus a fighter escort, to attack the two
carriers that had been sighted.[24]

To calculate a course to the target, Fletcher depended heavily on his
staff air officer, Commander Murr E. Arnold, a 1923 Academy graduate
who had previously commanded the bombing squadron on *Yorktown*, and
who had been central to all the operations in the Coral Sea, including the
battle of May 7–8. By now, Fletcher and Arnold had developed a close
friendship and mutual confidence. In collaboration with Pete Pederson,

the Yorktown's air group commander (CYAG), Arnold calculated a course of 230 to the enemy. More important, he and Pederson sat down with all four of the squadron commanders to discuss it. Arnold and Pederson told the pilots that if they arrived at the coordinates and didn't find the enemy, it might mean that the Kidō Butai had turned north. Under those circumstances, they suggested, they should probably turn to the northeast. This, of course, was exactly right, but equally important was the fact that all the participants had a chance to talk it over fully beforehand. Pederson recalled that "they all agreed that this made good sense."[25]

Equally important was the decision by Fletcher and Buckmaster that morning to employ a "normal departure" rather than the deferred departure that Miles Browning had imposed on the carriers of Task Force 16. In a normal departure, the slower and most heavily laden planes launched first and proceeded immediately toward the target while the lighter and faster planes launched afterward and caught up with the others in a "running rendezvous." Consequently, the Dauntless dive-bombers of Leslie's VB-3, each carrying a 1,000-pound bomb, went first, followed in the same deck load by the Devastators of Lance "Lem" Massey's VT-3. Leslie's bombers were to circle for only fifteen minutes before heading off toward the target; Massey's torpedo planes were not to circle at all but to proceed with the mission as soon as they formed up. The speedy Wildcat fighters were launched in the second deck load and caught up with the attack planes en route. Because of this, there was a minimum of circling and waiting, and the entire air group successfully executed a running rendezvous on the way to the target.

Finally, the Yorktown's air attack differed from those of the other two carriers in the role assigned to the escorting fighter planes. The fighters of VF-3 were commanded by Lieutenant Commander John S. "Jimmy" Thach. Like most Academy grads, Thach had acquired his nickname during plebe summer. Thach's older brother James had graduated from the Academy in 1923, the same year that John became a plebe. The upperclassman who introduced the new plebe to the customs of the institution insisted on calling him Jimmy—his brother's nickname—perhaps as a reminder that he was nothing special. Like most Academy nicknames, it stuck. Jimmy Thach was a thoughtful and creative fighter pilot. Just before the war, he had developed an innovative defense maneuver for fighters flying in groups of four. He called it the "beam defense position," though it subsequently became universally known as the Thach weave. Thach had commanded VF-3 on the *Saratoga* until she was torpedoed in January and sent stateside for repairs. His squadron was then transferred to the *Lexington* until she was sunk in the Coral Sea. Now he and his squadron were on the *Yorktown*. A superstitious person might have worried about that track record, but Thach was a confident pilot with a "sunny disposition."[26]

Like his Naval Academy classmate Pat Mitchell on the *Hornet*, Thach thought that his fighters should go with the torpedo planes. But unlike John Waldron, who had lobbied hard for fighter cover, Lem Massey, the commander of VT-3, demurred. Because the Zeros were likely to be high, he proposed that the fighters go with the dive-bombers. No, no, said Leslie, the dive-bomber commander, the fighters should go with the torpedo planes because they were more vulnerable. Amused by this Alphonse-and-Gaston routine, Thach said, "How about letting me decide it?" Both Massey and Leslie said that was fine with them, but as it happened none of them got the final say. Instead, it was Pete Pederson, the CYAG, who made the decision.[27]

In his official report on the Battle of the Coral Sea, Pederson had recommended that in future engagements the escorting fighters "should take position up sun from, and at least 5–6,000 feet above the torpedo planes. From this position," he wrote, "they can readily observe any attack coming in and can dive down and break it up." At Midway, Pederson took his own advice and ordered that Thach's Wildcat fighters should fly in between the high-flying bombers and the low-flying Devastators at 5,000 to 6,000 feet. That way Thach would be high enough to dive down on any Zeros that attacked the torpedo planes, but not so high as to be out of touch with them. It also meant that Thach's planes didn't have to burn all that fuel climbing to 20,000 feet. As a result of collaborative decision making, battle experience, and efficient execution, the *Yorktown* air group was the only one that arrived over the target in a timely fashion and effected a coordinated attack without any argument, insubordination, or error.[28]

■ Jimmy Thach in the cockpit of his Wildcat. Thach was a creative tactical innovator, but with only six Wildcats, he was unable to protect the lumbering Devastators of Lem Massey's VT-3. (U.S. Naval Institute)

The planes of the *Yorktown* air group flew almost directly to the Kidō Butai and found it in just over an hour, at about 10:00 a.m. Massey's low-flying Devastators saw the Japanese first, led to the target by the black smoke generated by the Japanese cruisers. Massey led his squadron from 2,500 feet down to 150 feet as he prepared to make his torpedo run. Two and a half miles above him, Max Leslie, leading the dive-bombers, called him on the radio to ask if he was ready to start a coordinated attack. Massey replied that he was. Almost at once, however, Massey reported "frantically" that he was under attack by enemy fighters. As a result, in the end there was no coordinated attack, for, as one Devastator pilot put it, "We were forced to go in on our own attack as soon as possible to prevent all of the torpedo planes from being shot down."[29]

By now, despite all their success, some of the Zero pilots must have felt a bit whipsawed. Having fought off one American attack from the northeast, then another from the south, here was yet another from the northeast. And not only were many of the Zero pilots nearly out of the 20 mm ammunition, they were now facing new attackers that had a fighter escort.

That fighter escort consisted of only six Wildcats. Of the eighteen Wildcats on the *Yorktown*, Fletcher had kept six for CAP and reserved another six to accompany Wally Short's VS-5 for the attack on the two "missing" carriers if and when they were located. That decision annoyed Jimmy Thach; his defensive weave pattern could be executed only when his fighters maneuvered in groups of four. He complained to Arnold that six was not divisible by four. Arnold told him that the decision had come from the flag bridge. Thach, disappointed, was nonetheless determined to do the best he could. When his fighters caught up with Massey's torpedo bombers en route to the target, he signaled Warrant Officer Tom Cheek to position his two-plane section just behind the torpedo bombers while Thach himself, with a four-plane section, flew above them at about 5,500 feet.[30]

Thach first saw the outer screen of the Kidō Butai about ten miles out. Colored shell bursts began to explode around him—directional signals from the screening warships to guide the Zeros to the new target. And soon enough, they came. Thach tried to count them and figured "there were around twenty." In fact, there were more than twice that number. By now, Nagumo's four carriers had launched every Zero they had, including the reserves, a total of forty-two. Because Thach's Wildcats had launched last rather than first, and because they had flown at 5,500 feet instead of 20,000 feet, they arrived with enough fuel in their tanks to engage in aerial combat. But there was not a lot six Wildcats could do against forty-two Zeros.

The Japanese pilots attacked both the torpedo planes and the escorting fighters. Ensign Edgar Bassett, occupying the trailing spot in Thach's four-plane formation, was attacked from below, and his plane fell smoking into the sea. Bassett never got out of the cockpit. Other Zeros "were streaming in right past us and into the torpedo planes," Thach recalled. "The air was like a bee hive." He found he could not seize the initiative against such over-whelming numbers. Though his mission was to protect the torpedo planes, it was all he could do to defend himself from the swarming Zeros. Because only one of his surviving wingmen was familiar with his "beam defense maneuver," Thach had to improvise. When a Zero came up behind them, he led his three surviving planes in a sharp right turn, which forced the Zero pilot to attempt a side shot. Then, as the Zero followed him through the turn, Thach turned sharply left. As the swift Zero flew past them, it gave Thach a shot at him from behind. After a long burst from Thach's .50-caliber machine guns, the Zero exploded and went down. Despite their agility, and the deadliness of their 20 mm cannons, the poorly armored Zeros suc-cumbed quickly when they were hit.[31]

Nonetheless, the Zeros had the numbers, and they savaged Massey's torpedo bombers just as they had Waldron's and Lindsey's. Massey's plane was one of the first to be taken out. "It just exploded," Thach recalled.

Machinist Harry Corl, flying a Devastator in Massey's section, remembered that it "went down in flames with no hope of anybody surviving." The steadily decreasing number of torpedo planes tried to hold a straight course to give their own gunners, who were firing continuously, a steady platform. The value of having fighter cover was not that the Wildcats fended off the Zeros but rather that they occupied some of the Zeros that might otherwise have focused exclusively on the Devastators. Somewhat bitterly, Thach wrote in his after-action report that "six F4F-4 airplanes cannot prevent 20 or 30 Japanese VF from shooting down our slow torpedo planes."[32]

Thach's 21-year-old wingman, "Ram" Dibb, was the only pilot in the squadron to whom Thach had explained the principles of his "beam defense maneuver." Before flying out that day, they had agreed to try it if circumstances allowed. In the midst of the air battle, Thach heard Dibb call out, "There's a Zero on my tail! Get him off!" Dibb and Thach were flying side by side but widely separated, and in accordance with the plan, they turned toward each other. As they closed on one another, Thach ducked under Dibb's plane to come up face-to-face with the onrushing Zero. The two planes sped toward each other at a combined 500 miles per hour. "I was really angry," Thach remembered later. "I probably should have decided to duck under this Zero, but I lost my temper a little bit, and decided I'm going to keep my fire going into him and he's going to pull out." As the two planes flashed past each other, only feet apart, flames began spouting from the Zero, and Thach watched it fall away into the sea.[33]

The five planes of Massey's squadron that survived this onslaught dropped their torpedoes, turned, and headed for home, seeking cloud cover to hide from the relentless Zeros. Wilhelm Esders recalled that the Zeros "continued to make passes at us" for more than twenty miles before they finally gave up the pursuit and returned to the Kidō Butai. Esders planned to use his YE homing system to plot a course for the Yorktown, and asked his backseat radioman/gunner, Aviation Radioman Second Class Robert B. Brazier, to change the radio coils so he could activate the system. Brazier had been hit three times and had bullets through both legs and one in his back. He replied weakly that he didn't think he could do it. Several minutes later, however, Brazier called Esders on the intercom to report that he had changed the coils. Because of that, Esders was able to get a signal from *Yorktown* and he headed for home. As he approached the task force, however, he saw that the *Yorktown* was herself under air attack (it was 12:40 by now), and, virtually out of gas, he had to ditch in the water about ten miles away. He managed to get Braziers out of the cockpit and into the raft, but Braziers' wounds were too serious for him to survive such rough handling; he died in the raft. A Japanese dive-bomber returning from his attack on the *Yorktown* flew past and turned back for a second look. Esders ducked under the water and waited for the inevitable strafing. But instead, Lieutenant Junior Grade Art Brassfield, flying CAP over Task Force 17, came to the rescue, shooting down the Val dive-bomber, his fourth of the day. Esders was picked up the next day by the destroyer *Hammann*.[34]

Of the forty-one Devastator torpedo planes launched from three American aircraft carriers that morning, only four made it back to their carriers, and one of those was so badly damaged as to be of no further service. Three more ditched in the water trying to make it back to the carriers, though their crews were later rescued. Despite those horrific losses, not a single torpedo struck home. Indeed, since 7:00 that morning, the Americans had hurled a total of ninety-four airplanes at the Kidō Butai in eight separate and uncoordinated attacks, and not a single bomb or torpedo had found its mark. The Japanese had shot down most of those planes and sent the rest fleeing. Nagumo had still not managed to get the planes of his own strike force up onto the flight deck for launch. To do so, all he needed was a short respite.

He was not going to get it. Three miles above the handful of retiring American torpedo planes, Max Leslie's dive-bombers from *Yorktown* were preparing to attack, astonished that there was no enemy CAP over the target. Simultaneously, and coincidentally, the long-delayed bombing and scouting squadrons from *Enterprise* under Wade McClusky were arriving from the south. It was 10:20 a.m., and the battle had reached a pivotal moment.

**14**

# The Tipping Point
## (7:00 a.m. to 10:30 a.m.)

While Japanese and American pilots had a frenetic morning on June 4, the submarine forces of both sides were considerably less active. The Japanese had committed nineteen submarines to the campaign, and the Americans twelve. Yet so far those subs had played no role in the engagement. As noted previously, the Japanese submarines got a late start leaving Japan, and a layover in Kwajalein put them hopelessly behind schedule; some were further delayed by the failed effort to reprise Operation K. The consequence was that the submarine cordons that Yamamoto counted on to give the Kidō Butai advance warning of the approach of the American carriers were not fully established until June 4, by which time the carriers of both sides were already engaged.

For their part, the Americans committed a dozen submarines to the operation, yet to this point they had played no active role, or indeed any role, in the battle. The American subs were simply too slow to catch up to the swift Japanese carriers. Most American submarines could make 17–20 knots on the surface but only about eight knots submerged. Since the

Japanese surface ships operated routinely at 20–25 knots, they could simply outrun the American subs. Nimitz hoped that his submarines could be vectored toward enemy vessels that had been crippled by air attack, and after several of the planes operating from Midway reported that they had left Japanese warships burning, he ordered several submarines toward the coordinates. None of those reports proved accurate, however, and so far there had been no cripples for the American subs to attack. An old submarine hand himself, Nimitz lamented in his battle report that "all submarines were ordered to close on the enemy Striking Force but the only submarine attack of the day was by *Nautilus*." That one exception, however, proved to be very important indeed.[1]

At 7:00 a.m., as *Hornet* and *Enterprise* were preparing to launch their air groups, the USS *Nautilus* (SS-168), was running on the surface 150 miles north of Midway in the middle of a fan-shaped semicircle of ten submarines that Nimitz had placed north and west of the atoll. Launched back in 1930, the *Nautilus* had just completed an overhaul on the West Coast. She had arrived in Pearl Harbor on April 27 and put to sea on her first war patrol a month later, on May 24, four days before the *Hornet* and *Enterprise* left for Point Luck. If the *Nautilus* was not a new boat, she was a big boat. At 350 feet long and displacing more than 2,700 tons, she was as big as many destroyers. When commissioned in 1931, she had been the largest submarine in the world. She was also heavily armed. Her two big 6-inch guns (one on the foredeck and another aft of the conning tower) were more powerful than most of the guns on a destroyer. Her principal weapons, however, were the three dozen torpedoes that could be fired from her ten torpedo tubes. These torpedoes were the Mark 14 variety with the flawed detonators, though that fact was still unacknowledged by the Bureau of Ordnance.

The commanding officer of the *Nautilus* was 37-year-old Lieutenant Commander William H. Brockman, Jr., yet another member of the Naval Academy class of 1927. Brockman was a big man—at the Academy he had played both football and lacrosse. He no longer competed in athletics and had begun to put on weight. He had a round face, a genial manner, and a ready smile. He was also a determined warrior.[2]

■ Lieutenant Commander William H. Brockman, Jr., was the skipper of the American submarine *Nautilus* (SS-168) at Midway. His prolonged duel with Commander Watanabe's destroyer *Arashi* proved crucial. (U.S. Naval Institute)

At exactly 6:58, the topside lookout on the *Nautilus* reported a northbound flight of six aircraft. They were flying low, he reported, but aside from determining that they were friendlies, the lookout could not identify the airplane type. They were, in fact, the six new Avenger torpedo planes of VT-8 under "Fieb" Fieberling, en route to make the first of five attacks on the Kidō Butai by Midway-based aircraft. Minutes later, the lookout reported black puffs of antiaircraft gunfire bursts in the sky to the north, and what looked like smoke from falling bombs. Clearly the American planes had found a worthwhile target. Brockman ordered his crew to general quarters and altered course to approach what could only be a Japanese surface force.[3]

At the time, the Kidō Butai was still steaming southward toward Midway and was therefore on a converging course with the northbound *Nautilus*. At five minutes to eight, with the *Nautilus* now at periscope depth, Brockman spotted the masts of big ships "dead ahead." He had little time to study them, for at almost the same moment, a Japanese Zero, spotting the shadow of his sub just below the surface, began a strafing run, and Brockman had to dive. As he maneuvered underwater, he could hear the ominous pinging sound of echo ranging—what the Americans called sonar—which meant that enemy surface ships were searching for him. Nevertheless, he crept back up to periscope depth to have a look. Through his viewfinder, he saw "a formation of four ships." He was pretty sure that one of them was a battleship and that the other three were cruisers. They were, in fact, the battleship *Kirishima*, the cruiser *Nagara*, and two destroyers—the advance screen of the Kidō Butai. Deciding to attack the battleship, which was on his starboard bow, Brockman maneuvered to obtain an angle on the bow. As he did so, however, the wake created by his periscope breaking the surface—called a feather—was spotted by one of the circling Zeros and he was again forced to dive. After that, a ship that Brockman identified as a cruiser of the *Jintsu* class closed on his position and began to drop depth charges. That attacking surface ship was actually the destroyer *Arashi*, skippered by Commander Watanabe Yasumasa, and at that moment Brockman and Watanabe began a duel that would last almost two hours and have a profound effect on the outcome of the Battle of Midway.[4]

Between 8:00 and 8:10, while Nagumo was contemplating his response to the news that there was at least one American carrier to the north of him, and while his Zeros fought off the attack by Joe Henderson's dive-bombers, Watanabe and the *Arashi* dropped five depth charges on the *Nautilus*. Japanese depth charges were smaller than the American version, with a 220-pound charge (American depth charges had a 290-pound charge), but they were deadly enough to the fragile hull of a submarine. The real weakness of Japanese depth charges, however, was that they had only two depth settings: forty feet and two hundred feet. Since Watanabe knew that the American boat had not had time to go deep, he almost certainly set the charges for forty feet. Brockman went to ninety feet and stayed there, but while that protected him from the worst effects of the depth charges, it also meant that the valuable targets above him had a chance to speed past him at 25 knots or more. Even if Watanabe did not destroy this pesky American sub, he would be doing his job if he simply kept it underwater, where its top speed was only eight knots, and where it could not fire any torpedoes, until after the Kidō Butai had moved on.[5]

This was the first time that anyone on board the *Nautilus* had experienced a depth-charge attack, and it was a particularly unpleasant experience. First of all, it was impossible to fight back. "Once you have to go down," one sub skipper recalled, "you don't have any offensive weapon. You just feel like

you're a sitting duck." Second, the aural and physical sensations were terrifying. When a depth charge exploded, the concussion hit the boat twice.
First came the shock wave, which made a sharp metallic clang, "like a hammer hitting the hull." Then, a second or two later, came the sound wave. That
was much louder—a giant wham—but if you heard it, you could breathe
out, because it meant the shock wave had not opened the hull of the boat.
Indeed, as long as there were two distinct sounds for each detonation—
the metallic bang of the shock wave, followed by the much louder boom
of the sound wave—the charge had exploded at a relatively safe distance.
It was when the two sounds came close together that there was cause for
worry. And if they occurred simultaneously, it was probably the last thing
anyone on board ever heard. In this case, the two sounds were separate and
distinct, and Brockman estimated that the Japanese were dropping their
charges about 1,000 yards away.[6]

After the explosions stopped, Brockman again heard the pinging sound
of underwater echo ranging as Watanabe continued to search for him. The
Japanese skipper waited seven minutes to see if any debris floated to the
surface or if his echo ranging could locate the American sub, and then he
dropped six more depth charges. During this second attack, the concussion
from one explosion sheared off the retaining pin on one of the torpedoes
on the *Nautilus*. The torpedo's propeller began spinning, generating a loud,
high-pitched whine that Brockman feared would be picked up by Japanese
sensors. At the same time, bubbles of escaping exhaust gas left a telltale
mark on the surface. There was also a chance that the spinning propeller
would arm the warhead, which had a magnetic exploder. No one on board
the *Nautilus* knew for sure whether the sub's own metal hull would trigger
the detonator. There was nothing to do but wait it out. As it happened, the
warhead did not explode, though Brockman continued to worry that the
whine of the spinning propeller would betray their position.[7]

Brockman kept the *Nautilus* at ninety feet, at which depth he hoped its
shadow would not be seen by circling enemy planes. Guided, perhaps, by
the noise of the torpedo running hot inside the *Nautilus*, Watanabe closed
in and dropped nine more depth charges. The first was fairly close, though
each successive one exploded further away. When the pinging faded and

the torpedo's propeller finally stopped running, Brockman eased back up to periscope depth to have another look. When he put his face to the rubber gasket around the viewfinder, what he saw shocked him. While he had played possum at ninety feet, the Kidō Butai, still moving southward, had closed with his position. He now found himself in the middle of the Japanese fleet. As he peered through the lens, he saw an image that he had "never experienced in peacetime practices." As one of his officers put it, "There were ships all over the place." They were moving at high speed and signaling to one another by flag hoist and blinker signal; searchlights from several of them were aimed directly at his periscope. The battleship *Kirishima* fired her broadside at the feather of his periscope, and the *Arashi* charged in again, this time from astern. Despite all that, Brockman made a quick estimate of the course and speed of the battleship before dropping the periscope. He estimated the range at 4,500 yards, which was the maximum range for the Mark 14 torpedo at the high-speed setting. He reported the angle on the bow at 80 degrees and her speed at 25 knots. He fed that information into the boat's torpedo data computer,* and when it generated a solution, he ordered "Fire one!" and then almost immediately, "Fire two!" with a one-degree offset on the second torpedo. Then he dove. The torpedo room reported that the number 1 tube did not fire, and only one torpedo was running. He did not know that as soon as he had fired, the battleship changed course away from him; in accordance with doctrine, the Japanese battleship skipper was presenting his ship's stern to the threat to narrow the target and extend the range. And, once again, here came the *Arashi*.[8]

The sound of enemy echo ranging was now "continuous and accurate" as Brockman dove to 150 feet, and as the boat angled downward, depth charges began exploding all around him. The explosions, he reported later, "sounded like a severe hammer blow on the hull." Nonetheless, the sub's hull remained intact, and after waiting several minutes Brockman began once again to ease back up to periscope depth. The battleship and the other large ships were still in sight, but out of range. Only the *Arashi* remained

---

* The Mark III Torpedo Data Computer (TDC) was an early electromagnetic analog computer used for calculating fire-control solutions on American submarines.

nearby, still echo sounding; she had clearly been left behind to hunt him down. Brockman remained submerged for ten more minutes, then took another look. The battleship was now out of sight, but almost due north and only about eight miles away he spotted the unmistakable profile of an aircraft carrier. He noted that it "was changing course continually," and that it "was overhung by anti-aircraft bursts." Though Brockman could not know it, the Zeros from the Kidō Butai were chasing off the last of the American attackers from Midway, and the carriers were maneuvering to avoid them.[9]

Brockman could not surface to chase the carrier because the *Arashi* was still lurking above him. He decided to take care of his tormentor first, maneuvering to fire a torpedo at the *Arashi*. Watanabe was expecting it and easily avoided it. Moreover, the wake of that torpedo gave Watanabe a guide to the *Nautilus's* likely position, and the *Arashi* closed in to drop six more depth charges. Brockman noted laconically that "these were more accurately placed than previous charges." Brockman ordered the *Nautilus* back down to 150 feet (her maximum depth was 300). He then changed course and ordered silence about the boat while it crept away. Watanabe guessed that Brockman had gone deep and adjusted the settings on his depth charges. Two more exploded quite near the *Nautilus*; gauges jumped, lights flickered, and deck plates rattled—but the hull remained intact.[10]

This time Brockman stayed down for forty minutes. He did not know that at almost the very moment that he dove—around 9:17—Nagumo and the Kidō Butai had changed course and turned north. While Brockman was submerged, the Zeros flying CAP were busy tearing apart the American torpedo planes. At five minutes to ten, Brockman could no longer hear the noise of echo ranging. He eased back up to periscope depth. As he turned the view finder around 360 degrees, he saw that "the entire formation first seen, including the attacking cruiser [*Arashi*] had departed." "The carrier previously seen was no longer in sight." Brockman no doubt feared that he had lost his chance to fire a torpedo at an enemy carrier, though later that day he would have a second chance. In fact, however, without knowing it he had already made his greatest contribution to American victory.[11]

Watanabe and the *Arashi* had persecuted the *Nautilus* for nearly two hours—from 8:00 to almost 10:00. When the Kidō Butai turned north,

Watanabe had stayed behind, determined to keep his foe submerged and therefore impotent. Just before 10:00, not having seen or heard anything of the American sub for forty minutes, and with the Kidō Butai well away over the northern horizon, Watanabe concluded that he had done his job. He may also have run out of depth charges. The *Arashi* carried thirty-six depth charges, and Brockman reported twenty-eight explosions, plus another attack by an unspecified number. None of those depth charges had proved fatal, but this hardly mattered, for even if the American sub was still down there, by now it would never be able to catch up to the Kidō Butai. Watanabe ordered the helm over and turned the *Arashi* northward. To catch up with the main body, now steaming to the northeast at 25 knots, he would have to go at nearly full speed, which for the *Arashi* was 35 knots. At that speed, his ship generated a broad white V-shaped wake.

---

While Brockman dueled with Watanabe, Wade McClusky's thirty-three dive-bombers from the *Enterprise* were winging their way southwestward toward a presumed intercept of the Kidō Butai. McClusky had been a naval aviator his entire career, most of it as a fighter pilot. Based on his looks alone, few would have picked him out as one. Short and stout, he had neatly parted dark hair, a generous nose, full lips, and just a hint of a double chin. McClusky had been an effective commander of Fighting 6 during the several raids on the Marshall Islands, Wake, and Marcus Islands. Then in April he had fleeted up to become the commander, *Enterprise* air group, or CEAG. He was the oldest active pilot on board, having turned forty just three days before on June 1.

As CEAG, McClusky traded his Wildcat for a Dauntless, and his airplane was in the lead as the two squadrons of dive-bombers flew toward the presumed coordinates of the Japanese carrier force. McClusky flew with the seventeen planes of Earl Gallaher's Scouting Six, with two of those planes acting as his wingmen. Each plane was armed with one 500-pound bomb and two 100-pound bombs under the wings. Behind and above this formation were the fifteen planes of Dick Best's Bombing Six—each of his planes armed with one 1,000-pound bomb. Early on, one of the planes in Gallaher's squadron developed mechanical problems and had to return to the ship, so in the end, a total of thirty-two bombers, including McClusky's, flew to the target.[12]

■ Lieutenant Commander Clarence Wade
McClusky was the air group commander on
the USS *Enterprise* and led the strike of VS-6
and VB-6 against *Kaga* and *Akagi* on June 4.
(U.S. Naval Institute)

Visibility was good, with light winds and only light scattered clouds between 1,500 and 2,500 feet. For more than an hour, this two-tier formation
flew toward the southwest. Best recalled that he could see the ocean "getting
a lighter and lighter blue then turning to a light green" as the water shoaled
toward Midway. He could see the plume of black smoke from the Midway
airfield and wondered if they had gone too far to the south. At around 9:20
McClusky arrived in the general area where he had calculated that the Kidō
Butai would be. Nothing was below him but empty ocean. At that moment,
seventy or so miles to the north, John Waldron was ordering his torpedo
bombers to attack the Kidō Butai, but neither McClusky nor anyone else
in his bomber group picked up his transmissions. Moreover, because of the
circling and waiting above the *Enterprise* before Spruance had turned them
loose, as well as the long climb to altitude, the fuel gauges on some of the
bombers already showed less than half full. Ensign Lew Hopkins, in Best's
squadron, looked at his fuel gauge and concluded that it was going to be a
one-way flight. "I knew, and most everybody else knew," he recalled later,
"that we didn't have enough fuel to get back." Despite that, McClusky decided to continue the search until the fuel situation became hopeless. Had
Spruance not decided to send him off without waiting for the Devastators,
he would not have been able to do even that.[13]

McClusky turned the formation slightly to the right and flew due west for thirty-five miles; then he turned right again to the northwest, intending to conduct a standard box search. He scanned the horizon eagerly for a sign of any surface ships, his binoculars "practically glued" to his eyes. After fifteen more minutes, he turned right again to the northeast. By now, fuel had become a serious problem, especially for the pilots in Best's squadron, who were lugging the big 1,000-pound bombs. Two of them, Ensign Eugene Greene and Ensign Troy Schneider, fell out of the formation, out of fuel, and landed in the water. Schneider and his radioman/gunner were rescued three days later, but Greene and his backseat gunner were never found.[14]

Nor was fuel the only problem. Best's wing man, Lieutenant Junior Grade Ed Kroeger, used hand signals to indicate to Best that his cylinder had run out of oxygen. Best could simply have signaled Kroeger to drop down to a lower level where he could breathe the air without an oxygen mask, but he did not want to break up what was left of his squadron. Instead he removed his own mask, holding it up to show Kroeger that he had done so and then began a gradual descent, leading his thirteen remaining planes down to 15,000 feet where the air was still thin, but breathable. That downward glide put him well below McClusky and Gallaher, and about a quarter mile behind them.[15]

Then, at about 9:55, well north of the plotted intercept position, McClusky noticed a ship, all by itself, proceeding northward at great speed, its bow wave making a broad wake that looked for all the world like a white arrow painted on the surface of the blue sea. It was, of course, Commander Watanabe in the *Arashi*, racing northward at 35 knots to catch up to the main body. McClusky guessed at once that it was a laggard from the Kidō Butai, and using that V-shaped bow wave as a guide, he altered course and followed the arrow just east of due north. Ten minutes later, at 10:05, he saw dark specks on the horizon ahead of him. As he flew closer, the specks resolved themselves into surface ships. Thanks to Brockman's persistence, Watanabe had provided the crucial signpost that enabled McClusky's air group to find the Kidō Butai.[16]

By now, the box formation of the four Japanese carriers had completely disintegrated. Each ship had maneuvered independently to avoid the persistent torpedo attacks of the Americans, and any resemblance to the original formation had long since disappeared. The southernmost of the four carriers, and therefore the first one spotted by McClusky's bombers, was the giant *Kaga*. Two miles ahead of it and "five to seven miles" off to the right was Nagumo's flagship, *Akagi*. Another fourteen miles beyond them, the *Hiryū* was under attack from Lem Massey's torpedo planes, and another six miles beyond her and all but out of sight was the *Sōryū*. Cruisers, battleships, and destroyers maneuvered between and around these four behemoths apparently at random.[17]

Unbeknownst to McClusky, Max Leslie's dive-bomber squadron from *Yorktown* was nearing the Kidō Butai at the same moment. Though the *Yorktown* planes had launched almost two hours after McClusky's, the more efficient launch sequence and the more accurate course of her air group put her bombers over the target at the same moment. (It is noteworthy that while the *Hornet*'s air group flew some eighty miles north of the Kidō Butai, and the *Enterprise* bomber group flew eighty miles south of it, the *Yorktown*'s air group flew almost directly to it.) Despite the near simultaneous arrival of McClusky and Leslie over the Kidō Butai, the Americans did not conduct a coordinated attack. McClusky approached from the south and Leslie from the east, each of them unaware that the other was there. Had they targeted the same ships, there might have been great confusion when they intruded into one another's air space. Instead, each targeted the first carrier he saw: Leslie the *Sōryū*, and McClusky the *Kaga* and *Akagi*, and because those carriers were widely dispersed, the Americans did not interfere with each other.[18]

There was considerable confusion, however, between the two squadrons of McClusky's air group. According to doctrine, each squadron was to attack a different capital ship. To do that, the lead squadron, which was Gallaher's, should fly past the first carrier and attack the more distant one, while the trailing squadron (Best's) attacked the near target. That would ensure that the attacks occurred nearly at the same time, so that the attack on the first ship did not alert the second. Another element of American dive-bombing doctrine was that the planes carrying the heavier 1,000-pound bombs should attack the nearest target simply because of their heavier

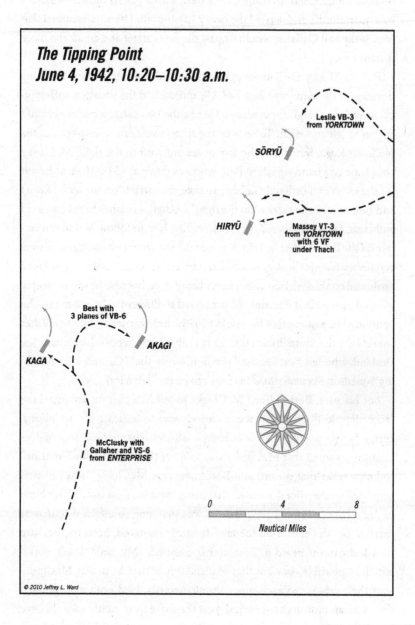

**The Tipping Point**
**June 4, 1942, 10:20–10:30 a.m.**

Leslie VB-3
from *YORKTOWN*

*SŌRYŪ*

*HIRYŪ*

Massey VT-3
from *YORKTOWN*
with 6 VF
under Thach

Best with
3 planes of VB-6

*AKAGI*

*KAGA*

McClusky with
Gallaher and VS-6
from *ENTERPRISE*

0       4       8

Nautical Miles

© 2010 Jeffrey L. Ward

ordnance load. On both counts, Dick Best, whose planes trailed Gallaher's by a quarter mile and carried the heavy 1,000-pound bombs, assumed that McClusky and Gallaher would fly past the first carrier and attack the more distant one.

But McClusky, the former fighter pilot, had not internalized bombing doctrine in the same way Best had. He approached the situation with typical American straightforwardness. He saw the two carriers not as near and far but as left and right. To be sure, the *Akagi* was a few miles ahead of the plodding *Kaga*, but it was also five or six miles off to the right. McClusky could not give hand signals to Best, who was down at 15,000 feet, so he got on the radio and ordered Gallaher to take the carrier "on the left" (*Kaga*) and Best to take the carrier "on the right" (*Akagi*). Gallaher heard him loud and clear. He remembered McClusky telling him to follow him to the carrier on the left and that he told Best "to take the carrier on the right." That is certainly what McClusky intended. But for such a simple order, it produced profound confusion. Best either never heard it, or, because he was so deeply steeped in standard doctrine, he processed it differently. In either case, he continued to assume that he would take the near carrier and that Gallaher would take the more distant one. In his subsequent report, Lieutenant Joe Penland, who led Best's second division, wrote that "Commander Bombing Squadron Six *understood* his target to be the 'left hand' CV."[19]

For his part, Best radioed McClusky to tell him that he was attacking "according to doctrine." It was a curious way to indicate his intentions, certainly less specific than McClusky's left-right distinction. Such a declaration assumed that McClusky was sufficiently familiar with "doctrine" to know what that meant, and Best knew that McClusky "was not well informed on bomber doctrine." That being the case, Best would have been better advised simply to say that he was planning to attack the "closest carrier," or "the carrier on the left." It hardly mattered, however, because McClusky never heard it. Best later speculated, "My radio didn't work," which is possible, but another explanation is that Best and McClusky sent their reports to each other simultaneously. Had both men pressed the transmit buttons on their radios at the same time, neither would have heard the other. In any event, this confusion meant that *both* squadrons under McClusky's command prepared to dive on the *Kaga*. Though the Americans had gained a great advantage by arriving over the Kidō Butai at a critical moment, the confusion in assigning targets threatened to throw that advantage away.[20]

Flying at 15,000 feet, Best turned his squadron toward the *Kaga* and "put the planes in echelon so that they were no more than 150 feet apart." His pilots prepared to dive by shifting to low blower and low prop pitch, cracking open the hatches of their cockpits to reduce the likelihood of the windscreen fogging up, and opening their split flaps. Best did not know that a mile above him, Gallaher's pilots were doing the same thing until, just as he was about to push over, the sixteen bombers of VS-6, plus McClusky's, all came flashing down past him, avoiding a catastrophic collision only by a matter of yards. In Best's words: "God! Here came McClusky and Gallaher from Scouting Six pouring right in front of me." Best's first thought was: "They had jumped my target!" Thinking fast, he closed his flaps and waggled his ailerons as a signal to the rest of his squadron to hold back. Too late. Already committed to the dive, ten of the pilots of VB-6 joined the onslaught on the *Kaga*. They almost certainly never saw Best's last-minute effort to recall them. Only Best's two wingmen, Kroeger and Ensign Frederick Weber, were close enough to see his frantic signals and hold up. As a result, no fewer than twenty-seven Dauntless dive-bombers plunged out of the sky to target the *Kaga*.[21]

Until that moment, the Japanese on *Kaga* had been entirely unaware of this new threat. Lacking radar, they were fully dependent on the sharp eyes of their lookouts. This time, however, the lookouts on the screening vessels had let them down. At 10:22, with the first of the bombers already screaming down toward them at 250 knots, first one, and then many observers on the *Kaga* pointed skyward and shouted "*Kyukoka!*" ("Dive-bombers!") Jimmy Thach, who was still trying to fend off the Zeros from Lem Massey's few remaining torpedo bombers, looked up and saw the sun glinting off silver wings. To him "it looked like a beautiful silver waterfall, those dive-bombers coming down."[22]

Because the Zeros were still focused on Massey's torpedo bombers, they were unable to interfere even minimally with the attack. Moreover, the guns of *Kaga*'s antiair battery were all still at low angle. With the shouted warnings, the gun crews furiously began to crank the ship's sixteen five-inch guns up to the vertical position, but it took only about forty seconds for the first of the plunging American bombers to reach the release point. The skipper of the *Kaga*, Captain Okada Jisaku, ordered the ship hard to port in order to throw them off. However, the 42,000-ton *Kaga* was slow to respond and had barely begun her turn when the first bombs came hurtling down.[23]

The first three bombs all missed, but the fourth plane, piloted by Earl Gallaher himself, placed its 500-pound bomb squarely on the flight deck of the big flattop. It was the first time all morning that American ordnance had found a target. The 500-pound bombs had a fuse with a 0.01-second delay, so that it pierced the flight deck before exploding in the crew's berthing compartments, starting the first of many fires that would eventually consume the big ship. That hit was followed by two more misses, and then by several hits in succession. One bomb struck on or near the forward elevator and penetrated to the hangar deck; another smashed into the flight deck amidships, and yet another hit squarely on the *Kaga*'s small island structure, killing Captain Okada and most of his senior officers, rendering the *Kaga* leaderless.[24]

As with the attack on the *Shōhō* a month before, the bombers simply overwhelmed the *Kaga*. Following these four hits by 500-pound bombs from Gallaher's squadron, the ten bombers of Best's VB-6 added several 1,000-pound bombs to the smoking wreck. Thach claimed later, "I'd never seen such superb dive bombing. It looked to me like almost every bomb hit." Watching from 12,000 feet, Best tried to count the number of hits. "They were hitting from stem to stern," he recalled later. At "four or five second intervals there would be a fresh blast and fire would come up and smoke would pour out." At least one 1,000-pound bomb exploded on the packed hangar deck crowded with fully fueled planes armed with torpedoes. The historians Jon Parshall and Anthony Tully estimate that a total of 80,000 pounds of ordnance "lay scattered" there. Some of it was on the big Kate torpedo bombers, some was still on the bomb carts, and some was "simply shoved against the hangar bulkheads." One of the first bomb hits had wrecked both of the *Kaga*'s fire mains, and the damage-control parties were helpless against the raging fires. The leaderless ship became an inferno fed by explosives and aviation fuel. A series of secondary explosions rocked the big carrier—one of them so powerful it sent the *Kaga*'s forward elevator platform spiraling up hundreds of feet into the air.[25]

While most of McClusky's dive-bombers assailed the doomed *Kaga*, Best led his three-plane section toward the carrier "on the right," which was Nagumo's flagship, *Akagi.* The three Dauntless bombers had dropped down to 12,000 feet before Best had been able to recall them, so now they had to climb back up to 14,000 feet for the attack run. As Best climbed, he was astonished that "there was no gunfire, no fighters aloft." Thanks to the sacrifice of the torpedo squadrons, the circling Zeros were all at low altitude and the ships' antiaircraft guns all at low angle. As a result, Best's three planes were entirely unmolested. Nonetheless, it was uncertain what his three airplanes might accomplish against the flagship. Despite his experience attacking targets in the Marshalls, and on Wake and Marcus Islands, this was the first time Best had ever attacked a carrier. Having only three planes meant that he could not order a conventional echelon attack or divide his command into sections to attack from different angles. Moreover, the fuel

■ Lieutenant Richard Best commanded Bombing Six (VB-6) in the Battle of Midway. He and Norman "Dusty" Kleiss of VS-6 were the only pilots to land bombs on two Japanese carriers in the same day. (U.S. Navy)

situation dictated that there was no time to maneuver for a bows-on attack. Best and his two wingmen therefore approached the *Akagi* from abeam, which meant they would have only the carrier's relatively narrow 100-foot width rather than its 850-foot length as a target. Even a slight misjudgment would result in a near miss rather than a hit.[26]

His two wingmen tucked in behind their commanding officer, one on each side, and flew toward the *Akagi* in a shallow V formation. Best signaled, and they opened their flaps and nosed over into "a long easy dive." It was "a calm placid morning," he recalled, and he remembered thinking that it felt just like "regular individual battle practice drill." He put his bombsight in the middle of the *Akagi*'s flight deck, just forward of her small island. Like *Kaga*, *Akagi* had only a few Zero fighters on her flight deck because she was still actively rotating CAP for the air battle. As he dove, Best saw a Zero taking off to rejoin the CAP. He remembered thinking, "*Best, if you're a real hero, when you've dropped your bomb, you'll aileron around and shoot that son-of-a-bitch.*" But he knew that his job was to bomb carriers, not shoot at fighters. There were other Japanese flattops out there, and he decided that after he hit this one he would head back to the *Enterprise* to get another bomb.[27]

Best released his bomb at about 1,500 feet. His wingmen dropped at almost the same moment. Though doctrine called for them to retire at once at low level, Best could not resist turning to look back and see the results. He watched his 1,000-pound bomb land squarely in the middle of the *Akagi*'s flight deck. Other explosions erupted at her bow and stern as well, and he subsequently reported "three 1000 lb bomb hits." In fact, however, the bombs from Kroeger and Weber had both hit close alongside. While they probably opened up holes in the skin of the *Akagi*'s hull below the water line, Best's was the only direct hit. But it was enough.[28]

Best's 1,000-pound bomb penetrated the flight deck and exploded on the *Akagi*'s crowded hangar deck. The immediate damage was extensive. The secondary damage was catastrophic. As on the *Kaga*, *Akagi*'s hangar deck was crowded with big Kate torpedo bombers, eighteen of them, every one with fuel tanks filled to the top and armed with the big Type 91 torpedoes. Other ordnance lay on the carts and on the racks along the bulkhead. Within minutes, that ordnance began to cook off. Once the explosions started, the aviation fuel from the wrecked planes fed the fires. Under most circumstances, a big carrier like *Akagi* could be expected to absorb four or five bomb hits and still function, but Best's one bomb had hit at just the right moment and in just the right place to do the most damage. By 10:25, both *Kaga* and *Akagi* were burning out of control. Ensign Weber's near miss astern had jammed the *Akagi*'s rudder hard over, so that she continued to turn in a tight circle out of control, burning furiously.[29]

Best did not try to shoot down the enemy Zero after dropping his bomb. Having descended to low altitude, however, there were now plenty of them around. Several flashed by just below him as they continued to target the hapless Devastators of Lem Massey's VT-3 from *Yorktown*. Instead of lingering to join the fray, Best led his three planes eastward back toward the *Enterprise*. His last view of the Kidō Butai left him with the impression that "everything was blowing up."[30]

The death throes of the *Kaga* and *Akagi* were terrifying and spectacular, but there were two more Japanese carriers a dozen miles away with enough striking power to turn the battle around.

While Best was diving on the *Akagi*, twenty miles to the north Max Leslie was preparing to dive on the *Sōryū*. There was some initial confusion there, too. When Leslie led the seventeen bombers of VB-3 away from the *Yorktown* at 9:00 that morning, he had assumed that Wally Short's VS-5 was right behind him, unaware that Fletcher had decided to keep Short's squadron on board as a reserve. Consequently, when the Kidō Butai came into view at about 10:00, Leslie called Short on the radio and ordered him to attack the carrier to the west (*Hiryū*) while he took the other (*Sōryū*). He got no reply. Next he called Massey to ask if he was ready to begin a coordinated attack. Massey replied that he was. Then, almost immediately, Massey reported that he was under furious attack from Japanese Zeros. Massey's radio went dead. Leslie concluded that the planned coordinated strike was not going to happen and decided he "had better get going before our presence was discovered." While Massey's surviving torpedo bombers attempted to fight their way through the intercept to attack the *Hiryū*, and

Jimmy Thach tried out his "beam defense maneuver" in their support, Leslie took his bombers off to the right, to approach the *Sōryū* from out of the sun. He gave the signal and pushed over from 14,500 feet at 10:25.[31]

Leslie led the attack even though by now his plane no longer carried a bomb. The planes of his squadron had recently been equipped with a new electrical release that was supposed to make dive-bombing more accurate. Instead of pulling back on a lever, which sometimes threw off the bomb's trajectory, all the pilot had to do now was press a button on top of his control stick. The electrical release system was not armed during takeoffs, so after departing the *Yorktown*, Leslie prepared to arm it. Much to his astonishment, when he did so, his bomb dropped away. Three other pilots in the squadron did the same thing, and fifteen thousand feet below them four bombs exploded on the surface, startling the pilots of the torpedo planes and their escorting Wildcats. Leslie broke radio silence to warn the other pilots not to arm their release devices. As a result of this mishap, four of his seventeen bombers had lost their principal weapon. They flew on anyway, Leslie because it was his command, and the others because they could still use their .50-caliber machine guns to strafe the enemy.[32]

When Leslie pushed over at 10:25, the crew of the *Sōryū* was on full alert. Minutes before, a bugle had sounded over the intercom system and a voice had announced that *Kaga* was under air attack. Indeed, crewmen crowding the rails on the *Sōryū* could see smoke rising from the big carrier off to the south. Then, just as Dick Best was diving on the *Akagi*, an American dive-bomber emerged from out of the clouds north of the *Sōryū*. Then another. Captain Yanagimoto Ryūsaku ordered the *Sōryū* hard to port, to throw off the bombers and to unmask his own antiaircraft battery, which opened fire at once. Leslie later recalled that "the sides of the carrier turned into a veritable ring of flames as the enemy commenced firing small caliber and anti-aircraft guns."[33]

Leslie planned to strafe the flattop, but at 4,000 feet his guns jammed and he pulled out. The next plane in line was piloted by his wingman, Lieutenant Junior Grade Paul "Lefty" Holmberg. His bomb landed near the *Sōryū*'s forward elevator and exploded on the hangar deck. A second bomb, dropped by Lieutenant Harold Bottomly, penetrated deep into the carrier's engine spaces before detonating. Leslie described the result as "the greatest inferno and holocaust I could ever imagine . . . with debris and material flying in all directions." He counted a total five "direct hits" and three near misses by the planes of his squadron, though in fact only three bombs actually struck the *Sōryū*. Each one, however, landed in a different part of the carrier: one forward, one aft, and one amidships. In consequence, the *Sōryū* became, in Leslie's words, "an inferno of flame." She was so obviously a total loss that pilots in the trailing section of Leslie's squadron chose to attack other nearby targets, including a cruiser and a destroyer. A sailor on the *Hiryū* who watched the attack thought the *Sōryū* "looked like [she] . . . had been sliced in two" and recalled that "it was possible to see right through her to the other side." Like the *Kaga* and *Akagi*, the *Sōryū* had been mortally wounded. Though desperate damage-control

■ The *Sōryū* maneuvers radically in reaction to an attack by high-level B-17 bombers. Note the rising sun painted on the forward part of the flight deck. (U.S. Navy)

parties on all three ships fought valiantly to contain the raging fires, it was hopeless. In little more than five minutes, three of the four carriers of the Kidō Butai had been smashed beyond recovery.[34]

Witnessing all this, Nagumo was reluctant to face reality. Though the fires on his flagship were burning out of control and her communications system had been knocked out, he did not want to leave the ship. Urged to transfer to another vessel, he replied, "It is not time yet." But it was very nearly past time. The *Akagi*'s captain, Aoki Taijirō, urged Kusaka Ryūnosuke, Nagumo's chief of staff, "to leave this vessel as soon as possible." Kusaka pleaded with Nagumo. The *Hiryū* was still undamaged, and a swift counterstrike could still redeem the situation, but, he pointed out, Nagumo could not command the Kidō Butai from a ship whose radio communications had been destroyed. Reluctantly, Nagumo allowed himself to be transferred to the light cruiser *Nagara*. Perhaps victory could still be snatched from the jaws of defeat.[35]

# The Japanese Counterstrike
## (11:00 a.m. to 6:00 p.m.)

t was evident very quickly that the *Kaga* and the *Sōryū* were doomed. Though the *Kaga*'s heavy armored battleship hull allowed her to continue to limp along at two to three knots, she was obviously dying. Flames raged unchecked all along her hangar deck and black smoke poured out of her from stem to stern. As for the *Sōryū*, Lieutenant Harold Bottomley's 1,000-pound bomb had penetrated deep into the ship and destroyed her engineering spaces. Dead in the water and without power, the *Sōryū* was helpless. To save his men, Captain Yanagimoto Ryūsaku ordered abandon ship at 10:45, barely twenty minutes after the first bomb struck. He chose to stay on board. On *Akagi*, which had been hit only by Dick Best's single bomb, damage-control teams struggled to fight the fires while other men labored to get her engines working again. It was a losing fight, however, since exploding ordnance and especially the aviation fuel on the hangar deck continued to feed the inferno. Consistent with a preference for attack over defense, Japanese damage-control doctrine and equipment were less robust than on American ships, with little built-in redundancy. With the ship's main engines out, the water pumps didn't work, and there were no portable gasoline-powered pumps or generators. Desperate crewmen manned a hand pump on the anchor deck that produced a thin stream of sea water, but it was like spitting into a forest fire. Though efforts to save the flagship would continue until that evening, at 1:30 in the afternoon, Captain Aoki, in silent acknowledgement that the situation was hopeless, ordered the emperor's portrait removed and sent over to the destroyer *Nowaki*.[1]

Catastrophic as the situation was, Nagumo thought less about his losses than about how to strike back. Once he had reestablished himself aboard the cruiser *Nagara*, he reported to Yamamoto that three of his carriers were burning—a message that, when it arrived, produced only a low groan from the commander in chief. Reflecting a culture that valued heroic effort nearly as much as ultimate success, Nagumo's understanding of his duty compelled him to continue the fight even if it did not produce a victory. Though *Hiryū* was the only functioning carrier he had left, he was determined to find the American carriers and attack them. During his transfer to the *Nagara*, operational command

■ Rear Admiral Yamaguchi Tamon, the aggressive and well-liked commander of Carrier Division 2, flew his flag on the carrier *Hiryū* at Midway. (U.S. Naval Institute)

fell temporarily onto Rear Admiral Abe Hiroaki, commander of Cruiser Division 8. At 10:50, Abe signaled Yamaguchi Tamon in the *Hiryū* to "attack the enemy carriers."[2]

Yamaguchi hardly needed such an order. Very likely he felt vindicated by the horrific turn of events. At 8:30 that morning he had argued for an immediate strike—even a partial strike—against the enemy, and his advice had been rejected. Nagumo had been reluctant to send only thirty-six dive-bombers without a significant fighter escort to attack the Americans; now he would have to do so with only half that number. In response to Abe's order, Yamaguchi had replied, "All our planes are taking off now," but that did not mean a full deck load. The *Hiryū* launched only eighteen Val dive-bombers—all there were—accompanied by six Zero fighters. Yamaguchi also had nine Kate torpedo bombers on board (one more, a refugee from *Akagi*, would land a half hour later). They were not ready to go, however, and rather than wait for them, he sent off what he had. It was far short of the "armored gauntlet" that Nagumo had expected to hurl at the Americans.*

These circumstances emboldened Yamaguchi to offer more unsolicited advice to his commander. By blinker signal to the new flagship, he insisted that only a single destroyer should be left behind to watch the three crippled carriers; everything else should be sent at once to attack the Americans. It was not the first time Yamaguchi had offered his views, but this time the syntax of his message was that of an order: "Leave one destroyer with the damaged carriers and have the others proceed on the course of attack." This was more than presumption, it was insolence. Either Nagumo ignored the "order" or his staff never showed it to him, for there was no acknowledgment from the flagship, only the order from Abe to "attack the enemy carriers."[3]

---

* Altogether, Yamaguchi and the *Hiryū* could count up to sixty-four aircraft. That included twenty-seven Zero fighters from all four carriers, most of them still flying CAP. There were an additional ten Zeros on the *Hiryū*'s hanger deck, the eighteen Val dive bombers, and nine Kate torpedo planes, plus one more orphaned Kate from the *Akagi*.

The *Hiryū's* eighteen Val dive-bombers were in the air by 11:00 a.m., merely thirty-five minutes after the first American bomb had landed on the *Kaga*. Lieutenant Kobayashi Michio commanded the mission, which included six Zeros under Lieutenant Shigematsu Yasuhiro. All of the pilots were experienced veterans. They headed east toward the most recent contact location sent in by a scout pilot from the cruiser *Chikuma*. Though the initial contact that morning had identified Spruance's Task Force 16, this newest sighting was of Fletcher's *Yorktown* group.

As Kobayashi's strike force flew eastward, Nagumo reorganized what was left of the Kidō Butai into two groups: a battleship-cruiser group in the lead, followed by Yamaguchi's lone carrier, which was surrounded by a circular screen. Despite Yamaguchi's "advice" to leave only one destroyer behind, Nagumo delegated six of them (two each) to try to save the stricken carriers, or, at worst, to rescue their crews. Meanwhile he directed his much-reduced and reorganized Kidō Butai to steam to the northeast (course 060), toward the Americans, who, according to an 11:10 scouting report, were now only ninety miles away. That report inspired Nagumo to think about the possibility of getting close enough for a surface attack by his battleships and heavy cruisers. He was encouraged in this line of thought by a noon message from Admiral Kondō, who reported that he was bringing his two battleships and four cruisers north to join the Kidō Butai. If air strikes from the *Hiryū* crippled one or more of the American carriers, it might allow Kondō's battleships to get close enough to finish them off with their 14-inch guns, or so Nagumo imagined. Much, therefore, depended on the success of the air strike by Kobayashi's eighteen Vals.[4]

En route to the target, Kobayashi saw what he thought were four American torpedo bombers below him. They were, in fact, dive-bombers: a section of Earl Gallaher's VS-6 under Lieutenant Charles Ware, returning to the *Enterprise* from the successful strike on the *Kaga*. Eager for a fight, Kobayashi's escorting Zeros dove on them, expecting to make quick work of it. But the American pilots were flying low, which restricted the Zeros' maneuvering room, and they were flying in formation, which meant the backseat gunners were able to put up a heavy curtain of .30-caliber machine gun fire. In the ensuing fight, the Zeros not only failed to shoot down any of the American dive-bombers, two of the Zeros were badly mauled.* The two crippled Zeros turned back toward the *Hiryū*, and only one of them made it, the other crashing into the sea nearby. Moreover, the remaining four Zeros spent so much time vainly assailing Ware's bombers that the eighteen Vals they were supposed to be escorting had to begin their attack on the *Yorktown* without fighter cover.[5]

*Yorktown*'s radar picked up Kobayashi's inbound Vals forty-six miles out. At 11:59, Radio Electrician V. M. Bennett reported "thirty to forty" bogeys approaching. Buckmaster ordered preparations to receive them: the crew purged the fuel lines, locked down the watertight doors, and pushed an 800-gallon auxiliary gas tank over the side. Jimmy Thach's six Wildcats had just been recovered on the *Yorktown*, but the last of them, flown by Machinist Tom Cheek, had failed to catch a wire and crashed into the barrier. That delayed the landing of the bombers of Max Leslie's squadron, returning from their strike on the *Sōryū*. Pete Pederson, the *Yorktown*'s air group commander, ordered them to stay aloft and join the Wildcats that were flying CAP, vectoring all of them out toward the inbound bogeys. Leslie himself could do little since his guns had jammed while he was diving on the *Sōryū*, but other planes of his squadron, though already low on gas, joined the attack on the inbound bombers. Once again, radar had played a crucial role, for without it the *Yorktown* might easily have been caught recovering airplanes when the Japanese arrived. Instead, the attacking Vals came under a furious air attack while they were still twenty to thirty miles out from their target.[6]

---

* Though the Zeros failed to shoot down any of Ware's dive bombers, none of the American planes made it back to the *Enterprise*, presumably because they subsequently ran out of gas. The crew of one of them—Ensign Frank W. O'Flaherty and his backseat gunner, Aviation Machinist's Mate First Class Bruno Gaido—ditched in the water and were subsequently taken prisoner by the Japanese destroyer *Makigumo*. Gaido was the man who had won Halsey's approbation four months earlier by attempting to fight off a Japanese Nell from the stern of the *Enterprise* during the raid on the Marshall Islands (see chapter 4). After the Japanese interrogated the two Americans, they tied weights to their ankles and dropped them over the side.

The onslaught of the American fighters broke up Kobayashi's attack formation and the air battle turned into a free-for-all. From the deck of the *Yorktown*, the fight looked like a swirling, chaotic mass. Buckmaster reported that "planes were seen flying in every direction, and many were falling in flames." Once the four Zeros that had survived the skirmish with Ware's dive-bombers joined the fray, a total of some fifty airplanes swirled and looped in the crowded sky.[7]

Pederson sought to bring order out of the chaos. Though he would have preferred to lead his air group in person, his role as onboard fighter director foreshadowed future Navy doctrine in which commanders managed air battles from a shipboard Combat Information Center. Pederson did not have a Combat Information Center, but he anticipated its function by using a search plot to keep track of inbound bogeys and a fighter director board to keep track of his own air assets. Using the *Yorktown*'s call sign "Scarlet," he addressed the pilots collectively and individually over the radio as he sought to turn a chaotic free-for-all into a coordinated attack. The transcript of the radio transmissions suggests something of the nature of the fight:

> "All Scarlet planes keep a sharp look-out, a group of planes is coming in at 255 unidentified."
> "All Scarlet planes, bandits eight miles, 255."
> "This is Scarlet 19. Formation seems to be breaking up."
> "O.K. Break 'em up."
> "Tally ho!"

The radar allowed Pederson to vector specific planes to particular contacts.

> "Scarlet 19, investigate plane bearing 235. . . . Distance ten to twelve miles, altitude low.
>     Go get 'em."
> "O.K. got him. Have bogey in sight."[8]

Thus directed, the Wildcats were able to splash eleven of the inbound bombers. Lieutenant Junior Grade Arthur J. Brassfield (who was "Scarlet 19") shot down the lead bomber, then pulled left into a wingover and found another Val at close range. "I watched my tracers going into the engine and lacing on back into the cockpit," he remembered; then, "suddenly it blew up." A third bomber headed for cloud cover. Brassfield chased it, fired off two short bursts, and it, too, fell in flames.

Occasionally Pederson forgot to use the call sign and lapsed into the familiar: "Art," he radioed to Brassfield, "go out and investigate a bogey down low, 3,000 feet." It turned out to be the plane that was closing in on downed pilot Bill Esders and his badly wounded gunner in their raft. If the Japanese pilot had been planning to strafe the downed flyers, he changed his mind when Brassfield came charging at him, and he instead fled for home at high speed. Pederson warned Brassfield not to chase him too far, but Brassfield's blood was up and he took off in pursuit. Because of the extreme range, he tried lifting the nose of his plane and arcing his tracers in toward the target. He remembered that the tracers "looked like a swarm of bees looping high through the sky." Soon the Val began smoking, and Brassfield had his fourth kill of the day.[9]

In addition to the attacking bombers, the Americans also shot down three of the four Zeros—only Shigematsu himself survived. Indeed, so many Japanese planes were falling from the sky that one witness on the *Yorktown* thought "it looked like a curtain coming down." The Dash-4 Wildcats had only about twenty seconds of firepower and quickly began to run out of bullets. To indicate they needed to land and reload, the pilots flew past the *Yorktown*'s bridge and communicated using hand signals: they shook their fists if they needed ammo, or raked their hands along the outside of the fuselage where the gas tank was to show that they were low on fuel. Landing planes in the midst of an air attack was impossible, however, because the *Yorktown* was maneuvering radically to throw off the attacking bombers. Pederson directed the planes that were low on ammo or fuel to head for Task Force 16, some forty miles to the southeast, and he called on *Enterprise* (call sign Red) for help.[10]

"Red from Scarlet. We need some VFs."

"Scarlet from Red. Repeat."

"Red from Scarlet, we need relief for our combat patrols, getting low on ammunition."

"Scarlet from Red, we are sending the Blue patrol to assist. . . . Blue patrol being launched now."[11]

Before the Wildcats from Task Force 16 could arrive, seven of the Val bombers that had survived the air battle entered the envelope of the antiaircraft fire from the circle of surface ships screening the *Yorktown*. As the American pilots veered off to avoid being hit by friendly fire, Buckmaster ordered the *Yorktown* sharply to port to throw off the attackers. The two cruisers and five destroyers of her protecting screen opened up with scores of 5-inch guns, 1.1-inch "pom pom" guns, 20 mm guns, and .50-caliber machine guns. Leslie thought it looked like "a fire works display at a Fourth of July celebration."[12]

Through this virtual cloud of antiair fire, the seven surviving Val dive-bombers of Kobayashi's command pressed home their attack. Two more fell into the sea, victims of the heavy antiair fire, but not before one of them released its bomb, which hit the *Yorktown* "just abaft No. 2 elevator on the starboard side." That bomb exploded near a 1.1-inch antiaircraft gun, slaughtering its crew and starting several fires. Only seconds later, a second bomb hit the *Yorktown* squarely amidships, passing through both the *Yorktown*'s flight deck and hangar deck and exploding on level three among the engine uptakes, extinguishing the fires in five of the ship's boilers. A third bomb hit near the *Yorktown*'s forward elevator, starting a fire in a rag-storage area. That one forced Buckmaster to flood the ship's forward magazine.[13]

Like *Sōryū*, *Yorktown* had been hit by three bombs—one forward, one amidships, and one astern. One important difference was that the bombs that had hit the *Sōryū* had been 1,000-pound bombs; those that hit the *Yorktown* were 250-kilogram (551-pound) bombs. More importantly, unlike *Sōryū*, *Yorktown*'s hangar deck was not packed with volatile ordnance because of the advance warning provided by the *Yorktown*'s radar. Though a fully fueled Dauntless armed with a 1,000-pound bomb sat on the hangar deck near where the first bomb exploded, the hangar-deck officer, Lieutenant Alberto Emerson, quickly activated the sprinkler system, and the better-equipped American damage control parties successfully contained the fire before any ordnance cooked off.[14]

Nevertheless, it was a dire moment. With main propulsion out, the big *Yorktown* began to lose speed, and by 12:40 she was dead in the water. Black smoke from the mutiple fires roiled up so high into the air that it was visible from Task Force 16 forty miles away. Immobile, and with three gaping holes in her flight deck, *Yorktown* could not conduct air operations. Her radar had been knocked out, meaning that any future attack would find her a sitting duck. Driven from his battle station in flag plot by thick smoke, Fletcher assessed the situation. "I can't fight a war from a dead ship," he told Buckmaster, and soon afterward, just past one o'clock, he left the *Yorktown* in Buckmaster's care and prepared to transfer to the heavy cruiser *Astoria*. The only way off the ship was to climb down a knotted rope. Fletcher was not sure he could do it. "I'm too damn old for this sort of thing," he muttered. In the end, two sailors had to lower him down to the *Astoria*'s motor whaleboat.[15]

The damage to the *Yorktown* compelled all of her planes still aloft to seek sanctuary on *Hornet* and *Enterprise*. Aboard the *Hornet*, most of the planes from the "flight to nowhere" had landed by now except for Ruff Johnson's bombers, which would return from Midway that afternoon. Unfortunately, the *Hornet*'s run of bad luck was not over. One of the *Yorktown*'s refugee pilots was Ensign Daniel C. Sheedy, whose Wildcat had been badly shot up during the strike on the Kidō Butai, wounding him in the leg. As a result, he had trouble bringing his fighter in for a landing. Though Sheedy did not know it, one of the two Japanese bullets that had punched through his instrument panel had disabled the switch that put his own machine guns on "safe." When his damaged Wildcat hit the deck, his left landing gear collapsed and his plane swerved toward the *Hornet*'s island. The impact also set off his machine guns. A burst of .50-caliber bullets sprayed both the island and a group of men standing nearby. Three Marines and a sailor were killed, as was Lieutenant Royal R. Ingersoll, son of the commander of the U. S. Atlantic Fleet, Admiral Royal E. Ingersoll.[16]

Meanwhile, back on board the wounded *Yorktown*, damage-control parties worked feverishly. Some fought the fires, others worked on the engines, and still others labored to repair the holes in the flight deck. To sustain them, the executive officer, Dixie Keefer, ordered the ship's store opened and distributed candy ("gedunk") to all hands, both to boost morale and to keep up their energy level. In place of the small national flag that normally flew from the bridge, Buckmaster ordered the crew to raise the fifteen-foot-long "holiday" flag, which provoked cheers from the crew. On

■ Damage-control parties repair a hole in the flight deck of the *Yorktown* after the attack by Lieutenant Kobayashi's dive-bombers from *Hiryū*. (U.S. Naval Institute)

the flight deck, men constructed a frame made of 4 by 6 wooden timbers across the gaping holes in the deck, then nailed quarter-inch steel plates over the framework. It was a makeshift patch, but it was good enough. Technicians managed to get the radar working again.

The biggest problem was in the engine spaces, where the second Japanese bomb had taken out five of the ship's nine boilers. Water Tenderman First Class Charles Kleinsmith and a crew of volunteers donned gasmasks so they could stay in the engine room and maintain pressure in boiler number 1, which provided the power the damage-control parties needed to run their equipment. By 1:30, other crewmen of the "black gang" had boilers 4, 5, and 6 back on line, and ten minutes after that, the chief engineer reported that he could generate steam for twenty knots. As the crew cheered, the *Yorktown* began to move, slowly at first, then faster, and soon she was a warship again. With the fires under control, Buckmaster ordered the crew to resume fueling the Wildcats of Jimmy Thach's squadron.[17]

The refueling had barely started, however, when the radar on the cruiser *Pensacola* picked up another group of inbound planes. The *Yorktown*'s 1MC public address system blared out: "Stand by for air attack." Once again, radar prevented the *Yorktown* from being caught unready. The fueling was halted immediately and the lines purged with $CO_2$ gas. The *Yorktown* had only six Wildcats aloft, including several from Task Force 16. Pederson was eager to get Thach's squadron back into the air as well. But there were two problems. The first was that although the *Yorktown* had by now worked its way up to about sixteen knots, the light winds that day meant that the fighters would have to get airborne with relatively low wind speed across the deck. The second problem was that since the refueling had been halted, most of the Wildcats had only about 23 gallons of gas in their tanks. They took off nonetheless.[18]

The inbound bogeys were ten Kate torpedo bombers protected by six more Zeros. The Kate was the best weapon in the Japanese air arsenal, but Yamaguchi now had only these ten. As a measure of just how much and how quickly the fortunes of war had turned, early that morning Lieutenant Tomonaga had led 108 bombers and fighters in the attack on Midway Island, leaving 140 more behind as a reserve. Now the ten Kate torpedo bombers that Tomonaga led against the *Yorktown* represented almost the last available striking force of the Kidō Butai, nearly the final arrow in the quiver.[19]

Nagumo had agreed to hurl them against the enemy because at this point he was still clinging to the hope that he could turn the battle around by forcing a surface engagement. Only five of the eighteen dive-bombers that Yamaguchi had sent against the *Yorktown* had returned, but they reported that they had left a mortally wounded American carrier dead in the water and burning. If Tomonaga's ten Kates could inflict similar damage on a second American carrier, a surface attack by Nagumo's battleships and cruisers might be able to finish them off. Failing that, Nagumo would still have the opportunity to launch a night attack with his destroyers, armed with the deadly Type 93 "Long Lance" torpedoes that had a twenty-mile range.

He knew that the Kidō Butai would be exposed to renewed American air attack in the interim, but he also knew, having witnessed it himself, that the Americans had suffered extremely heavy air losses that morning, including the near-annihilation of their torpedo squadrons, which significantly minimized the air threat. Attempting a surface battle was risky. Nonetheless, so long as there was even the least chance of success, Nagumo was determined to grasp it.

Even before Tomonaga took off, however, two key pieces of information ought to have brought Nagumo back to earth. At 12:40, a message from *Chikuma's* number 5 scout plane reported an undamaged American carrier task force 130 miles away, much too far for any surface attack to be realistic. And twenty minutes after that, Nagumo received another piece of information from Commander Watanabe on the destroyer *Arashi*. Watanabe's crew had plucked one of the pilots from Lem Massey's VT-3 from the water. It was Ensign Wesley Frank Osmus, a 24-year-old product of the AVCAD program from Illinois. Osmus had apparently failed to retrieve the life raft from his Devastator, for the Japanese found him, weak and dehydrated, swimming all alone in the middle of the Pacific Ocean. Hauled aboard the *Arashi*, the Japanese interrogated him aggressively, threatening him with a sword. Osmus revealed that there were three American carriers in the area, the *Hornet*, *Enterprise*, and *Yorktown*, and that the *Yorktown* was operating separately from the other two. Once they completed the interrogation, the Japanese carried Osmus to the stern to throw him back over the side. Realizing their intent, Osmus grabbed on to the ship's stern railing, and to break his grip the Japanese smashed his head with a fire ax. Osmus' body tumbled into the ship's wake.[20]

Consequently, Nagumo now knew that there were two undamaged American carriers out there somewhere, and thus that there was no realistic hope of forcing a surface engagement. With only the *Hiryū* and its ten Kates, plus perhaps a score of Zeros, it was evident that it was now time—indeed past time—for the Kidō Butai to cut its losses and run for it. Nevertheless, Nagumo approved Yamaguchi's decision to send Tomonaga and the ten Kates out to do what they could.

One factor in that decision may have been that Admiral Yamamoto had at last put his oar in. He had considered breaking radio silence at 7:45 a.m. that morning, when the *Yamato* had picked up the report by Petty Officer Amari that there were ten American ships to the northeast. At the time, Yamamoto had turned to his chief of staff and said, "I think we had better order Nagumo to attack at once." But in the end he had decided not to interfere, and now he very likely regretted it. At 12:20 Yamamoto broke radio silence to send a series of orders directing Kondō's battleships and heavy cruisers to close on the Kidō Butai from the south and Kakuta's two carriers off the Aleutians to abort their mission, send the transports back to Japan, and steam south. Rather than cut his losses, Yamamoto was prepared to double down in the hope of winning the pot. As for Nagumo, by dispatching Tomonaga's handful of torpedo bombers against the Americans at 1:30, he had staked everything on their success.[21]

When Tomonaga took off from the *Hiryū*, he knew that he would not be coming back. During the attack on Midway that morning, his left-wing fuel tank had been punctured and was no longer serviceable. Consequently, though he had enough gas to find the enemy, he would not have enough to return. He joked with his fellow pilots that with the Americans only ninety miles away, he would have enough fuel to make it, but everyone recognized it as bravado. Yamaguchi himself came down to the flight deck to shake Tomonaga's hand and tell him goodbye, and to remind him that it was essential to find and cripple a second American carrier. One had been badly wounded, perhaps sunk, but there were two more out there.[22]

After leading his small squadron eastward for not quite an hour, Tomonaga saw the wakes of an American task force on the surface. At the center of that task force was an apparently undamaged carrier making an estimated twenty knots and launching aircraft. Clearly this could not be the cripple that Kobayashi's dive-bombers had left dead in the water and burning only two hours ago. He used hand signals to indicate the target and split his ten planes into two divisions to conduct a classic anvil attack. Despite outward appearances, his target was indeed the *Yorktown*, returned to operational status by her efficient damage-control teams. Consequently,

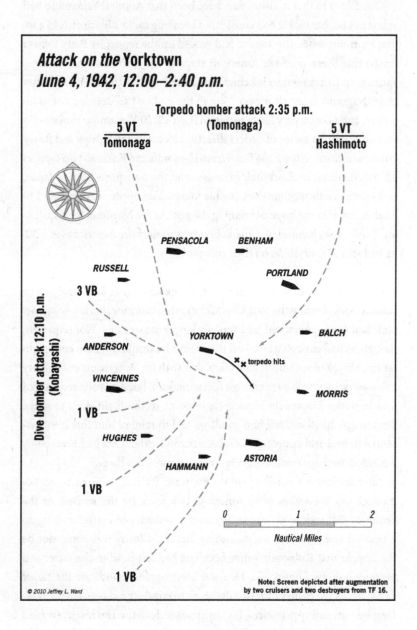

**Attack on the** Yorktown
**June 4, 1942, 12:00–2:40 p.m.**

Torpedo bomber attack 2:35 p.m.
(Tomonaga)

5 VT
Tomonaga

5 VT
Hashimoto

Dive bomber attack 12:10 p.m.
(Kobayashi)

PENSACOLA

BENHAM

RUSSELL

PORTLAND

3 VB

YORKTOWN

BALCH

ANDERSON

✕✕ torpedo hits

VINCENNES

MORRIS

1 VB

HUGHES

ASTORIA

HAMMANN

1 VB

0        1        2

Nautical Miles

1 VB

© 2010 Jeffrey L. Ward

Note: Screen depicted after augmentation
by two cruisers and two destroyers from TF 16.

instead of hitting a second carrier, Tomonaga's Kates were about to expend their fury on the same carrier that Kobayashi had hit, while the two carriers of Task Force 16 remained undiscovered and unharmed.

Tomonaga led one division of five planes against the *Yorktown*'s starboard side, while Lieutenant Hashimoto Toshio took the other five planes out to the left to attack its port side. As the Kates bore down on the *Yorktown*, Thach's eight Wildcats were struggling to get airborne. The *Yorktown*'s own 5-inch guns had already started firing when the first of the Wildcats rolled down the deck, and the pilots could feel their jolting recoil as they took off. On the one hand this launch at the last possible moment was fortuitous because, with only twenty-three gallons of gas, the Wildcats were spared having to burn fuel flying out to the contact. On the other hand, it also meant that the air battle took place inside the envelope of the antiair fire from the escorts of the task force. That escort was even more powerful now than it had been two hours before, for Spruance had sent two cruisers (*Pensacola* and *Vincennes*) and two destroyers (*Benham* and *Balch*) to reinforce *Yorktown*'s screen. Consequently, Wildcats, Zeros, and Kates maneuvered and shot at each other from close range as thousands of rounds of ordnance flew past them from the screening cruisers and destroyers. It was like fighting an air battle in the middle of a target range.[23]

One of the Wildcats was piloted by a 22-year-old ensign with the unlikely name of Milton Tootle IV, the son of a prominent St. Louis banker. Tootle's plane had barely cleared the deck in his takeoff when he made a hard right turn and saw a Kate making its torpedo run on the *Yorktown*. Tootle did not even have time to crank up his landing gear before he fired a long burst at the Kate and shot it down. When he pulled up, however, he entered the free-fire zone of the *Yorktown*'s own antiaircraft battery, and his plane was hit by friendly fire. As his cockpit filled with smoke, he knew he was too low to bail out, so he climbed to 1,500 feet before jumping. His whole flight had lasted less than five minutes.[24]

Jimmy Thach almost didn't get airborne at all. He flew the only Wildcat that had been fully fueled, which made it heavier, and in the light winds, it virtually fell off the end of the flight deck; Thach had to nurse it up into the air. As he began to gain altitude, he too saw an enemy torpedo plane streaking in toward the *Yorktown*, and he turned to go after it. As he closed in, he saw that its tail bore "a bright red colored insignia shaped like feathers . . . that no other Japanese aircraft had." It was Tomonaga's command plane, flying very low, barely fifty feet off the water, and heading straight for *Yorktown's* starboard side. Thach made a side approach and triggered a long burst of .50-caliber bullets. The Kate began to smoke, and flames issued from the engine, but Tomonaga somehow held his course. Thach recalled that "the whole left wing was burning, and I could see the ribs [of the plane] showing through the flames," but still Tomonaga flew on. Thach was impressed in spite of himself. "That devil still stayed in the air until he got close enough and dropped his torpedo." Only after that did Tomonaga's plane smash into the sea and disintegrate. No doubt Tomonaga died satisfied that he had done his full duty. But despite his sacrifice, his torpedo missed, as did those of the other planes in his section.[25]

Hashimoto's second division had better luck. Threading their way through the heavy antiair fire, four of the Kates in his section managed to get close enough to launch their torpedoes. That morning, Petty Officer Hamada Giichi had watched the destruction of *Kaga*, *Akagi*, and *Sōryū* from the deck of the *Hiryū* and had resolved to make the Americans pay. Now, after his pilot dropped his torpedo and pulled out over the *Yorktown's* flight deck, Hamada leaned out of the cockpit and shook his fist at it. The Americans who saw him yelled and gestured back. It was an intensely personal moment in a battle dominated by impersonal weapons. Within seconds, at 2:43 p.m., the first torpedo struck the *Yorktown* flush on the port side at about frame 90.[26]

"It was a real WHACK," Ensign John "Jack" Crawford remembered. "You could feel it all through the ship. . . . I had the impression that the ship's hull buckled slightly." The blast knocked out six of the ship's nine boilers and opened a large hole in the hull fifteen feet below the water line. Fires spread into the other boiler rooms and knocked out all propulsion. The *Yorktown* began to slow and take on a slight list. Then, just moments later, a second torpedo struck near frame 75. The two strikes were so close together that combined they created a single giant sixty-by-thirty-foot hole in the *Yorktown's* port side. The inrushing sea flooded the generator room and knocked out power throughout the ship; the emergency generators failed too, and the ship went dark. The *Yorktown* continued to lose way and the list became more pronounced. Soon she was again dead in the water. Eventually the ship heeled over at a 26-degree angle—so steep that it was difficult to walk on the flight deck. Commander Clarence Aldrich, the damage-control officer, reported to Buckmaster that without power none of the pumps feeding the fire hoses were working, nor could he effect counterflooding to prevent the *Yorktown* from listing further. Charles Kleinsmith, whose crew had kept boiler number one in operation after the first attack, had been killed. Lacking power, unable to fight the fires, and fearing that the big flattop "would capsize in a few minutes," trapping the whole crew underwater, at 2:55, Buckmaster ordered abandon ship.[27]

There was no panic. Men came up from the darkened spaces below, some carrying the wounded. The kapok-filled life vests were stowed in giant canvas bags suspended from the overhead on the hangar deck, and they spilled onto the deck in a heap. As they had on the *Lexington* in the Coral Sea, men stripped off their shoes for swimming and lined them up on the deck. Because Buckmaster feared the ship might roll over at any moment, he directed the men to evacuate from the starboard (high) side. From there, it was some sixty feet from the flight deck to the sea, and the men had to lower themselves down knotted ropes thrown over the side. One recent graduate of the Naval Academy began to lower himself with his legs splayed out at a 45-degree angle as he had been taught to do in gym class. Then, appreciating that this was not gym class, he wrapped his legs tightly around the rope as he continued his descent. Seaman E. R. "Bud" Quam successfully lowered himself down into the sea, then found that the water soaking into his heavy anti-flash overalls made them heavy and threatened to drag him down. He was floundering badly when a pair of strong arms pulled him out of the water and into a rubber raft. He looked up at his rescuer and was astonished to see that it was Peter Newberg, a high school classmate from Willmar, Minnesota.[28]

Morale remained high, even in the water. Those bobbing in life vests put out their thumbs to those in the rafts, as if hitching a ride. A few called out "Taxi! Taxi!" and there was a lot of joshing and joking—one group

■ The USS *Balch* (DD-363), at right, picking up survivors from the badly listing *Yorktown* on the afternoon of June 4. (U.S. Naval Institute)

began singing "The Beer Barrel Polka." The escorting destroyers closed in to pick up the survivors, and eventually some 2,280 men were recovered; USS *Balch* alone picked up 725. Buckmaster wanted to ensure that he was the last one off the *Yorktown.* All alone, he conducted a tour of the spaces that were still above water to make sure that no one had been overlooked. With the *Yorktown* listing near 30 degrees and the decks and ladders slippery with oil, he had to move "hand-over-hand" to stay vertical. By now the water was lapping at the hangar deck. Buckmaster made his way to the stern, stepped off into the sea, and swam away from the ship. He was soon picked up and taken on board Fletcher's new flagship, *Astoria.*[29]

As the *Yorktown* was fighting for her life, Bill Brockman on the *Nautilus* was getting his second good look that day at an enemy aircraft carrier. After finding himself alone on the surface at 10:00 that morning, he had continued northward for half an hour when he spotted a tall cloud of smoke on the horizon. Because of enemy airplanes in the vicinity, he went to periscope depth, where he had to rely on the boat's electric power. He was concerned about how long his batteries would last. However, deciding that they had enough juice to last until nightfall he continued submerged until, at 11:45, he "identified the source of the smoke as a burning carrier" guarded by what he thought were two cruisers, but which were the destroyers *Hagikaze* and *Maikaze*. Closing this formation proved difficult since the burning carrier was still making headway at one or two knots, and with her depleted batteries, the submerged *Nautilus* herself was only marginally faster. As Brockman watched through his periscope, it seemed to him that the two "cruisers" were making preparations to take the carrier under tow. He thought about attacking the escorts, but in the end he decided it was more important to finish off the carrier.[30]

At two o'clock, about the time that Tomonaga was beginning his attack run on the *Yorktown*, Brockman calculated the range and the angle on the bow. He and the other officers carefully studied the ship identification books—"to make sure this couldn't possibly be one of ours." Satisfied that it was not, he fired a spread of four torpedoes at what he thought was a *Sōryū*-class carrier but was instead the mortally wounded *Kaga*. One of the torpedoes misfired, and two missed. The fourth ran straight and true and struck the *Kaga* flush on her starboard side. At the time, Brockman's enthusiasm led him to imagine that he saw it explode and reignite fires on the big carrier. In fact, however, when the torpedo hit the *Kaga*'s armored battleship hull, it did not explode, and instead broke in half. The heavy nose containing the unexploded warhead sank from sight, and the after section floated harmlessly nearby. Ironically, several Japanese crewmen who had evacuated the *Kaga* used it as a flotation device until they were picked up by one of the destroyers.[31]

Brockman had no time for a lengthy assessment, since the *Kaga*'s two escorts immediately charged toward him and he had to dive. He went down to three hundred feet—as deep as the boat would go. The Japanese destroyers dropped eleven depth charges, but their deepest setting was two hundred feet, and all of them exploded well above him. Despite that, the multiple concussions at such an extreme depth started several leaks in the boat's hull, and the dripping water led to some tense moments on board the *Nautilus*. Brockman stayed deep for almost two hours, then crept back up to periscope depth just past 4:00 p.m. The carrier was still there, smoke pouring out of her. The duty officer on the *Nautilus* watched the towering column of smoke climbing up "to the height of a thousand feet" and told Brockman with evident satisfaction that it reminded him of the smoke that rose up from the USS *Arizona* on December 7.[32]

By then, Nagumo had finally, and reluctantly, given up on the idea of forcing a surface action. At 3:40 he ordered what was left of the Kidō Butai to change course from northeast to northwest. It was the right decision, if somewhat tardy. By now *Hiryū* had only nine attack planes left (four Vals and five Kates), plus perhaps a dozen Zeros. Though Yamaguchi reported (incorrectly) that his two air strikes had "accounted for 2 carriers damaged," another report from a scout plane informed Nagumo that there were still two more undamaged American carriers east of him. For his part, Yamaguchi was planning one more desperate attack at dusk. He hoped to launch his last nine attack planes, plus six Zeros, at about 6:00 p.m. and hit the Americans at twilight when they would not be expecting it. Though the pilots were woozy with exhaustion, the planes were ready and waiting on the hangar deck. Meanwhile, Yamaguchi kept an active CAP flying over what was left of the Kidō Butai.[33]

The Americans, too, were planning a strike that afternoon, and they had many more tools to hand. Without question, their morning losses had been heavy and sobering. All three of the torpedo squadrons had been virtually annihilated, and whatever happened from now on would depend entirely on the rugged and dependable Dauntless dive-bombers. Of the thirty-two dive-bombers that Wade McClusky had led away from the *Enterprise* that morning, however, only eleven had returned, and two of those were so badly damaged as to be of no further use. These losses were due less to enemy fire than to the long flight and lengthy search; most of the planes had simply run out of gas on the way back and ditched in the water. The vast majority of their pilots would eventually be recovered, but for now *Enterprise* had only about as many attack planes left as *Hiryū* did: seven from Earl Gallaher's Scouting Six and four from Dick Best's Bombing Six. There was, however, Max Leslie's Bombing Three from *Yorktown*. When Leslie's bombers had returned from their strike on the *Sōryū* to find the *Yorktown* under attack, Pederson had ordered them to help defend the task force and then sent them off to find refuge on the *Enterprise*. Leslie himself and two others ran out of gas en route and ditched in the water, but fourteen of them had made it, and those fourteen were on board *Enterprise* now. Adding them to the remnants of Gallaher's and Best's squadrons gave the *Enterprise* a strike force of twenty-five dive-bombers.[34]

As for the *Hornet*, thanks to the "flight to nowhere," her air group had not been in action at all that day save for Waldron's martyred Torpedo Eight. Despite that, ten Wildcats had been lost, and only three of Ruff Johnson's planes from Bombing Eight had returned. *Hornet* still had all eighteen dive-bombers of Walt Rodee's squadron, plus the three planes of Johnson's squadron, so that altogether Spruance had more than forty bombers that he could commit to a second strike.

Certainly the pilots were eager for it. After landing on the *Enterprise*, Dick Best climbed out of his cockpit and hurried up to the flag bridge to convince Spruance to send out another strike at once. Miles Browning intercepted him, and Best made his case. "There are three carriers aflame and burning," he told Browning. "But there's a fourth one up to the north. He requested that he be "rearmed and sent out right away." Before Browning could reply, McClusky came up to make his report. Commander Walter Boone noticed that blood was running down McClusky's arm and dripping onto the deck: "My God, Mac, you've been shot!" he exclaimed. In fact, McClusky had parts of five bullets in his arm and shoulder, and he was hustled off to sick bay.[35]

Browning and Spruance were surprised to learn of a fourth undamaged carrier. At 2:04, Spruance had notified Nimitz, "All four CV believed badly damaged." Yet Best's report, and the attack on *Yorktown*, proved that at least one undamaged enemy carrier was still operating. Even so, Spruance did not launch at once. The losses among the American strike aircraft that morning had been "horrific," and he was aware that if he launched a second strike now, the planes would probably have to return in the dark. Most important, he didn't know with any certainty where that fourth carrier was other than, in Best's words, somewhere "up to the north." He therefore rejected Browning's suggestion to launch at once and decided to wait until he had more information.[36]

It came in at 2:45. That morning, as we've seen, Fletcher had kept the planes of Wally Short's Scouting Five back from the strike in anticipation of finding the presumed second group of Japanese carriers. At 11:30, just twenty minutes before Kobayashi's attack, he sent ten of them off on a combination search and attack mission. Short's ten planes flew in five two-plane sections in order to cover an arc of the sea from 280 degrees (almost due west) to 020 degrees (almost due north)—see map, p. 334. They were to fly two hundred miles out, turn left for sixty miles, then fly back. At 150 miles, most of them encountered a thick fog bank. "We'd fly through thick fog for five or ten minutes," one pilot recalled, "and then break out into the open for a few miles, then back into a fog bank again." Nevertheless, at 2:45 p.m., just as Tomonaga was attacking the *Yorktown*, Lieutenant Samuel Adams called in a sighting. Adams was in a buoyant mood, for he had received word just that morning that his wife had given birth back in the States. Perhaps somewhat giddy as a result, he had flown off the *Yorktown* still wearing his blue pajamas under his flight jacket. Now, however, he was all business. Finding no enemy ships in his assigned sector, he took the initiative to fly further south and at 2:45 reported "One carrier, two battleships, three heavy cruisers, four destroyers. Course north, speed 20 knots." The enemy ships bore 278 degrees from Task Force 16 and they were only 110 miles away. Adams's radioman/gunner, Joseph Karrol, sent in the sighting report, and when Adams asked him to send it again, Karrol interrupted him: "Mr. Adams, would you mind waiting a minute. There's a Zero on our tail." Karrol transferred from the radio to the twin .30-caliber machine guns to fend off the Zero, then went back to the radio to send the voice message.[37]*

---

* Because the *Yorktown* was out of action by the time these scouts returned, all of them had to land on board the carriers of Task Force 16. When Adams climbed out of his Dauntless on board the *Enterprise* still wearing his pajamas, he provoked a laugh when he claimed to be the only one who had come prepared to spend the night.

▓ The popular and boyish-looking Lieutenant Samuel Adams spotted the *Hiryū* on the afternoon of June 4 and reported her location. (U.S. Naval Institute)

After receiving that news, Spruance ordered *Enterprise* and *Hornet* to "prepare to launch attack group immediately." For whatever reason, that order never reached the *Hornet*. So far the day had been an unalloyed fiasco for the *Hornet*. It would get no better in the afternoon. Anticipating an order to launch a second strike, Mitscher had spotted Walt Rodee's scout bombers on the *Hornet*'s flight deck. Then just a few minutes before 3:00, Mitscher learned that the eleven bombers of Ruff Johnson's VB-8 that had landed on Midway that morning were at last returning. Mitscher decided to "break the spot" (as it was called) and push the planes of Rodee's strike force forward in order to recover Johnson's bombers. As a result, when at 3:17 Spruance ordered both carriers to begin launching at 3:30, the *Hornet* was not ready. *Enterprise* began launching at 3:25; the *Hornet* did not get her first plane into the air until after 4:00.[38]

That first plane lifted off at 4:03, and one by one, sixteen Dauntless bombers got airborne. Almost at once, however, two of them reported engine failure and had to return. By the time they were back aboard, it was past 4:30, and, deciding it was too late now to continue launching, Mitscher turned the *Hornet* west to the point-option course. That decision stranded fifteen planes of the *Hornet*'s strike force that were still on the hangar deck. Worse, among those fifteen were the planes of Stanhope Ring, the air group commander, and Walt Rodee, the squadron commander. Mitscher's report is silent on how he learned of this latest snafu. Did Ring and Rodee come running up to the bridge to ask why they had been left behind? Did they then consult the roster to find out who the senior officer with the strike group was? In any case, only after he was in the air did Lieutenant Edgar Stebbins learn that he was in charge of the mission. It was yet another humiliation for the hapless *Hornet*, her frustrated commanding officer, and her even more frustrated air group commander.[39]

As for the *Enterprise*, once she had launched her strike group, she began recovering the orphaned Wildcats from the stricken *Yorktown*. Jimmy Thach was the last to come aboard, and when he climbed out of his cockpit, he was told that Admiral Spruance wanted to see him. Thach rushed up to the flag bridge, where the sober-faced admiral was waiting for him. He asked Thach how he thought things were going. "Admiral, we're winning this battle," Thach replied. "I saw with my own eyes three big carriers burning so furiously they'll never launch another airplane." He told Spruance that he felt that they ought to go after the fourth one. Thach remembered that Spruance "kind of smiled" at that, which was about as demonstrative as Spruance got.[40]

The *Enterprise* strike force of twenty-four planes (one of Gallaher's planes had to return because of engine trouble) flew toward the target at 13,000 feet in three squadrons. Each squadron was a mere shadow of what it had been that morning. Earl Gallaher's VS-6 had only six planes; Dick Best's VB-6 had four; and Max Leslie's VB-3 from *Yorktown* had fourteen. Neither McClusky nor Leslie could take part—McClusky because of his shoulder wound and Leslie because his plane had never made it to the *Enterprise*. That made Earl Gallaher the senior man, with Lieutenant Dave Shumway leading the *Yorktown* planes. Gallaher planned to have the ten *Enterprise* planes (his own and Dick Best's) attack the enemy carrier, and he wanted Shumway's fourteen planes from *Yorktown* to hit the escorting battleships. This was a curious decision, since battleships—though big and impressive—were of little operational importance compared to the carrier. Very likely, Gallaher was remembering the doctrine that called for two squadrons flying together to select different targets. But with the American squadrons so reduced by battle damage, and with only one enemy carrier left, it would have been understandable in this case for all the planes to attack the primary target. Despite doctrine, that is exactly what happened.

The strike force from *Enterprise* spotted the Kidō Butai just before 5:00. Gallaher led his group of twenty-four planes up to 19,000 feet and around to the west in order to attack out of the setting sun. The Japanese had a handful of Zeros flying CAP at altitude, but they did not discover the threat until Gallaher was nearly ready to push over, and for the second time that day the Japanese were caught by surprise when American dive-bombers came hurtling down on them. Despite that, they put up an impressive curtain of antiaircraft fire. In the growing darkness, the gunfire flashes along both sides of the carrier were clearly visible.[41]

Gallaher began his dive just as the *Hiryū* made a radical turn to port. The *Hiryū* was agile for a big ship, and it turned tighter than Gallaher had calculated. He was already committed to his dive, so he tried to adjust for the *Hiryū*'s sharp turn by pulling up abruptly when he released his bomb, hoping to "throw" the bomb at the rapidly retreating carrier. The bomb missed astern, and Gallaher succeeded only in wrenching his back so badly that after he landed back on the *Enterprise* he had to be lifted bodily out of his cockpit.[42]

The next two bombs also missed, and after witnessing that, Shumway decided to forget about the battleships and lead his squadron against the carrier. It was the right decision, though it caused some confusion, since his group and Best's four-plane section both dove on the *Hiryū* at the same time. Once again, Best had to maneuver at the last moment while he was preparing to dive. That gave the Zeros flying CAP a second chance at him, and they shot down one of Best's wingmen, Ensign Fred Weber. Then, as Shumway targeted the *Hiryū*'s starboard bow, Best led his other three planes against her port bow.[43]

The first to hit the *Hiryū* was Ensign Richard Jaccard. His 500-pound bomb struck the forward elevator, blowing a section of it into the air and propelling it back against the *Hiryū*'s small island. Three more hits quickly followed, one of them Dick Best's—his second of the day. Norman "Dusty" Kleiss, who had landed a bomb on the *Kaga* that morning, also got a second hit on *Hiryū*. All four American bombs landed forward of the ship's island and created a single, massive crater in her flight deck; the *Hiryū* looked as if a giant's hand had reached down and scooped out her bow section, leaving

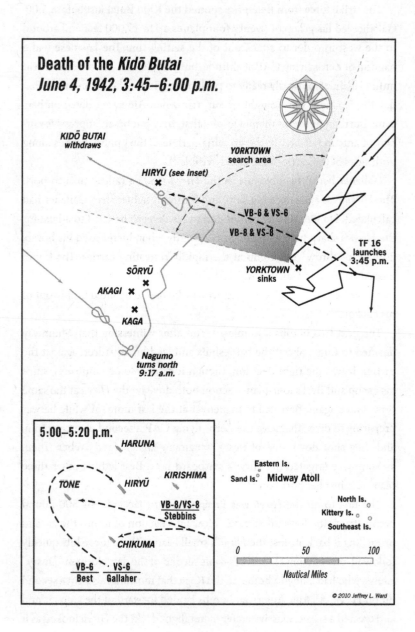

**Death of the *Kidō Butai***
**June 4, 1942, 3:45–6:00 p.m.**

KIDŌ BUTAI
withdraws

YORKTOWN
search area

HIRYŪ (see inset)
✕

VB-6 & VS-6

VB-8 & VS-8

TF 16
launches
3:45 p.m.

SŌRYŪ
✕

AKAGI ✕

YORKTOWN
sinks
✕

KAGA ✕

Nagumo
turns north
9:17 a.m.

**5:00–5:20 p.m.**

HARUNA

KIRISHIMA

TONE    HIRYŪ

VB-8/VS-8
Stebbins

Eastern Is.
Sand Is.    Midway Atoll

North Is.
Kittery Is.
Southeast Is.

CHIKUMA

VB-6    VS-6
Best    Gallaher

0          50          100

*Nautical Miles*

© 2010 Jeffrey L. Ward

a gaping cavern. The *Hiryū* suffered less secondary damage than the other Japanese carriers because there was less ordnance to cook off on the hangar deck, but the primary damage was enough. Like her sister ships, she had been wrecked beyond recovery.[44]

Only then did Stebbins' fourteen planes from *Hornet* arrive on the scene. Seeing that the Japanese carrier was already smashed and "burning throughout its entire length," Stebbins led his squadron against the heavy cruisers *Chikuma* and *Tone*. Based on the pilots' assessments, Mitscher later reported three hits on a battleship and two on a heavy cruiser, though in fact none of the bombs from the *Hornet*'s planes hit home.[45]

In an epilogue to this very long day, a dozen Army B-17s—six from Midway and six from Barking Sands Airfield on Kauai Island—appeared overhead just at dusk and dropped more than thirty 500-pound bombs on what was left of the Kidō Butai. They scored no hits, though they returned to base claiming one hit on a carrier and the sinking of a destroyer.[46]

By the time all the Navy planes were back aboard the carriers, it was full dark.\* Spruance called Fletcher on the TBS to ask if he had any orders. "Negative," Fletcher replied; "will conform to your movements," in effect releasing Spruance to operate his task force independently, a vote of confidence that Spruance greatly appreciated. Spruance's first decision was to turn Task Force 16 to the east, away from the enemy. He was aware that this might allow the remnants of the Kidō Butai to escape during the night. He knew, however, that four Japanese carriers had been hit, and he was sensitive to the possibly of a Japanese night attack by their heavy battleships or by destroyers launching torpedoes. As he put it in his subsequent report to

---

\* There was one more American air strike that night. At 5:00 p.m., a PBY from Midway reported a "burning carrier" off to the northwest—almost certainly the *Kaga*. Major Ben Norris lifted off with twelve planes from the Eastern Island airfield at 7:15, and Simard sent out eight PT boats, each of them carrying a 200-gallon auxiliary gas tank to enable them to make the long run out to the target. But by the time any of them arrived, the *Kaga* was no longer afloat. At 6:25 she suffered another massive explosion and went under at around 7:25, taking some eight hundred men out of her crew of 1,800 down with her. During the return flight, Norris got disoriented in the dark with no visual references and flew his plane into the sea.

Nimitz, "I did not feel justified in risking a night encounter with possibly superior enemy forces, but on the other hand, I did not want to be too far away from Midway the next morning." Though Spruance's decision was subsequently controversial, it was a sound one. Nimitz had told him—and Fletcher—not to risk the fleet.[47]

As for Nagumo, with his last carrier in flames, and lacking any aircraft beyond the few scout planes on the heavy cruisers and battleships, he at last faced reality and directed the remnants of his command to head west into the setting sun.

# 16

# Denouement

The battle was not over. Though Yamamoto was a gambler, he was also a realist. Nonetheless, for several more hours he continued to behave as if victory were still possible. When Spruance turned Task Force 16 eastward after dark, Yamamoto sent a radio message to all units that the American fleet, which he announced had "practically been destroyed," was retiring to the east and that the landing on AF (Midway) would proceed. His purpose in sending such a message may have been to boost morale, but his subsequent orders suggest that he was still clinging to the hope that he could make it happen. At 9:20 p.m. he ordered Kondō's two battleships and four cruisers to head northeast at high speed, to seek a night surface engagement with the retiring American carrier task force. He also directed Kurita's four heavy cruisers, which were covering the "Transport Group," to proceed to Midway to shell the airfield. He announced that the main body, including his flagship, *Yamato*, was coming up to rendezvous with what was left of the Kidō Butai. Finally, he authorized Ugaki to relieve Nagumo of his command and put Kondō in charge of the battle. Kondō led his big surface ships to the northeast, spreading them out into a scouting line in anticipation of finding the American carriers in the dark.[1]

Yamamoto also had to decide what to do about Nagumo's wrecked flagship. Though the *Akagi* was virtually destroyed, she remained stubbornly afloat. It was unrealistic to imagine that she could be salvaged and towed all the way back across the Pacific, but the alternatives were appalling: abandoning her to the enemy or sinking her with torpedoes. One of Yamamoto's staff officers worried that if she were abandoned, the Americans would turn her into "a museum piece on the Potomac River," a horrifying scenario. But the idea of sinking one of the emperor's capital ships was equally horrifying. The decision belonged to Yamamoto, and after listening to the discussion he told his staff, "I will apologize to the Emperor for the sinking of the *Akagi*," and he gave orders for her destroyer screen to send her to the bottom. After receiving those orders, the screen commander fired four torpedoes at the *Akagi*, one from each of his four destroyers, like a firing squad. At least two of them struck home, and the majestic *Akagi* slipped beneath the waves.[2]

That made the *Hiryū* the last Japanese carrier afloat. For some time, Yamaguchi hoped that he could salvage his flagship and get her back to Japan, and throughout the evening and into the night her crews fought the fires. Then, just past midnight, the *Hiryū* was rocked by another internal explosion. The exhausted damage-control parties continued to labor, but it was now evident to all that it was hopeless. At 2:00 a.m., Yamaguchi ordered them to stop working and to assemble on the flight deck aft of the gaping holes left by the American bombs. There, he addressed them. He took full responsibility for the loss of the *Hiryū* and ordered the seven hundred or so survivors to live, so that they could become the core of a new and revitalized Imperial Navy. He asked them to face west, toward Tokyo, and called for three banzai cheers as the flag was lowered to the strains of the national anthem. Then, at 3:15 a.m., he ordered abandon ship. His last two messages consisted of an apology to Nagumo and an order to Captain Abe Toshio, commanding the destroyer screen, to sink the *Hiryū* with torpedoes once the crew had left the ship. Yamaguchi himself remained aboard. Several members of his staff came to him to say that they, too, wished to go down with the ship. No, Yamaguchi told them. They must survive so they could carry on the war. He did, however, accept the request of the *Hiryū*'s captain, Kaku Tomeo, to remain aboard, and the two of them stood together on what was left of the bridge to watch the orderly evacuation and admire the brightness of the moon.[3]

At ten minutes past five, after the *Hiryū*'s crew had been plucked from the water, and with the sun just coming up, Commander Fujita Isamu, captain of the destroyer *Makigumo*, fired a Type 93 "Long Lance" torpedo at the smoldering flattop. The first one ran underneath the hull and failed to detonate. A second struck home and exploded. Fujita, perhaps eager to wash his hands of this unpleasant duty, steamed off to the west. Some members of his crew reported that they saw survivors on board the *Hiryū* waving at them, but, perhaps assuming that these were patriots who preferred to go down with the ship, Fujita kept going.[4]

By then Yamamoto had abandoned whatever hope he had had of forcing a surface action. By midnight, two things had become clear. First, that Kondō was not going to catch the American carriers before dawn, and second, that Kurita's cruisers could not reach Midway before sunrise left them exposed to air attack. There was no avoiding what was now evident—he had to acknowledge defeat and call off the whole operation. Yamamoto's gunnery officer, Watanabe Yasuji, who had argued so passionately for the Midway plan before the Naval General Staff back in April, suggested that the battleships *Haruna* and *Kirishima* could be sent to join Kurita's four cruisers in the bombardment of Midway. Their big guns could neutralize the Midway airfield, he declared, and gain more time for Kondō's battleships to catch up with and finish off the American carriers. Victory was still possible. Listening to his enthusiastic young staff officer, Yamamoto "turned very calm and quiet," then replied, "It is too late now for such an operation." He suggested to Watanabe, not unkindly, that as in *shogi*, "too much fighting causes all-out defeat." Instead, Yamamoto recalled both Kondō and Kurita, ordering them to fall back on the main body.[5]

There was a delay in the transmission of those orders, perhaps a deliberate one. Watanabe acknowledged that "everyone was crazy to recover the situation and fight the enemy." Kurita's recall order was sent first to the wrong cruiser division and he did not get his orders until 2:30 a.m. By then, his four cruisers were less than ninety miles from Midway—three more hours would have put them within gun range of the atoll. To be so close to the objective and have to turn around was galling, but orders were orders. Worse, dawn was now only two hours away, so that even at their top speed of 35 knots, Kurita's four cruisers would be no more than 160 miles from Midway when the sun came up on June 5. They would be isolated, without air cover, and within easy range of the Midway airfield; Kurita knew it was unlikely he would get away undiscovered.[6]

For Kurita and his cruiser force, however, there were other dangers that night besides airplanes. In the pitch darkness of the early hours of June 5, while Yamaguchi addressed the crew of the doomed *Hiryū*, the American submarine USS *Tambor* (SS-198) was running on the surface eighty-nine miles west of Midway. At 2:15 a.m., her commanding officer, Lieutenant Commander John W. Murphy, Jr., spotted "the loom of four large ships on the horizon." They were, of course, Kurita's four heavy cruisers, at that time still closing on Midway for a dawn shelling of the airfield. In the dark of night and three miles away, however, Murphy could not tell if the ships were friend or foe. His orders had cautioned him and all other sub commanders that "encounters with friendly surface forces during night [were] possible," and that they should be sure of their targets. Murphy therefore turned the *Tambor* to the east to parallel the unidentified vessels, hoping to catch them in the moonlight so he could "identify them by silhouette." Instead he lost them in the dark. He did not regain contact until 2:38, by which time they had changed course to the north in response to Yamamoto's recall order. Now they were heading almost directly toward him.[7]

Murphy sent out a contact report, but it was necessarily vague and specified only that he had spotted "many unidentified ships." He was hoping that Midway could tell him whether these vessels were likely to be friends or enemies. Meanwhile, he maintained intermittent contact but was unable to get in position for an attack mainly because the cruisers were barreling along at 28 knots and the *Tambor* had a top speed of 21 knots. At 3:06 a.m., Murphy got an acknowledgment to his initial report, which did not contain any news about whether any U.S. surface forces were in the area. Not until 4:12, when the sky had lightened enough to enable him to study the profile of the ships against the gray dawn, was Murphy satisfied that these were enemy cruisers. He had no time for an updated report, however, because one of the two accompanying destroyers detached itself from the column and came charging toward him. Murphy stepped back from the periscope and yelled out: "Dive! Dive! Dive! Take her down and rig for depth charge attack!"[8]

Murphy took the *Tambor* deep and stayed down for twenty minutes before easing back up to periscope depth. In the growing light of dawn, he saw two cruisers of the *Mogami* class, moving now at only about 17 knots and signaling to one another. Murphy tried to get close enough for an attack. Despite his efforts, however, the range actually increased from 9,000 yards to 13,000 yards (over seven miles). He sent in an updated contact report noting that the two cruisers were now headed due west on a course of 270 degrees. He also reported that "the trailing cruiser had about forty feet of her bow missing."[9]

Though he did not know it, Murphy and the *Tambor* were primarily responsible for that missing bow section. The wounded ship was, in fact, the heavy cruiser *Mogami*, namesake of the class. The *Mogami*-class cruisers were big ships, heavily armed with ten 8-inch guns in five two-gun turrets packed into a 661-foot long hull. At 2:35, Kurita's cruisers had just completed their turn northward in response to Yamamoto's recall order when one of the lookouts on Kurita's flagship, *Kumano*, spied the low silhouette of the *Tambor* almost dead ahead on the northern horizon. Kurita ordered an emergency simultaneous turn to port. The *Kumano*, at the head of the column, and the *Mikuma*, which was third in line, both turned sharply left at near 90 degrees, but the number 2 ship (*Suzuya*) and the trailing ship (*Mogami*) each turned at 45 degrees. The *Suzuya* barely missed colliding with the *Kumano*, and the *Mogami* drove herself headlong into the four-inch-thick armor belt on the port side of the *Mikuma*, just forward of her bridge. The *Mikuma* was only superficially damaged, but warships of the Second World War were not built for ramming, and the sheer bow of the *Mogami* crumpled like a crash-test car hitting a concrete wall.[10]

Quick and effective damage control prevented the *Mogami* from going down, but she could no longer make 28 knots, or even 20. With dawn approaching, Kurita could not slow the whole formation to wait for her. He ordered the two lead ships to proceed, and directed the wounded *Mogami*, accompanied by the *Mikuma* and the two destroyers, to follow at best speed. At first that best speed was only about eight or ten knots, as the *Mogami* pushed her blunt bow into the sea. Her captain, Soji Akira, did everything he could to regain speed: his men cut away the wreckage and threw overboard all nonessential materials, including all twenty-four of the expensive and valuable Type 93 torpedoes (a decision that would have important consequences later). Gradually the *Mogami* worked her way back up to 20 knots, which allowed her to run away from the *Tambor*. But when dawn arrived at 4:15, Midway was only a hundred miles away. It was only a matter of time before an American patrol plane found these two ships struggling along under the bright sun.[11]

Sure enough, at 6:30, a PBY out of Midway reported sighting "two battleships" 125 miles to the west. Simard ordered out what was left of his attack group: six Dauntlesses under Marine Captain Marshall Tyler and six Vindicators under Marine Captain Richard Fleming. They found the two cruisers and dropped their bombs, but the poor luck of the Marine bombers continued. Fleming's plane was shot down, and despite the cruisers' relatively slow speed, all of the American bombs missed. Eight Army B-17s from Midway tried their luck next, but they, too, failed to make any hits. The commanding officers of the two cruisers began to hope that they might get away after all.[12]

Spruance also got word of the two "battleships" west of Midway, and his task force now possessed a robust strike force of more than sixty bombers with the addition of Wally Short's Scouting Five from *Yorktown* and the return of Ruff Johnson's Bombing Eight from Midway. Spruance did not launch at once, however. Battleships were valuable targets but not as important as carriers, and another report at 8:00 a.m. indicated a crippled Japanese carrier off to the northwest. It was, in fact, the *Hiryū*. Despite the torpedo from the *Makigumo* that was supposed to have sunk her, the *Hiryū* continued to drift along, powerless but afloat. Moreover, forty or so men from the engine rooms who had been overlooked when she was abandoned had made their way up to the flight deck and were still on board. Spruance did not know any of this; all he knew was that there was still an enemy carrier out there, and he wanted to go get it.

Yamamoto found out that the *Hiryū* was still afloat about the same time that Spruance did. At 7:20 that morning, a search plane from the small carrier *Hōshō*, which was accompanying Yamamoto's Main Body, sent in a sighting report of the *Hiryū*, including the information that there were still men on board her who had waved when the scout plane flew past. The pilot's backseat gunner took pictures of the crippled carrier, still smoking and with a gigantic hole in her forward flight deck, but on an even keel and in no apparent danger of sinking. Yamamoto was displeased, for now he had to order a destroyer to go back and rescue the men on the carrier and then ensure that the *Hiryū* was sent to the bottom. Ironically, as Spruance was pondering sending a force to find and sink the *Hiryū*, the Japanese

■ The *Hiryū*, as photographed by a scout pilot from *Hōshō* on June 6. When Yamamoto learned that the *Hiryū* was still afloat, he dispatched the destroyer *Tanikaze* to finish her off. (U.S. Naval Institute)

destroyer *Tanikaze* was dispatched on a mission to accomplish precisely the same goal.[13]

Conflicting sighting reports led Spruance to hold off from attacking immediately, and by the time these reports were sorted out, it was early afternoon. Another problem was that the sighting reports put the *Hiryū* some 230 miles away, and the need to turn away from the target into the wind to launch meant that it would be closer to 270 miles away by the time the strike force set out. Though this was well beyond the ideal range of the Dauntless dive-bombers, Browning wanted to launch at once. He pointed out that if Task Force 16 steamed toward the target during the outbound flight, it would reduce the length of the return trip. Moreover, he wanted all the planes to carry 1,000-pound bombs, which were unquestionably more effective than 500-pound bombs, but which significantly reduced the fuel efficiency—and therefore the range—of the bombers. The planes on *Enterprise* that would be assigned this task were mostly refugees from the *Yorktown*, and the two squadron commanders, Dave Shumway and Wally Short, were leery of lugging 1,000-pound bombs to a target more than 250 miles away. After talking it over between themselves, they decided to talk to the CEAG, Wade McClusky, who was down in sick bay recovering from his wounds of the day before. McClusky listened to their concerns and agreed that the order was unwise. He got out of bed to go with them back up to the bridge to see Browning.[14]

Browning was annoyed at having his orders challenged. He was not only the senior aviator on board, in his mind he was the representative—in spirit, if not in fact—of the absent Bull Halsey, and he refused to reconsider. As McClusky put it, "Browning was stubborn." Unintimidated by his blunt refusal, McClusky pressed the issue. He reminded Browning that most of the planes in his own squadron had run out of gas returning from their attack on the *Kaga* and *Akagi* the day before—and those targets had been only 170 miles away. He pointedly asked Browning whether he had ever flown an SBD carrying a 1,000-pound bomb and a full load of gas from a carrier deck. Browning admitted that he had not. McClusky then formally requested a one-hour delay in the launch in order to close the range, and, further, that the bomb loads on all the planes be changed to

500-pounders. Browning was starting to reject McClusky's request when Spruance, who had been quietly listening nearby, interrupted him, saying evenly, "I will do what you pilots want." Browning was furious to be publicly overridden. Without another word, he left the bridge and stalked off to his cabin. A contemporary likened it to Achilles sulking in his tent.[15]

Spruance's decision meant not only an hour's delay in the launch but rearming all the strike planes with 500-pound bombs, which took additional time. As a result, the strike against the *Hiryū* was not launched until after 3:00 in the afternoon. The *Hornet* launched first—and this time Stanhope Ring made sure that he was not left behind. He led Walt Rodee's VS-8 and Ruff Johnson's VB-8 (plus one orphan from Wally Short's VS-5), thirty-two planes altogether. At about the same time, Shumway and Short led thirty-three planes from the *Enterprise*. Thus a total of sixty-five bombers headed out to finish off the crippled *Hiryū*.

Though none of them knew it, the *Hiryū* had already sunk, going down without any further assistance from either American bombs or Japanese torpedoes shortly after 9:00 that morning, less than twenty minutes after the last sighting had been called in. Stanhope Ring was bound on another "flight to nowhere."*

The Americans flew low in a long scouting line to ensure that they did not miss the target. When they reached the reported coordinates at twilight, around 6:00 p.m., "the enemy was nowhere in sight." Grimly determined, Ring pressed on. At 6:20, he spotted a single vessel, initially identified as a light cruiser but which was in fact the destroyer *Tanikaze* bound on the same mission he was: to find and sink the *Hiryū*. Ring led his air group past the *Tanikaze*, looking for bigger game. After flying more than three hundred miles and seeing nothing, Ring decided to go back and sink that light cruiser. It was the first enemy ship he had seen since the battle began, and he was not going back

---

* Before the *Hiryū* went down, the roughly forty Japanese survivors still on board her (though not Yamaguchi or Captain Kaku) successfully evacuated in a cutter stocked with supplies. They spent the next two weeks hoping to be rescued by their countrymen. Instead they were spotted by a PBY out of Midway and picked up by the U.S. submarine tender USS *Ballard* on June 19. Not until then did Spruance learn for certain that the *Hiryū* had sunk.

this time without striking a blow. He reported the sighting to both Shumway and Short, and since neither of them had found a target either, all sixty-five American dive-bombers prepared to attack the hapless *Tanikaze*. Her captain, Commander Katsumi Tomoi, may have wondered what he had done to merit such attention.[16]

Katsumi had been skeptical of his assignment from the outset. When ordered to return to the *Hiryū*, rescue her crew, and then sink her, he considered the mission "suicidal." Now he announced to the crew on the ship's loudspeaker that they "should be prepared to die with dignity." At the same time, however, he was determined to make the best defense he could. He ordered lookouts to lean out the bridge windows, facing almost straight up, and to report the flight path of each approaching American bomber. They would call out, "Dive-bombers approaching from aft starboard!" and Katsumi would order the helmsman: "Port helm. Full speed." When another dove from the port side, he reversed helm. "I never saw a ship go through such radical maneuvers at such high speed," Ring later wrote.[17]

In the gathering darkness, the American dive-bomber pilots jostled among themselves to attack this one lone destroyer. One by one, sixty-five American dive-bombers plunged down to release their bombs, and they pressed the attack to the limit—the lookout on the *Tanikaze* later recalled that the bombers dove so low he could see the pilots' goggles and white scarves. In spite of that, all the American bombs missed. Whether it was the small size of the target, the gathering darkness, or Katsumi's maneuvers, not a single bomb hit home.* Lieutenant Abbie Tucker of Ruff Johnson's squadron managed a near miss that damaged the *Tanikaze*'s hull near the waterline, but that was it. Moreover, Sam Adams, perhaps still in his blue

---

* For Ring himself it was another day of hair-pulling frustration. As he dove at last on an enemy warship, he discovered to his horror that his bomb would not release. Frantically, he continued to press the release button, to no avail, and in the end he had to return to the *Hornet* with his bomb still attached. Afterward, a rumor circulated within Ruff Johnson's squadron that Ring did not know how to drop a bomb. While perhaps unfair, it suggested how alienated Ring had become from the pilots he commanded. That night in his quarters, Ring asked Ensign Clayton Fisher to demonstrate to him how to use the emergency bomb release lever in case it ever happened again.

pajamas, was shot down by antiair fire. He and his backseat gunner, Joseph Karrol, were never found. Because Adams was an especially popular member of Short's VS-5, this loss significantly dampened the mood on the return trip. Johnny Nielsen thought, "*We might better have lost a cruiser than lost Sam.*"[18]

Returning low on gas after a very long flight, the pilots now had to find the carriers in the dark, and most of them had never attempted a night landing, even in training. At 7:30, worried that the pilots didn't have time to look for the task force, and knowing they would be low on gas, Spruance ordered both carriers to turn on their big 36-inch searchlights, pointing them straight up like beacons despite the danger of attracting the attention of Japanese submarines. The searchlights were turned off at 8:00, but the *Enterprise* kept her sidelights burning for another two and a half hours.* As a result, Adams was the only pilot who failed to return, though in the dark some of the pilots landed on the wrong carrier. Only after the strike force was back aboard did Spruance learn that several of the planes from *Hornet* had flown off with 1,000-pound bombs despite his orders to carry 500-pounders. He said nothing at the time, but the news added to a lengthening list of concerns he had about the *Hornet*'s performance in the battle, and about Mitscher's capacity for command.[19]

This time, instead of heading east during the night hours, away from the enemy, Spruance ordered the task force to maintain a westerly course, though he did so at a reduced speed, both to avoid running into Japanese battleships in the dark and to conserve fuel. Then he went to bed.[20]

---

While Spruance slept, Lieutenant Commander Tanabe Yahachi on the Japanese submarine I-168 was heading northward on the surface toward a set of coordinates that Nagumo had forwarded to him. Early that morn-

---

* Just over two years later, during the Battle of the Philippine Sea in June of 1944, Marc Mitscher, by then commanding the American fast carrier task force of fifteen carriers and seven fast battleships, ordered the carriers to turn on their lights to assist pilots returning from a long-range strike. Almost certainly, his inspiration for that decision was Spruance's action during the Battle of Midway.

ing, the *Chikuma*'s number 4 floatplane had reported a *Yorktown*-class carrier "listing to starboard and drifting," and with the surviving Japanese surface ships now in full retreat, only Tanabe's sub was close enough to respond. Concealed by darkness, Tanabe and the I-168 stayed on the surface under diesel power, both to save the batteries and to make better speed. Just before 4:00 a.m., only minutes before dawn on June 6, Tanabe identified the looming shadow of a big carrier, apparently under tow and surrounded by a screen of five destroyers, and as the eastern sky began to lighten, he submerged.

Buckmaster had ordered the evacuation of the *Yorktown* thirty-six hours earlier because it had seemed to him that she was about to capsize, which would have trapped the whole crew of nearly three thousand men under the water. Fletcher had ordered the destroyer *Hughes* to stay by the abandoned flattop on the night of June 4 and to sink her if there was any chance that the enemy might capture her. But she was still afloat on June 5, and during the day the minesweeper *Vireo*, ordered there from French Frigate Shoals by Nimitz, took her under tow. The big flattop, riding low in the water and somewhat down by the bow, was a lot of dead weight for the *Vireo*. In addition, the *Yorktown*'s rudder was jammed hard over so that she yawed badly; it was almost like towing her sideways. Consequently, during the night of June 5–6, there was little progress eastward.[21]

By then, Buckmaster had decided that since the *Yorktown* appeared to have stabilized, he would take a volunteer crew back aboard to try to salvage her. He called for volunteers from her former crew members who were with him on the *Astoria* and, ranging up alongside the destroyers *Benham* and *Balch*, solicited more volunteers. Those who raised their hands—twenty-nine officers and 141 enlisted men—were transferred to the destroyer *Hammann* by breeches buoy. Early on June 6, the *Hammann* closed on the *Yorktown* so that the volunteers could make their way back on board the ship that they had abandoned two days before. The big flattop was still canted over at a 26-degree angle, and a few fires were still burning, including the one in the rag storage area forward. But it was the quiet that was most disturbing. The big ship was "dark, dead, and silent" as the volunteers came aboard. Machinist Lew Williams experienced "an eerie, unearthly dream-like feeling" as he made his way through the ship. It soon passed as he and the others got to work.[22]

Using electric power and steam pressure supplied by the *Hammann*, which was tied up alongside, the volunteers suppressed the last of the fires and corrected some of the list with counterflooding. They cut away anything they could from the lower (port) side to reduce weight, and the *Yorktown* slowly began to right herself, listing now at only 22 degrees. By noon, Buckmaster and his hardworking volunteers began to believe that they were on their way to saving the ship. Fletcher had informed Nimitz that the *Yorktown* was "badly damaged and dead in the water," but also that, unless Nimitz directed otherwise, he planned to "protect and salvage" his flagship. Nimitz agreed, and he informed Fletcher that he was sending tugs and salvage officers to the scene.[23]

By the time Fletcher got that message, it was already too late. At noon, the crew on the *Hammann* passed food over to the salvage crew, and many of the volunteers took a break to eat. It was a warm, calm day, with "a glassy sea with perfect visibility" and some of the men sat on the deck to eat. Then at 1:30, first one sailor, and then others, spotted the white wakes of torpedoes heading toward them. Tanabe had somehow managed to work his way through the screen of five destroyers to loose a spread of four Type 95 torpedoes from 1,200 yards. The *Yorktown*'s klaxon sounded general quarters, and gunners manning the antiaircraft guns aimed their weapons at the head of the wakes, hoping to detonate the torpedoes prematurely.[24]

It was to no avail. The first torpedo hit the *Yorktown* near the bow, and the big ship shuddered. Seconds later another slammed into the destroyer *Hammann* tied up alongside. A third torpedo hit the *Yorktown* astern near frame 95, and a fourth missed astern. The *Hammann* was literally cut in half. Many in her crew were killed outright, knocked unconscious, or blown into the sea by the impact. The *Hammann* began to sink almost immediately, while on her stern men assigned to the depth-charge racks worked frantically to ensure that the safety forks were inserted into the canisters so that when the stern did sink, the charges would not explode. Their effort remained vivid to one witness sixty years later. "I can still see them," William Burford recalled, "working on the depth charges on the stern . . . trying to put them on safety." But there was not enough time, and the stern of the *Hammann* went down with at least some of her depth charges still set in the active mode. As the destroyer's hull plunged downward, the depth charges began to go off, the big explosions damaging the hull of the *Yorktown* further and killing scores of men flailing in the water nearby.[25]

One of those men was the *Yorktown*'s gunnery officer, Commander Ernest J. Davis, who had been blown over the side of the carrier by the impact of the torpedo. He had grabbed a rope and was in the act of climbing back aboard the *Yorktown* when the depth charges went off. Only his lower torso was still submerged, which allowed him to survive, though he sustained a number of internal injuries. The concussion in the water was so great that the gold watch he had in his pocket was flattened to "the thickness of a silver dollar against his thigh." Others, fully immersed in the water, were less fortunate. One witness recalled seeing the heads of swimming survivors simply disappear after the depth-charge explosion. One minute there were scores of swimmers in the water, and then "they were all gone."[26]

For the second time in three days, Buckmaster ordered abandon ship. The tug *Vireo* cut the towing cable and came alongside to collect the survivors (plus sixteen bodies) from the *Yorktown*. Even then, however, Buckmaster wondered if the big ship could be saved. The torpedoes had blasted holes in the *Yorktown*'s starboard side so that while she now lay very low in the water, her list was less pronounced—only about 17 degrees. But the big ship continued to settle lower and lower in the water, until at two minutes before 5:00 a.m. on June 7, as Buckmaster saluted from a nearby destroyer, she disappeared.[27]

While Buckmaster and his volunteer crew sought to save the *Yorktown*, Spruance and the pilots of Task Force 16 were seeking to complete the destruction of the Japanese armada—or as much of it as was still within range. Just past dawn on June 6, while Tanabe was studying the silhouette of the *Yorktown* through his periscope, Spruance sent eighteen scout bombers from the *Enterprise* to conduct a search to the westward. At 6:45, Ensign William D. Carter sighted what he thought was a battleship or battlecruiser and a cruiser screened by three destroyers 128 miles away and heading west at a leisurely ten knots. It was the crippled *Mogami* and the *Mikuma* with two (not three) destroyers, looking like a battleship and a cruiser because one was forty feet longer than the other. Carter told his radioman, Oral "Slim" Moore, to send the message "Sighted one CA [cruiser] and one CB [battlecruiser]" But Moore had never heard of a "CB" and over the intercom it sounded like "CV" [carrier], so that's what he sent. Spruance did not react at once. Having dispatched his planes on a wild goose chase the day before, he wanted to make sure of the target this time. Rather than order an immediate launch, he directed floatplanes from two of the cruisers in his screen (*Minneapolis* and *New Orleans*) to verify the contact and stay in the area, so that they could guide the strike to the target, which they could do because of their long-range capability.[28]

At 7:30, with the float planes still en route to the sighting, Ensign Roy Gee, whose flying skills had drawn Mitscher's ire back in March during the *Hornet*'s shakedown cruise, flew over the *Enterprise* and dropped a beanbag on the deck. The attached note accurately reported two cruisers and two destroyers 133 miles to the southwest. Though this was a confirmation of the same group reported earlier, Spruance now wondered if there were *two* groups of enemy ships out there, one of them with a carrier. He decided to hedge his bets, ordering *Hornet* to launch her air group at once, but keeping the planes of the *Enterprise* back as a reserve, as Fletcher had done two days before, on the morning of June 4. The *Hornet* began launching at 8:00 a.m.

It was Stan Ring's third opportunity to strike the enemy, and he was grimly determined that this time nothing should go wrong. He led eleven planes of VB-8 under Ruff Johnson and fourteen from VS-8 under Walt Rodee. Mitscher sent along eight Wildcats to strafe the target and to suppress antiaircraft fire. As Ring's formation circled the *Hornet* and prepared to depart, the *Enterprise* was busy recovering planes from the morning search. From their pilots, Spruance learned that the sighting had involved a *battleship*, not a carrier, and, fearful that Ring might ignore the battleship and waste time seeking a nonexistent carrier, he authorized a radio message to tell him: "Target may be a battleship instead of a carrier. Attack."[29]

Ring took his air group westward, and an hour later, at 9:30, Ruff Johnson was the first to spot the *Mogami* and *Mikuma*, plus their two destroyers.

He reported the sighting to Ring: "Stanhope from Robert, Enemy below on port bow." Apparently, the Japanese were monitoring the same radio frequency, for soon afterward an unidentified radioman came on the circuit, speaking in "a very oriental tone," to say, "Stanhope from Robert, Return to base." It fooled no one, and Ring led his air group around to the east to attack out of the sun. At last, Ring had an opportunity to strike at a major element of the enemy fleet.[30]

The fourteen planes of Walt Rodee's Scouting Eight dove on the *Mogami*, while the eight planes of Johnson's Bombing Eight attacked the *Mikuma*, which most of the pilots reported as a battleship. Rodee's bombers scored two hits. One bomb landed squarely on top of *Mogami*'s turret number five, blowing off the roof and killing every man inside, and another hit the cruiser astern. Neither hit was fatal, however, in part because Captain Soji had jettisoned all his torpedoes, and there were no secondary explosions. The *Mikuma* escaped altogether. Ruff Johnson himself scored a near miss (a "paint scraper" as he called it) on the *Mikuma*, but no one scored a direct hit, and the heavy antiair fire claimed two of the American pilots. Ensign Don Adams landed a 500-pound bomb on the destroyer *Asashio*, and the Wildcat pilots strafed both destroyers and cruisers.

On the whole, the strike was disappointing. Thirty-three planes had attacked two cruisers, one of them already crippled, and two destroyers, and failed to sink any of them. The already-damaged *Mogami* had been hit twice but continued to steam at better than 20 knots. Captain Sakiyama reported only "light damage" to the *Mikuma*. All four ships continued to steam southward, seeking to get inside the 700-mile radius from Wake Island and the protection of land-based air cover. Even at 28 knots, however, it would take them another twenty hours to get there, and there were still eight hours of daylight left.[31]

As the *Hornet* planes were attacking, the *Enterprise* was launching a second strike of thirty-one more bombers, escorted by twelve Wildcats— forty-three planes in all, with Wally Short in command. In case there was a carrier out there after all, Spruance decided at the last minute to send along his last three torpedo planes as well. He worried about risking them; they were the last three operational torpedo bombers in the Pacific Fleet.

He told Lieutenant Junior Grade Robert Laub, who commanded the section, that he was not to attack unless the dive-bombers and fighters had completely suppressed enemy antiaircraft fire. "If there is one single gun firing out there," he instructed Laub, "under no circumstances are you to attack. Turn around and bring your torpedoes home. I am not going to lose another torpedo plane if I can help it. Do you understand?"[32]

The forty-six planes from *Enterprise* were aloft by noon. The bombers climbed to 22,500 feet, with the three torpedo planes behind and below them at 1,500 feet. En route to the target, Johnny Nielsen saw a small motor boat, leaving "a tiny white wake, that was heading eastward in the direction of San Francisco." It may have been the cutter from the *Hiryū* containing the last of the survivors from that ship, though why it would be heading east was a mystery.[33]

Soon after that, the pilots spotted a trail of oil on the surface that led off to the southwest, and they followed it to the two cruisers. By now the *Mogami* had worked her way back up to 28 knots, and both cruisers were trying desperately to get within the envelope of air cover from Wake. The American bombers flew past them for thirty miles to be sure there was neither a carrier nor a battleship in the area. Jim Gray took his Wildcat down to 10,000 feet to look over the cruisers, and noting that one was shorter than the other, he concluded, correctly, that they were the "battleship and cruiser" that had been reported earlier, and he radioed Short to that effect.

All formality was dispensed with as Shumway and Short prepared to attack. "Wally, this is Dave," Shumway radioed. "I'll take the cruiser to the northeast." Short replied that he would take "the other one." The Americans dove at nearly 90 degrees, and although there was heavy antiair fire, all the flak exploded well behind them. The pilots got two more hits on the *Mogami* and devastated the "battleship" *Mikuma* with five bombs. Johnny Nielsen watched as one bomb went down the smoke stack and detonated. "That stack just lifted up off the deck," Neilsen recalled, "tumbled over in the air, splashed into the water, and disappeared." White steam gushed up through the black smoke. The *Mikuma* slowed and then stopped, burning furiously. The almost giddy mood of the American pilots was evident in the recorded message traffic. "Tojo, you Son-of-a-Bitch," said one, "send out the rest and we'll get those, too."[34]

Even as this strike by the planes from the *Enterprise* was in progress, Spruance authorized the *Hornet* air group to rearm and go out again. In effect, he was tag-teaming the *Mogami* and *Mikuma*, with the two carriers taking turns. This time, however, Stanhope Ring did not go along with the *Hornet* air group. The radio on his plane was not working, and Mitscher used that as a reason to hold him back. Ring could have flown another plane had Mitscher deemed it useful. Instead, as Ring recalled it, "Capt. Mitscher decided . . . that I should not accompany the final attack group which was being readied for takeoff." Perhaps Mitscher had finally concluded that Ring was not a particular asset.[35]

Walt Rodee led the *Hornet*'s second strike and found the smoking and burning cruisers at about 2:30 in the afternoon. The *Mikuma* was dead

■ The wrecked and burning Japanese heavy cruiser *Mikuma* as photographed by Lieutenant Junior Grade Cleo Dobson on June 6. She sank soon afterward. (U.S. Naval Institute)

in the water and burning furiously. The Americans hit it again and put another bomb into the *Mogami*, while strafing the two destroyers. Both cruisers were now badly hurt, but the *Mikuma* was in extremis, burning from end to end. On the radio net, one pilot blurted out, "Look at that battleship burn!"[36]

Back on *Enterprise*, Shumway and Short were pleading with Spruance to let them go back out for another strike. Spruance was pleased by their enthusiasm but uncertain what a fourth strike would accomplish. It was late afternoon by now, the target was getting closer to the envelope of air cover from Wake, and Spruance had to consider the fuel situation. As his destroyers had run low on fuel, Spruance had sent them back one by one to the fuel rendezvous site, and he now had only four destroyers left to accompany his two carriers. Finally, given the pilot reports, it was not clear that the target was worth another strike. In fact, Spruance did not know for sure what the target had been. Shumway thought they had hit a battleship and a cruiser; Short reported that both ships had been cruisers. Johnny Neilsen joined the group and Spruance turned to him to ask what kind of ship he had hit. "A heavy cruiser," Neilsen answered. "Very much like our own Indianapolis class."* Spruance asked him whether he was sure it wasn't a battleship. Nielsen told him he was positive it was a cruiser. [37]

In the end, Spruance decided against a fourth strike, but he did send out two Dauntless bombers to reconnoiter and to take photographs of the damaged enemy ships. Flying one of those scout bombers, Lieutenant Junior Grade Cleo Dobson arrived at the coordinates and saw the wrecked and burning *Mikuma* with "lots of bodies lying on the deck, and lots more were lying on the stern." There were also "about 400 to 500 saliors [*sic*] in the water all around the ship," he recalled. On the way out, he had decided that if he saw any survivors in the water, he would strafe them, as the Japanese had done to American survivors. When he saw those heads bobbing in the water, however, he couldn't bring himself to do it. *"Boy I would hate to be in*

---

* Neilson's comparison was spot on. The *Portland*-class *Indianapolis* displaced 12,000 tons and carried nine 8-inch guns. The *Mogami*-class cruisers displaced 11,200 tons and carried ten 8-inch guns.

*the shoes of those fellows,"* he remembered thinking. *"I might be in their shoes some day."* He took his photographs and flew back.[38]

As it turned to full dark on June 6, Spruance assessed the value of continuing the pursuit. Despite the remarkable successes of the past three days, there were a number of reasons for caution. By the time the sun came up on June 7, whatever targets were left would very likely be protected by land-based air from Wake Island, and with tired pilots, low fuel, and only four destroyers on hand, he decided to call it off. As he wrote later, "I had a feeling, an intuition perhaps, that we had pushed our luck as far to the westward as was good for us." Once the two scout planes were recovered, he turned Task Force 16 back east toward the fuel rendezvous.[39]

# EPILOGUE

"The efforts and sacrifices of the Army, Navy, and Marine Corps forces involved in the Battle of Midway have been crowned with glorious success and I firmly believe have already changed the course of the war."

—Admiral Chester Nimitz

June 7 was a Sunday morning, and it dawned on a changed world. It was six months to the day after that other Sunday morning when the Japanese had surprised the world by attacking the American battle fleet in Pearl Harbor. Now the instrument of that attack had been smashed beyond recovery. Japan still had the *Shokaku* and *Zuikaku*, as well as a number of smaller carriers, plus her large battleship and cruiser fleet, but the concentrated Kidō Butai that had dominated the Pacific for half a year was no more. The only prize the Japanese had won for their massive effort and astounding losses was the occupation of the tiny islands of Attu and Kiska in the Aleutian archipelago, and, as Commander Miyo had prophesied back in April, those outposts proved more of a burden than a benefit. The living conditions were horrible. The Japanese occupiers spent most of their time huddled in poorly insulated barracks trying not to freeze to death. Rear Admiral Theobald could not figure out why they wanted the islands in the first place, or why they stayed there. "There is no manner in which a force could be made self-sufficient in this area," he wrote. "Food, ammunition, and military supplies . . . have to flow to the Japanese forces in a steady stream and in considerable volume." It just made no sense. He wondered whether the Japanese wanted to fish the surrounding waters. More likely they remained simply because it was all they had to show for the loss of five capital ships,[1] hundreds of combat airplanes, and thousands of men.[2]

The full extent of the American victory at Midway became evident only gradually. In a cable to Stalin, Roosevelt described the outcome of the battle as "indecisive" as late as June 6. Nimitz, Fletcher, and Spruance did not learn that all four of the Japanese carriers had gone down until the seaplane tender *Ballard* rescued the last of the *Hiryū*'s survivors from their small cutter on June 19. In fact, the Battle of Midway was the most complete naval victory since Horatio Nelson's near annihilation of the Spanish and French fleets at Trafalgar in 1805, and, like that battle, it had momentous strategic consequences. The previous April, the Japanese had been in a position to choose from among half a dozen strategic options. Now those options had narrowed to one: a perimeter defense designed to wear out the Americans and force them to the negotiating table. The war had three more years to run, but the Japanese never again seized the strategic initiative; their only hope was to hold out long enough for the Americans to tire of the struggle.[3]

The battle had the opposite effect on the Americans. They had suffered too, of course. The loss of the *Yorktown* on June 7 was a severe blow. Nonetheless, the return that same day of the repaired *Saratoga* gave Nimitz three carriers—soon to be four, since the *Wasp* was at that moment on her way to the Pacific. With four carrier task groups, Nimitz and the Americans had operational superiority over their foe for the first time in the war, and that encouraged Ernie King to renew his push for an early offensive against the Japanese. He wrote to Army Chief of Staff George Marshall, insisting, "It is urgent, in my opinion, that we lose no time in taking the initiative." Once it became evident that there would be no cross-channel invasion of occupied France in 1942, King pushed even harder for a Pacific offensive that would begin no later than August 1 "or shortly thereafter."[4]

MacArthur, too, saw the victory at Midway as opening the door for an offensive. He insisted that it "should be exploited at the earliest possible date."

Given Roosevelt's commitment to the Germany First concept, a complete re-orientation of the war to the Pacific was unlikely. The president made it clear that he was "opposed to an American all-out effort in the Pacific." MacArthur nonetheless sought 40,000 soldiers to begin an offensive against Rabaul and appealed to Marshall for support. Marshall was more receptive to such an appeal than he might have been a month earlier, for he was disappointed—even angered—by British unwillingness to accept the American proposal for a cross-channel invasion of occupied France in 1942.[5]

King was as eager as anyone to obtain more resources for an offensive in the Pacific, but he was adamant that the Navy and not the Army should have direction of what he conceived of as a naval war. Instead of advancing directly to Rabaul from Australia, as MacArthur envisioned, King proposed approaching the Japanese citadel along the axis of the Solomon Islands, beginning with landings on Tulagi and Guadalcanal, where the Japanese were building an airstrip. Moreover, he insisted that such amphibious operations were the provenance of the Navy and Marine Corps. "In my opinion," he wrote to Marshall, "this part of the operation must be con-ducted under the direction of the Commander in Chief Pacific Fleet [Nim-itz], and cannot be conducted in any other way." In a kind of preemptive strike, on June 25 he ordered Nimitz to assemble the forces needed "for commencing offensive operations about one August."[6]

King's move forced Marshall to choose between MacArthur and the Navy. Marshall had great respect for MacArthur, who had been Army Chief of Staff back when Marshall was a mere colonel. King, on the other hand, was a powerful advocate of the argument that since the Army had control of the European theater, the Navy should have oversight in the Pacific. In a kind of compromise, Marshall agreed to move the theater boundary between Nimitz's and MacArthur's commands one degree (sixty miles) to the west in order to put Guadalcanal within Nimitz's theater. As a result of that decision, on August 7, just two months after the Battle of Midway, ten thousand U.S. Marines went ashore on Guadalcanal to seize the airfield (which they named for Major Lofton Henderson, the martyred VMSB-241 commander at Midway) and to inaugurate what turned into a savage fourteen-month campaign of attrition.

During those fourteen months, American soldiers and Marines fought their way westward from Guadalcanal to other places with exotic names: Rendova, Kolombangara, Vella Lavella, and Bougainville. The Japanese fought ferociously, but they lost more than they could afford in a futile defense of these sparsely populated jungle outposts. In their prewar plan, their defense of the empire's perimeter was supposed to diminish the American battle fleet as it moved westward. Like a wave running up a sloping beach, the Americans would lose power and momentum as they advanced. Instead, the longer the campaign lasted, the stronger American forces became.

In May 1943, the new-construction carrier USS *Essex* (CV-9) joined the Pacific fleet, the first of an eventual twenty-four ships of her class. The foolishness of the Japanese decision to launch a war against an industrial juggernaut like the United States was thus fully revealed. The second *Essex*-class carrier had been prospectively named the *Bonhomme Richard* in honor of John Paul Jones's flagship during the American Revolution, but after Midway she was rechristened *Yorktown* (CV-10). The existence of two carriers both named *Yorktown* still causes confusion for some students of the Second World War, but there is something symbolic about it. Three times the Japanese believed that they had sunk the *Yorktown*: once in the Coral Sea and twice at Midway. Even after she finally succumbed, she reemerged again only months later in a newer and bigger form. To the Japanese, the Americans must have seemed like the mythical Hydra, which grew two new heads whenever one was decapitated.

For their part, the Japanese never recovered from the loss of the four big fleet carriers sunk at Midway. They simply did not have the industrial capacity to produce a score of new carriers in the midst of war. Even more critically, Japan never recovered from the loss of so many of her airplanes and trained carrier pilots. The battles of the Coral Sea, Midway, and especially the grinding Solomons campaign claimed hundreds of frontline aircraft and the lives of a disproportionate number of her frontline pilots. Genda Minoru later observed despondently, "One after another, our best pilots were lost, and green, inexperienced men came in as replacements." The Japanese had no option but to rely on these young and untested pilots who, however earnest and determined, lacked the training, and especially the experience, of their predecessors.[7]

By the time the Solomons campaign came to an end in the fall of 1943, the United States boasted seven new *Essex*-class aircraft carriers whose hanger decks were packed with a thousand new planes from American factories, and which were manned by thousands of new pilots who streamed out of American training programs. In November of 1943, the United States began an island-hopping campaign that led them to the Gilberts, the Marshalls, the Marianas, Iwo Jima, Okinawa, and finally to the very doorstep of Japan's home islands. The Japanese continued to fight courageously, and they inflicted heavy casualties, but they never succeeded in halting the American advance. In hindsight, it is evident that the course of the war— and with it the course of history—had tilted on the fulcrum of the Battle of Midway.

**Chester Nimitz** remained as CinCPac for the duration of the war and directed the Pacific campaign right up to the signing of the instrument of surrender on the deck of the battleship *Missouri* in Tokyo Bay. In December of 1944, President Roosevelt promoted him to the newly established rank of five-star fleet admiral, and he remains one of only nine men ever to hold that rank. At war's end, he relieved King as chief of naval operations and retired from the Navy two years later. He died at his quarters on Yerba Buena Island in San Francisco Bay in February 1966.

**Frank Jack Fletcher** never received the credit he deserved for the victory at Midway; some accounts of the battle even imply that it was Spruance and not Fletcher who commanded the American carrier forces in the battle. For the most part this was the result of subsequent events. Two months after Midway, Fletcher commanded the fleet protecting the Guadalcanal landing force. He initially expected to keep a three-carrier task force there for three days, but because the landings were proceeding well, he recommended that the carriers be withdrawn after two days in order to limit their exposure in the confined waters around the Solomon Islands. That provoked angry criticism from the American amphibious commander, Richmond Kelly Turner, and reignited questions in the mind of Ernie King about Fletcher's determination. Later that month, after his flagship, *Saratoga*, was torpedoed by a Japanese sub, Fletcher brought her back to Pearl Harbor for repairs and Nimitz sent Fletcher Stateside for two weeks' recuperation. Afterward, rather than return him to the front, King sent Fletcher to command the Thirteenth Naval District at the Puget Sound Navy Yard in Washington State. It was the end of Fletcher's sea service. After the war, Fletcher headed the Navy's General Board, a largely ceremonial post. He retired from the Navy as a four-star admiral in 1947 and died at his farm in southern Maryland in 1973 at the age of 87.

**Raymond Spruance** became Nimitz's chief of staff after the Battle of Midway. Over the next thirteen months, he worked closely with his boss, living with him under the same roof and walking to work with him every day. In the process he learned the nuances of theater command. Nimitz came to admire Spruance's quiet work ethic, which closely resembled his own. In the fall of 1943, as the United States geared up for the island-hopping campaign that would take it to the shores of Japan, Nimitz tapped Spruance for command of the Fifth Fleet, essentially the offensive arm of the U.S. Navy in the Pacific. In that capacity, Spruance directed operations against Tarawa in the Gilberts, Kwajalein in the Marshalls, and Saipan in the Marianas. When Nimitz became CNO in 1945, Spruance took over as CinCPac. After the war, he served as president of the Naval War College from 1946 until he retired in 1948. He died in 1969 at his home in Pebble Beach, California, at age 83.

**William Halsey** recovered from his skin condition and returned to active duty in September of 1942, replacing the disappointing Robert L. Ghormley in command of the South Pacific. After that, Halsey and his former subordinate Raymond Spruance took turns commanding the "Big Blue Fleet," which was called Third Fleet when Halsey commanded it and Fifth Fleet when Spruance did so. Halsey never lost his pugnacious edge, though it got him into trouble at least twice: once during the Battle of Leyte Gulf in October of 1944, when he charged off after an enemy carrier fleet, leaving a critical strait unguarded, and once when he failed to take adequate precautions against a powerful typhoon in December 1944. That latter incident resulted in the deaths of eight hundred men and the loss of

146 airplanes. After a subsequent encounter with another typhoon, a board of inquiry recommended that Halsey be reassigned, but Nimitz intervened on his behalf. In December 1945, Halsey joined Nimitz as a five-star fleet admiral and retired two years later in 1947. He died in 1959 at the age of 86.

**Marc "Pete" Mitscher** was never officially called to account for his error-plagued performance at Midway. Spruance knew that Mitscher's report was flawed, however, and he very likely suggested to Nimitz that Mitscher should no longer command a carrier task force. After the battle, Nimitz transferred Mitscher to the command of Patrol Wing Two, a shore-based billet, and Mitscher remained there in a kind of exile until December. In April 1943 he became commander of air assets in the Solomons and gradually worked his way back into Nimitz's good graces. In January of 1944 he received command of the Fast Carrier Task Force, called Task Force 58 since it was associated with Spruance's Fifth Fleet. Based on his success in that role, he was promoted to vice admiral in March. With overwhelming superiority over the enemy, Mitscher emerged as "the Bald Eagle" and "the Magnificent Mitscher," winning several decorations. After the war, he became the deputy CNO for Air, and then, as a four-star admiral, commander of the Atlantic Fleet. Mitscher's health was never good; he died in February 1947 at the age of 60 while still on active duty.

**Miles Browning**'s postbattle career was as rocky and uneven as his performance at Midway. Aware of Browning's many lapses during the battle, Spruance did not recommend him for a medal. When Halsey returned to active duty that fall, he made up for it by putting Browning in for a Distinguished Service Medal. The citation claimed that Browning was "largely responsible" for the American victory at Midway, an assertion that some historians have taken seriously but which is manifestly untrue. Halsey brought Browning back onto his staff, but after problems continued during the Solomons campaign, including a messy and public affair with the wife of a fellow officer, Secretary of the Navy Knox insisted that he be replaced. Browning got another chance as the commanding officer of the new-construction USS *Hornet* (CV-12), a replacement for the original *Hornet* (CV-8) which was lost in the Battle of the Santa Cruz Islands in October 1942. Once again, however, Browning's volatility drew criticism, and he was removed for cause in May 1944. His only child, a daughter, gave birth to Cornelius Crane, who became a comedian and changed his name to Chevy Chase. Browning retired as a captain in 1947 and died in 1954.

**Stanhope Ring** went ashore with Pete Mitscher when Mitscher became Commander of Patrol Wing Two. His punctiliousness and loyalty continued to win him promotions, and as the war neared its end in May of 1945 he got command of the new escort carrier USS *Siboney* (CVE-112), though by the time that ship arrived in Pearl Harbor, the war had ended. Ring also briefly commanded the USS *Saratoga*, but only long enough to steer her to Bikini Atoll where, in July of 1946, she performed her last service as a target ship for an atomic bomb test. Ring proved to be an excellent peacetime officer, and won promotions to rear admiral and then vice admiral before he died in 1963.

**Clarence Wade McClusky** was granted leave back to the States to recover from his multiple wounds and was replaced as CEAG by Max Leslie. He returned to active duty later in the war and commanded the escort carrier USS *Corregidor* (CVE-58). He also served in the Korean War and commanded the Glenview Naval Air Station near Chicago. He was promoted to rear admiral upon his retirement in 1956 and died in 1976.

**Richard Best**, who put bombs into two enemy carriers on the same day, had the most curious postbattle experience of anyone. After landing his airplane following his successful strike on the *Hiryū*, Best began to feel queasy and started vomiting. He went to see the ship's doctor and told him that during the morning flight, when he had first put on his oxygen mask, he had smelled "caustic soda." He thought that might be the cause of the problem. Best became weaker by the minute and had to be carried back to his room on a stretcher. He could not hold down any food and lost weight dramatically. Eventually he was diagnosed with tuberculosis, and by August he was in a Navy hospital, where he stayed for two years. Best never flew again, and he retired on full disability in 1944. The disease was not fatal, however, and he lived in Santa Monica, California, until 2001, when he died at the age of 91.

**John S. "Jimmy" Thach** returned to the United States to formulate a new set of air tactics for the fleet. Afterward, he served as operations officer for Vice Admiral John S. McCain (grandfather of the Arizona senator) and ended the war as a captain. He commanded the escort carrier *Sicily* (CVE-118) during the Korean War and afterward the full-sized carrier *Franklin D. Roosevelt* (CV-42). He was promoted to rear admiral in 1955, to vice admiral in 1960, and ended his career as a four-star admiral in command of U.S. Naval Forces, Europe. He died in 1981 just short of his 76th birthday.

**Joseph Rochefort**'s singular contributions to the American victory at Midway went unacknowledged for many years. The work of the code-breakers was necessarily secret. (After the battle, the Chicago *Tribune* ran a headline proclaiming: "NAVY HAD WORD OF JAP PLAN TO STRIKE AT SEA"; King wanted to arrest the publisher for treason.) But Rochefort's work went unacknowledged officially as well. Though Nimitz recommended him for the Distinguished Service Medal, King, after consulting with John Redman, turned down the nomination, justifying his decision by saying that Rochefort had been simply doing his job and that it was unfair to single out any one person for work performed by a team of cryptanalysts. Of course, by that standard, no one would ever receive a medal. Rochefort was as prickly as King. When King reassigned him to duties unrelated to cryptanalysis, Rochefort refused the assignment. Despite that, he ended up in California, supervising the construction of a floating drydock in Tiburon. In the spring of 1944 he went to Washington to work under Joe Redmond, John's brother and the director of Naval Communications. There, his job was to run the Pacific Strategic Intelligence Section, assessing Japan's naval and military capabilities as part of the planning for an invasion of the home islands. He retired as a captain in 1953. Only when the role of the code breakers was declassified in the 1970s did Rochefort begin to get his due. He died in 1976, and, a decade later, he was posthumously awarded the President's National Defense Service Medal.

**Yamamoto Isoroku** tried to be philosophical about the outcome of the Battle of Midway. Whatever he may have felt privately, he accepted full responsibility for its outcome. He remained at the head of the Combined Fleet mainly because replacing him would require public disclosure of the defeat—news of which the government kept secret. But the defeat at Midway cost Yamamoto his leverage with the Naval General Staff, and in any case his options were severely limited by the crippling of the Kidō Butai. After the string of defeats in the Solomons in late 1942 and early 1943, Yamamoto decided to tour the front to bolster morale. His itinerary was transmitted in code to the various bases he was to visit, and the message was intercepted and decrypted by the code-breakers. The question of what to do with that information went all the way to the desk of President Roosevelt. FDR told Frank Knox that if they had a chance to get Yamamoto, they should do it. As a result, long-range Army Air Corps P-38 Lightning fighters intercepted him, and Yamamoto died when his plane was shot down on April 18, 1943. Yamamoto was 59.

**Nagumo Chūichi**, who was not by nature a cheerful man, became positively morose after Midway. Yamamoto had promised him a second chance and kept his word, appointing Nagumo commander in chief of what was called the Third Fleet, which included both *Shokaku* and *Zuikaku*, now redesignated as CarDiv 1. In August he tangled with Fletcher again in the Battle of the Eastern Solomons (August 24–25, 1942). Though Nagumo's pilots inflicted significant damage on the *Enterprise*, they failed to put Henderson Field out of action, and the Americans sank the small carrier *Ryūjō*. After another battle off the Santa Cruz Islands in October, which cost the Americans the *Hornet*, Nagumo retuned to Japan to command the naval bases at Sasebo and Kure. Then in March of 1944 (the same month that Mitscher got command of the Fast Carrier Task Force), Nagumo was charged with the defense of Saipan in the Marianas, which was about to be targeted by Spruance's Fifth Fleet. By now the disparity of forces between the two sides was overwhelming, and Nagumo's only prospect was to make the Americans pay a heavy price for their conquest. American Marines went ashore on Saipan on June 15, 1944, and quickly drove inland. The Japanese fought furiously, as they did everywhere in the Pacific, but they were soon forced back into a tiny enclave where they fought from a number of small caves. Two years before, Nagumo had commanded the most powerful naval striking force ever assembled, effectively the ruler of the vast Pacific Ocean. Now, at age 57 and suffering from arthritis, he sat in a cave as his world collapsed around him. In a dark recess of that cave, he put his pistol to his head and pulled the trigger.

# ACKNOWLEDGMENTS

Because most of my earlier work focused on the nineteenth century, I am more indebted than usual to the many people who offered assistance and advice in the preparation of this book. My first debt, as always, is to my wife, Marylou, best friend and life partner, and also a superb editor and patient sounding board. As usual, she was a full partner in the writing of this book.

Of the several World War II scholars who generously shared their time and expertise, my greatest debt is to John B. Lundstrom, Jonathan Parshall, and Ronald W. Russell, each of them careful and meticulous scholars of the Pacific War. As I was working on Midway, John Lundstrom was writing a history of the Ninth Minnesota Regiment in the Civil War. We worked out a mutually useful arrangement whereby we read each other's manuscripts and offered suggestions and ideas. I am sure that I gained much more from this exchange than John did, and I am grateful to him for his help. Jon Parshall, coauthor of the excellent book *Shattered Sword*, which focuses on the Japanese side of the battle, read the second half of the book and generously offered suggestions and corrections. Ronald Russell, who manages the website for veterans and students of the Battle of Midway (http://www.midway42.org), read the entire manuscript and offered many corrections and suggestions. In addition, Bert Kinzey and Richard B. Frank each read sections of the manuscript and were generous in sharing their expertise. Vice Admiral Yoji Koda (Ret.), now at Harvard, and Lee Pennington at the Naval Academy helped me understand

and appreciate the Japanese side of the story. Though all these scholars patiently tried to steer me away from error, it hardly needs to be said that any factual mistakes that remain, and all the interpretive conclusions, are mine alone.

At Oxford University Press, my excellent editor, Tim Bent, sought to limit my tendency toward the overly dramatic, Joellyn Ausanka steered the book through the production process, and Ben Sadock was a superb copy editor. Once again, I am in debt to this team of professionals at OUP.

Among the many librarians and archivists who guided me to resources, I want to thank Barbara (Bobbi) Posner, Curtis Utz, John Hughes, and John Greco of the Naval History and Heritage Command at the Washington Navy Yard. Thanks are due as well to Evelyn Cherpak at the Naval War College Archives, and to my longtime friend John Hattendorf as well as Doug Smith of the Naval War College faculty. Ginny Kilander welcomed me to the American Heritage Center on the campus of the University of Wyoming in Laramie; Bob Clark, Matt Hanson, and Mark Renovich provided assistance at the Franklin Delano Roosevelt Library in Hyde Park, New York; and Elizabeth Navarro was my guide at the Hornbake Library at the University of Maryland. At the Naval Academy, Barbara Manvel and the Interlibrary Loan librarian, Flo Todd, helped me as always. In the Special Collections room, where I spent many days alternating between studying manuscripts and enjoying the beautiful view of the Severn River, I was assisted by the archivist Jennifer Bryan as well as David D'Onofrio and Dorothea (Dot) Abbot. Jeffrey Ward created the thirteen maps in the book, and Janis Jorgensen at the U.S. Naval Institute assisted me in finding the illustrations, as did Robert Hanshew at the Naval Historical Foundation Photo Archives. My friend Tom Cutler helped me with details about naval procedures.

I also want to thank several people who helped me simply because of their love of the Battle of Midway. These include Phil Hone, Alvin Kernan, Bill Price, and Peter Newberg. I particularly appreciate the interest and assistance of many Midway veterans who offered their help, especially John "Jack" Crawford, Norman "Dusty" Kleiss, Donald "Mac" Showers, and Bill Houser.

# APPENDIX A

## American and Japanese Aircraft Carriers

| Hull# | Name | Year comm. | Tons | Aircraft capacity | Speed |
|-------|------|------------|------|-------------------|-------|
| CV-1 | *Langley* | 1920 | 13,000 | 34 | 15.5 |

NOTES: Built on hull of the collier *Jupiter*, the *Langley* was converted to a seaplane tender in 1937; sunk by Japanese air attack, February 27, 1942.

| | | | | | |
|-------|------|------------|------|-------------------|-------|
| CV-2 | *Lexington* | 1927 | 51,000 | 90 | 34 |

NOTES: Built on hull of a battle cruiser following the Washington Naval Arms Treaty of 1922; sunk in Battle of the Coral Sea, May 8, 1942.

| | | | | | |
|-------|------|------------|------|-------------------|-------|
| CV-3 | *Saratoga* | 1927 | 50,000 | 90 | 34 |

NOTES: Sister ship of *Lexington*; she was torpedoed by a Japanese submarine January 11, 1942. After repair in Bremerton, she left the West Coast for Hawaii on June 1, 1942, but did not arrive until June 6.

| | | | | | |
|-------|------|------------|------|-------------------|-------|
| CV-4 | *Ranger* | 1934 | 14,576 | 76 | 29 |

NOTES: First U.S. carrier built as such from the keel up. Too small for effective offensive operations, she served throughout the war in the Atlantic.

| | | | | | |
|-------|------|------------|------|-------------------|-------|
| CV-5 | *Yorktown* | 1937 | 19,800 | 81 | 32.5 |

NOTES: The prototype for both *Enterprise* and *Hornet*, she served at Coral Sea and Midway as flagship of TF-17. Sunk at Midway.

| | | | | | |
|-------|------|------------|------|-------------------|-------|
| CV-6 | *Enterprise* | 1938 | 19,800 | 81 | 32.5 |

NOTES: Flagship of TF-16; fought at Midway.

*Continued*

| Hull# | Name | Year comm. | Tons | Aircraft capacity | Speed |
|-------|------|-----------|------|-------------------|-------|
| CV-7 | *Wasp* | 1940 | 15,000 | 76 | 29.5 |

NOTES: Left Norfolk for Pacific June 6, 1942; arrived in the first week of July.

| Hull# | Name | Year comm. | Tons | Aircraft capacity | Speed |
|-------|------|-----------|------|-------------------|-------|
| CV-8 | *Hornet* | 1941 | 19,800 | 85 | 32.5 |

NOTES: Commissioned in October 1941 but not ready for battle until March 1942. She carried Doolittle's bombers to Tokyo and fought at Midway as part of TF 16.

(NOTE: USS *Essex*, the first of an eventual twenty-four carriers of her class that would be built during the war, was launched in July 1942 and commissioned in December. She and each of her sister ships displaced 36,000 tons and carried 90–100 aircraft.)

## Imperial Japanese Navy Aircraft Carriers up to June 1942

| Name | Year comm. | Tons | Aircraft capacity | Speed |
|---|---|---|---|---|
| Hōshō | 1922 | 7,500 | 8 | 25 |

NOTES: Converted from an oiler; small and slow, she nevertheless remained in commission and served with the Main Body at Midway.

| Akagi | 1927 | 41,300 | 91 | 31 |
|---|---|---|---|---|

NOTES: Built from a battle-cruiser hull; flagship of the Kidō Butai at Midway.

| Kaga | 1928 | 42,541 | 90 | 28 |
|---|---|---|---|---|

NOTES: Built from a battleship hull; part of Kidō Butai at Midway

| Ryūjō | 1933 | 12,500 | 36 | 29 |
|---|---|---|---|---|

NOTES: A failed effort to build a CV under 10,000 tons, the Ryūjō was a poor compromise and used mostly in support functions. During the Midway campaign, her planes attacked Dutch Harbor in the Aleutians on June 3.

| Sōryū | 1937 | 18,800 | 71 | 34.5 |
|---|---|---|---|---|

NOTES: Part of the Kidō Butai at Midway.

| Hiryū | 1939 | 20,250 | 73 | 34.5 |
|---|---|---|---|---|

NOTES: Part of the Kidō Butai at Midway.

| Zuiho | 1940 | 12,000 | 30 | 28 |
|---|---|---|---|---|

NOTES: Converted from the sub tender Takasaki in 1940; accompanied the support fleet at Midway.

| Shōhō | 1942 | 14,000 | 30 | 28 |
|---|---|---|---|---|

NOTES: Converted from the sub tender Tsurugisaki in late 1941; sunk in the Coral Sea in May 1942

| Shōkaku | 1941 | 32,105 | 72 | 34 |
|---|---|---|---|---|

NOTES: Along with her sister ship Zuikako, one of Japan's best carriers; missed the Battle of Midway because of damage received in the Coral Sea in May.

| Zuikaku | 1941 | 32,105 | 72 | 34 |
|---|---|---|---|---|

NOTES: Though undamaged in the Coral Sea, her air wing was badly weakened and she was therefore kept out of the Battle of Midway.

*Continued*

| Name | Year comm. | Tons | Aircraft capacity | Speed |
|------|-----------|------|-------------------|-------|
| *Hiyo* | 1942 | 24,000 | 44 | 24 |

NOTES: Both *Hiyo* and *Jun'yō* were converted from luxury liners and were too slow to operate with the Kidō Butai.

| Name | Year comm. | Tons | Aircraft capacity | Speed |
|------|-----------|------|-------------------|-------|
| *Jun'yō* | 1942 | 24,000 | 44 | 24 |

NOTES: During Midway campaign, planes from *Jun'yō* attacked Dutch Harbor in the Aleutians on June 3 and 5, 1942.

# APPENDIX B

| American and Japanese Aircraft | | | | | |
|---|---|---|---|---|---|
| **Allied Nickname** | **Type/ Function** | **Builder** | **Designation** | **Date** | **Speed (knots)** |
| *A. American Aircraft* | | | | | |
| *Dauntless | Dive-Bomber | Douglas | SBD-2/3 | 1940 | 222 |
| *Devastator | Torpedo Bomber | Douglas | TBD-1 | 1937 | 179 |
| *Avenger | Torpedo Bomber | Grumman | TBF-1 | 1942 | 239 |
| *Buffalo | Fighter | Brewster | F2A-3 | 1939 | 261 |
| *Wildcat | Fighter | Grumman | F4F-3/4 | 1940 | 287 |
| *Vindicator | Scout Bomber | Vought | SB2U-3 | 1937 | 218 |
| Flying Fortress | Four-Engine Bomber | Boeing | B-17 | 1938 | 249 |
| Mitchell | Two-Engine Bomber | North American | B-25 | 1940 | 275 |
| Marauder | Two-Engine Bomber | Martin | B-26 | 1941 | 250 |

*Continued*

| Allied Nickname | Type/ Function | Builder | Designation | Date | Speed (knots) |
|---|---|---|---|---|---|
| **B. Japanese Aircraft** | | | | | |
| *Val | Dive-Bomber | Aichi | D3A1, Type 99 | 1940 | 205 |
| *Kate | Torpedo Bomber | Nakajima | B5N2, Type 97 | 1937 | 204 |
| *Zeke (Zero) | Fighter | Mitsubishi | A6M2, Type 0 | 1940 | 287 |
| Nell | Two-Engine Bomber | Mitsubishi | GM3, Type 96 | 1935 | 203 |
| Betty | Two-Engine Bomber | Mitsubishi | GM4, Type 1 | 1939 | 230 |
| Jake | Fighter/ Float Plane | Aichi | E13A | 1941 | 203 |
| Emily | Four-Engine Seaplane | Kawanishi | H8K, Type 2 | 1938 | 208 |

* Carrier capable

# APPENDIX C

## American Order of Battle at Midway

(carriers in bold face)

Commander in Chief, Pacific (CincPac), ADM Chester Nimitz, USN

Commander, Carrier Strike Force, RADM Frank Jack Fletcher, USN

---

### Task Force 17 (1 carrier, 2 cruisers, 5 destroyers)

---

Commander, Task Force 17, RADM Frank Jack Fletcher, USN

**USS *Yorktown* (CV-5), CAPT Elliott Buckmaster, USN**

Commander, *Yorktown* Air Group, LCDR Oscar Pederson, USN
Commander, VF-3, LCDR John S. Thach, USN (from *Saratoga*)
Commander, VS-5, LT Wallace C. Short, Jr., USN (formerly VB-5)
Commander, VB-3, LCDR Maxwell F. Leslie, USN (from *Saratoga*)
Commander, VT-3, LCDR Lance E. Massey, USN (from *Saratoga*)

Commander Task Group 17.2 (Cruiser Force), RADM William W. Smith, USN
USS *Astoria* (CA-34), CAPT Francis W. Scanland, USN
USS *Portland* (CA-33), CAPT Laurance T. Du Bose, USN

Commander Task Group 17.4 (Destroyer Screen), CAPT Gilbert C. Hoover, USN
Destroyer Squadron Two
USS *Morris* (DD-417), CDR H. B. Jarrett, USN
USS *Russell* (DD-414), LCDR Glenn R. Hartwig, USN
USS *Hammann* (DD-412), CDR Arnold E. True, USN
USS *Anderson* (DD-411), LCDR John K. B. Ginder, USN
USS *Hughes* (DD-410), LCDR Donald J. Ramsey, USN

---

## Task Force 16 (2 carriers, 5 cruisers, 1 light cruiser, 8 destroyers)

---

Commander, Task Force 16, RADM Raymond Spruance, USN
Chief of Staff, CAPT Miles R. Browning, USN

**USS *Enterprise* (CV-6), CAPT George D. Murray, USN**

Commander, *Enterprise* Air Group, LCDR Clarence Wade McClusky, USN
Commander, VF-6, LT James S. Gray, USN
Commander, VS-6, LT Wilmer E. Gallaher, USN
Commander, VB-6, LT Richard H. Best, USN
Commander, VT-6, LCDR Eugene E. Lindsey, USN

**USS *Hornet* (CV-8), CAPT Marc A. Mitscher, USN**

Commander, *Hornet* Air Group, CDR Stanhope C. Ring, USN
Commander, VF-8, LCDR Samuel G. Mitchell, USN
Commander, VS-8, LCDR Walter F. Rodee, USN
Commander, VB-8, LCDR Robert R. Johnson, USN
Commander, VT-8, LCDR John C. Waldron, USN

Commander, Task Group 16.2 (Cruiser Group), RADM Thomas C. Kinkaid, USN
USS *Minneapolis* (CA-36), CAPT Frank J. Lowry, USN
USS *New Orleans* (CA-32), CAPT Howard J. Good, USN
USS *Vincennes* (CA-44), CAPT Frederick L. Riefkohl, USN
USS *Northampton* (CA-26), CAPT William D. Chandler, USN
USS *Pensacola* (CA-24), CAPT Frank L. Lowe, USN
USS *Atlanta* (CL-51), CAPT Samuel P. Jenkins, USN

Commander Task Group 16.4 (Destroyer Screen), CAPT Alexander R. Early, USN
Destroyer Squadron One, CAPT Early
USS *Phelps* (DD-360), LCDR Edward L. Beck, USN
USS *Aylwin* (DD-355), LCDR George R. Phelan, USN
USS *Monaghan* (DD-354), LCDR William P. Burford, USN
USS *Worden* (DD-352), LCDR William G. Pogue, USN

Destroyer Squadron Six, CAPT Edward P. Sauer, USN
USS *Balch* (DD-363), LCDR Harold L. Tiemroth, USN
USS *Conyngham* (DD-371), LCDR Henry C. Daniel, USN
USS *Benham* (DD-397), LCDR Joseph M. Worthington, USN
USS *Ellet* (DD-398), LCDR Francis H. Gardner, USN
USS *Maury* (DD-401), LCDR Gelzer L. Sims, USN

---

## Fueling Group

---

USS *Cimarron* (AO-22), CDR Russell M. Ihrig, USN
USS *Platte* (AO-24), CAPT Ralph H. Henkle, USN

USS *Dewey* (DD-349), LCDR Charles F. Chillingworth, USN
USS *Monssen* (DD-436), CDR Roland N. Smoot, USN

Midway Relief Fueling Unit
USS *Guadaloupe* (AO-32), CDR Harry R. Thurber, USN
USS *Blue* (DD-387), CDR Harold N. Williams, USN
USS *Ralph Talbot* (DD-390), CDR Ralph Earle, Jr., USN

## Submarine Force

Commander, Submarine Force (ComSubPac), RADM Robert H. English, USN
Task Force 7
USS *Cachalot* (SS-170), LCDR George A. Lewis, USN
USS *Flying Fish* (SS-229), LCDR Glynn R. Donaho, USN
USS *Tambor* (SS-198), LCDR John W. Murphy, Jr., USN
USS *Trout* (SS-202), LCDR Frank W. Fenno, USN
USS *Grayling* (SS-209), LCDR Eliot Olsen, USN
USS *Nautilus* (SS-168), LCDR William H. Brockman, Jr., USN
USS *Grouper* (SS-214), LCDR Clarence E. Duke, USN
USS *Dolphin* (SS-169), LCDR Royal L. Rutter, USN
USS *Gato* (SS-212), LCDR William G. Myers, USN
USS *Cuttlefish* (SS-171), LCDR Martin P. Hottel, USN
USS *Gudgeon* (SS-211), LCDR Hyland B. Lyon, USN
USS *Grenadier* (SS-210), LCDR Willis A. Lent, USN

**Task Force 7.2**

USS *Narwhal* (SS-167), LCDR Charles W. Wilkins, USN
USS *Plunger* (SS-179), LCDR David C. White, USN
USS *Trigger* (SS-237), LCDR Jack H. Lewis, USN

**Task Force 7.3**

USS *Tarpon* (SS-175), LCDR Lewis Wallace, USN
USS *Pike* (SS-173), LCDR William A. New, USN
USS *Finback* (SS-230), LCDR Jesse L. Hull, USN
USS *Growler* (SS-215), LCDR Howard W. Gilmore, USN

## Midway-Based Aircraft

Commander, Midway Naval Air Station, CAPT Cyril T. Simard, USN
Air Commander for Battle of Midway, CDR Logan C. Ramsey, USN

Commander Patrol Wing Two, RADM Patrick N. Bellinger
VP-23, VP-24, VP-44, VP-53, and a detachment of VT-8
(31 PBY Catalinas, and 6 TBF Avengers)

Commander, Marine Aircraft Group 22, LCOL Ira L. Kimes, USMC
   Commander, VMF-221, MAJ Floyd B. Parks, USMC
      (21 F2A-3 Buffaloes, 7 F4F-3 Wildcats)
   Commander, VMSB-241, MAJ Lofton R. Henderson, USMC
      (19 SBD Devastators, 21 SB2U Vindicators)

7th Army Air Corps, Bomber Command, MGEN Willis P. Hale, USA
   431st Bomber Squadron, LCOL Walter C. Sweeny, Jr., USA
      (19 B-17 Flying Fortresses)
   69th Bomber Squadron, CAPT James F. Collins, USA
      (4 B-26 Marauders)

# APPENDIX D

## Japanese Order of Battle at Midway

(carriers in bold face)

Commander, Japanese Combined Fleet (CinC), ADM Yamamoto Isoroku, IJN

---

**Main Body (3 heavy battleships, 1 small carrier, 1 light cruiser, 9 destroyers)**

Commander, Main Body, ADM Yamamoto, IJN
Chief of Staff, RADM Ugaki Matome, IJN

Battleship Division One
  BB *Yamato* (flagship), CAPT Takayanagi Gihachi, IJN
  BB *Nagato*, CAPT Yano Hideo, IJN
  BB *Mutsu*, CAPT Yamazumi Tejiro, IJN

Carrier Group Accompanying Main Body
  **Light Carrier *Hōshō*, CAPT Kaoru Umetani, IJN**
  Commander, *Hōshō* Air Group, LT Irikiin Yoshiaki, IJN
  DD *Yukaze*, LCDR Kajimoto Shizuka

  Commander, Destroyer Squadron 3, RADM Hashimoto Shintarō, IJN
  CL *Sendai*, CAPT Morishita Nobue, IJN

  Commander, Destroyer Division 11, CAPT Shōji Kichirō, IJN
  DD *Fubuki*, CDR Yamashtia Shizuo, IJN
  DD *Shirayuki*, CDR Sugahara Rokorō, IJN
  DD *Murakumo*, CDR Higaashi Hideo, IJN
  DD *Hatsuyuki*, LCDR Kamiura Junnari, IJN

  Commander, Destroyer Division 19, CAPT Oe Ranji, IJN
  DD *Isonami*, CDR Sugama Ryōkichi, IJN

DD *Uranami*, CDR Hagio Tsutomu, IJN
DD *Shikinami*, CDR Kawahashi Akifumi, IJN
DD *Ayanami*, CDR Sakuma Eiji, IJN

Fueling Unit, CAPT Nishioka Shigeyasu, IJN
AO *Naruto*, CAPT Nishioka

The Main Body also included a "Special Force" of two tenders carrying midget submarines, plus a supply ship.

---

## First Carrier Strike Force (The Kidō Butai)
### (4 carriers, 2 battleships, 2 cruisers, 1 light cruiser, 12 destroyers)

---

Commander, First Carrier Strike Force, VADM Nagumo Chūichi, IJN
Chief of Staff, RADM Kusaka Ryūnosuke, IJN
Senior Air Officer, CDR Fuchida Mitsuo, IJN

Commander, Carrier Division 1, VADM Nagumo

**CV *Akagi* (flagship), CAPT Aoki Taijirō, IJN**
Commander, *Akagi* Air Group, CDR Fuchida
Commander, Fighter Planes (Kansen Buntai), LT Itaya Shigeru, IJN
Commander, Bombing Force (Kanbaku Buntai), LT Chihaya Takehiro, IJN
Commander, Torpedo Planes (Kanko Buntai), LCDR Murata Shigeharu, IJN
Plus 6 fighters intended for Midway garrison

**CV *Kaga*, CAPT Jisaku Okada, IJN**
Commander, *Kaga* Air Group, LCDR Kusumi Tadashi, IJN
Commander, Fighter Planes (Kansen Buntai), LT Satō Masao, IJN
Commander, Bombing Force (Kanbaku Buntai), LT Ogawa Shō-ichi, IJN
Commander, Torpedo Planes (Kanko Buntai), LT Kazuraki Masuhiko, IJN
Plus 9 fighters and 2 bombers intended for Midway garrison

Commander, Carrier Division 2, RADM Yamaguchi Tamon, IJN
Air Officer, LCDR Egusa Takashige, IJN

**CV *Hiryū* (flagship), CAPT Kaku Tomoeo, IJN**
Commander, *Hiryu* Air Group, LT Tomanga Joichi, IJN
Commander, Fighter Planes (Kansen Buntai), LT Mori Shigeru, IJN
Commander, Bombing Force (Kanbaku Buntai), LT Kobayashi Michio, IJN
Commander, Torpedo Planes (Kanko Buntai), LT Kikuchi Rokurō, IJN
Plus 3 fighters intended for Midway garrison

**CV *Sōryū*, CAPT Yanagimoto Ryusaku, IJN**
Commander, *Soryu* Air Group, LCDR Egusa, IJN
Commander, Fighter Planes (Kansen Buntai), LT Suganami Masaji, IJN
Commander, Bombing Force (Kanbaku Buntai), LT Ikeda Masatake, IJN

Commander, Torpedo Planes (Kanko Buntai), LT Abe Heijirō, IJN
Plus one reconnaissance plane and 3 fighters intended for Midway garrison

Commander, Cruiser Division 8, RADM Abe Haroaki, IJN
  CA *Tone* (flagship), CAPT Okada Tametsugu, IJN
  CA *Chikuma*, CAPT Komura Keizō, IJN

Battleship Division 3
  BB *Haruna*, CAPT Koma Tamotsu, IJN
  BB *Kirishima*, CAPT Iwabughi, IJN

Commander, Destroyer Squadron 10, RADM Kimura Susumu, IJN
  CL *Nagara* (flagship), CAPT Naoi Toshio, IJN

  Commander, Destroyer Division 4, CAPT Ariga Kosaku, IJN
  DD *Nowaki*, CDR Yoshida Masayoshi, IJN
  DD *Arashi*, CDR Watanabe Yasumasa, IJN
  DD *Hagikaze*, CDR Iwagami Juichi, IJN
  DD *Maikaze*, CDR Nakasugi Seiji, IJN

  Commander, Destroyer Division 10, CAPT Abe Toshio, IJN
  DD *Kazagumo*, CDR Yoshida Masayoshi, IJN
  DD *Yugomo*, CDR Semba Shigeo, IJN
  DD *Makigumo*, CDR Fujita Isamu, IJN

  Commander, Destroyer Division 17, CAPT Kitamura Masayuki, IJN
  DD *Urakaze*, CDR Shiraishi Nagayoshi, IJN
  DD *Isokaze*, CDR Toshima Shunichi, IJN
  DD *Tanikaze*, CDR Katsumi Motoi, IJN
  DD *Jamakaze*, CDR Orita Tsuneo, IJN

Plus 5 small oilers escorted by DD *Akigumo*, CDR Soma Shohei

---

### Close Support Group (4 cruisers, 2 destroyers)

---

Commander, Close Support Group, VADM Kurita Takeo, IJN
Commander, Cruiser Division 7, VADM Kurita
  CA *Kumano* (flagship), CAPT Tanaka Kikumatsu, IJN
  CA *Suzuya*, CAPT Kimura Masatomi, IJN
  CA *Mikuma*, CAPT Sakiyama Shakao, IJN
  CA *Mogami*, CAPT Soji Akira, IJN

Commander, Destroyer Division 8, CDR Ogawa Nobuki, IJN
  DD *Asashio*, CDR Yoshii Gorō, IJN
  DD *Arashio*, CDR Kuboki Hideo, IJN

Plus an oiler, the *Nichiel Maru*

---

## Midway Invasion Force (1 small carrier, 2 battleships, 4 cruisers, 1 light cruiser, 8 destroyers)

---

Commander, Midway Invasion Force, VADM Kondō Nobutake, IJN
Chief of Staff, RADM Shiraishi Kazutaka, IJN

Commander, Battle Division 3, Section 1, RADM Mikawa Gunichi, IJN
  BB *Kongo* (flagship), CAPT Koyanagi Tomiji, IJN
  BB *Hiei*, CAPT Nishida Masao, IJN

Cruiser Division 4, Section 1
  CA *Atago* (invasion force flagship), CAPT Ijuin Matsuji, IJN
  CA *Chokai*, CAPT Hayakawa Mikio, IJN

Commander, Cruiser Division 5, VADM Takagi Takeo, IJN
  CA *Myoko* (flagship), CAPT Miyoshi Teruhiki, IJN
  CA *Haguro*, CAPT Mori Tomoichi, IJN

Commander, Destroyer Squadron 4, RADM Nishimura Shōji, IJN

  CL *Yura* (flagship), CAPT Satō Shirō, IJN
  Commander, Destroyer Division 3, CAPT Tachibana Masao, IJN
  DD *Murasame*, CDR Suenaga Naoji, IJN
  DD *Samidare*, CDR Matsubara Takisaburo, IJN
  DD *Harusame*, CDR Kamiyama, IJN
  DD *Yudachi*, CDR Kikkawa Kiyoshi, IJN

  Commander, Destroyer Division 9, CAPT Satō Yasuo, IJN
  DD *Asagumo*, CDR Iwahashi Tōru, IJN
  DD *Minegumo*, CDR Suzuki Yasuatsu, IJN
  DD *Natsugumo*, CDR Tsukamoto Moritarō, IJN

Commander, Escort Carrier Group, CAPT Obayahi Sueo, IJN
  **Light Carrier *Zuihō*, CAPT Obayashi**
  Commander, Fighter Planes (Kansen Buntai), LT Hidaka Moriyasu, IJN
  Commander, Torpedo Planes (Kanko Buntai), LT Matsuo Kaji, IJN
  DD *Mikazuki*, LCDR Maeda Saneho, IJN

The Midway Invasion force was accompanied by 4 oilers and a supply ship.

---

### Transport Group (1 light cruiser, 10 destroyers, 13 transports)

---

Commander, Transport Group, RADM Tanaka Raizō, IJN
Commander, Destroyer Squadron 2, RADM Tanaka

  CL *Jintsu* (flagship), CAPT Kozai Torazō, IJN

  Commander, Destroyer Division 15, CAPT Satō Torajirō, IJN

DD *Kuroshio*, CDR Ugaki Tamaki, IJN
DD *Oyashio*, CDR Arima Tokikichi, IJN

Commander, Destroyer Division 16, CAPT Shibuya Shirō, IJN
DD *Yukikaze*, CDR Tobita Kenjirō, IJN
DD *Amatsukaze*, CDR Hara Tameichi, IJN
DD *Tokitsukaze*, CDR Nakahara Giichirō, IJN
DD *Hatsukaze*, CDR Takahashi Kameshirō, IJN

Commander, Destroyer Division 18, CAPT Mikyasaka Yoshito, IJN
DD *Shiranuhi*, CDR Akasawa Jisuo, IJN
DD *Kasumi*, CDR Tomura Kiyoshi, IJN
DD *Kagero*, CDR Yokoi Minoru, IJN
DD *Arare*, CDR Ogata Tomoe, IJN

Commander, Landing Force, COL Ichiki Kiyonao, IJA
(5,000 soldiers carried in 13 transport and supply ships)

---

## Submarine Force (15 submarines)

---

Commander, Submarine Force, VADM Komatsu Teruhishi, IJN
Chief of Staff, RADM Mito Hisashi, IJN
Commander, Submarine Squadron 3, RADM Kono Chirnaki, IJN

Submarine Division 11
I-174, LCDR Kusaka Toshi, IJN
I-175, LCDR Uno Kameo, IJN

Submarine Division 12
I-168, LCDR Tanabe Yahachi, IJN
I-169, LCDR Watanabe Katsuji, IJN
I-171, LCDR Kawasaki Rokuro, IJN

Submarine Division 13 (CAPT Miyazaki Takeharu)
I-121, LCDR Fujimori Yasuo, IJN
I-122, LCDR Norita adatoshi, IJN
I-123, LCDR Ueno Toshitake, IJN

Commander, Submarine Squadron 5, RADM Tadashige Daigo, IJN
Submarine Division 19 (CAPT Ono Ryōjirō)
I-156, LCDR Ōhashi Katsuo
I-157, LCDR Nakajima Sakae, IJN
I-158, LCDR Kitamura Soshichi, IJN
I-159, LCDR Yoshimatsu Tamori, IJN

Submarine Division 30 (CAPT Teraoka Masao)
    I-162, LCDR Kinashi Takakuzu, IJN
    I-165, LCDR Harada Hakue, IJN
    I-166, LCDR Tanaka Makio, IJN

---

### The Aleutians Force (5th Fleet) (1 carrier, 1 light carrier, 3 cruisers, 3 destroyers)

Commander, Aleutians Force, VADM Hosogaya Moshirō, IJN
Chief of Staff, CAPT Nakazawa Tasuku, IJN

CA *Nachi* (flagship), CAPT Kiyota Takahiko, IJN
DD *Inazuma*, CDR Takeuchi Hajime, IJN
DD *Irazuchi*, LCDR Kudo Shunsaku, IJN

Commander, 2nd Carrier Striking Force, RADM Kakuta Kakuji, IJN
**Light Carrier *Ryūjō* (flagship), CAPT Kato Tadao, IJN**
Commander, *Ryūjō* Air Group, LT Kobayashi Minoru, IJN
Commander, Fighter Planes (Kansen Buntai), LT Kobayashi
Commander, Torpedo Planes (Kanko Buntai), LT Yamagami Masayuki, IJN

**CV *Jun'yō*, CAPT Ishii Shizue, IJN**
Commander *Jun'yō* Air Group, LT Shiga Yoshio, IJN
Commander, Fighter Planes (Kansen Buntai), LT Shiga
Commander, Bombing Force (Kanbaku Buntai), LT Abe Zenji, IJN

Cruiser Division 4, Section 2
    CA *Maya*, CAPT Nabeshima Shunsaku, IJN
    CA *Takeo*, CAPT Asakura Bunji, IJN

Commander, Destroyer Division 7, CAPT Konishi Kaname, IJN
    DD *Akebono*, LCDR Nakagawa Minoru, IJN
    DD *Ushio*, CDR Uesugi Yoshitake, IJN
    DD *Sazanami*, LCDR Uwai Hiroshi, IJN

---

### Attu Invasion Force (1 light cruiser, 4 destroyers, plus transports)

Commander, Attu Invasion Force, RADM Ōmori Sentarō
    CL *Abukuma* (flagship), CAPT Murayama Seiroku, IJN

Commander, Destroyer Division 21, CAPT Shimizu Toshio, IJN
    DD *Wakaba*, LCDR Kuroki Masakichi, IJN
    DD *Nenohi*, LCDR Terauchi Saburō, IJN
    DD *Hatsuharu*, CDR Makino Hiroshi, IJN
    DD *Hatsushimo*, LCDR Migihama Satoru, IJN

Army North Seas Detachment (1,200 soldiers), MAJ Hozumi Matsuoshi, IJA
Plus 3 oilers, 3 supply ships, and 2 minelayers

---

### Kiska Invasion Force (2 light cruisers, 3 destroyers, 4 support vessels, 3 minesweepers)

Commander, Kiska Invasion Force, CAPT Ono Takeji, IJN
Cruiser Division 21
    CL *Kiso*, CAPT Ono
    CL *Tama*, CAPT Kawabata Masaharu, IJN

Commander, Destroyer Division 6, CAPT Yamada Yusuke, IJN
    DD *Hibiki*, LCDR Ishii Hagumu, IJN
    DD *Atatsuki*, CDR Takasuka Osamu, IJN
    DD *Hokaze*, LCDR Tanaka Tomō, IJN

Plus 4 support vessels and 3 minesweepers

---

### Submarines Assigned to Aleutians Group (6 submarines)

Commander, Submarine Squadron 1, RADM Yamazaki Shigenaki, IJN
    I-9 (flagboat), CDR Fujii Akiyoshi, IJN

    Submarine Division 2, CAPT Imazato Hiroshi, IJN
    I-15, CDR Ishikawa Nobuo, IJN
    I-17, CDR Nishino Kozo, IJN
    I-19, CDR Narahara Seigo, IJN

    Submarine Division 4, CAPT Nagai Mitsuru
    I-25, CDR Togami Meiji, IJN
    I-26, CDR Yokota Minoru, IJN

---

### Aleutians Guard Force (4 battleships, 2 light cruisers, 12 destroyers)

Commander, Guard Force, VADM Takasu Shirō, IJN
Chief of Staff, RADM Kobayashi Kengō, IJN

Battleship Division 1
    BB *Hyuga* (flagship), CAPT Matsuda Chiaki, IJN
    BB *Ise*, CAPT Takeda Isamu, IJN
    BB *Fuso*, CAPT Kinoshita Mitsuo, IJN
    BB *Yamashiro*, CAPT Kogure Gunji, IJN

Commander, Cruiser Division 9, RADM Kishi Fukuji, IJN

CL *Kitakami* (flagship), CAPT Norimitsu Saiji, IJN
CL *Oi*, CAPT Narita Mōichi

Commander, Destroyer Division 20, CAPT Yamada Yuji, IJN
DD *Agagiri*, CDR Maekawa Nisaburo, IJN
DD *Yugiri*, CDR Motokura Masayoshi, IJN
DD *Shirakumo*, CDR Hitomi Toyoji, IJN
DD *Amagiri*, CAPT Ashida Buichi, IJN

Commander, Destroyer Division 24, CAPT Hirai Yasji, IJN
DD *Umikasa*, CDR Sugitani Nagahide, IJN
DD *Yamakaze*, CDR Hamanaka Shuishi, IJN
DD *Kawakase*, CDR Wakabayashi Kazuo, IJN
DD *Suzukaze*, CDR Shibayama Kazuo, IJN

Commander, Destroyer Division 27, CAPT Yoshimura Matake, IJN
DD *Ariake*, CDR Yoshida Shōichi, IJN
DD *Yugure*, CDR Kamo Kiyoshi, IJN
DD *Shigure*, CDR Seo Noboru, IJN
DD *Shiratsuyu*, LCDR Hashimoto Kimmatsu, IJN

# APPENDIX E

## How Much Did the U.S. Know

## of Japanese Plans?

Though it was long kept a secret, the contribution of the code breakers to American victory in the Battle of Midway is now well known. At the center of that story, however, is a continuing mystery about a particular message: the detailed twelve-part Japanese operational order dated May 20 that Joseph Rochefort says he took with him to the meeting with Chester Nimitz on May 25. According to the oral testimony of several cryptanalysts at both Melbourne and Pearl Harbor who claim to have seen it, this message contained the complete Japanese order of battle as well as their prescribed route, the bearing to Midway, and even the timing of the air attack. In many subsequent histories of the battle, this document is credited with giving the Americans the decisive edge against their superior foe and making American victory not only possible but even inevitable.* The problem is that no copy of this intercept has survived.

At least six men later testified that they saw and handled the document. Petty Officer Bill Tremblay, who found it, Lieutenant Commander Gil Richardson, the duty officer at FRUMEL, who sent it on to Hypo, Ensign (later Rear Admiral) Ralph Cook who was at FRUMEL during the effort to break the message, Ensign (later Rear Admiral) Donald "Mac" Showers, and Lieutenant (later Captain) Jasper Holmes at FRUPAC, who worked on it, and of course Commander (later Captain) Joseph Rochefort, who took it with him to his meeting with Nimitz on May 25. It is improbable that all six men should invent such a document and cling to the story of it so consistently over seventy years. Nevertheless, the document itself has never been found. Such a mystery has led some scholars to wonder if it ever existed at all.

Edwin Layton, who was the person in the best position to know, insisted for the rest of his life that no such document ever existed and, moreover, that the code breakers

---

* This includes my own own book, *Decision at Sea: Five Naval Battles that Shaped American History* (New York: Oxford University Press, 2005), which acknowledges that the May 20 intercept was a "series of recently intercepted Japanese messages" but attributes to them far more specificity than they actually contained (p. 210).

never had the complete Japanese order of battle for Midway. In an interview with Etta Belle Kitchen on May 31, 1970, Layton declared emphatically that "everything that has been written about that is absolutely, unqualifiedly false," and that "there was no such message." When Kitchen pressed him, asking "to make it perfectly clear, [that] there never was a complete battle order as it reported in some of the books," Layton replied: "Never was. Not available to us" (Layton Oral History, 125–27).

Why, then, do so many people remember it? An investigation of the Layton Papers at the Naval War College in Newport, Rhode Island, suggests a possible explanation. Layton kept a personal (and highly confidential) journal during his time as Nimitz's intelligence officer. The physical journal itself offers insight into the kind of mind that is drawn to cryptanalysis, for it is written in four colors and in tiny—almost microscopic—handwriting; reading it today requires the use of a magnifying glass. In this journal, Layton carefully recorded all the intercepted messages that he considered important each day. There is no record in that journal of a unified twelve-part message on May 20, but it does indicate a dramatic upswing in the volume of message traffic that day. Some of the messages concerned a planned Japanese "fleet exercise," but a dozen others obviously referred to a forthcoming operation. One revealed the presence of "occupation forces" for both Midway and Alaska. Another mentioned that Japanese forces would approach the target from the northwest. As the Hypo analysts worked on these messages, the results would have been collated and compared so that Rochefort could present the collected findings to Nimitz. Very likely, therefore, the men who achieved this intelligence coup recalled their effort as having focused on a single message rather than a group of shorter messages. If so, instead of one lengthy and detailed operational order, the May 20 decrypt remembered by several of the Hypo analysts and reported in several histories of the battle may well have been a composite of a dozen shorter messages.

Another important correction to the record is that the extent of the detail about Japanese plans contained in these messages has been significantly exaggerated. Though the messages did indicate the presence of four carriers, they did not, for example, specify that they would be operating as a single unit, which had important consequences for the battle. If the Hypo analysts had been able to provide such information, it might have avoided the calamitous "flight to nowhere" on the morning of June 4. Nor did those messages show that Yamamoto himself was at sea with the "Main Body" including the massive battleship *Yamato*. Though the code breakers at Hypo and Belconnen made a signal and significant contribution to American victory at Midway, they did not provide a detailed blueprint of the enemy's operational plans, as is sometimes asserted. The decrypts of May 20 were not the equivalent, for example, to the discovery of Robert E. Lee's famous War Order No. 191, at Frederick, Maryland, on the eve of the Battle of Antietam during the Civil War.

None of this detracts from the crucial contributions of the code breakers, but it does remind us that the subsequent decisions made by the commanders on the scene were more complex and open-ended than might otherwise be assumed. The Battle of Midway was not won by the code breakers alone but by the analysts, the decision makers who trusted them, and finally by the men who drove the ships, manned the guns, and flew the planes at the point of contact. Certainly there is enough glory for all of them.

# APPENDIX F

## The Flight to Nowhere

For nearly fifty years after the Battle of Midway, historians accepted Marc Mitscher's official report on Midway more or less at face value. After all, by 1944 he had become the much-celebrated commander of the Fast Carrier Task Force that fought its way from the Marianas to the shores of Japan, and, in the words of his biographer, the "Magnificent Mitscher." At the Naval Academy, Mitscher Hall stands directly across from the sprawling dormitory of Bancroft Hall, and any subsequent challenge to Mitscher's veracity seemed nearly unpatriotic. Even at the time, however, there were doubts about the accuracy of his Midway report. In his own report on the battle, Raymond Spruance wrote, "Where discrepancies exist between *Enterprise* and *Hornet* reports, the *Enterprise* report should be taken as more accurate." This was an astonishing statement to make in an official report, and it comes close to asserting that Mitscher's report was not to be trusted. Alas, since neither Stanhope Ring nor any of the four squadron commanders filed a report at all, Mitscher's was very nearly the only official source on the role of the *Hornet*'s air group in the battle. As a result, most twentieth-century accounts of the Battle of Midway dutifully recorded the *Hornet*'s air group as proceeding along a course of 239 or 240 degrees, and maps depicting the battle show the same thing—including the map that Mitscher submitted with his report, which is duplicated as part of map 9 in this book (p. 257). Whatever doubts there were, there was no evidence that what Mitscher reported was not, in fact, what had happened.

Mitscher's story began to unravel when compared with Japanese records, for Mitscher had asserted (or at least he signed the report that asserted) that Stanhope Ring and his air group had flown a course of 239 degrees, and that it had missed the Kidō Butai because Nagumo had turned north instead of continuing toward Midway. The problem was that Nagumo did not turn north until 9:17 a.m. (something Mitscher did not know at the time he signed the report), which meant that if Ring had flown a course of 239, he very likely would have intercepted the Kidō Butai either before it turned north or just as it did so. Waldron found the Kidō Butai at 9:18, and he commanded the last launched and the slowest flying element of the *Hornet* air group. Consequently, if Ring *had* flown a course 239 or 240 degrees, he might well have found the Kidō Butai too.

In the 1980s, a lawyer and retired Marine major named Bowen Weisheit began looking into the death of one of Pat Mitchell's Wildcat pilots. The pilot was a former all-American lacrosse player from the University of Maryland named Mark Kelly, a close friend of Weisheit. When Weisheit learned that Kelly's empty life raft had been recovered in a position utterly inconsistent with Mitscher's report, he decided to interview each of the surviving members of Mitchell's squadron to ask them what had happened. What he found was that with one or two exceptions, the pilots themselves remembered that they had flown not to the southwest at 239 or 240 degrees, but "westerly," "almost due west," or, more precisely, "at 265 degrees." One, Troy Guillory, initially said that they flew "westerly." When Weisheit suggested that it must have been to the southwest at 239 degrees, Guillory said no: "We went the wrong way to start with," and finally, pointing to the chart, he said "to the 265 line." Ensign Ben Tappan stated simply, "We were going west," and Ensign John McInerny stated that "Commander Ring was 35 degrees off." Even the commander of Scouting Eight, Lieutenant Commander (later Rear Admiral) Walt Rodee stated bluntly: "We took the bearing and the course they gave us. It was about 265. . . . . It was almost due west." Rodee never had an opportunity to make a similar statement in an official after-action report, but he did write it down in his flight log, which he kept. Finally, the radar operator on board the *Hornet* recalled tracking the air group as it flew away from the task force, and he stated that as far as the CXAM radar would reach, the *Hornet* air group had flown on a course of 265 degrees. The transcripts of all these interviews are in the Nimitz Library at the U.S. Naval Academy, and Wesiheit's conclusions are in his book *The Last Flight of C. Markland Kelly*.

Not every veteran agreed. Clayton Fisher, who flew as Ring's wing man until the very end of the Flight to Nowhere, remained convinced his whole life that "we flew a southwest course of about 235 to 240," and that "we were between Midway and the enemy force"—that is, south of the Kidō Butai.

Explaining this obvious discrepancy is difficult, and the story will always retain a certain amount of mystery, but if the *Hornet* air group did indeed fly north of the Kidō Butai on a course of 265, as most of the evidence suggests, the possible explanations of how this may have happened fall into three categories: technological, computational, and conspiratorial.

Attributing Ring's course to flawed technology is the simplest explanation, but also the least likely. Some have suggested that the *Hornet*'s magnetic compass was off by 15 or 20 degrees that day, and that her radar was malfunctioning (she did get a new radar set after the battle). It is an appealing solution, for it absolves all the decision makers of error. The problem is that the pilots in both Mitchell's fighter squadron and Walt Rodee's bomber squadron did not *think* they were flying at 239 degrees and accidentally find themselves going the wrong way. They knew *at the time* that they were flying at 265 degrees. It was not, therefore, an error with the ship's compass that sent Ring's air group in the "wrong" direction.

The second possibility is that Stanhope Ring was such a bad navigator that his calculation was 25 degrees off, and that Mitscher accepted his flawed solution in order to support his air group commander. The problem with this explanation is that it assumes that Marc Mitscher, the most experienced and confident pilot on board, would have neglected to compute his own solution to the target and that he simply took Ring's word for it. Such a scenario is utterly inconsistent with Mitscher's character. And even if this is what happened, it still casts both Mitscher and Ring in the role of conspirators for agreeing to suppress the actual course in the subsequent report, and pretending that the air group had flown 240 degrees when it had not.

The only explanation that fits both the circumstances and the personalities of the principal decision makers is that Mitscher himself decided it was his duty to find the two "missing" Japanese carriers that had not yet been reported by any of the scouts. Like Fletcher and Spruance, Mitscher did not learn that all four Japanese carriers were operating together until the afternoon. He knew that the air group from *Enterprise* was going after the two carriers that had been sighted, and he very likely calculated that a course of 265 was most likely to lead his air group to the other two carriers that were presumably operating separately behind the first two. By the time Mitscher learned that all four enemy carriers were operating together, he also knew the details of the various mutinies that had taken place during the Flight to Nowhere. A truthful and complete report of that flight would not only have exposed his own error in sending the *Hornet* air group the wrong way, but it would also have compelled him to consider pressing formal charges against Waldron, McInerny, Mitchell, Johnson, Rodee, and perhaps others for abandoning the group commander. That was hardly the kind of press the Navy wanted after the Battle of Midway. So instead of court-martialing his squadron commanders, he recommended all of them for medals. Of the mutiny by Waldron's Torpedo Eight, Mitscher (or someone on his staff) wrote: "Torpedo Squadron Eight, flying low, beneath the broken clouds, became separated from the remainder of the group, which flew at higher levels. They found the enemy carriers, those at high altitude did not." Technically, each word of that is true, but it is also deliberately misleading.

At the time, at least, the squadron commanders went along with this solution. Certainly they knew they had a responsibility to complete a report. The form itself declared that it was "to be filled out by unit commanders immediately upon landing after each action or operation," and specifically enjoined each recipient: "Do not 'gun deck' this report." Perhaps they each filed a report and Mitscher's staff suppressed them, or more likely Mitscher told the squadron commanders that he (or his staff) would write the report and not to bother writing one themselves. In any case, it is clear that at some point Mitscher decided that only one report would be submitted by the *Hornet*, that he assigned his staff to write it, and that he signed it knowing it was misleading. It is hard to argue, even now, that he made the wrong decision. With victory in hand, what was to be gained by acknowledging the confusion, insubordination, and failure of the Flight to Nowhere?

# NOTES

## Abbreviations Used in Notes

Action Reports — *U.S. Navy Action and Operational Reports from World War II, Pacific Theater, PART I: CINCPAC* (16 microfilm reels), Bethesda, MD: University Publications of America

AHC — American Heritage Center, University of Wyoming, Laramie

BOMRT — "The Battle of Midway Roundtable," a website for Midway veterans, at http://www.midway42.org/

FDRL — Franklin D. Roosevelt Library and Archives, Hyde Park, New York

NHHC — Operational Archives, Naval History and Heritage Command, Washington Navy Yard, Washington, D.C.

NMPW — National Museum of the Pacific War, Fredericksburg, Texas

NWC — U.S. Naval War College, Newport, Rhode Island

UMD — Maryland Room, Hornbake Library, University of Maryland, College Park, Maryland

USNA — U.S. Naval Academy, Annapolis, Maryland

## Introduction

1. Several Midway veterans make the case for divine intervention, among them Bryan Crisman, who was the disbursing officer on the USS *Yorktown*, and Stanford Linzey, who wrote a book entitled *God Was at Midway: The Sinking of the USS Yorktown (CV-5) and the Battles of the Coral Sea and Midway* (San Diego, CA: Black Forest, 1996). See also Ronald W. Russell, *No Right to Win: A Continuing Dialogue with Veterans of the Battle of Midway* (New York: iUniverse, 2006), 172.
2. Leo Tolstoy, *War and Peace*, trans. Anthony Briggs (London: Penguin, 2006), 1098.

## Chapter 1

1. Frank DeLorenzo, "Admiral Nimitz Arrives at Pearl Harbor," BOMRT; E. B. Potter, *Nimitz* (Annapolis, MD: Naval Institute Press, 1976), 16.
2. DeLorenzo, "Admiral Nimitz Arrives"; Potter, *Nimitz*, 16.
3. Joseph Rochefort oral history (Oct. 5, 1969), U.S. Naval Institute Oral History Collection, USNA, 1:223; 1905 *Lucky Bag*, USNA; Potter, *Nimitz*, 156.

4. Potter, *Nimitz*, 16; John B. Lundstrom, *Black Shoe Carrier Admiral: Frank Jack Fletcher at Coral Sea, Midway, and Guadalcanal* (Annapolis, MD: Naval Institute Press, 2006), 45.

5. *Annual Report of the Secretary of the Navy, 1941* (Washington, DC: Government Printing Office, 1941), 1; Bruce Catton, *The War Lords of Washington* (New York: Harcourt, Brace, 1948), 9–12.

6. George H. Lobdell, "Frank Knox," in *American Secretaries of the Navy*, ed. Paolo E. Coletta (Annapolis, MD: Naval Institute Press, 1980), 2:677–81; Harold L. Ickes, *The Secret Diary of Harold L. Ickes* (New York: Simon & Schuster, 1953–54), 2:718 (diary entry of Sept. 9, 1939); Henry L. Stimson and McGeorge Bundy, *On Active Service in Peace and War* (New York: Harper, 1948), 323–24.

7. Lobdell, "Frank Knox,"682; Senate Committee on Naval Affairs, *Nomination of William Franklin Knox: Hearings before the Committee on Naval Affairs, United States Senate on the Nomination of William Franklin Knox to be Secretary of the Navy*, 76th Cong., 3rd sess., 1940, 42; Ickes, *Secret Diary*, 2:717; "Attack Upon Pearl Harbor," 77th Cong., 2nd sess., 1942, S. Doc. 159, 20. See also Knox's sycophantic letters to FDR in 1940 in President's Secretary's file, box 62, FDRL.

8. Thomas B. Buell, *Master of Sea Power: A Biography of Fleet Admiral Ernest J. King* (Boston: Little, Brown, 1980), 111; Floyd Thorn interview (Aug. 14, 2000), NMPW.

9. Eric Larrabee, *Commander in Chief: Franklin Delano Roosevelt, His Lieutenants, and Their War* (New York: Harper & Row, 1987; reprint Annapolis, MD: Naval Institute Press, 2004), 171; Robert William Love, Jr., "Ernest Joseph King," in *The Chiefs of Naval Operations*, ed. Robert William Love, Jr. (Annapolis, MD: Naval Institute Press, 1980), 139–40; Ernest J. King and Walter Muir Whitehill, *Fleet Admiral King: A Naval Record* (New York: Norton, 1952), 350–51.

10. B. Mitchell Simpson, "Harold Raynsford Stark," in Love, *Chiefs of Naval Operations*, 131, 119–20; Samuel Eliot Morison, *History of United States Naval Operations in World War II*, vol. 1, *The Battle of the Atlantic, September 1939–May 1943* (Boston: Little, Brown, 1947), 41. Stark's memos to FDR, signed "Betty," are in the President's Secretary's Files, FDRL, box 62. Stark subsequently went to England as commander, U.S. Naval Forces Europe. The memo making King both CominCh and CNO is dated March 12, 1942, and is in the King Papers, Series I, box 1. It is also printed in Buell, *Master of Sea Power* as Appendix 4.

11. Potter, *Nimitz*, 9; King's comment about Nimitz is quoted in Larrabee, *Commander in Chief*, 356.

12. A. T. Mahan, *The Influence of Sea Power Upon History, 1660–1783* (Boston: Little, Brown, 1890).

13. Norman Jack (Dusty) Kleiss to the author, July 31, 2009.

14. Potter, *Nimitz*, 62, 122–34.

15. Ibid., 135–61.

16. Kimmel's plan for the employment of the carriers is in the "Briefed Estimate," Dec. 10, 1941, Nimitz Papers, NHHC, box 1:13; Stark's order is Stark to Kimmel, Dec. 15, 1941, Nimitz Papers, NHHC, box 1:49–50; Lundstrom, *Black Shoe Carrier Admiral*, 23.

17. Stark to Pye, and Pye to Stark, both Dec. 22, 1941, both in Nimitz Papers, NHHC, box 1, 72; Lundstrom, *Black Shoe Carrier Admiral*, 31; Edward Layton oral history (May 30, 1970), U.S. Naval Institute Oral History Collection, USNA, 106.

18. Stark to Pye, Dec. 27, 1941, Nimitz Papers, NHHC, box 1, 120; Knox to Kimmel, Jan. 9, 1941, Kimmel Papers, AHC, box 2; Lundstrom, *Black Shoe Carrier Admiral*, 39, 45. Circumstantial evidence suggests that that FDR may have subsequently blocked Pye's appointment to command the South Pacific.

19. The officer who likened Nimitz's arrival to opening a window in a stuffy room was Raymond Spruance in an interview with Gordon Prange (Sept. 5, 1964), Prange Papers, UMD, box 17.

20. Lundstrom, *Black Shoe Carrier Admiral*, 6.

21. Edward P. Stafford, *The Big E: The Story of the USS Enterprise* (New York: Random House, 1962; Annapolis, MD: Naval Institute Press, 2002), 23–24. Citations are to the Naval Institute Press edition.

22. Edward S. Miller, *War Plan Orange: The U.S. Strategy to Defeat Japan, 1897–1945* (Annapolis, MD: Naval Institute Press, 1991); *Annual Report of the Secretary of the Navy* (1940), 27–33.

23. Stark to Knox, Nov. 12, 1940, original in FDRL; also available online at http://docs.fdrlibrary.marist.edu/psf/box4/a48b01.html.

24. Ibid.

25. Ibid.

26. Joint Committee on the Investigation of the Pearl Harbor Attack, *Pearl Harbor Attack: Hearings before the Joint Committee on the Investigation of the Pearl Harbor Attack*, 79th Cong., 1st sess., 1945, part 15, 1505. The text of Rainbow 5 is in Steven T. Ross, ed., *American War Plans, 1919–1941* (New York: Garland, 1992), 5:100.

27. Knox to ALNAV (all Navy personnel), Dec. 7, 1941, Nimitz Papers, NHHC, box 1, 5; Joel Ira Holwitt, *"Execute against Japan": The U.S. Decision to Conduct Unrestricted Submarine Warfare* (College Station: Texas A&M University Press, 2009).

28. Buford Rowland and William B. Boyd, *U.S. Navy Bureau of Ordnance in World War II* (Washington, DC: Bureau of Ordnance, 1953), 90; Thomas Wildenberg and Norman Polmar, *Ship Killer: A History of the American Torpedo* (Annapolis, MD: Naval Institute Press, 2010), 102 ff. See also Robert Gannon, *Hellions of the Deep: The Development of American Torpedoes in World War II* (University Park: Pennsylvania State University Press, 1996), 75–76, 89.

29. Nimitz to Mrs. Nimitz, Dec. 28, 1941, and Jan. 29, 1942, both in Nimitz Diary #1 (serial letters from Nimitz to his wife), NHHC.

## Chapter 2

1. The number of planes carried by the Kidō Butai is from Mark R. Peattie, *Sunburst: The Rise of Japanese Naval Air Power, 1909–1941* (Annapolis, MD: Naval Institute Press, 2001), 152. John B. Lundstrom offers the slightly lower figure of 387 airplanes for the Kidō Butai in *Black Shoe Carrier Admiral: Frank Jack Fletcher at Coral Sea, Midway, and Guadalcanal* (Annapolis, MD: Naval Institute Press, 2006), 151. A total of 360 aircraft were assigned to the Pearl Harbor strike, but there were ten aborts; in addition, the Japanese launched two "Jake" floatplanes, though they

did not participate in the attack. I am grateful to Richard Frank, Vice Admiral Yoji Koda, and Lee Pennington for their help with this chapter.

2. The "feminine delicacy" observation is from Matsunaga Keisuke, who is quoted by Hiroyuki Agawa in *The Reluctant Admiral: Yamamoto and the Imperial Navy*, trans. John Bester (Tokyo: Kodansha International, 1979), 131, 139. The "recent scholar" is Sadao Adasa, in *From Mahan to Pearl Harbor: The Imperial Japanese Navy and the United States* (Annapolis, MD: Naval Institute Press, 2006), 275. The American officer was Edwin T. Layton, from his oral history (May 30, 1970), U.S. Naval Institute Oral History Collection, USNA. Jonathan B. Parshall and Anthony P. Tully discuss Yamamoto's personality in *Shattered Sword: The Untold Story of the Battle of Midway* (Washington, DC: Potomac Books, 2005), 22–23. Yamamoto's involvement with carrier aircraft is from Asada, *From Mahan to Pearl Harbor*, 182–84.

3. Agawa, *Reluctant Admiral*, 139.

4. Ibid., 124.

5. Ibid., 95–96, 118; Ronald H. Spector, *Eagle against the Sun: The American War with Japan* (New York: Free Press, 1985), 36–37; Samuel Eliot Morison, *History of United States Naval Operations in World War II*, vol. 3, *The Rising Sun in the Pacific, 1931–April 1942* (Boston: Little, Brown, 1948), 13.

6. The text of the "Fundamental Principles": is available at http://www.ibiblio.org/pha/timeline/144app01.html. See also Spector, *Eagle against the Sun*, 42.

7. Asada, *From Mahan to Pearl Harbor*, 164–66, 194–97.

8. Yamamoto is quoted in Peattie, *Sunburst*, 83. See also Agawa, *Reluctant Admiral*, 46–52.

9. Agawa, *Reluctant Admiral*, 13.

10. Yamamoto to Admiral Shimada, Sept. 4, 1939, quoted in Donald M. Goldstein and Katherine V. Dillon, eds., *The Pearl Harbor Papers: Inside the Japanese Plans* (Washington, DC: Brassey's, 1993), 114; Agawa, *Reluctant Admiral*, 13, 124, 186; Matome Ugaki, *Fading Victory: The Diary of Admiral Matome Ugaki, 1941–1945*, ed. Donald M. Goldstein and Katherine V. Dillon, trans. Masataka Chihaya (Annapolis, MD: Naval Institute Press, 1991), 6. To some extent, the Imperial Japanese Navy acquiesced to the pact with Germany in exchange for assurances that it would get an increase in steel allocation in the budget. In effect, therefore, national policy was subordinated to service ambitions. See Asada, *From Mahan to Pearl Harbor*, 243.

11. Yamamoto to Navy Minister Oikawa, Jan. 7, 1941, quoted in Goldstein and Dillon, *Pearl Harbor Papers*, 115; Asada, *From Mahan to Pearl Harbor*, 238; Peattie, *Sunburst*, 83; Agawa, *Reluctant Admiral*, 192.

12. H. P. Willmott, *The Barrier and the Javelin: Japanese and Allied Pacific Strategies, February to June 1942* (Annapolis, MD: Naval Institute Press, 1983), 28–30.

13. Atsushi Oi, "The Japanese Navy in 1941," in *The Pacific War Papers: Japanese Documents of World War II*, ed. Donald M. Goldstein and Katherine V. Dillon (Washington, DC: Potomac Books, 2004), 16; Agawa, *Reluctant Admiral*, 127, 195.

14. Peattie, *Sunburst*, 76.

15. Jisaburo Ozawa, "Outline Development of Tactics and Organization of the Japanese Carrier Air Force," in Goldstein and Dillon, *Pacific War Papers*, 78–79; Peattie, *Sunburst*, 149, 151.

16. Agawa, *Reluctant Admiral*, 264; Gordon Prange interview of Genda (Sept. 5, 1966), Prange Papers, UMD, box 17; Ugaki, *Fading Victory*, 13 (diary entry of Oct. 22, 1941).

17. The quotation is from Admiral Yonai Mitsumasa and is quoted by Hiroyuki Agawa in *The Reluctant Admiral: Yamamoto and the Imperial Navy*, trans. John Bester (Tokyo: Kodansha International, 1979), 191.

18. Yamamoto to Navy Minister Oikawa, Jan. 7, 1941, quoted in Goldstein and Dillon, *Pearl Harbor Papers*, 116; Parshall and Tully, *Shattered Sword*, 14–15.

19. Masataka Chihaya, "Concerning the Construction of Japanese Warships," in Goldstein and Dillon, *Pacific War Papers*, 86.

20. The "modern expert" is Mark Peattie, in *Sunburst*, 100. See also Oi, "The Japanese Navy in 1941," 22–23.

21. Peattie, *Sunburst*, 166; Parshall and Tully, *Shattered Sword*, 89; Agawa, *Yamamoto*, 202; Oi, "The Japanese Navy in 1941," 12.

22. Parshall and Tully, *Shattered Sword*, 130; John Campbell, *Naval Weapons of World War Two* (London: Conway Maritime, 1985); Peattie, *Sunburst*, 95. The Kate was also used as a level bomber against land targets when it carried a heavy (1,760-pound) explosive (fragmentation) bomb whose purpose was to suppress antiaircraft fire from a surface target. Such bombs wrecked the superstructure of the USS *Arizona* in the attack on Pearl Harbor.

23. Peattie, *Sunburst*, 91–92; Parshall and Tully, *Shattered Sword*, 78; and Spector, *Eagle against the Sun*, 46–47.

24. Parshall and Tully, *Shattered Sword*, 256; Oi, "The Japanese Navy in 1941," 25.

25. John B. Lundstrom, *The First Team: Pacific Naval Air Combat from Pearl Harbor to Midway* (Annapolis, MD: Naval Institute Press, 1984), 455 (Appendix 1).

26. Oi, "The Japanese Navy in 1941," 23; Peattie, *Sunburst*, 133–34; Lundstrom, *First Team*, 455–56.

27. Ugaki, *Fading Victory*, 48 (diary entry of Dec. 9, 1941). The notion that Nagumo ought to have attacked the U.S. oil-tank farm on Oahu is mostly hindsight. The tank farm was not part of the initial target list, and even if Nagumo had launched a third strike, its purpose would most likely have been to mop up elements of the fleet that remained afloat.

28. Martin Middlebrook and Patrick Mahoney, *Battleship: The Loss of the Prince of Wales and the Repulse* (London: Lane, 1977).

## Chapter 3

1. Steve Wiper, *Yorktown Class Carriers* (Tucson, AZ: Classic Warships, 2000); Robert Cressman et al., *"A Glorious Page in Our History": The Battle of Midway, 4–6 June 1942* (Missoula, MT: Pictorial Histories, 1990), 202. I am grateful to Bert Kinzey and to Ronald W. Russell for their help with this chapter.

2. John B. Lundstrom, *Black Shoe Carrier Admiral: Frank Jack Fletcher at Coral Sea, Midway, and Guadalcanal* (Annapolis, MD: Naval Institute Press, 2006), 100.

3. Thomas Wildenberg, *All the Factors of Victory: Admiral Joseph Mason Reeves and the Origins of Carrier Airpower* (Washington, DC: Brassey's, 2003), 155.

4. William F. Halsey and J. Bryan III, *Admiral Halsey's Story* (New York: Whittlesey House, 1947), 50–55. The quotation is from 52.

5. Ibid., 14.

6. The "modern scholar" is John B. Lundstrom in *Black Shoe Carrier Admiral*, 21; 1902 *Lucky Bag*, USNA; Samuel Eliot Morison, *History of United States Naval Operations in World War II*, vol. 3, *The Rising Sun in the Pacific, 1931–April 1942* (Boston: Little, Brown, 1948), 211n.

7. Noel Gayler oral history (Feb. 15, 2002), 4, Naval Historical Foundation.

8. Stephen D. Regan, *In Bitter Tempest: The Biography of Admiral Frank Jack Fletcher* (Ames: Iowa State University Press, 1994), viii; 1906 *Lucky Bag*, USNA. The critic was Lieutenant Richard Best, in an interview (Aug. 11, 1995), 30, NMPW.

9. Lundstrom, *Black Shoe Carrier Admiral*, 53.

10. J. J. Clark, with Clark G. Reynolds, *Carrier Admiral* (New York: McKay, 1967), 78; Lundstrom, *Black Shoe Carrier Admiral*, 55.

11. John B. Lundstrom, *The First Team: Pacific Naval Air Combat from Pearl Harbor to Midway* (Annapolis, MD: Naval Institute Press, 1984), 51.

12. Harold L. Buell, *Dauntless Helldivers: A Dive-Bomber Pilot's Epic Story of the Carrier Battles* (New York: Orion Books, 1991); Barrett Tillman, *The Dauntless Dive Bomber of World War II* (Annapolis, MD: Naval Institute Press, 1976); Cressman et al., *Glorious Page*, 206.

13. The quotations are from ENS Clayton Fisher, who flew in VB-8, "The SBD in Combat," BOMRT, available at http://www.midway42.org/fisher-sbd.htm. See also Buell, *Dauntless Helldivers*, 61.

14. The pilot was Max Leslie, skipper of VB-3 on *Yorktown*, in Leslie to Smith, Dec. 15, 1964, Prange Papers, UMD, box 17. Bill Burch made the same analogy. See Stuart D. Ludlum, *They Turned the War Around at Coral Sea and Midway: Going to War with Yorktown's Air Group Five* (Bennington, VT: Merriam, 2000), 86.

15. N. J. "Dusty" Kleiss, "Remembrance of a Rear-Seater," BOMRT, posted April 27, 2007, http://www.midway42.org/vets-kleiss.html; Richard Best interview (Aug. 11, 1995), NMPW, 16; Cressman et al., *Glorious Page*, 209.

16. Richard Best interview (Aug. 11, 1995), NMPW, 25; Frederick Mears, *Carrier Combat* (Garden City, NY: Doubleday, Doran, 1944), 22; Clayton E. Fisher, "Officer and Enlisted Airmen," BOMRT, *The Roundtable Forum*, issue 2010–15, April 10, 2010.

17. John S. Thach oral history (Nov. 6, 1970), U.S. Naval Institute Oral History Collection, USNA, 1:231; Richard Best interview (Aug. 11, 1995), NMPW, 18.

18. John Campbell, *Naval Weapons of World War Two* (London: Conway Maritime, 1985), 206; Mears, *Carrier Combat*, xv.

19. Captain P. R. White, USN, June 6, 1942, Action Reports, reel 3.

20. Masatake Okumiya and Jiro Horikoshi, with Martin Caidin, *Zero! The Story of the Japanese Navy Air Force, 1937–1945* (London: Cassell, 1957).

21. Barrett Tillman, *Wildcat: The F4F in WWII*, 2nd ed. (Annapolis, MD: Naval Institute Press, 1990); William Wolf, *Victory Roll! The American Fighter Pilot and Aircraft in World War II* (Atglen, PA: Schiffer Books, 2001), 38; John S. Thach oral history (Aug. 26, 1942); Cressman et al., *Glorious Page*, 209.

22. Edward P. Stafford, *The Big E: The Story of the USS Enterprise* (Annapolis, MD: Naval Institute Press, 2002), 46, 54; Lundstrom, *First Team*, 63.

23. Lundstrom, *First Team*, 55–56.

24. Mears, *Carrier Combat*, 18.
25. The statistics are from Lundstrom, *First Team*, Appendix 6, "List of U.S. Navy Fighter Pilots," 490–95; Stephen Jurika oral history (Dec. 3, 1975), U.S. Naval Institute Oral History Collection, USNA, 1:171. Buell, in *Dauntless Helldivers* (28–29) tells the story of one American flight instructor who was chastised for being too tough in his standards.
26. Buell, *Dauntless Helldivers*, 27.
27. Mears, *Carrier Combat*, 20; Clayton E. Fisher, *Hooked: Tales and Adventures of a Tailhook Warrior* (Denver: Outskirts, 2009), 27.
28. Wolf, *Victory Roll*, 21–24.
29. Mears, *Carrier Combat*, 25. See also Lundstrom, *First Team*, 490–95.
30. Paolo E. Coletta, *Bald Eagle: Admiral Marc A. Mitscher and U.S. Naval Aviation* (Lewiston, NY: Mellen, 1997), 107; Ludlum, *They Turned the War Around*, 10; Richard Best interview (Aug. 11, 1995), NMPW, 31.

## Chapter 4

1. The quotation is from King to Frank Knox, Feb. 8, 1942, King Papers, NHHC, Series I, box 1. Curtin's concerns are reflected in a memo from Casey to King, Jan. 26, 1942, King Papers, NHHC, Series I, box 1. See also Ernest J. King and Walter Muir Whitehill, *Fleet Admiral King: A Naval Record* (New York: Norton, 1952), 373; Samuel Eliot Morison, *History of United States Naval Operations in World War II*, vol. 3, *Rising Sun in the Pacific, 1931–April 1942* (Boston: Little, Brown, 1948), 259–60; John B. Lundstrom, *The First Team: Pacific Naval Air Combat from Pearl Harbor to Midway* (Annapolis, MD: Naval Institute Press, 1984), 56–57; and Stephen D. Regan, *In Bitter Tempest: The Biography of Admiral Frank Jack Fletcher* (Ames: Iowa State University Press, 1994), 85.
2. Nimitz to King, and King to Nimitz, both dated Jan. 5, 1942, Nimitz Papers, NHHC, box 1:139–40.
3. King to Nimitz, Jan. 20, 1942, Nimitz Papers, NHHC, box 1:179; Running Summary, Jan. 21 and 23, 1942, Nimitz Papers, NHHC, box 1:158, 183. See John B. Lundstrom, *Black Shoe Carrier Admiral: Frank Jack Fletcher at Coral Sea, Midway, and Guadalcanal* (Annapolis, MD: Naval Institute Press, 2006), 59–62.
4. Edward P. Stafford, *The Big E: The Story of the USS Enterprise* (Annapolis, MD: Naval institute Press, 2002), 44; William F. Halsey and J. Bryan III, *Admiral Halsey's Story* (New York: Whittlesey House, 1947), 89.
5. Fletcher's op order, dated Jan. 25, 1942, is in Action Reports, reel 2. See also Lundstrom, *Black Shoe Carrier Admiral*, 65–67.
6. Lundstrom, *First Team*, 78; Lundstrom, *Black Shoe Carrier Admiral*, 65–67; Stuart D. Ludlum, *They Turned the War Around at Coral Sea and Midway: Going to War with Yorktown's Air Group Five* (Bennington, VT: Merriam, 2000), 25–26.
7. Pederson to Buckmaster, Feb. 5, 1942, Action Reports, reel 2; Ludlum, *They Turned the War Around*, 27.
8. Lundstrom, *First Team*, 79; Ludlum, *They Turned the War Around*, 27. Jocko Clark later criticized Fletcher for not spending more time to search for the downed pilots. J. J. Clark, with Clark G. Reynolds, *Carrier Admiral* (New York: David McKay, 1967), 85.

9. Lundstrom, *First Team*, 78–80; Ludlum, *They Turned the War Around*, 29.
10. Lundstrom, *First Team*, 65–66; Richard Best interview (Aug. 11, 1995), NMPW, 13.
11. Stafford, *Big E*, 49.
12. Lundstrom, *First Team*, 66.
13. Halsey to Nimitz, Feb. 7, 1942, Action Reports, reel 1.
14. Stafford, *Big E*, 47–50; Lundstrom, *First Team*, 67–69.
15. Stafford, *Big E*, 50.
16. Stafford, *Big E*, 51; Richard Best interview (Aug. 11, 1995), NMPW, 27.
17. Stafford, *Big E*, 51–52.
18. McCluskey to CEAG, and Massey to CEAG, both Feb. 2, 1942, and Halsey to Nimitz, Feb. 9, 1942, all in Action Reports, reel 1; Halsey and Bryan, *Admiral Halsey's Story*, 92; Stafford, *The Big E*, 51–54; Morison, *Rising Sun*, 262–63.
19. Best to CEAG, Feb. 2, 1942, Action Reports, reel 1; Richard Best interview (Aug. 11, 1995), NMPW, 28.
20. Stafford, *The Big E*, 56–57; Halsey and Bryan, *Admiral Halsey's Story*, 93.
21. Stafford, *The Big E*, 56–57.
22. Murray to Halsey, Feb. 2, 1942, Action Reports, reel 1; Halsey to Brown, Feb. 7, 1942, Map room files, FDRL, box 41; Halsey and Bryan, *Admiral Halsey's Story*, 94; Stafford, *Big E*, 58; Lundstrom, *First Team*, 74. Gaido tried to keep his identity a secret, but Halsey found out who he was and promoted him on the spot to aviation machinist's mate first class. Gaido was subsequently captured by the Japanese during the Battle of Midway and executed. See chapter 15.
23. Lundstrom, *First Team*, 75.
24. Halsey to Nimitz, Feb. 9, 1942, Action Reports, reel 1; Halsey and Bryan, *Admiral Halsey's Story*, 96; Stafford, *Big E*, 58–59.
25. Fletcher to Nimitz, Feb. 9, 1942, Action Reports, reel 1.
26. King to Nimitz, Jan. 27, 1942, Nimitz to King, Jan. 29 and 31, 1942, and King to Nimitz, Feb. 15, 1942, all in Nimitz Papers, NHHC, box 8:204–6.
27. Russell D. Buhite and David W. Levy, eds., *FDR's Fireside Chats* (Norman: University of Oklahoma Press, 1992), 209; King to FDR, March 5, 1942, King Papers, NHHC, Series I, box 2; Running Summary, Feb. 9 and Feb. 11, 1942, Nimitz Papers, NHHC, box 8:211, 213.
28. Brown's operation order for the Rabaul raid is in the Nimitz Papers, NHHC, box 8:541–42; Brown's report to Nimitz that he was withdrawing due to an "acute fuel shortage" is COMTASKFOR 11 (Brown) to CINCPAC (Nimitz), Feb. 20, 1942, Nimitz Papers, NHHC, box 1:250. See also H. P. Willmott, *The Barrier and the Javelin: Japanese and Allied Pacific Strategies, February to June 1942* (Annapolis, MD: Naval Institute Press, 1983), 56.
29. Brown to Nimitz, Feb. 20, 1942, Nimitz Papers, NHHC, box 8:250; Lundstrom, *Black Shoe Carrier Admiral*, 21.
30. Louis Brown, *A Radar History of World War II: Technical and Military Imperatives* (Bristol, UK: Institute of Physics, 1999).
31. Steve Ewing and John B. Lundstom, *Fateful Rendezvous: The Life of Butch O'Hare* (Annapolis, MD: Naval Institute Press, 1997), 127.
32. Ewing and Lundstrom, *Fateful Rendezvous*, 130–31; Lundstrom, *First Team*, 101–4, 106, 107.

33. Lundstrom, *First Team*, 104–5.

34. John S. Thach oral history (Nov. 6, 1970), 1:284.

35. Brown to Nimitz, Feb. 20 and 23, 1942; Nimitz to Task Force Commanders, Feb. 25, 1942; Brown to Nimitz, Feb. 26, 27, and 28, 1942; and Nimitz to King, Feb. 28, 1942, all in Nimitz Papers, NHHC, box 8:253, 255, 256, 257; Morison, *Rising Sun*, 267.

36. Running Summary, Feb. 12, 1942, Nimitz Papers, NHHC, box 8:214; Halsey and Bryan, *Admiral Halsey's Story*, 97–98.

37. Nimitz to Halsey, Feb. 25, 1942, Nimitz Papers, NHHC, box 8:543; Halsey and Bryan, *Admiral Halsey's Story*, 98; Richard Best interview (Aug. 11, 1995), NWPW, 30; Lundstrom, *First Team*, 117–19.

38. On March 18, FDR wrote Churchill: "Australia must be held and, as I telegraphed you, we are willing to do that. India must be held and you must do that." FDR to Churchill, March 18, 1942, in *Roosevelt and Churchill: Their Secret Wartime Correspondence*, ed. Francis Loewenheim et al. (London: Barrie & Jenkins, 1975), 268–69.

39. King to Leary, Feb. 12, 1942, King Papers, NHHC, Series I, box 1; King to FDR, Feb. 12, 1942, King Papers, NHHC, Series I, box 1. See also John Costello, *The Pacific War, 1941–1945* (New York: Rawson, Wade, 1981; reprint New York: Harper Perennial, 2002), 203. Nimitz had suggested Pye for the job, but FDR vetoed the idea.

40. King to Leary and Leary to King, Feb. 17, 1942, King Papers, NHHC, Series I, box 1.

41. Nimitz's remarks about securing Australia are in a "Briefed Estimate of the Situation," Feb. 5, 1942, Nimitz Papers, NHHC, box 8:233; Nimitz's reply to King's proposal to maintain two carriers in the south is Nimitz to King, Feb. 25, 1942, and King's reply dated Feb. 26, both in Nimitz Papers, NHHC, box 8:256, 545.

42. Running Summary, Feb. 26, 1942, Nimitz Papers, NHHC, box 8:246.

43. King to Nimitz, and Brown to Nimitz, both Feb. 26, 1942, Nimitz Papers, NHHC, 8:242, 244, 255.

44. Lundstrom, *First Team*, 124–27.

45. Running Summary, Feb. 23 and 25, 1942, Nimitz Papers, NHHC, box 8:243–44, 245; Ludlum, *They Turned the War Around*, 37–38; Morison, *Rising Sun*, 387–89; Lundstrom, *First Team*, 131; Roosevelt to Churchill, March 17, 1942, in *Churchill and Roosevelt: The Complete Correspondence*, ed. Warren F. Kimball (Princeton, NJ: Princeton University Press, 1984), 1:415–16.

46. Nimitz to King, March 23, 1942, Nimitz Papers, NHHC, box 8:548; Lundstrom, *Black Shoe Carrier Admiral*, 96; Running Summary, March 11, 1942, Nimitz Papers, NHHC, box 8:267. Captain James M. Steele replaced McCormick as the keeper of the Running Summary in April.

47. Willmott, *Barrier and Javelin*, 74–76.

## Chapter 5

1. H. P. Willmott, *The Barrier and the Javelin: Japanese and Allied Pacific Strategies, February to June 1942* (Annapolis, MD: Naval Institute Press, 1983), 15; John J. Stephan, *Hawaii under the Rising Sun: Japan's Plans for Conquest after Pearl Harbor* (Honolulu: University of Hawaii Press, 1984), 124.

2. H. P. Willmott, *Empires in the Balance: Japanese and Allied Pacific Strategies to April 1942* (Annapolis, MD: Naval Institute Press, 1982), 436.

402 ■ Notes to Pages 90-104

3. Stephan, *Hawaii under the Rising Sun*, 96.

4. Sadao Asada, *From Mahan to Pearl Harbor: The Imperial Japanese Navy and the United States* (Annapolis, MD: Naval Institute Press, 2006), 171–72, 246–50.

5. Hiroyuki Agawa, *The Reluctant Admiral: Yamamoto and the Imperial Navy*, trans. John Bester (Tokyo: Kodansha International, 1979), 213, 225; Asada, *From Mahan to Pearl Harbor*, 250–52, 281.

6. Jonathan B. Parshall and Anthony P. Tully, *Shattered Sword: The Untold Story of the Battle of Midway* (Washington, DC: Potomac Books, 2005), 27.

7. Prange interview of Watanabe Yasuji (Sept. 25, 1964), Prange Papers, UMD, box 17; Willmott, *Barrier and Javelin*, 43–44; Stephan, *Hawaii under the Rising Sun*, 107; Agawa, *Reluctant Admiral*, 294; Matome Ugaki, *Fading Victory: The Diary of Admiral Matome Ugaki*, ed. Donald M. Goldstein and Katherine V. Dillon, trans. Masataka Chihaya (Annapolis, MD: Naval Institute Press, 1991), 68 (diary entry of Jan. 5, 1942).

8. Quoted in Willmott, *Barrier and Javelin*, 79; Prange interview of Watanabe (Feb. 3–4, 1966), Prange Papers, UMD, box 17.

9. Paul S. Dull, *A Battle History of the Imperial Japanese Navy, 1941–1945* (Annapolis, MD: Naval Institute Press, 1978), 108–9.

10. Mark R. Peattie, *Sunburst: The Rise of Japanese Naval Air Power, 1909–1941* (Annapolis, MD: Naval Institute Press, 2001), 67–70.

11. Dull, *Battle History*, 109–10.

12. Donald MacIntyre, *Fighting Admiral: The Life of Admiral of the Fleet Sir James Somerville, G.C.B., G.B.E., D.S.O* (London: Evans Brothers, 1961), 179.

13. Stephan, *Hawaii under the Rising Sun*, 485; Asada, *From Mahan to Pearl Harbor*, 184–86; Inoue Shigeyoshi, "A New Theory on the Armament Plan," Jan. 1941, quoted in Agawa, *Reluctant Admiral*, 224–25.

14. Willmott, *Barrier and Javelin*, 61, 64–65; Parshall and Tully, *Shattered Sword*, 32.

15. Agawa, *Reluctant Admiral*, 294–95; Parshall and Tully, *Shattered Sword*, 32–37.

16. Agawa, *Reluctant Admiral*, 264; Stephan, *Hawaii under the Rising Sun*, 90–91. According to Lieutenant Commander Ishiguro Susumu, Yamaguchi's communications officer, Yamaguchi was eager to attack again and was angry when Nagumo ignored him. Ishiguro interview, Goldstein Collection, Prange Papers, Archives Service Center, University of Pittsburgh, box 21, folder 37. I am grateful to Jon Parshall for bringing this interview to my attention.

17. Ugaki, *Fading Victory*, 62 (diary entry of Dec. 25, 1941); Yamamoto to Navy Minister Oikawa, Jan. 7, 1941, quoted in Donald M. Goldstein and Katherine V. Dillon, eds., *The Pearl Harbor Papers: Inside the Japanese Plans* (Washington, DC: Brassey's 1993), 117.

18. Ugaki, *Fading Victory*, 75 (diary entry of Jan. 14, 1942); Parshall and Tully, *Shattered Sword*, 28.

19. Stephan, *Hawaii under the Rising Sun*, 109–21; Parshall and Tully, *Shattered Sword*, 33.

20. Craig L. Symonds, *Decision at Sea: Five Naval Battles that Shaped American History* (New York: Oxford University Press, 2005), 206–7.

21. Ibid.

22. Parshall and Tully, *Shattered Sword*, 51; Willmott, *Barrier and Javelin*, chapter 2.

23. Parshall and Tully, *Shattered Sword*, 48–51; Willmott, *Barrier and Javelin*, 81–82.

24. Agawa, *Reluctant Admiral*, 284; Hugh Bicheno, *Midway* (London: Cassel, 2001), 73–77.
25. The substance of this argument comes from interviews of Miyo by Robert E. Barde (January, 1966), in Barde, "The Battle of Midway: A Study in Command" (Ph.D. dissertation, University of Maryland, 1971), 32–33, and of Watanabe by Gordon Prange (Feb. 3–4, 1966 and Sept. 25, 1964), in Prange Papers, UMD, box 17. See also Agawa, *Reluctant Admiral*, 295–96; Willmott, *Barrier and Javelin*, 68–71; and Mitsuo Fuchida and Masatake Okumiya, *Midway: The Battle that Doomed Japan, the Japanese Navy's Story* (Annapolis, MD: Naval Institute Press, 1955), 82–85.
26. Prange interviews of Watanabe (Feb. 3–4, 1966) and (Sept. 25, 1964), both in Prange Papers, UMD, box 17.
27. Prange interview of Watanabe (Feb. 3–4, 1966), and Miyo (May 6, 1966), both in Prange Papers, UMD, box 17; Willmott, *Barrier and Javelin*, 72.
28. Willmott, *Barrier and Javelin*, 76.
29. Parshall and Tully, *Shattered Sword*, 37–38.

**Chapter 6**

1. Theodore Taylor, *The Magnificent Mitscher* (New York: Norton, 1954; Annapolis, MD: Naval Institute Press, 1991), 20–21. Citations are to the Naval Institute Press edition.
2. Ibid., 20–27; 1910 *Lucky Bag*, USNA.
3. Taylor, *Magnificent Mitscher*, 30; Paolo E. Coletta, *Bald Eagle: Admiral Marc A. Mitscher and U.S. Naval Aviation* (Lewiston, NY: Mellen, 1997), 18.
4. Mitscher to Frances Mitscher, Aug. 17, 1917, Mitscher Papers, NHHC.
5. Coletta, *Bald Eagle*, 16, 25–30; Taylor, *Magnificent Mitscher*, 63–66.
6. Taylor, *Magnificent Mitscher*, 78.
7. Mitscher to Frances Mitscher, Aug. 17, 1942, Mitscher Papers, NHHC; Bernard M. Stern (1974), 47, and Stephen Jurika (April 1, 1976), 1:492–3, both in U.S. Naval Institute Oral History Collection, USNA.
8. The shipmate was Tookies Bright; the 18-year-old helmsman was Richard Nowatski. Both are quoted in Coletta, *Bald Eagle*, 91, 108. The exchange with Gee is in Taylor, *Magnificent Mitscher*, 110–11.
9. Taylor, *Magnificent Mitscher*, 112.
10. D. B. Duncan to King, Feb. 4, 1942, King Papers, NHHC, Series I, box 1. At the end of Duncan's report, King scrawled the comment: "Excellent, K."
11. Duane Schultz, *The Doolittle Raid* (New York: St. Martin's, 1988), 5–10.
12. Ibid., 17.
13. King to FDR, March 5, 1942, King Papers, Series I, box 1, NHHC. The document is also printed as Appendix V in Thomas B. Buell, *Master of Sea Power: A Biography of Fleet Admiral Ernest J. King* (Boston: Little, Brown and Company, 1980), 532.
14. Buell, *Master of Sea Power*, 532; Lowell Thomas and Edward Jablonski, *Doolittle: A Biography* (Garden City, NY: Doubleday, 1976), 158.
15. James H. "Jimmy" Doolittle, with Carroll V. Glines, *I Could Never Be So Lucky Again: An Autobiography* (New York: Bantam Books, 1991), 28–34; Thomas and Jablonski, *Doolittle: A Biography*, 13–45; Schultz, *The Doolittle Raid*, 25.

16. Doolittle and Gaines, *I Could Never* , 98; Dik Alan Daso, *Doolittle: Aerospace Visionary* (Washington, DC: Brassey's, 2003), 18–21; Schultz, *Doolittle Raid*, 31–32.
17. James A. Doolittle oral history (Aug. 3, 1987), U.S. Naval Institute Oral History Collection, USNA, 12.
18. Henry Miller (May 23, 1973), 1:30–32; and James A. Doolittle oral history (Aug. 3, 1987), 10, both in U.S. Naval Institute Oral History Collection, USNA.
19. Henry Miller oral history (May 23, 1973), 33.
20. Richard Cole interview (Aug. 8, 2000), NMPW, 27.
21. James A. Doolittle oral history (Aug. 3, 1987), USNA, 20. This story is repeated in virtually every Doolittle biography, but Doolittle seems to have told it first to Carroll V. Glines, who included it in his book *Doolittle's Tokyo Raiders* (Princeton, NJ: Van Nostrand, 1964), 53–54.
22. Nimitz to Mrs. Nimitz, March 22, 1942, Nimitz Diary #1, NHHC; William F. Halsey, with J. Bryan III, *Admiral Halsey's Story* (New York: Whittlesey House, 1947), 101.
23. James A. Doolittle oral history (Aug. 3, 1987), 15–16.
24. Prange et al., *Miracle at Midway* (New York: McGraw Hill, 1982), 111; James A. Doolittle oral history (Aug. 3, 1987), 22.
25. James A. Doolittle oral history (Aug. 3, 1987), 31. The Japanese routinely kept all their planes on the hangar deck, bringing them up only for launching. That was one reason why they carried fewer planes on their carriers.
26. Henry Miller oral history (May 23, 1973), 1:37; and James A. Doolittle oral history (Aug. 3, 1987), 27. Mitscher to Nimitz, April 28, 1942, Action Reports, reel 2.
27. Clayton Fisher, "Officer and Enlisted Airmen," *The Roundtable Forum*, April 24, 2010; Stephen Jurika oral history (March 17, 1976), 1:457; Henry Miller oral history (May 23, 1973), 1:43; James A. Doolittle oral history (Aug. 23, 1978), 15.
28. Richard E. Cole interview (Aug. 8, 2000), 36, NMPW; Mitscher to Nimitz, April 28, 1942, Action Reports, reel 2.
29. Richard Best interview (Aug. 11, 1995), NMPW, 23.
30. Ibid.; Thomas and Jablonski, *Doolittle: A Biography*, 178–79; Doolittle and Gaines, *I Could Never*, 4.
31. Halsey and Bryan, *Admiral Halsey's Story*, 101.
32. John B. Lundstrom, *The First Team: Pacific Naval Air Combat from Pearl Harbor to Midway* (Annapolis, MD: Naval Institute Press, 1984), 148; interview of Gilbert Martin and Paul McKay (Sept. 2000), NMPW, 181.
33. Thomas and Jablonski, *Doolittle: A Biography*, 181.
34. James A. Doolittle oral history (Aug. 3, 1987), 19, and Stephen Jurika oral history (March 17, 1976), 1:470–71.
35. Doolittle to Arnold, June 5, 1942, available at http://www.ibiblio.org/hyperwar; Doolittle and Glines, *I Could Never*, 8; James H. Macia interview (July 21, 2000), NMPW.
36. James A. Doolittle oral history (Aug. 3, 1987), 6.
37. Ibid.; Doolittle and Glines, *I Could Never*, 8–9.
38. Quentin Reynolds, *The Amazing Mr. Doolittle: A Biography of Lieutenant General James H. Doolittle* (New York: Appleton-Century-Crofts, 1953), 209–12; Doolittle and Glines, *I Could Never*, 10–11.

39. The propaganda is quoted in Glines, *Doolittle's Tokyo Raiders*, 337; Watanabe's statement is from an interview by Gordon Prange (Sept. 25, 1964), Prange Papers, UMD, box 17.

## Chapter 7

1. Two excellent general summaries of the code-breaking wars in early 1942 are Ronald Lewin, *The American Magic: Codes, Ciphers and the Defeat of Japan* (New York: Farrar Straus Giroux, 1982), and John Prados, *Combined Fleet Decoded: The Secret History of American Intelligence and the Japanese Navy in World War II* (New York: Random House, 1995). Also essential are the memoirs of W. J. Holmes, *Double-Edged Secrets: U.S. Naval Intelligence Operations in the Pacific during World War II* (Annapolis, MD: Naval Institute Press, 1979), and Edwin T. Layton, with Roger Pineau and John Costello, *And I Was There: Pearl Harbor and Midway— Breaking the Secrets* (New York: Morrow, 1985). I am indebted to William Price and Rear Admiral Donald "Mac" Showers, USN (Ret.) for their help with this chapter.

2. Prados, *Combined Fleet Decoded*, 210–14; Layton, *And I Was There*, 29; Holmes, *Double-Edged Secrets*, 13; David Kahn, *The Reader of Gentlemen's Mail: Herbert O. Yardley and the Birth of American Codebreaking* (New Haven, CT: Yale University Press, 2004).

3. Layton, *And I Was There*, 32.

4. Holmes, *Double-Edged Secrets*, 3; Layton, *And I Was There*, 33; Ronald W. Russell, *No Right to Win: A Continuing Dialogue with Veterans of the Battle of Midway* (New York: iUniverse, 2006), 38; Joseph J. Rochefort oral history (Aug. 14, 1969), U.S. Naval Institute Oral History Collection, USNA, 5.

5. Rochefort oral history (Aug. 14, 1969), 6.

6. John Winton, *Ultra in the Pacific: How Breaking Japanese Codes and Ciphers Affected Naval Operations against Japan 1941–45* (London: Cooper, 1993), 6.

7. Rochefort oral history (Aug. 14, 1969), 104.

8. Ibid., 99.

9. Edward Layton oral history (May 30, 1970), U.S. Naval Institute Oral History Collection, USNA, 137; Frederick D. Parker, *A Priceless Advantage: U.S. Navy Communications Intelligence and the Battles of Coral Sea, Midway, and the Aleutians* (Ft. Meade, MD: Center for Cryptologic History, National Security Agency, 1993), 16.

10. Holmes, *Double-Edged Secrets*, 16; William Price, "Why There Was a Battle of Midway," lecture presented at the U.S. Navy Memorial, Washington, DC, June 4, 2009.

11. Lewin, *American Magic*, 55. The example of how "east" might be encrypted is borrowed from Russell, *No Right to Win*, 28–30.

12. Rochefort oral history (Aug. 14, 1969), 131; the decrypted message (050202) is from the Layton Papers, NWC, box 26, folder 4. See also Jonathan B. Parshall and Anthony P. Tully, *Shattered Sword: The Untold Story of the Battle of Midway* (Washington, DC: Potomac Books, 2005), 60.

13. Holmes, *Double-Edged Secrets*, 54

14. Interview of Rear Admiral Donald "Mac" Showers by the author (May 4, 2010); Rochefort oral history (Aug. 14, 1969), 110–17, 126. Some of those who worked

with Rochefort in the "dungeon" were subsequently angered by the popular portrayal of him as weirdly eccentric, though Rochefort himself later remarked, "If you desire to be a real cryptanalyst, being a little nuts helps." Rochefort oral history (Aug. 14, 1969), 13.

15. Rochefort oral history (Aug. 14, 1969), 34; Layton oral history (May 31, 1970), 124–25.

16. Parker, *Priceless Advantage*, 16–17; Layton, *And I Was There*, 259.

17. Layton oral history (May 30, 1970), 167.

18. King to Nimitz, May 4, 1942, Nimitz Papers, NHHC, box 1:431; Layton oral history (May 30, 1971), 14–15.

19. Layton oral history (May 30, 1970), 79.

20. Parker, *Priceless Advantage*, 19, 22. MacArthur in particular was skeptical of the conclusions offered by the cryptanalysts and preferred to rely on "hard" intelligence gleaned by scout planes and submarines.

21. Ibid., 108; Rochefort oral history (Aug. 14, 1969), 26; Rochefort oral history (Sept. 21, 1969), 145.

22. Holmes, *Double-Edged Secrets*, 65; Parker, *Priceless Advantage*, 18, 20; John B. Lundstrom, *Black Shoe Carrier Admiral: Frank Jack Fletcher at Coral Sea, Midway, and Guadalcanal* (Annapolis, MD: Naval Institute Press, 2006), 120–22.

23. Layton oral history (May 30 and 31, 1970), 108, 120; Holmes, *Double-Edged Secrets*, 72; author interview of Donald Showers (May 4, 2010).

24. Parker, *Priceless Advantage*, 25; Frederick C. Sherman, *Combat Command: The American Aircraft Carriers in the Pacific War* (New York: Dutton, 1950), 92; Nimitz to King, April 9, 1942; Running Summary, April 18, 1942 (italics in original); and King to Nimitz, April 18, 1942, all in Nimitz Papers, NHHC, box 1:501–5.

25. Traffic Intelligence Summary, Combat Intelligence Unit, Fourteenth Naval District (April 22, 1942), 3:154; Holmes, *Double-Edged Secrets*, 72.

26. Nimitz to King, April 17, 1942, Nimitz Papers, Operational Archives, NHHC, box 1:514.

27. Layton, *And I Was There*, 367–68; Prados, *Combined Fleet Decoded*, 300; Layton oral history (May 31, 1970), 137; Parker, *Priceless Advantage*, 18.

28. Rochefort oral history (Sept. 21, 1969), 174–75.

29. "Estimate of the Situation," April 22, 1942, and Nimitz to Fitch, April 19, 1942, both in Nimitz Papers, NHHC, box 1:375, 516, 518–19. See also Lundstrom, *Black Shoe Carrier Admiral*, 124–26.

30. Fletcher to Leary (copy King), March 29, 1942, and King to Fletcher, March 30, 1942, both in Nimitz Papers, NHHC, box 1:322; Joseph M. Worthington (June 7, 1972), U.S. Naval Institute Oral History Collection, USNA, 193 (Worthington was commanding officer of the USS *Benham*); Judson Brodie interview (March 13, 2007), NMPW, 24–25.

31. King to Nimitz, April 24, 1942, and Running Summary, April 24, 1942, both in Nimitz Papers, NHHC, box 1:409, 411; "Minutes of Conversation between CominCh and CinCPac, Saturday, April 25, 1942," King Papers, NHHC, Series II, box 10; Lundstrom, *Black Shoe Carrier Admiral*, 126–27. By coincidence, April 29th was also Fletcher's birthday—he turned 57.

32. Lewin, *American Magic*, 92.

33. E. B. Potter, *Nimitz* (Annapolis, MD: Naval Institute Press, 1976), 68–69.

**Chapter 8**

1. John B. Lundstrom, *Black Shoe Carrier Admiral: Frank Jack Fletcher at Coral Sea, Midway, and Guadalcanal* (Annapolis, MD: Naval Institute Press, 2006), 136.

2. Richard W. Bates, *The Battle of the Coral Sea, May 1 to May 11 Inclusive, 1942: Strategical and Tactical Analysis* (Newport, RI: Naval War College, 1947), 7–12; Prange interview of Genda Minoru (Sept. 5, 1966), Prange Papers, UMD, box 17.

3. Jonathan B. Parshall and Anthony P. Tully, *Shattered Sword: The Untold Story of the Battle of Midway* (Washington, DC: Potomac Books, 2005), 61–63. See also chapter 9.

4. Nimitz to Fletcher, April 22, 1942, Nimitz Papers, NHHC, box 1:399.

5. John B. Lundstrom, "A Failure of Radio Intelligence: An Episode in the Battle of the Coral Sea," *Cryptologia* 7, no. 2 (1983), 115.

6. Nimitz to King, Feb. 25, 1942, Nimitz Papers, NHHC, box 8:545; Lundstrom, *Black Shoe Carrier Admiral*, 141.

7. Richard W. Bates, in the semiofficial study *The Battle of the Coral Sea, May 1 to May 11 Inclusive, 1942,* insisted that by sending Takagi and Hara around the eastern end of the Solomon Islands, they were seeking a "Cannae"—a double envelopment—of American forces in the Coral Sea and concluded that Fletcher was irresponsible to let Hara get in behind him. John Lundstrom, however, points out that the initial objective of the Japanese end run was an attack on the Australian air bases. Bates, *Battle of the Coral Sea*; Lundstrom, *Black Shoe Carrier Admiral*, 137–40. See also H. P. Willmott, *The Barrier and the Javelin: Japanese and Allied Pacific Strategies, February to June 1942* (Annapolis, MD: Naval Institute Press, 1983), 87.

8. John B. Lundstrom, *The First South Pacific Campaign: Pacific Fleet Strategy, December 1941–June 1942* (Annapolis, MD: Naval Institute Press, 1976), 98; Willmott, *Barrier and Javelin*, 208.

9. Bates, *Battle of the Coral Sea*, 32; Lundstrom, *Black Shoe Carrier Admiral*, 145.

10. In his postwar memoir, the captain of the *Lexington*, Frederic "Ted" Sherman, called Fletcher's decision to withhold fighter support for the attack force a "serious mistake." Had Hara's carriers been within range, it might well have proved so. Sherman, *Combat Command: The American Aircraft Carriers in the Pacific War* (New York: Dutton, 1950), 93.

11. One reason the *Okinoshima* survived was that the American bombs were armed with impact fuses, so that, while the ship suffered significant topside damage, no bombs penetrated to her vital engineering spaces. Nimitz to King, June 17, 1942, Action Reports, reel 2, p. 3; Samuel Eliot Morison, *History of United States Naval Operations in World War II*, vol. 4, *Coral Sea, Midway and Submarine Actions, May 1942–August, 1942* (Boston: Little, Brown, 1949), 25–26; Lundstom, *Black Shoe Carrier Admiral*, 146, 149; Bates, *Battle of the Coral Sea*, 36; Willmott, *Barrier and Javelin*, 217–18.

12. Stuart D. Ludlum, *They Turned the War Around at Coral Sea and Midway: Going to War with Yorktown's Air Group Five* (Bennington, VT: Merriam, 2000), 70.

13. Nimitz to King, June 17, 1942, Action Reports, reel 2, p. 3; Paul S. Dull, *A Battle History of the Imperial Japanese Navy, 1941–1945* (Annapolis, MD: Naval Institute Press, 1978), 120; Lundstrom, "Failure of Radio Intelligence," 113.

14. Nimitz to Fletcher, May 5, 1942, CinCPac message file, Nimitz Papers, Operational Archives, NHHC, box 1:422. See Lundstrom, *First South Pacific Campaign*, 103–4, as well as Lundstrom, "Failure in Radio Intelligence," 108–10, 115; and Willmott, *Barrier and Javelin*, 234–35.

15. Neilson is quoted in Ludlum, *They Turned the War Around*, 73–74; John B. Lundstrom, *The First Team: Pacific Naval Air Combat from Pearl Harbor to Midway* (Annapolis, MD: Naval Institute Press, 1984), 193.

16. Lundstrom, *Black Shoe Carrier Admiral*, 165; Lundstrom, *First Team*, 194–96. Fletcher is quoted in Ludlum, *They Turned the War Around*, 77.

17. Lundstrom, *Black Shoe Carrier Admiral*, 165.

18. Ludlum, *They Turned the War Around*, 74.

19. Lundstrom, *Black Shoe Carrier Admiral*, 176–77; Lundstrom, *First Team*, 191; Dull, *A Battle History*, 124.

20. Lundstrom, *First Team*, 200; Ludlum, *They Turned the War Around*, 78.

21. Both Burch and Taylor are quoted in Ludlum, *They Turned the War Around*, 76–77.

22. Office of Naval Intelligence, *Combat Narrative: The Battle of the Coral Sea* (Washington, DC: Office of Naval Intelligence, United States Navy, 1943), 15–16; Lundstrom, *First Team*, 199, 205; Lundstrom, *Black Shoe Carrier Admiral*, 169; Ludlum, *They Turned the War Around*, 79, James H. Belote and William M. Belote, *Titans of the Seas: The Development and Operations of Japanese and American Carrier Task Forces during World War II* (New York: Harper & Row, 1975), 76; Sherman, *Combat Command*, 100.

23. The conversation was remembered by Taylor and is recorded in Ludlum, *They Turned the War Around*, 80.

24. For the rest of this life, Biard (who died in 2010) insisted that Fletcher missed a great opportunity by not listening to him. It is possible that Biard's assertions found their way to Washington and contributed to Admiral King's growing unease about Fletcher's aggressiveness. Author's interview of RADM Donald "Mac" Showers (May 4, 2010). See also Lundstrom, *Black Shoe Carrier Admiral*, 78, 167–68, 170–71.

25. Belote and Belote, *Titans of the Seas*, 76–77; Lundstrom, *First Team*, 212.

26. Lundstrom, *Black Shoe Carrier Admiral*, 176–77; Sherman, *Combat Command*, 102; Ludlum, *They Turned the War Around*, 82; Judson Brodie interview (March 13, 2007), NMPW, 28.

27. Lundstrom, *Black Shoe Carrier Admiral*, 176–77; Belote and Belote, *Titans of the Seas*, 77. In his memoir, Sherman insisted that postwar evidence proved that the Japanese carriers had been just where he claimed they were—only thirty miles away—and this proved that Fletcher should have ordered a night surface attack. In fact, postwar evidence places those carriers about a hundred miles to the east, in which case a night surface attack would have been futile and probably dangerous. Sherman, *Combat Command*, 102.

28. Matome Ugaki, *Fading Victory: The Diary of Admiral Matome Ugaki, 1941–1945*, ed. Donald M. Goldstein and Katherine V. Dillon, trans. Masataka Chihaya

(Annapolis, MD: Naval Institute Press, 1991), 128 (diary entry of May 18, 1942). Burch is quoted in Ludlum, *They Turned the War Around*, 80.

29. The official Navy reports credit the sighting by Smith without mentioning Dixon, though Dixon's postwar testimony makes it clear that he, too, played a crucial role. Buckmaster to Nimitz, May 25, 1942, Action Reports, reel 2, p. 3; Belote and Belote, *Titans of the Seas*, 78; Ludlum, *They Turned the War Around*, 84–85.

30. Pederson to Buckmaster, May 16, 1942, Action Reports, reel 2; Dull, *Battle History*, 126; Samuel Eliot Morison, *History of United States Naval Operations in World War II*, vol. 4, *Coral Sea, Midway and Submarine Action, May 1942–August, 1942* (Boston: Little, Brown, 1949), 47–48; Ludlum, *They Turned the War Around*, 87.

31. Burch and Short are quoted in Ludlum, *They Turned the War Around*, 87–88; Office of Naval Intelligence, *Battle of the Coral Sea*, 24–25.

32. Pederson to Buckmaster, May 16, 1942, Action Reports, reel 2. American torpedo plane pilots reported dropping nine torpedoes and making four hits. See Office of Naval Intelligence, *Battle of the Coral Sea*, 23. Taylor's quotation is in Ludlum, *They Turned the War Around*, 86.

33. Noel Gayler oral history (Feb. 15, 2002), Naval Historical Foundation, 6; Morison, *Coral Sea*, 49–51.

34. Sherman, *Combat Command*, 31.

35. Ibid., 109–10.

36. Buckmaster to Nimitz, May 25, 1942, Action Reports, reel 2, pp. 7, 40.

37. Frederick D. Parker, *A Priceless Advantage: U.S. Navy Communications Intelligence and the Battle of the Coral Sea, Midway, and the Aleutians* (Ft. Meade, MD: Center for Cryptologic History, National Security Agency, 1993), 29–30.

38. Ronald Russell, "Sam Laser in Sky Control," transcript available at BOMRT, http://www.midway42.org/vets-laser.html.

39. Sherman, *Combat Command*, 111, 114; Buckmaster to Nimitz, May 25, 1942, Action Reports, reel 2, p. 10; Paul Stroop oral history (Sept. 13, 1969), 144, U.S. Naval Institute Oral History Collection, USNA; Judson Brodie interview (March 13, 2007), NMPW, 30.

40. Sherman, *Combat Command*, 115; Judson Brodie interview (March 13, 2007), NMPW, 31.

41. Ludlum, *They Turned the War Around*, 96.

42. Ugaki, *Fading Victory*, 128 (diary entry of May 18, 1942).

43. Ludlum, *They Turned the War Around*, 96, 100; Lundstrom, *Black Shoe Carrier Admiral*, 194.

44. Sherman, *Combat Command*, 117; Walter Lord, *Incredible Victory* (New York: Harper & Row, 1967), 11; Ugaki, *Fading Victory*, 122 (diary entry of May 7, 1942).

## Chapter 9

1. Hiroyuki Agawa, *The Reluctant Admiral: Yamamoto and the Imperial Navy*, trans. John Bester (Tokyo: Kodansha International, 1979), 302; Matome Ugaki, *Fading Victory: The Diary of Admiral Matome Ugaki, 1941–1945*, ed. Donald M. Goldstein and Katherine V. Dillon, trans. Masataka Chihaya (Annapolis, MD: Naval Institute Press, 1991), 118 (diary entry of May 1, 1942).

2. RADM Ko Nagasawa, quoted in Robert E. Barde, "The Battle of Midway: A Study in Command" (Ph.D. diss., University of Maryland, 1972), 43; Ugaki, *Fading Victory*, 118 (diary entry of May 1, 1942); Sanematsu to Lord, Jan. 22, 1967, Walter Lord Collection, NHHC, box 18.

3. The Japanese observer at the war game was Chihaya Masataka, who wrote an analysis of the Imperial Japanese Navy a few years later. He is quoted in Donald M. Goldstein and Katherine Dillon, eds., *The Pearl Harbor Papers: Inside the Japanese Plans* (Washington, DC: Brassey's, 1993), 348. See also Mitsuo Fuchida and Masatake Okumiya, *Midway: The Battle that Doomed Japan, the Japanese Navy's Story* (Annapolis, MD: Naval Institute Press, 1955), 91–92; and Office of Naval Intelligence, *The Japanese Story of the Battle of Midway: A Translation*, OPNAV P32–1002, (Washington, DC: Government Printing Office, 1947), 2.

4. Fuchida and Okumiya, *Midway*, 96; Agawa, *Reluctant Admiral*, 303; Jonathan B. Parshall and Anthony P. Tully, *Shattered Sword: The Untold Story of the Battle of Midway* (Washington, DC: Potomac Books, 2005), 61–62.

5. Ugaki, *Fading Victory*, 119, 120 (diary entry of May 4, 1942).

6. Gordon Prange interview with Watanbe Yasuji (Oct. 6, 1964), Prange Papers, UMD, box 17; Gordon Prange, Donald M. Goldstein, and Katherine V. Dillon, *Miracle at Midway* (New York: McGraw-Hill, 1982), 35. Yamamoto is quoted in John Deane Potter, *Admiral of the Pacific: The Life of Yamamoto* (London: Heinemann, 1965), 44.

7. The "knowledgeable scholars" are Parshall and Tully, *Shattered Sword*, 62–63.

8. Ugaki, *Fading Victory*, 120 (diary entry of May 5, 1942). Turret no. 5 on *Hyūga* was removed, the barbette roofed over, and antiaircraft guns were put there. I am indebted to John Lundstrom for this information.

9. Agawa, *Reluctant Admiral*, 305; Ugaki, *Fading Victory*, 123–24 (diary entry of May 7, 1942).

10. Ugaki, *Fading Victory*, 125 (diary entry of May 10, 1942).

11. Ugaki, *Fading Victory*, 127 (diary entry of May 17, 1942).

12. Parshall and Tully, *Shattered Sword*, 66.

13. Ibid., 64–65.

14. Frederick D. Parker, *A Priceless Advantage: U.S. Navy Communications Intelligence and the Battles of Coral Sea, Midway, and the Aleutians* (Ft. Meade, MD: Center for Cryptologic History, National Security Agency, 1993), 43–45; CINCPAC Intelligence Briefs, OP-20G File (May 10, 1942), Special Collections, Nimitz Library, USNA, 75.

15. Joseph Rochefort oral history (Oct. 5, 1969), 203, and Thomas Dyer oral history (Sept. 14, 1983), 241, both in U.S. Naval Institute Oral History Collection, USNA; author's interview of RADM Donald "Mac" Showers (May 4, 2010). The list of known designators (060710) is in the Layton Papers, NWC, box 26, folder 4.

16. Rochefort oral history (Oct. 5, 1969), 203. See John B. Lundstrom, *The First South Pacific Campaign: Pacific Fleet Strategy, December 1941–June 1942* (Annapolis, MD: Naval Institute Press, 1976).

17. Traffic Intelligence Summaries, Combat Intelligence Unit, Fourteenth Naval District (July 16 1941—June 30 1942), Special Collections, Nimitz Library, USNA, 3:326; King to Nimitz, May 15, 1942, Nimitz Papers, NHHC, box 1:468.

18. Nimitz to King, May 16, 1942, and the Running Summary, May 16, 1942, are both in Nimitz Papers, NHHC, box 1:471, 482; King to Nimitz, May 15, 1942, is also in the Nimitz Papers, but in box 8, unnumbered page, date-time group 152130.

19. Nimitz to Halsey, May 17,1942, and King to Spenavo, May 18, 1942, both in Nimitz Papers, NHHC, box 1:491, 492.

20. King to Nimitz, May 17 and 18, 1942, both in Nimitz Papers, NHHC, box 1:490, 492.

21. Nimitz to King, May 17 and May 21, 1942, both in Nimitz Papers, NHHC, box 1:488, 490.

22. The summary of air strength on Midway is from the Nimitz Papers, NHHC, box 1:505. Spruance's handwritten note shows 115 airplanes on Midway: Spruance Papers, NWC, box 2, folder 4. See Appendix C.

23. There has been a lot of discussion about who came up with the idea for the bogus message. The account here relies heavily on RADM "Mac" Showers, who recalls the conversation between Rochefort and Holmes that took place as they were standing next to his desk in the Dungeon. See W. J. Holmes, *Double-Edged Secrets: U.S. Naval Intelligence Operations in the Pacific during World War II* (Annapolis, MD: Naval Institute Press, 1979), 90; Rochefort oral history (Oct. 5, 1969), 211; and Dyer oral history (Sept. 14, 1983), 241.

24. The message (Com 14, 200050) is in Edwin Layton's handwritten journal, May 20, 1942, Layton Papers, NWC, box 29, folder 3. William Price asserts that the man who discovered the key intercept was Yeoman Second Class William Tremblay who worked at Belconnen, though others recall that the initial discovery took place in "the Dungeon" at Hypo. What is clear is that both units played an important role in the final decryption of the messages. William Price interview (May 4, 2010). See also Russell, *No Right to Win*, 30–33.

25. See the list of decrypts in Appendix III of Edwin Layton's unpublished manuscript, "The Role of Radio Intelligence in the American-Japanese War" (which he submitted in September of 1942), in Layton Papers, NWC, box 15, folder 1. Interview of RADM Donald "Mac" Showers by the author (May 4, 2010); Henry F. Schorreck, "The Role of COMINT in the Battle of Midway," *Cryptologic Spectrum* 5, no. 3 (Summer 1975), 3–11; "Estimate of the Situation" (May 26, 1942), Nimitz Papers, NHHC, box 1:544. Rochefort's words are from his oral history (Oct. 5, 1969), 219.

26. Rochefort oral history (Oct. 5, 1969), 217–19. See also the Traffic Intelligence Summaries, 3:381.

27. David Kahn, *The Codebreakers: The Story of Secret Writing* (London: Weidenfeld & Nicolson, 1967), 569–70.

28. "Estimate of the Situation" (May 26, 1942), Nimitz Papers, NHHC, box 1:516, 520.

29. E. B. Potter, *Bull Halsey* (Annapolis, MD: Naval Institute Press, 1985), 84.

30. Ibid., 118; Gordon Prange interview of Spruance (Sept. 5, 1964), Prange Papers, UMD, box 17; C. J. Moore interview (Nov. 28, 1966) in Spruance Papers, NWC, box 2, series 4, folder 1; John B. Lundstrom, *Black Shoe Carrier Admiral: Frank Jack Fletcher at Coral Sea, Midway, and Guadalcanal* (Annapolis, MD: Naval Institute Press, 2006), 225.

31. Quoted in Thomas B. Buell, *The Quiet Warrior: A Biography of Admiral Raymond A. Spruance* (Boston: Little, Brown, 1974), 122.

32. Ashford to Walter Lord, Feb. 26, 1966, Lord Collection, NHHC, box 18; Potter, *Bull Halsey*, 78.

33. Nimitz to Navy Yard, Pearl Harbor, May 28, 1942, Nimitz Papers, NHHC, box 8, no page, date-time group 280233.

34. Potter, *Bull Halsey*, 79; Nimitz to Navy Yard, Pearl Harbor, May 28, 1942, and Fletcher to Nimitz, May 11, 1942, both in Nimitz Papers, NHHC, box 8, no page number, date-time group 280233 and 092102; E. B. Potter, *Nimitz* (Annapolis, MD: Naval Institute Press, 1976), 85.

35. Craig L. Symonds, *Decision at Sea: Five Naval Battles that Shaped American History* (New York: Oxford University Press, 2005), 202.

36. Nimitz to King, May 10, 1942, Nimitz Papers, NHHC, box 8, no page number, date-time group 092219.

37. King to Fletcher, March 30, 1942, Nimitz Papers, NHHC, box 1:322; King to Dudley Pound, May 21, 1942, King Papers, NHHC, Series I, box 2; King to Nimitz, May 11, 1942, and Fletcher to Nimitz, May 15, 1942, both in Nimitz Papers, NHHC., box 1:468, 469. See Lundstrom, *First South Pacific Campaign*, 68–70; and *Black Shoe Carrier Admiral*, 116–17.

38. Fletcher to Nimitz, May 28, carbon copy in King Papers, NHHC, Series I, box 2; Potter, *Nimitz*, 86.

39. Nimitz to King, May 29, 1942, King Papers NHHC, Series I, box 2.

40. Examples of King's use of the phrase are in King to J. H. Ingram, March 14, 1942, and King to Freeman, March 17, 1942, both in King Papers, NHHC, Series I, box 2. Nimitz's use of it (italics mine) is in Nimitz to King, May 29, 1942, King Papers, NHHC, Series I, box 2.

41. Nimitz to Commander Striking Forces, May 28, 1942, Action Reports, reel 2, pp. 1, 6. See also Wayne P. Hughes, Jr., "Clear Purpose, Comprehensive Execution: Raymond Ames Spruance (1886–1969)," in *Nineteen-Gun Salute: Case Studies of Operational, Strategic, and Diplomatic Naval Leadership during the 20th and Early 21st Centuries*, ed. John B. Hattendorf and Bruce A. Elleman (Newport, RI: Naval War College Press, 2010), 52.

42. Nimitz to Spruance, May 28, 1942, Nimitz Papers, NHHC, box 8/280105.

43. Interview of Captain John W. "Jack" Crawford, USN (Ret.) by the author (May 5, 2004).

44. Nimtiz's visit is discussed in a questionnaire completed by LT Clarence E. Aldrich, in Walter Lord Collection, NHHC, box 18.

## Chapter 10

1. Jonathan B. Parshall and Anthony P. Tully, *Shattered Sword: The Untold Story of the Battle of Midway* (Washington, DC: Potomac Books, 2005), 90–91.

2. Beardall to King, Jan. 12, 1942, King Papers, NHHC, Series I, box 1; King Secret File, Feb. 1, 1942, Gruening to Ickes, Feb. 14, 1942, and Ickes to FDR, Feb. 18, 1942, all in King Papers, NHHC, Series I, box 2.

3. Nimitz to Theobald, May 20, 1942, Nimitz Papers, NHHC, 1:496.

4. Marshall and King Memo, April 16, 1942, King Papers, NHHC, Series I, box 2; Nimitz to King, May 20, 1942, Nimitz Papers, NHHC, box 1:496.

5. Robert Theobald, "Memorandum for Whom it May Concern," July 2, 1942, King Papers, NHHC, Series I, box 2, p. 8 (hereafter Theobald Memorandum); Samuel Eliot Morison, *History of United States Naval Operations in World War II*, vol. 4, *Coral Sea, Midway and Submarine Actions, May 1942–August, 1942* (Boston: Little, Brown, 1949), 170.

6. Theobald Memorandum, 9; interview of VADM William D. Houser by the author (May 5, 2004).

7. Morison, *Coral Sea*, 175–76; Gordon Prange, Donald M. Goldstein, and Katherine V. Dillon, *Miracle at Midway* (New York: McGraw-Hill, 1982), 153.

8. J. W. Reeves to King, June 13, 1942, King Papers, NHHC, Series I, box 2; Theobald Memorandum, 4.

9. Theobald Memorandum, 11.

10. Ibid., 11–12.

11. J. W. Reeves to King, June 13, 1942, King Papers, NHHC, Series, I, box 2. In a handwritten comment on this message, King wrote: "The basic trouble was that CTF8 [Theobald] did not set up a Joint Air Command until about 20 June."

12. Morison, *Coral Sea*, 178.

13. It was Commander Miyo who proposed Operation K at the April 5 conference with the Naval General Staff in Tokyo. See Robert E. Barde, "The Battle of Midway: A Study in Command" (Ph.D. diss., University of Maryland, 1972), 41–42, 41n.

14. Alec Hudson, "Rendezvous," *Saturday Evening Post*, Aug. 2 and 9, 1941, quotation from the Aug. 9 issue, 32; Steve Horn, *The Second Attack on Pearl Harbor: Operation K and Other Japanese Attempts to Bomb America in World War II* (Annapolis, MD: Naval Institute Press, 2005), 73–74.

15. Horn, *Second Attack on Pearl Harbor*, 65–90.

16. Edward T. Layton, with Roger Pineau and John Costello, *"And I was there": Pearl Harbor and Midway—Breaking the Secrets* (New York: Morrow, 1985), 374.

17. The Hypo intercepts are in the Layton Papers, NWC, box 26, folder 5.

18. Horn, *Second Attack on Pearl Harbor*, 175–77.

19. Prange interviews with Watanabe (Sept. 26 and Oct. 6, 1964), Prange Papers, UMD, box 17. See also Barde, "Battle of Midway," 42, 45–46.

20. Mitsuo Fuchida and Masatake Okumiya, *Midway: The Battle that Doomed Japan, the Japanese Navy's Story* (Annapolis, MD: Naval Institute Press, 1955; repr., 1992), 155; Prange et al., *Miracle at Midway*, 145.

21. Nimitz to Midway garrison, June 2, 1942, Nimitz Papers, NHHC, box 1:550. The "criminal waste" passage is from John S. McCain to "Frog" Low, March 14, 1942, King Papers, NHHC, Series I, box 2. See also King to Marshall, March 19, King Papers, NHHC, Series I, box 2.

22. Prange et al., *Miracle at Midway*, 160–61.

23. Ibid., 162–63.

24. Ibid.

25. The details of the sighting come from a letter from Reid to Gordon Prange dated Dec. 10, 1966. It is cited in Prange et al., *Miracle at Midway*, 162–64. See also Potter, *Nimitz*, 91; Symonds, *Decision at Sea*, 225.

26. Layton to Walter Lord, Feb. 10, 1967, Walter Lord Collection, NHHC, box 17; Nimitz to Mrs. Nimitz, June 2, 1942, Nimitz Diary # 1, NHHC; Layton, *And I was There*, 436; Potter, *Nimitz*, 92.

27. Quoted in Prange et al., *Miracle at Midway*, 170.

28. Prange et al., *Miracle at Midway*, 173.

29. Dick Knott, "Night Torpedo Attack," *Naval Aviation News*, June 1982, 10–13; Gerald Astor, *Wings of Gold: The U.S. Naval Air Campaign in World War II* (New York: Ballantine Books, 2004), 87–88; and Prange et al., *Miracle at Midway*, 174–76.

30. James C. Boyden to Walter Lord, Jan., 24, 1966, Walter Lord Collection, NHHC, box 18; Lieutenant Junior Grade Douglas Davis interview (Oct. 1, 2000), NMPW; and Stuart D. Ludlum, *They Turned the War Around at Coral Sea and Midway: Going to War with Yorktown's Air Group Five* (Bennington, VT: Merriam, 2000), 106.

31. John B. Lundstrom, *Black Shoe Carrier Admiral: Frank Jack Fletcher at Coral Sea, Midway, and Guadalcanal* (Annapolis, MD: Naval Institute Press, 2006), 236.

## Chapter 11

1. Mitsuo Fuchida and Masatake Okumiya, *Midway: The Battle that Doomed Japan, the Japanese Navy's Story* (Annapolis, MD: Naval Institute Press, 1955), 75; Jonathan B. Parshall and Anthony P. Tully, *Shattered Sword: The Untold Story of the Battle of Midway* (Washington, DC: Potomac Books, 2005), 123.

2. The numbers used here are from Parshall and Tully, *Shattered Sword*, 90–91.

3. Fuchida and Okumiya, *Midway*, 184–85.

4. Fuchida and Okumiya, *Midway*, 185. The discovery that the Japanese did not bring the second strike force onto the flight deck is a particular contribution of Jonathan Parshall and Anthony Tully, who were the first to combine an analysis of Japanese carrier doctrine with the battle photos of the Kidō Butai to conclude that the decks of the four Japanese carriers were largely bare throughout the morning. They note that "at no time during the morning prior to 1000 was the reserve strike force ever spotted on the flight decks." (*Shattered Sword*, 131.) Another important contribution is the time-motion study, based on interviews of Japanese crewmen, done by Dallas Isom to determine both the process and the time needed to arm (and rearm) the Japanese planes. See Dallas Woodbury Isom, *Midway Inquest: Why the Japanese Lost the Battle of Midway* (Bloomington: Indiana University Press, 2007), 116–28.

5. Thomas Wildenberg, "Midway: Sheer Luck or Better Doctrine?" *Naval War College Review* 58 (Winter 2005):121–35. In his after-action report, Nagumo acknowledged that, "under such weather conditions, it is believed that the number of recco planes should be increased." See "CINC First Air Fleet Detailed Battle Report No. 6," *ONI Review* 5 (May 1947), available on line at http://www.ibiblio.org/hyperwar/Japan/IJN/rep/Midway/Nagumo/. See also Parshall and Tully, *Shattered Sword*, 146–48.

6. Craig L. Symonds, *Decision at Sea: Five Naval Battles that Shaped American History* (New York: Oxford University Press, 2005), 228–29.

7. Douglas C. Davis interview (Oct. 1, 2000), NMPW.

8. Fletcher to Nimitz, June 14, 1942, Action Reports, reel 2.

9. "Pertinent Extracts from Communications Logs Relative to Midway Attack," Action Reports, reel 2; Fletcher to S. E. Morison, Dec. 1, 1947, Fletcher Papers, AHC, box 1; interview of Howard P. Ady by Walter Lord (April 9, 1966), Lord Collection, NHHC, box 18.

10. Communications Log Relative to Midway Attack, Action Reports, reel 2; James R. Ogden oral history (March 16, 1982), 76–77, U.S. Naval Institute Oral History Collection, USNA.

11. Interview with John F. Carey by Gordon Prange (July 1, 1966), Prange Papers, UMD, box 17; Robert J. Cressman et al., "A Glorious Page in Our History": The Battle of Midway, 4–6 June 1942 (Missoula, MT: Pictorial Histories, 1990), 62; statement of Captain John F. Carey, USMC, June 6, 1942, Action Reports, reel 3; Kirk Armistead to Walter Lord, Feb. 15, 1967, Walter Lord Collection, NHHC, box 18.

12. Statement of Captain John F. Carey, USMC, June 6, 1942, Action Reports, reel 3; Cressman et al., Glorious Page, 62.

13. Statement of Captain John F. Carey, and statement of Capt. P. R. White, both June 6, 1942, Action Reports, reel 3. The story of Kurz and the "stiff shots" is from Cressman et al., Glorious Page, 64.

14. John B. Lundstrom, Black Shoe Carrier Admiral: Frank Jack Fletcher at Coral Sea, Midway, and Guadalcanal (Annapolis, MD: Naval Institute Press, 2006), 237–43.

15. Fletcher to Nimitz, June 14, 1942, Action Reports, reel 2; Parshall and Tully, Shattered Sword, 134–35; Lundstrom, Black Shoe Carrier Admiral, 242. John Lundstrom notes that Spruance did not acknowledge Fletcher's order and that Fletcher had to send a follow-up message fifteen minutes later. By then, Spruance was already heading toward the southwest (Black Shoe Carrier Admiral, 242). Interestingly, Spruance does not mention getting this order from Fletcher in his own after-action report (Spruance to Nimitz, June 16, 1942, Action Reports, reel 3.) In 1947, when Samuel Eliot Morison asked both Fletcher and Spruance who had commanded the combined American carrier task forces at this time, both men replied that it was Fletcher. "I ordered Spruance to attack," Fletcher wrote, "but as we were well separated he was left to select his own point option." Curiously, however, Task Force 16 did not set a point option. Fletcher to Morison, Dec. 1, 1947, Fletcher Papers, AHC, box 1.

16. Richard Best interview (Aug. 11, 1995), NMPW, 37–38.

17. Clark Reynolds, "The Truth About Miles Browning," in Cressman et al., Glorious Page, 214–15; Richard Best interview (Aug. 11, 1995), NMPW; Gordon Prange interview of Spruance (Sept. 5, 1964), Prange Papers, UMD, box 17.

18. Communications Log Relative to the Battle of Midway, Action Reports, reel 2.

19. Kimes to Nimitz, June 7, 1942, Action Reports, reel 2; Nimitz to King, June 4, 1942, Nimitz Papers, NHHC, box 8, no page number, date-time group 042007; Parshall and Tully, Shattered Sword, 301–2.

20. Gordon Prange, with Donald M. Goldstein, and Katherine V. Dillon, Miracle at Midway (New York: McGraw-Hill, 1982), 206; Fuchida and Okumiya, Midway, 156; Parshall and Tully, Shattered Sword, 149.

21. Albert K. Earnest and Harry Ferrier, "Avengers at Midway," *Foundation* 17, no. 2 (Spring 1996), 1–7; Robert J. Mrazek, *A Dawn Like Thunder: The True Story of Torpedo Squadron Eight* (New York: Little, Brown, 2008), 6–10.

22. Willard Robinson interview (July 20, 2003), NMPW.

23. Ibid.; Albert Earnest interview (July 20, 2003), NMPW; Mrazek, *Dawn Like Thunder*, 61, 121; Cressman et al., *Glorious Page*, 70.

24. The details of Earnest's saga come from interviews conducted by Robert Mrazek in February 2006. See Mrazek, *Dawn Like Thunder*, 122–23, 142–145.

25. Recollections of Frank Melo, as told to Charles Lowe, Lowe Diary, BOMRT; Parshall and Tully, *Shattered Sword*, 152; Cressman et al., *Glorious Page*, 72–73. Fuchida Mitsuo recalled that one of the B-26 bombers tried to crash into the *Akagi*, but Fuchida very likely conflated Jim Muri's plane, which flew very low over the *Akagi*'s deck, with that of First Lieutenant Herbert Mayes, which cartwheeled into the sea after being shot down. I am grateful to Jon Parshall for his insights about this particular attack.

26. Nagumo's chief of staff was RADM Kusaka Ryūnosuke, who made these remarks in an interview with Gordon Prange (no date), Prange Papers, UMD, box 17. See also Parshall and Tully, *Shattered Sword*, 153.

27. Dallas Isom describes the rearming process in detail in *Midway Inquest*, 124–28; Parshall and Tully, *Shattered Sword*, 157.

28. "CINC First Air Fleet Detailed Battle Report No. 6" ; Fuchida and Okumiya, *Midway*, 148. It was Fuchida who sustained for so long the notion that the delay in launching *Tone*'s search plane no. 4 was a piece of horrible luck that doomed the Japanese at Midway. Jonathan Parshall and Anthony Tully have suggested that his motive was to imply that the Japanese defeat at Midway was a fluke of timing and circumstance rather than the product of doctrinal error or command failure. See Parshall and Tully (*Shattered Sword*, 132, 159, 161), who render Amari's first name as Hiroshi.

29. Credit for figuring out this irony belongs to Dallas Isom, "The Battle of Midway: Why the Japanese Lost," *Naval War College Review* 53, no. 3 (Summer 2000), 68–70. Isom makes the same point in *Midway Inquest*, 114–16.

30. Kusaka's recollection is taken from a questionnaire he completed for Gordon Prange in 1966, Prange Papers, UMD, box 17. In that same document, Kusaka asserts that "it was not before 0500 [8:00 a.m.] that the said report reached our ears." Based partly on this, Prange and Isom both argue that the message probably did not reach the bridge on the *Akagi* until 8:00. Isom in particular makes a strong case that Nagumo did not learn of the sighting until 8:00 and concludes that this was why Nagumo could not get his strike launched until after 10:20. Parshall and Tully argue for the 7:45 time, citing not only the Japanese message log but also the intercept by Station Hypo. Isom suggests that the 7:47 notation in the Hypo log was added after the fact to comport with the reconstructed Japanese message log. See Prange et al., *Miracle at Midway*, 217; Isom, *Midway Inquest*, 133–37; and Parshall and Tully, *Shattered Sword*, 159–60. See also Isom's article "Battle of Midway."

31. "CINC First Air Fleet Detailed Battle Report No. 6"; Parshall and Tully, *Shattered Sword*, 162.

32. Isom, *Midway Inquest*, 158–59; Parshall and Tully, *Shattered Sword*, 155.
33. R. D. Heinl, Jr., *Marines at Midway* (Washington, DC: Historical Section, Division of Public Information, U.S. Marine Corps, 1948), 34–35.
34. Cressman et al., *Glorious Page*, 79; Statement of Captain R. L. Blain, USMC., no date, Action Reports, reel 3.
35. Second Lt. George Lumpkin, USMC, quoted in Heinl, *Marines at Midway*, 38.
36. Interview of Kusaka by Gordon Prange (1966), Prange Papers, UMD, box 17; "CINC First Air Fleet Detailed Battle Report No. 6"; Kusaka questionnaire, 1966, Prange Papers, UMD, box 17.
37. Agawa, *Reluctant Admiral*, 264.
38. Parshall and Tully, *Shattered Sword*, 165–66; interview of Kusaka by Gordon Prange (1966), Prange Papers, UMD, box 17. See also the discussion of the impact of doctrine on operational decisions in Parshall and Tully, *Shattered Sword*, 404–5.

## Chapter 12

1. The young officer was LT James James E. Vose, who was interviewed by Barrett Tillman in June 1973 and quoted in Tillman, *The Dauntless Dive Bomber of World War II* (Annapolis, MD: Naval Institute Press, 1976), 66. The sailor on the *Enterprise* was Alvin Kernan, in *The Unknown Battle of Midway: The Destruction of the American Torpedo Squadrons* (New Haven, CT: Yale University Press, 2005), 73.
2. Robert J. Mrazek, *A Dawn Like Thunder: The True Story of Torpedo Squadron Eight* (New York: Little, Brown, 2008), 18–20; Kernan, *Unknown Battle of Midway*, 71–75.
3. Peter C. Smith treats Ring more positively in *Midway: Dauntless Victory; Fresh Perspectives on America's Seminal Naval Victory of World War II* (Barnsley, UK: Pen & Sword Maritime, 2007), 59–60, though most of the supportive comments about him come from Ring's superiors. Barrett Tillman tells the story of Ring grounding pilots for refusing to come to attention in *Wildcat: The F4F in WW II*, 2nd ed. (Annapolis, MD: Naval Institute Press, 1990), 50. Ring's insistence that the *Hornet* pilots remain on duty at Ewa Field is from E. T. Stover and Clark G. Reynolds, *The Saga of Smokey Stover* (Charleston, SC: Tradd Street, 1978), 29.
4. Troy Guillory interview (March 14, 1983), 33, by Bowen Weisheit, in Weisheit, "The Battle of Midway: Transcripts of Recorded Interviews," Nimitz Library, USNA (hereafter Weisheit, "Transcripts"); Clay Fisher and Roy Gee are quoted in Ronald W. Russell, *No Right to Win: A Continuing Dialogue with Veterans of the Battle of Midway* (New York: iUniverse, 2006), 128–29; J. E. McInerny interview (1981), Weisheit, "Transcripts," 41. The story of Ring's navigational error is in a letter from K. B. White to Bill Vickery, which was read aloud at a BOMRT event in 2003. See Russell, *No Right to Win*, 129. See also Kernan, *Unknown Battle of Midway*, 73–74.
5. George Gay, among several others, asserted that few of the pilots slept on June 3. Gay also reported that five of the pilots of VT-8 had not made a single carrier landing until they reached the Pacific. George Gay, *Sole Survivor: The Battle of Midway and Its Effect on His Life* (Naples, FL: Naples Ad/Graphics, 1979), 64. The "one-eyed sandwich" is described by LT Jim Gray in "Decision at Midway," BOMRT,

http://www.midway42.org/aa-reports/vf-b.html. Interview of Troy Guillory (March 14, 1983), Weisheit, "Transcripts," 4; Tillman, *Wildcat*, 50.

6. Gay, *Sole Survivor*, 115; Mrazek, *Dawn Like Thunder*, 105–6, 110–11; Clayton E. Fisher, *Hooked: Tales and Adventures of a Tailhook Warrior* (Denver: Outskirts, 2009), 76–77; interview of Ben Tappan (1981), Weisheit, "Transcripts," 39–40; Roy P. Gee, "Remembering Midway," BOMRT (2003), http://www.midway42.org/vets-gee.html.

7. John B. Lundstrom, *The First Team: Pacific Naval Air Combat from Pearl Harbor to Midway* (Annapolis, MD: Naval Institute Press, 1984), 142.

8. Interview of S. G. Mitchell (1981), Weisheit, "Transcripts," 16–17.

9. George Gay interview (no date), World War II Interviews, Operational Archives, NHHC, box 11; Gay, *Sole Survivor*, 59; Mrazek, *Dawn Like Thunder*, 13–14, 86–87; Kernan, *Unknown Battle of Midway*, 64–67. Kernan quotes Waldron's letter to his nephew on p. 68.

10. Interview of Ben Talbot, Weisheit, "Transcripts," 8; Lundstrom, *First Team*, 324.

11. Interview of S. G. Mitchell (1981), Weisheit, "Transcripts," 17–18; Waldron's effort to get a single fighter to fly with his squadron is in Gay, *Sole Survivor*, 115.

12. "Pertinent Extracts from Communications Logs Relative to Midway Attack," Action Reports, reel 2; John B. Lundstrom, *Black Shoe Carrier Admiral: Frank Jack Fletcher at Coral Sea, Midway, and Guadalcanal* (Annapolis, MD: Naval Institute Press, 2006), 245–46. With Browning as his chief of staff, Halsey had used a deferred departure in his attacks in the Marshalls and Wake. Fletcher had used a normal departure in the Coral Sea.

13. Lewis Hopkins interview, NMPW, 17; Gee, "Remembering Midway."

14. Frederick Mears, *Carrier Combat* (Garden City, NY: Doubleday Doran, 1944), 18; Interview of Walt Rodee (1981), Weisheit, "Transcripts," 2; Stanhope Ring, letter of March 28, 1946, in Bruce R. Linder, "Lost Letter of Midway," *U.S. Naval Institute Proceedings* 125, no. 8 (August 1999), 31; interview of Ben Tappan (1981), Weisheit, "Transcripts," 46.

15. The fuel use numbers come from the interview of J. E. McInerny (1981), Weisheit, "Transcripts," 24, 37; Smith, *Midway, Dauntless Victory*, 75; Bowen P. Weisheit, *The Last Flight of Ensign C. Markland Kelly, Junior, USNR, Battle of Midway, June 4, 1942* (Baltimore: Ensign C. Markland Kelly, Jr., Memorial Foundation, 1993), 5; interview of S G. Mitchell (1981), Weisheit, "Transcripts," 17; interview of LT James E. Vose by Barrett Tillman (June 1973), quoted in Tillman, *Dauntless Dive Bomber*, 68.

16. Mitscher to Nimitz, June 13, 1942, Action Reports, reel 3, also available at http://www.history.navy.mil/docs/wwii/mid5.htm. The most telling piece of evidence that the *Hornet*'s air group flew a course of 265 is that Walt Rodee, commander of the scouting squadron (and later an admiral), wrote the course down in his log book. Still, not all of the contemporary testimony points to a course of 265. Ring's wingman, Clayton Fisher, remained adamant that they flew a course of 240. See Fisher, *Hooked*, 80–81, and Russell, *No Right to Win*, 134, 140.

17. John Lundstrom asserts that Mitscher made a deliberate decision "to go after the supposed second, trailing group of two Japanese carriers" in part because he was "contemptuous of the lack of aviation expertise of Fletcher and Spruance." Posting

to BOMRT, July 30, 2009. I am grateful to John Lundstrom for our conversations about this enigmatic event.

18. Nimitz to Commander Striking Force, May 28, 1942, Action Reports, reel 3, p. 3. The passage from Jurika's intelligence briefing is from the diary of E. T. "Smokey" Stover, Stover and Reynolds, *Saga of Smokey Stover*, 29 (entry of June 7). Fletcher's message to Spruance is quoted in Lundstrom, *Black Shoe Carrier Admiral*, 248. The Ring letter of March 28, 1946, is in Bruce R. Linder, "Lost Letter of Midway," *U.S. Naval Institute Proceedings* 125, no. 8 (August 1999), 31. It is interesting that both Mitscher and Ring employed the passive voice in their statements: Mitscher noted that the course "was calculated" and Ring notes that departure "was taken." Of course the passive voice was (and is) common in Navy documents, where special requests are worded: "It is requested that. . . ."

19. Gay, *Sole Survivor*, 116. In his memoir, Gay has Waldron telling him that he was planning to go "more to the north." This comports with Mitscher's report, which has Ring flying to the southwest and Waldron heading off to the north to find the Kidō Butai. Very likely, however, Gay relied on Mitscher's report to assist his memory thirty-seven years after the fact and adjusted the language of the remembered conversation to fit the report.

20. Interview of Troy Guillory (March 14, 1983), 28, 23; and Ben Tappan (1981), Weisheit, "Transcripts." The last response from Waldron is rendered here as a combination of what Tappan and Guillory recalled.

21. Interview of J. E. McInerny (1981), Weisheit, "Transcripts," 7; Weisheit, *Last Flight*, 17–18.

22. Interview of S. G. Mitchell (1981), Weisheit, "Transcripts," 24. See also Mrazek, *Dawn Like Thunder*, 132.

23. Interview of J. E. McInerny (1981), Weisheit, "Transcripts," 11, 13.

24. Enclosure (H) to Hornet Serial 0018 dated June 13, 1942, by Leroy Quillen, radioman/gunner for Ensign K. B. White, in VB-8, Action Reports, reel 2. Quillen remembered the initial call as "Johnny One to Johnny Two," but others recalled it as "Stanhope from Johnny One," which is more logical under the circumstances.

25. 1926 *Lucky Bag*, USNA; Gee, "Remembering Midway," 4; interview of Troy Guillory (March 14, 1983), Weisheit, "Transcripts," 26; Robert Johnson to Walter Lord, Feb. 21, 1967, Walter Lord Collection, NHHC, box 17.

26. Gee, "Remembering Midway"; Ring letter of March 28, 1946, in Linder, "Lost Letter," 32. Clay Fisher, Ring's designated wingman, sought to stay with him, but Ring had sent him to deliver a visual message to Rodee, and after VS-6 turned, Risher was unable to find Ring again. See Fisher, *Hooked*, 80.

27. Weisheit, *Last Flight*, 28–29.

28. Interview of S. G. Mitchell (1981), Weisheit, "Transcripts," 10–11.

29. "Battle of Midway, Rescues Performed by PBY's," *PBY Memorial Association Newsletter* 41, May 2002; interview of Jerry Crawford (Aug. 28, 1984), Weisheit, "Transcripts," 7.

## Chapter 13

1. George Gay recalled later how the moon was centered in the middle of his cowling during the flight, and, based on that and the position of the moon that day, Bowen

Wiesheit subsequently calculated that he was flying a course of 234 degrees. See George Gay, *Sole Survivor: The Battle of Midway and Its Effects on His Life* (Naples, FL: Naples Ad/Graphics, 1979), 117; Bowen P. Weisheit, *The Last Flight of Ensign C. Markland Kelly, Junior, USNA, Battle of Midway, June 4, 1942* (Baltimore: Ensign C. Markland Kelly, Jr., Memorial Foundation, 1993), 14. Weisheit's "plot of moon bearings" on June 4, 1942, is on p. 69.

2. On Larsen, see Robert J. Mrazek, *A Dawn Like Thunder: The True Story of Torpedo Squadron Eight* (New York: Little, Brown, 2008), 25–31; on Owens, see Gay, *Sole Survivor*, 97.

3. "Memorandum for the Commander in Chief," June 7, 1942, Action Reports, reel 2; Gay, *Sole Survivor*, 119.

4. Robert J. Cressman et al., *"A Glorious Page in Our History": The Battle of Midway, 4–6 June 1942* (Missoula, MT: Pictorial Histories, 1990), 91; Jonathan B. Parshall and Anthony P. Tully, *Shattered Sword: The Untold Story of the Battle of Midway* (Washington, DC: Potomac Books, 2005), 205.

5. Gay, *Sole Survivor*, 119; "Memorandum for the Commander in Chief," Action Reports, reel 2; Parshall and Tully, *Shattered Sword*, 207.

6. Gay, *Sole Survivor*, 120–21. Waldron's radio broadcasts were overheard by ARM3/c Leroy Quillen of VB-8 and reported in "Enclosure (H) to Hornet Serial 0018 dated June 13, 1942," in Action Reports, reel 2.

7. Frederick Mears, *Carrier Combat* (Garden City, NY: Doubleday, Doran, 1944), xiv; "Enclosure (H) to Hornet Serial 0018 dated June 13, 1942," in Action Reports, reel 2; Gay, *Sole Survivor*, 121.

8. Gay, *Sole Survivor*, 108.

9. Ibid., 121, 125.

10. Ibid., 125, 128–29; "George Gay's Fisheye View of Midway," *Naval Aviation News* 64, no. 6 (June 1982), 18–21.

11. Gay, *Sole Survivor*, 128–29. Gay later claimed that he remained in the middle of the Kidō Butai during the ensuing battle. Time-motion studies by Parshall and Tully and by Dallas Isom have suggested that this was unlikely.

12. 1927 *Lucky Bag*, USNA; Robert E. Barde interview of Wade McClusky (June 30, 1966), quoted in Barde, "The Battle of Midway: A Study in Command," (Ph.D. diss., University of Maryland, 1971), 176; Clarence Wade McClusky, "The Midway Story," unpublished manuscript in the Gordon Prange Papers, UMD, box 17. See Also Edward P. Stafford, *The Big E: The Story of the USS Enterprise* (Annapolis, MD: Naval Institute Press, 2002), 78.

13. Interview of Clarence Wade McClusky (June 30, 1966) by Gordon Prange, Prange Papers, UMD, box 17.

14. I am grateful to John Lundstrom for helping me unravel this launch sequence.

15. Gray to McClusky, June 8, 1942, Action Reports, reel 3; McClusky, "Midway Story"; Cressman et al., *Glorious Page*, 86–87.

16. Gray's recollection of Browning's instructions is from remarks Gray made at a 1988 Midway symposium and are quoted by Alvin Kernan in *The Unknown Battle of Midway: The Destruction of the American Torpedo Squadrons* (New Haven, CT: Yale University Press, 2005), 137; the discussion between Gray and Ely is in CAPT James S.

Gray, "Decision at Midway," USNA Museum, also available as part of the BOMRT archive at http://www.midway42.org/aa-reports/vf-6.html.

17. Gray, "Decision at Midway."

18. Ibid.

19. Laub to McClusky, June 4, 1942, Action Reports, reel 3.

20. The fellow pilot was Dick Best in an interview with Walter Lord (April 13, 1966), in Lord Collection, NHHC, box 18.

21. Ibid.; Cressman et al., *Glorious Page*, 94–95; Parshall and Tully, *Shattered Sword*, 213. Gray's remarks were made at a 1988 conference in Pensacola and are quoted in Kernan, *Unknown Battle of Midway*, 138. Gray's radio report is quoted in John B. Lundstrom, *Black Shoe Carrier Admiral: Frank Jack Fletcher at Coral Sea, Midway, and Guadalcanal* (Annapolis, MD: Naval Institute Press, 2006), 256–57.

22. Laub to McClusky, June 4, 1942, Action Reports, reel 3; Barde, "Battle of Midway," 179.

23. Barde, "Battle of Midway," 183–87.

24. See the various naval messages from Midway to CINCPAC, plus CINCPAC to Task Force Commanders, all dated June 4 from 8:20 a.m. to 11:01 a.m., in Nimitz Papers, NHHC, box 8. As late as the afternoon of June 5, Midway was still reporting to Nimitz, "Our patrols have seen only two carriers." By then, however, there were no carriers, since all four had been sunk. I thank John Lundstrom for directing my attention to these messages.

25. Lundstrom, *Black Shoe Carrier Admiral*, 249–50. Pederson is quoted on p. 249.

26. Steve Ewing and John B. Lundstrom, *Fateful Rendezvous: The Life of Butch O'Hare* (Annapolis, MD: Naval Institute Press, 1997), 93; 1927 *Lucky Bag*, USNA,

27. Thach oral history (Nov. 6, 1970), 230–31, U.S. Naval Institute Oral History Collection, USNA.

28. Pederson to Buckmaster, May 16, 1942, Action Reports, reel 2; Lundstrom, *Black Shoe Carrier Admiral*, 249; Lundstrom, *The First Team: Pacific Naval Air Combat from Pearl Harbor to Midway* (Annapolis, MD: Naval Institute Press, 1984), 340.

29. Esders was very specific in noting that he sighted the smoke of the Kidō Butai at 9:33, though Machinist Harry Corl, in his report, said it was at 10:00 a.m. Since LCDR Shumway also put the sighting at 10:00, and claims he called Massey at 10:20, the later time is probably more accurate. The reports of Esders and Corl are available at the BOMRT website: http://www.midway42.org/aa-reports/vt3-esders.pdf and http://www.midway42.org/aa-reports/vt3-corl.pdf. The radio exchange between Max Leslie and Lem Massey is in Shumway's squadron report, June 10, 1942, Action Reports, reel 3. The Devastator pilot was Esders, quoted in Stuart D. Ludlum, *They Turned the War Around at Coral Sea and Midway: Going to War with Yorktown's Air Group Five* (Bennington, VT: Merriam, 2000), 113.

30. Commanding Officer Yorktown Air Wing (Pederson), June 14, 1942, Action Reports, reel 2.

31. Lundstrom, *First Team*, 351–56; Parshall and Tully, *Shattered Sword*, 223–25.

32. John S. Thach oral history (Nov. 6, 1970), 1:245–46, U.S. Naval Institute Oral History Collection, USNA; Machinist Harry Corl Report, June 15, 1942, available

at http://www.midway42.org/aa-reports/vt3-corl.pdf; correspondence of Lloyd Childers to BOMRT, Nov. 8, 2004.

33. Thach oral history (Nov. 6, 1970), 1:248; Lundstrom, *First Team*, 355.

34. Report W. G. Esders, June 6, 1942, Action Reports, reel 3.

**Chapter 14**

1. Nimitz to King, June 28, 1942, Action Reports, reel 3. Also available at http://www. history.navy.mil/docs/wwii/mid1.htm.

2. 1927 *Lucky Bag*, USNA.

3. William H. Brockman, Jr., "U.S.S. Nautilus, Narrative of 4 June 1942," Action Reports, reel 3. Hereafter "Nautilus Narrative." Also available at http://www.hnsa. org/doc/subreports.htm.

4. Ibid.

5. John Campbell, *Naval Weapons of World War Two* (London: Conway Maritime, 1985), 89.

6. Roy S. Benson (executive officer of *Nautilus*) Questionnaire, n.d., Walter Lord Collection, NHHC, box 18; John F. Davidson oral history (Sept. 4, 1985), 196, and Slade Cutter oral history (June 17, 1985), 297, both in U.S. Naval Institute Oral History Collection, USNA.

7. Roy S. Benson Questionnaire, n.d., Walter Lord Collection, NHHC, box 18; "Nautilus Narrative."

8. "Nautilus Narrative"; Roy S. Benson oral history (March 18, 1980), U.S. Naval Institute Oral History Collection, USNA, 185.

9. "Nautilus Narrative." Brockman gives the time here as 9:00 a.m., but it was more likely around 8:30.

10. Ibid.

11. Ibid.

12. This is compiled from the action reports by McClusky, Gallaher, and Best. It is evident that Gallaher and Best collaborated on their reports, for not only do they agree in every particular, they also used identical language to do so. See Action Reports, reel 3, also available at http://www.cv6.org/ship/logs/action19420604.htm.

13. Richard Best interview (Aug. 11, 1995), NMPW, 39–40; Lew Hopkins interview (Jan. 15, 2004), NMPW, 17.

14. Clarence Wade McClusky, "The Midway Story," unpublished manuscript in the Gordon Prange collection, UMD, box 17.

15. Gordon Prange, Donald M. Goldstein, and Katherine V. Dillon, *Miracle at Midway* (New York: McGraw-Hill,1982), 260; Best to Walter Lord, Jan. 27, 1966, Lord Collection, NHHC, box 18.

16. Prange et al., *Miracle at Midway*, 259–60.

17. Best interview (Aug. 11, 1995), NMPW, 42.

18. Murray to Nimitz (via Spruance), June 13, 1942, Action Reports, reel 3. Also available at http://www.history.navy.mil/docs/wwii/mid1.htm.

19. Gallaher to Walter Lord, Feb. 26, 1967, Lord Collection, NHHC, box 18; Penland After-Action Report, Jun 10, 1942, Action Reports, reel 3. Italics added. Also available at http://www.cv6.org/ship/logs/action19420604-vb6.htm. Both carriers turned to

the northwest as McClusky approached, which put *Kaga* slightly ahead of *Akagi*. See schematic in Parshall and Tully, *Shattered Sword*, 222.

20. Best to Walter Lord, Jan. 27, 1966, Lord Collection, NHHC, box 18; Dick Best Action Report, June 6, 1942, 3 (also available at http://www.cv6.org/ship/logs/action19420604-vb6.htm); James T. Murray to Walter Lord, Feb. 26, 1967, Lord Collection, NHHC, box 18.

21. Best interview (Aug. 11, 1995), NMPW, 41–42; Best to Walter Lord, Jan. 27, 1966, Lord Collection, NHHC, box 18.

22. John S. Thach oral history (Nov. 6, 1970), U.S. Naval Institute Oral History Collection, USNA, 251.

23. Jonathan B. Parshall and Anthony P. Tully, *Shattered Sword: The Untold Story of the Battle of Midway* (Washington, DC: Potomac Books, 2005), 233–34.

24. Ibid., 234–35.

25. Thach oral history (Nov. 6, 1970), 252; Best interview (Aug. 11, 1995), NMPW, 17; Norman (Dusty) Kleiss, BOMRT, Sept. 3, 2010; Parshall and Tully, *Shattered Sword*, 250. Subsequently, Jon Parshall estimated that, including the small 100-pound bombs, a total of twelve bombs probably hit the *Kaga*. BOMRT, Aug. 25, 2010, http://www.midway42.org/Backissues/2010-28.htm.

26. Best interview (Aug. 11, 1995), NMPW, 19.

27. Ibid., 42.

28. Best to Walter Lord, Jan. 27, 1966, Lord Collection, NHHC, box 18.

29. Parshall and Tully, *Shattered Sword*, 253–55, 257.

30. Best interview (Aug. 11, 1995), NMPW, 42.

31. Leslie to Murray, June 10, 1942, Action Reports, reel 3 (also available at http://www.midway42.org/reports.html).

32. Leslie to Smith, Dec. 15, 1964, in Prange Papers, UMD, box 17; Parshall and Tully, *Shattered Sword*, 264.

33. Ibid.

34. Leslie to Smith, Dec. 15, 1964, Prange Papers, UMD, box 17; Parshall and Tully, *Shattered Sword*, 264.

35. Ibid., 259.

## Chapter 15

1. The death throes of the three carriers are described in detail in Jonathan B. Parshall and Anthony P. Tully in *Shattered Sword: The Untold Story of the Battle of Midway* (Washington, DC: Potomac Books, 2005), chaps. 14 and 15. See also Robert Cressman et al., *"A Glorious Page in Our History": The Battle of Midway, 4–6 June 1942* (Missoula, MT: Pictorial Histories, 1990), 104–5.

2. Parshall and Tully, *Shattered Sword*, 261–62, 268–69.

3. Ibid., 263.

4. Ibid., 264, 267.

5. Cressman et al., *Glorious Page*, 114–15; Parshall and Tully, *Shattered Sword*, 292–93.

6. Buckmaster to Nimitz, June 18, 1942, Action Reports, reel 3 (also available at http://www.history.navy.mil/docs/wwii/mid7.htm); Stuart Ludlum, *They Turned*

*the War Around at Coral Sea and Midway: Going to War with Yorktown's Air Group Five* (Bennington, VT: Merriam, 2000), 118.

7. Ibid.

8. The message traffic is from Enclosure C of Action Report, Commander in Chief, U.S. Pacific Fleet (Nimitz), June 28, 1942, Action Reports microfilm, reel 3.

9. Ludlum, *They Turned the War Around*, 119.

10. Judson Brodie interview (March 13, 2007), NMPW, 35; John S. Thach oral history (Nov. 6, 1970), U.S. Naval Institute Oral History Collection, USNA, 1:267.

11. Enclosure C of Nimitz's Action Report, June 28, 1942, Action Reports, reel 3.

12. Jeff Nesmith, *No Higher Honor: The U.S.S. Yorktown at the Battle of Midway* (Atlanta: Longstreet, 1999), 210–14; Leslie to Smith, Dec. 15, 1964, Prange Papers, UMD, box 17.

13. Buckmaster to Nimitz, June 18, 1942, Action Reports, reel 3.

14. Ibid.; Cressman et al., *Glorious Page*, 116–17.

15. Interview of Richard S. Brown by Ronald W. Russell (March 15, 2007), BOMRT; Buckmaster to Nimitz, June 18, 1942, Action Reports, reel 3; Robert E. Barde, "The Battle of Midway: A Study in Command," (Ph.D. diss., University of Maryland, 1971), 301.

16. Cressman et al., *Glorious Page*, 122.

17. Buckmaster to Nimitz, June 18, 1942, Action Reports, reel 3; Nesmith, *No Higher Honor*, 220–22; Barde, "Battle of Midway," 289–90.

18. Ludlum, *They Turned the War Around*, 122; Cressman et al., *Glorious Page*, 128.

19. Parshall and Tully, *Shattered Sword*, 267.

20. Ibid., 285; Peter C. Smith, *Midway: Dauntless Victory; Fresh Perspectives on America's Seminal Naval Victory of World War II* (Barnsley, UK: Pen & Sword Maritime, 2007), 185–86.

21. Yamamoto's comment is from an interview of Kuroshima Kameto by Robert E. Barde, quoted in Barde, "Battle of Midway," 285.

22. Mitsuo Fuchida and Masatake Okumiya, *Midway: The Battle that Doomed Japan, the Japanese Navy's Story* (Annapolis, MD: Naval Institute Press, 1955), 193.

23. Ludlum, *They Turned the War Around*, 121; Spruance to Nimitz, June 8, 1942, Spruance Papers, NWC, box 2, folder 4.

24. John Thach oral history (Nov. 6, 1970), 1:269; Cressman et al., *Glorious Page*, 130. Tootle was subsequently picked up by the destroyer *Anderson*. Ensign George Hopper's flight was even shorter. The last of the eight Wildcat pilots to take off, he had barely cleared the *Yorktown*'s bow when he was hit by 20 mm cannon fire from a Zero.

25. John Thach oral history (Nov. 6, 1970), 1:268; Craig L. Symonds, *Decision at Sea: Five Naval Battles that Shaped American History* (New York: Oxford University Press, 2005), 254–55; Parshall and Tully, *Shattered Sword*, 314. Thach did not know he had shot down Tomonaga's plane until it was revealed to him by historian John Lundstrom in 1974. Thach also thought that Tomonaga's torpedo hit the *Yorktown*, but a careful study by Parshall and Tully showed that it missed.

26. It was author Jeff Nesmith who learned the identity of the Japanese flyer who shook his fist at the *Yorktown*. Nesmith, *No Higher Honor*, 226.

27. Author's interview of Captain John "Jack" Crawford (May 5, 2004); Buckmaster to Nimitz, June 18, 1942, Action Reports, reel 3. That the two torpedoes created a single large hole was discovered only after the war when Navy divers explored the wreckage.

28. Nesmith, *No Higher Honor*, 232; John Crawford interview (May 5, 2004); Ronald Russell, "A Reunion in the Water," *Veteran's Biographies* (June 2006), BOMRT, http://www.midway42.org/vets-newberg.html; Ludlum, *They Turned the War Around*, 125.

29. John B. Lundstrom, *Black Shoe Carrier Admiral: Frank Jack Fletcher at Coral Sea, Midway & Guadalcanal* (Annapolis, MD: Naval Institute Press, 2006), 275; Cressman et al., *Glorious Page*, 135. As it turned out, two injured men were left aboard ship and were found when the *Yorktown* was reboarded the next day.

30. William H. Brockman, Jr., "U.S.S. Nautilus, Narrative of 4 June 1942," Action Reports, reel 3 (also available at http://issuu.com/hnsa/docs/ss-168_nautilus?mode=a_p).

31. Ibid.; Roy S. Benson oral history (March 18, 1980), U.S. Naval Institute Oral History Collection, USNA, 189; Parshall and Tully, *Shattered Sword*, 302-3.

32. Ibid.; Cressman et al., *Glorious Page*, 141. The *Kaga* was not scuttled until 7:25 p.m.

33. "CINC First Air Fleet Detailed Battle Report No. 6," *ONI Review* 5 (May 1947), available online at http://www.ibiblio.org/hyperwar/Japan/IJN/rep/Midway/Nagumo; Parshall and Tully, *Shattered Sword*, 323.

34. Gallaher to Murray, and Leslie to Murray, both June 10, 1942, Action Reports, reel 3. In the end, only twenty-four planes flew to the target, because one of the planes of Gallaher's section had engine trouble and had to return. Leslie was picked up and taken to Fletcher's new flagship, the cruiser *Astoria*.

35. Richard Best interview (Aug. 11, 1995), NMPW; Wade McClusky interview (June 30, 1966), Gordon Prange Papers, UMD, box 17.

36. Lundstrom, *Black Shoe Carrie Admiral*, 270-73.

37. Ludlum, *They Turned the War Around*, 117, 123, 127; Samuel Eliot Morison, *History of United States Naval Operations in World War II*, vol. 4, *Coral Sea, Midway, and Submarine Actions, May 1942–August 1942* (Boston: Little, Brown, 1949, repr., 1975, 136. John Lundstrom notes that Adams's report came in "almost to the minute when the *Yorktown* was torpedoed." Lundstrom, *First Team*, 411.

38. Cressman et al., *Glorious Page*, 136. Buell attributes the communications failure to poor staff work. See Thomas B. Buell, *The Quiet Warrior: A Biography of Admiral Raymond A. Spruance* (Boston: Little, Brown, 1974), 138-39.

39. Gallaher to Murray, June 10, 1942, Action Reports, reel 3 (also available at http://www.midway42.org/reports.html); Robert J. Mrazek, *A Dawn Like Thunder: The True Story of Torpedo Squadron Eight* (New York: Little. Brown, 2008), 166-67.

40. Thach oral history (Nov. 6 1970), 1:278-79.

41. Gordon Prange interview of Richard Best (May 15, 1966), Prange Papers, UMD, box 17.

42. Gallaher to Walter Lord, Feb. 26, 1967, Walter Lord Collection, NHHC, box 18.

43. Best interview (Aug. 11, 1995), NMPW, 44; Best to Lord, Jan. 27, 1966, Walter Lord Collection, NHHC, box 18.

44. Gallaher to Walter Lord, Feb. 26, 1967, Walter Lord Collection, NHHC, box 18; Parshall and Tully, *Shattered Sword*, 326–29.
45. Mitscher to Nimitz, June 13, 1942, Action Reports, reel 3 (also available at http://www.midway42.org/reports.html).
46. Parshall and Tully, *Shattered Sword*, 329; Cressman et al., *Glorious Page*, 139.
47. Spruance to Nimitz, June 5, 1942, Nimitz Papers, NHHC, box 8:89; Spruance to Nimitz, June 16, 1942, Action Reports, reel 3 (also available at http://www.midway42.org/reports.html). See also Buell, *Quiet Warrior*, 140; and Lundstrom, *Black Shoe Carrier Admiral*, 277.

## Chapter 16

1. "CINC First Air Fleet Detailed Battle Report No. 6," *ONI Review* 5 (May 1947), available online at http://www.ibiblio.org/hyperwar/Japan/IJN/rep/Midway/Nagumo; Prange interview with Watanabe (Nov. 24, 1964), Prange Papers, UMD, box 17; Jonathan B. Parshall and Anthony P. Tully, *Shattered Sword: The Untold Story of the Battle of Midway* (Washington, DC: Potomac Books, 2005), 342–43.
2. Prange interview of Watanabe (Nov. 24, 1964), Prange Papers, UMD, box 17; Parshall and Tully, *Shattered Sword*, 352–53.
3. Nagumo After-Action Report, 9; Parshall and Tully, *Shattered Sword*, 349–50; Barde, "Battle of Midway," 330–32; Walter Lord, *Incredible Victory* (New York: Harper-Collins, 1967), 250.
4. Parshall and Tully, *Shattered Sword*, 351–52.
5. Prange interview with Watanabe (Nov. 24, 1964), Prange Papers, UMD, box 17; Robert E. Barde, "The Battle of Midway: A Study in Command" (Ph.D. dissertation, University of Maryland, 1971), 332–34; Parshall and Tully, *Shattered Sword*, 344–45.
6. The orders intended for Kurita's CruDiv7 were sent first to CruDiv8. This may have been a simple error in transmission, but Watanabe admitted in a postwar interview that he was deliberately slow in forwarding the orders to retreat. Parshall and Tully, *Shattered Sword*, 344; Prange interview of Watanabe (Nov. 24, 1964), Prange Papers, UMD, box 17.
7. Robert Schultz and James Shell, "Strange Fortune," *World War II*, May/June 2010, 61–62; War Diary, Third War Patrol, USS *Tambor* (SS-198), Office of Naval Records and History (also available at http://www.hnsa.org/doc/subreports.htm).
8. War Diary, Third War Patrol, USS *Tambor* (SS-198), Office of Naval Records and History.
9. Ibid.
10. Parshall and Tully, *Shattered Sword*, 345–47.
11. Ibid., 346–48.
12. Ibid., 362–63.
13. Ibid., 361.
14. Prange interview with McClusky (June 30, 1966), Prange Papers, UMD, box 17. See also John B. Lundstrom, *Black Shoe Carrier Admiral: Frank Jack Fletcher at Coral Sea, Midway, and Guadalcanal* (Annapolis, MD: Naval Institute Press, 2006), 285.
15. Ibid.; Robert J. Cressman et al., *"A Glorious Page in Our History": The Battle of Midway, 4–6 June 1942* (Missoula, MT: Pictorial Histories, 1990), 149.

16. Shumway's Report of Action, June 10, 1942, and the Report of Bombing Squadron Five, June 7, 1942, both in Action Reports, reel 3 (also available at http://www. midway42.org/reports.html); Bruce R. Linder, "Lost Letter of Midway," U.S. Naval Institute Proceedings 125, no. 8 (August 1999), 33.

17. Katsumi is quoted by the Tanikaze's lookout, Masashi Shibato, in Clayton E. Fisher, Hooked: Tales and Adventures of a Tailhook Warrior (Denver: Outskirts, Inc., 2009), 96; Ring is quoted in Linder, "Lost Letter of Midway," 33.

18. Fisher, Hooked, 97; Stuart D. Ludlum, They Turned the War Around at Coral Sea and Midway (Bennington, VT: Merriam, 2000), 127.

19. One plane ditched in the water near the task force, but its crew was recovered. Parshall and Tully, Shattered Sword, 365; Cressman et al., Glorious Page, 34.

20. Cressman et al., Glorious Page, 151.

21. Samuel Eliot Morison, History of United States Naval Operations in World War II, vol. 4, Coral Sea, Midway, and Submarine Actions, May 1942–August 1942 (Boston: Little, Brown, 1949), 153–54; Lundstrom, Black Shoe Carrier Admiral, 288.

22. Interview of Francis Fabian (Feb. 6, 2009), 17–18, NWC; Parshall and Tully, Shattered Sword, 361; Cressman et al., Glorious Page, 153. Samuel Eliot Morison is critical of Buckmaster for prematurely ordering abandon ship and for not attempting a salvage operation sooner, though such judgments are easy enough to make after the fact. Morison, Coral Sea, Midway, and Submarine Actions, 153–54.

23. Fletcher to Nimitz, and Nimitz to Fletcher, both June 5, 1942, Nimitz Papers, NHHC, box 8; Joseph M. Worthington oral history (June 7, 1972) U.S. Naval Institute Oral History Collection, USNA, 185.

24. Worthington oral history (June 7, 1972), 186; interview of William P. Burford by Prange (Aug. 18, 1964), Prange Papers, UMD, box 20.

25. The Hammann's captain, Commander Arnold E. True, reported that "all depth charges had been set on safe when Hammann went alongside Yorktown," and he speculated that the subsequent underwater explosion may have been caused by one of the Hammann's torpedoes being set off by the initial explosion. Another possibility is that, in anticipation of imminent antisubmarine efforts, the depth-charge officer, Ensign C. C. Elmes, pulled the safety forks when the torpedo wakes were first spotted but did not have time to replace them all after the Hammann was hit. See CDR True to Nimitz, June 16, 1942, Action Reports, reel 3 (also available at http://www.midway42.org/reports.html); interview of William P. Burford by Prange (Aug. 18, 1964), Prange Papers, UMD, box 20; Fabian interview (Feb. 6, 2009), NWC, 20; Cressman et al., Glorious Page, 157.

26. Ernest Eller oral history (Aug. 25, 1977) U.S. Naval Institute Oral History Collection, USNA, 542; Jeff Nesmith, No Higher Honor: The U.S.S. Yorktown at the Battle of Midway (Atlanta: Longstreet, 1999), 253.

27. Fletcher to Nimitz, June 7, 1942, Nimitz Papers, NHHC, box 8:118; Cressman et al., Glorious Page, 161.

28. Interview of Oral Moore in Ronald W. Russell, Veterans' Biographies (San Francisco, 2007). I am grateful to Ron Russell for sharing this information. See also Parshall and Tully, Shattered Sword, 367; Lundstrom, Black Shoe Carrier Admiral, 290.

29. Cressman et al., Glorious Page, 154.

428 ■ Notes to Pages 352-361

30. Linder, "Lost Letter of Midway," 34.
31. Linder, "Lost Letter of Midway," 34; Cressman et al., *Glorious Page*, 155; Parshall and Tully, *Shattered Sword*, 369.
32. Quoted in Cressman et al., *Glorious Page*, 155.
33. Ludlum, *They Turned the War Around*, 128–29; Enclosure C, Action Report, Commander in Chief, U.S. Pacific Fleet, June 28, 1942, Action Reports, reel 3.
34. Message traffic is from Action Reports, reel 3.
35. Linder, "Lost Letter of Midway," 35.
36. Cressman et al., *Glorious Page*, 162.
37. Ludlum, *They Turned the War Around*, 129–30.
38. Cressman et al., *Glorious Page*, 162–63.
39. Worthington oral history (June 7, 1972), 202–4. Spruance's remarks are from his foreword to the American edition of Mitsuo Fuchida and Masatake Okumiya, *Midway: The Battle that Doomed Japan, the Japanese Navy's Story* (Annapolis, MD: Naval Institute Press, 1955).

## Epilogue

1. In addition to four carriers, the Japanese also lost the *Mikuma*, which sank not long after she was photographed by Lieutenant Junior Grade Dobson on June 6. The *Mogami*, on the other hand, survived. Though she was hit by five bombs, her captain's decision to jettison her torpedoes almost certainly saved her. Repaired at Truk, she returned to Japan, where her two rear turrets were removed and replaced with a short flight deck that could carry eleven reconnaissance planes. She finally sank in Surigao Strait during the Battle of Leyte Gulf on October 25, 1944.
2. Robert Theobald, "Memorandum for Whom it May Concern," July 2, 1942, NHHC, King Papers, Series I, box 2.
3. FDR to Stalin, June 6, 1942, quoted in Robert E. Sherwood, *Roosevelt and Hopkins: An Intimate History*, rev. ed. (New York: Enigma Books, 2001), 455.
4. King to Marshall, June 25, 1942, King Papers, NHHC, series I, box 2.
5. MacArthur to Joint Chiefs, June 8, 1942, Nimitz Papers, NHHC, 1:557; FDR Memorandum, July 16, 1942, quoted in Sherwood, *Roosevelt and Hopkins*, 473.
6. King to Marshall and Marshall to King, both June 26, 1942, and King to Nimitz, June 25, 1942, all in King Papers, NHHC, series I, box 2. See also Thomas B. Buell, *Master of Sea Power: A Biography of Fleet Admiral Ernest J. King* (Boston: Little, Brown, 1980), 207–8.
7. Prange interview of Genda (Nov. 28, 1949), Prange Papers, UMD, box 19.

# A NOTE ON SOURCES

Though the historical significance of the Battle of Midway was evident almost from the moment of the battle, there have been a number of milestone
studies in the seventy years since that have further illuminated the story.
The declassification of intelligence files in the 1960s and '70s exposed the
crucial role of code breaking in the Pacific War, and especially at Midway,
and thereby added a whole new perspective to the understanding of what
happened there. Memoirs by Edwin Layton, Jasper Holmes, and others
spawned a cottage industry in rewriting the history of the Battle of Midway.
The story about how the cryptanalysts at Hypo duped the Japanese into
revealing the meaning of "AF" became a classic and is now part of every
account of the battle. Indeed, in many cases there has been a tendency to
exaggerate the level of detail that was gleaned by the cryptanalysts, and to
suggest that the Americans had a full blueprint of the Japanese plan for the
Midway operation. Such a suggestion is a disservice to the American operational commanders, for as important as code breaking was to eventual
victory, the decision makers did not have a complete copy of the enemy's
playbook in their hands and therefore had to make a number of crucial
decisions based on other factors (see appendix E).

Another critical element of the struggle that was long overlooked was
the Japanese side of the story. The logs of the Japanese ships and other
primary-source materials went down with the carriers of the Kidō Butai.
In addition, most Western scholars did not read Japanese and relied on

translated documents and memoirs to flesh out the Japanese side of the narrative. Both Walter Lord and Gordon Prange conducted a number of interviews with Japanese survivors of the battle (often using intermediaries) and incorporated their views in their excellent histories. But among the sources in translation, the most influential was a memoir by Mitsuo Fuchida (with Masatake Okumiya) published in America as *Midway: The Battle that Doomed Japan, the Japanese Navy's Story* (Annapolis, MD: Naval Institute Press, 1955). Fuchida, a naval aviator who had led the attack on Pearl Harbor, was also to have led the air attack on Midway, and would have done so but for an untimely attack of appendicitis. Because of that, he was instead an interested and knowledgeable spectator on the bridge of the flagship *Akagi* during the battle. Because of the dearth of Japanese sources, and because of the persuasiveness of Fuchida's firsthand account, it had a tremendous influence on Western narratives of the battle. Alas, as Jonathan Parshall and Anthony Tully demonstrate in their book *Shattered Sword: The Untold Story of the Battle of Midway* (Washington, DC: Potomac Books, 2005), Fuchida had an agenda of his own, which was to suggest just how close the Japanese had come to delivering a coup de grâce against the Americans, and as a result, not everything in his book can be taken at face value. Parshall has charged that "it is doubtful that any one person has had a more deleterious long-term impact on the study of the Pacific War than Mitsuo Fuchida." (Parshall, "Reflecting on Fuchida, or 'A Tale of Three Whoppers,'" *Naval War College Review* 63, no. 2 (Spring 2010) 127–38.) Whatever the merits of that statement, Parshall and Tully made an immeasurable contribution to the historiography of the Battle of Midway by delving into the Japanese accounts and analyzing the battle from the perspective of the Imperial Japanese Navy.

Another individual who helped illuminate the Japanese side of the story is Dallas Woodbury Isom in his 2007 book *Midway Inquest: Why the Japanese Lost the Battle of Midway* (Bloomington: Indiana University Press, 2007). An attorney, Isom conducted his investigation like a trial lawyer (hence the title) and renders a "not guilty" verdict for Vice Admiral Nagumo, who is blamed by many in both Japan and America for poor leadership decisions at Midway. Isom concludes that Nagumo's decisions were entirely logical on the morning of June 4, and that the principal blame for Japanese failure belongs to Yamamoto.

The official sources for the Battle of Midway are voluminous, but two are especially important. The first is the secret and confidential naval message traffic between Ernest King and Chester Nimitz, and between Nimitz and his commanders. It is included in the papers of FADM Chester W. Nimitz in the Operational Archives at the Naval History and Heritage Command (NHHC) in the Washington Navy Yard in Washington, D.C. These messages, along with a "Running Summary" of daily events kept by Nimitz's staff, and occasional "Situation Reports," were all bound together in a series of eight thick volumes. These volumes make up boxes 1–8 of the Nimitz Papers. Volume 1 covers the period between December 7, 1941, and the end of June 1942; volume 8 is a collection of messages pertinent to the Battle of Midway and duplicates some of the material in volume 1. Over the years, scholars have often referred to this source as the "Gray Book" (even though the binding is navy blue) and cited it that way in their footnotes. In 2010, the American Naval Records Society scanned these volumes and made them available electronically at http://www.ibiblio.org/anrs/graybook.html. This version was not available as I prepared this book. I therefore cited these letters and documents as part of the FADM Chester W. Nimitz Papers. In the footnotes, I indicate author, recipient, date, and the box number (there is one volume in each box) and page number where the letter may be found. In Volume 8, the page numbers begin at 500 and then stop at 550. Then, after several hundred unnumbered pages, the numbers begin again at 1. For messages on the unnumbered pages, I cited the date/time group—a six-digit code in which the first two numbers indicate the date and the last four the time (in twenty-four-hour military time).

The other official source of special note is the microfilmed collection of after-action reports from combatants in the field. Throughout the war, every unit commander was required to submit a postaction report. This included not only the fleet and ship commanders but squadron commanders as well. These were collected and microfilmed after the war, and the entire sixteen-reel collection is available from University Microfilms. Most of the reports from the Battle of Midway are on reel 3. This source is largely complete, with one notable exception. One of the great mysteries of the Battle of Midway is what happened to the after-action reports of the air group commander and the squadron commanders on the USS *Hornet* for the action on June 4. Marc Mitscher submitted various enclosures with his own report (a list of casualties, recommendations for awards, etc.) but the only squadron commander report was the one from John S. "Jimmy" Thach (VF-3) who flew off the *Yorktown*, not the *Hornet*, on June 4. The requirement to produce such reports makes it extraordinary that none of the other squadron commanders, nor the CHAG (commander, *Hornet* air group) submitted a report. For a discussion of this, see appendix F.

In constructing the combat narratives for this book, I relied heavily on the oral histories and interviews of the participants. Such accounts are often rich with detail, but of course they are also subject to fading (or enhanced) memory. No doubt a few of the survivors were like Tolstoy's Nikolai Rostov in *War and Peace*, who "set out with every intention of describing exactly what had occurred, but imperceptibly, unconsciously, and inevitably, he drifted into falsehood" (Leo Tolstoy, *War and Peace*, trans. Anthony Briggs [New York: Penguin, 1005], 257). As one veteran of the battle wrote candidly to Walter Lord in 1967: "The more I think about what happened, the less I am sure about what happened" (V. L. Micheel to Walter Lord, March 2, 1967, Walter Lord Collection, NHHC, box 18). Still, by including the widest possible number of such personal memories, and using a historian's judgment about which ones to trust, a kind of pointillist image eventually emerges. In reconstructing the Battle of Midway, and the six months preceding it, I occasionally privileged oral memory over the documentary record. This is particularly true of the so-called Flight to Nowhere on June 4, where the collective memories of the participants conflict dramatically with the official published record. As noted above, a fuller discussion of this is in appendix F.

There are five collections of interviews and oral histories that are particularly rich. The most extensive and detailed interviews are those that were conducted as part of the U.S. Naval Institute's Oral History Program, run for many years by Paul Stilwell. Bound copies of these are available at a few sites; the ones I used are in the Special Collections of the Nimitz Library at the U.S. Naval Academy, and they are listed below. Another source is the collection of nine interviews conducted by Major Bowen Weisheit, a retired Marine officer and aeronautical specialist whose friend, Ensign C. Markland Kelly, was killed in the battle. In seeking to learn how and why his friend Kelly lost his life, Weisheit sought to unravel that long-standing mystery. His interviews of the surviving members of VF-8 proved crucial in helping to expose the history of the *Hornet* air group on June 4. A valuable and underutilized source of oral histories is the Archive at the National Museum of the Pacific War (NMPW) in Fredericksburg, Texas, and these, too, are listed below. Both Walter Lord and Gordon Prange conducted their own interviews while working on their histories of the battle. These are not listed individually below but can be found in their respective collections at the Navy History and Heritage Command at the Washington Navy Yard (Lord), and the Maryland Room at the Hornbake Library at the University of Maryland (Prange). Finally, Stuart D. Ludlum conducted many interviews with veterans from USS *Yorktown* and included them in his book *They Turned the War Around at Coral Sea and Midway: Going to War with Yorktown's Air Group Five* (Bennington, VT: Merriam, 2000).

All history is the product of human action, and biographies of the major players can offer invaluable insight into their motivations. Between them, Thomas B. Buell and E. B. "Ned" Potter wrote biographies of four of the principal decision makers at Midway. In the interest of full disclosure, I need to report that both men were personal friends. I served with Tom Buell when we were both in the Navy, and a few years ago I undertook to complete a project he had begun just before he died, the result of which is my book *Decision at Sea: Five Naval Battles that Shaped American History* (New York: Oxford University Press, 2005). Ned Potter was a colleague and friend in the History Department at the Naval Academy for more than twenty years. Buell wrote *Master of Sea Power: A Biography of Fleet Admiral Ernest J. King* (Annapolis, MD: Naval Institute Press, 1980) and *The Quiet Warrior: A Biography of Admiral Raymond A. Spruance* (Boston: Little, Brown, 1974), both excellent books. Potter's *Nimitz* (Annapolis, MD: Naval Institute Press, 1976) is a model of the historian's art, save for the frustrating fact that in lieu of footnotes Potter appended short paragraphs summarizing the sources of information for each chapter. Potter is also the author of the best book on William Halsey, *Bull Halsey* (Annapolis, MD: Naval Institute Press, 1985), though Halsey's own autobiography (with J. Bryan III), *Admiral Halsey's Story* (New York: Whittlesey House, 1947), is not to be missed. Frank Jack Fletcher, long dismissed as a secondary figure in the American victory, did not get his proper due until John B. Lundstrom's detailed and authoritative *Black Shoe Carrier Admiral: Frank Jack Fletcher at Coral Sea, Midway, and Guadalcanal* (Annapolis, MD: Naval Institute Press, 2006). On the Japanese side, Hiroyuki Agawa's biography of Yamamoto (Tokyo: Kodansha International, 1969), which was distributed in the United States by Harper & Row as *The Reluctant Admiral* (1979), is especially noteworthy.

The Internet has made available, at the click of a mouse, a wide variety of sources that scholars and students would otherwise have to travel long distances to read. Many veterans as well as students of the Battle of Midway are contributors to the website "The Battle of Midway Roundtable" (http://www.midway42.org), founded by William Price and now run by Ronald W. Russell, both of them knowledgeable and authoritative students of the battle in their own right. On this website, veterans and students of the battle share questions and recollections with one another. Many of these firsthand accounts are as fresh today as when they were first recalled, or for that matter, when their narrators participated in the most consequential naval battle of the twentieth century.

In addition, the following sites are also valuable: "Naval History and Heritage Command," at http://www.history.navy.mil/; and "HyperWar," at http://www.ibiblio.org/hyperwar. These contain many of the original after-action reports (some in facsimile format) and other original and secondary sources. When possible, notes indicate both the archival source and also the Internet address for the online source.

# BIBLIOGRAPHY

**Manuscript Sources**
American Heritage Center, University of Wyoming, Laramie
   Frank Jack Fletcher Papers
   Husband Kimmel Papers
Franklin D. Roosevelt Library, Hyde Park, New York
   Map Room Files
National Archives and Records Administration, Washington, D.C.
   CINCPAC Files, Record Group 38
   Record Group 457
Naval War College, Newport, Rhode Island
   Richard W. Bates Papers
   Ernest J. King Papers
   Edwin T. Layton Papers
   Raymond A. Spruance Papers
Operational Archives, Naval History and Heritage Command, Washington Navy Yard,
   Washington, D.C.
   Ernest J. King Papers
   Walter Lord Collection
   Marc A. Mitscher Papers
   Chester W. Nimitz Diary #1 [Serial letters to Mrs. Nimitz], Dec. 20, 1941–May 7,
      1945
   Papers of FADM Chester W. Nimitz ["Gray Book"]
   Raymond A. Spruance Papers
University of Maryland, Hornbake Library, College Park
   Gordon Prange Papers

**Oral Histories and Interviews**
National Museum of the Pacific War, Fredericksburg, Texas
   Richard H. Best Interview (Aug. 11, 1995)
   Judson Brodie Interview (March 13, 2007)
   Richard Byram Interview (April 14, 2005)
   Richard E. Cole Interview (Aug. 8, 2000)
   Eugene Conklin Interview (March 17, 2007)
   Douglas C. Davis Interview (Oct. 1, 2000)

Albert Earnest Interview (July 20, 2003)
Kaname Harada Interview (Oct. 7, 2007)
Byron K. Henry Interview (June 13, 2002)
John V. Hillard Interview (Feb. 28, 2002)
Henry Hise Interview (Sept. 30, 2000)
Lewis R. Hopkins Interview (Jan 15, 2004)
Jack Kleiss Interview (Sept. 29, 2000)
Sam Laser Interview (April 9, 2003)
Edwin T. Layton Interview (n.d.)
James H. Macia Interview (July 21, 2000)
Gilbert Martin and Paul McKay Interview (Sept. 2000)
Willard "Robbie" Robinson Interview (July 20, 2003)
William G. Roy Interview (June 6, 2003)
Ellis Skidmore Interview (June 3, 2005)
Floyd Thorn Interview (Aug. 14, 2000)
Richard Toler Interview (Nov. 11, 2003)
John E. Underwood Interview (Feb. 8, 2007)
Naval War College, Newport, Rhode Island
    Charles F. Barber Interview (March 1, 1996)
    Francis Fabian Interview (Feb. 6, 2009)
    Peter E. Karetka Interview (May 26, 2010)
    Hugh Moure Interview (July 30, 2008)
    John C. Powell Interview (Oct. 8 and 15, 2008)
Operational Archives, Naval History and Heritage Command
    Noel Gayler Interview (Feb. 15, 2002)
U.S. Naval Institute Oral History Collection, Naval Academy, Nimitz Library (Special
        Collections), Annapolis, MD
    Slade Cutter Oral History (June 17, 1985)
    John F. Davidson Oral History (Sept. 4, 1985)
    James Doolittle Oral History (Aug. 3, 1987)
    Thomas Dyer Oral History (Sept. 14, 1983)
    Earnest Eller Oral History (Aug. 25, 1977)
    Stephen Jurika Oral History (1973)
    Edwin Layton Oral History (May 30 and 31, 1970)
    Henry "Hank" Miller Oral History (May 23, 1973)
    Joseph Rochefort Oral History (Aug. 14, Sept. 21, and Oct. 5, 1969)
    Paul Stroop Oral History (Sept. 13 and 14, 1969)
    John S. Thach Oral History (Nov. 6, 1970)
    Joseph M. Worthington Oral History (June 7, 1972)
"The Battle of Midway: Transcripts of Recorded Interviews" by Major Bowen P.
        Weisheit, USMCR (Ret.), Nimitz Library, USNA.
    Ben Tappan Interview (1981)
    Samuel G. Mitchell Interview (1981)
    Richard Gray Interview (1981)
    Johnny A. Talbot Interview (March 31, 1981)

Humphrey L. Tallman Interview (April 4, 1982)
John E. McInerny Interview (1982)
Walter Rodee Interview (1982)
T. T. Guillory Interview (March 14, 23, and 24, 1983)
Jerry Crawford Interview (Aug. 28, 1984)
Interviews conducted by the author
John C. "Jack" Crawford Interview (May 5, 2005)
William D. Houser Interview (May 5, 2005)
William Price Interview (May 4, 2010)
Donald "Mac" Showers Interview (May 4, 2010)

**Official Records and Published Collections**
Goldstein, Donald M., and Katherine V. Dillon, eds. *The Pacific War Papers: Japanese Documents of World War II*. Washington, DC: Potomac Books, 2004.
——, eds. *The Pearl Harbor Papers: Inside the Japanese Plans*. Washington, DC: Brassey's, 1993.
Kimball, Warren F., ed. *Churchill and Roosevelt: The Complete Correspondence*. 3 vols. Princeton, NJ: Princeton University Press, 1984.
Loewenheim, Francis L., Harold D. Langley, and Manfred Jonas, eds. *Roosevelt and Churchill, Their Secret Wartime Correspondence*. London: Barrie & Jenkins, 1975.
Office of Naval Intelligence, *Combat Narrative: The Battle of the Coral Sea*. Washington, DC: Office of Naval Intelligence, United States Navy, 1943.
OP-20G File of CINCPAC Intelligence Bulletins (March 16–June 1, 1942), Special Collections, Nimitz Library, U.S. Naval Academy.
Spector, Ronald H., ed. *Listening to the Enemy: Key Documents on the Role of Communications Intelligence in the War with Japan*. Wilmington, DE: Scholarly Resources, 1988.
Traffic Intelligence Summaries, Combat Intelligence Unit, Fourteenth Naval District (July 16, 1941–June 30, 1942). 3 vols. Special Collections, Nimitz Library, U.S. Naval Academy.
U.S. Congress. Senate. Committee on Naval Affairs. *Hearings before the Committee on Naval Affairs on the Nomination of William Franklin Knox to be Secretary of the Navy*. 76th Cong., 3rd sess., 1940.
——. Joint Committee on the Investigation of the Pearl Harbor Attack, *Pearl Harbor Attack: Hearings before the Joint Committee on the Investigation of the Pearl Harbor Attack*. 79th Cong., 1st sess., 1945.
U.S. Navy Action and Operational Reports from World War II, Pacific Theater, Part I: CINCPAC (16 microfilm reels). Bethesda, MD: University Publications of America.
U.S. Navy, Office of Naval Intelligence. *The Japanese Story of the Battle of Midway*. Washington, DC: Government Printing Office, 1947. (Translation of "CINC First Air Fleet Detailed Battle Report No. 6." Published in *ONI Review* 5 (May 1947).

**Primary Sources and Memoirs**
Bates, Richard W. *The Battle of the Coral Sea, May 1 to May 11 Inclusive, 1942: Strategical and Tactical Views*. Newport, RI: Naval War College, 1947.

———. *The Battle of Midway Including the Aleutian Phase, June 3 to June 14, 1942: Strategical and Tactical Analysis*. Newport, RI: U.S. Naval War College, 1948.

Buell, Harold L. *Dauntless Helldivers: A Dive-Bomber Pilot's Epic Story of the Carrier Battles*. New York: Orion Books, 1991.

Clark, J. J., with Clark G. Reynolds. *Carrier Admiral*. New York: McKay, 1967.

Doolittle, James H. "Jimmy," with Carroll V. Glines. *I Could Never Be So Lucky Again: An Autobiography*. New York: Bantam Books, 1991.

Evans, David C., ed. *The Japanese Navy in World War II: In the Words of Former Japanese Naval Officers*. Translated by David C. Evans. 2nd ed. Annapolis, MD: Naval Institute Press, 1986.

Fisher, Clayton E. *Hooked: Tales and Adventures of a Tailhook Warrior*. Denver: Outskirts, 2009.

Forrestel, E. P. *Admiral Raymond A. Spruance, USN: A Study in Command*. Washington, DC: Government Printing Office, 1966.

Fuchida, Mitsuo, and Masatake Okumiya. *Midway: The Battle That Doomed Japan, the Japanese Navy's Story*. Annapolis, MD: Naval Institute Press, 1955, 1992.

Gay, George. *Sole Survivor: The Battle of Midway and Its Effects on his Life*. Naples, FL: Naples Ad/Graphics, 1979.

Halsey, William F., and J. Bryan III. *Admiral Halsey's Story*. New York: Whittlesey House, 1947.

Holmes, W. J. *Double-Edged Secrets: U.S. Naval Intelligence Operations in the Pacific during World War II*. Annapolis, MD: Naval Institute Press, 1979.

Ickes, Harold L. *The Secret Diary of Harold L. Ickes*. New York: Simon & Schuster, 1953–54.

Ito, Masanori, and Roger Pineau. *The End of the Imperial Japanese Navy*. Translated by Andrew Y. Kuroda and Roger Pineau. New York: Norton, 1962.

King, Ernest J., and Walter Muir Whitehill. *Fleet Admiral King: A Naval Record*. New York: Norton, 1952.

Layton, Edwin T., with Roger Pineau and John Costello. *"And I was there": Pearl Harbor and Midway—Breaking the Secrets*. New York: Morrow, 1985.

Ludlum, Stuart D. *They Turned the War Around at Coral Sea and Midway: Going to War with Yorktown's Air Group Five*. Bennington, VT: Merriam, 2000.

Mears, Frederick. *Carrier Combat*. Garden City, NY: Doubleday, Doran, 1944.

Robert R. Rea. *Wings of Gold: An Account of Naval Aviation Training in World War II; The Correspondence of Aviation Cadet/Ensign Robert R. Rea*. Edited by Wesley Phillips Newton and Robert R. Rea. Tuscaloosa: University of Alabama Press, 1987.

Rowland, Buford, and William B. Boyd. *U.S. Navy Bureau of Ordnance in World War II*. Washington, DC: Bureau of Ordnance, Department of the Navy, 1953.

Russell, Ronald W. *No Right to Win: A Continuing Dialogue with Veterans of the Battle of Midway*. New York: iUniverse, 2006.

Sherman, Frederick C. *Combat Command: The American Aircraft Carriers in the Pacific War*. New York: Dutton, 1950.

Sherwood, Robert E. *Roosevelt and Hopkins: An Intimate History*. Rev. ed. New York: Harper, 1950. Reprint, New York: Enigma Books, 2001.

Stimson, Henry L., and McGeorge Bundy. *On Active Service in Peace and War*. New York: Harper, 1948.

Stover, E. T., and Clark G. Reynolds. *The Saga of Smokey Stover*. Charleston, SC: Tradd Street, 1978.

Ugaki, Matome. *Fading Victory: The Diary of Admiral Matome Ugaki, 1941–1945*. Edited by Donald M. Goldstein and Katherine V. Dillon. Translated by Masataka Chihaya. Annapolis, MD: Naval Institute Press, 1991.

## Books

Agawa, Hiroyuki. *The Reluctant Admiral: Yamamoto and the Imperial Navy*. Translated by John Bester. Tokyo: Kodansha International, 1979.

Asada, Sadao. *From Mahan to Pearl Harbor: The Imperial Japanese Navy and the United States*. Annapolis, MD: Naval Institute Press, 2006.

Astor, Gerald. *Wings of Gold: The U.S. Naval Air Campaign in World War II*. New York: Ballantine Books, 2004.

Barde, Robert E. "The Battle of Midway: A Study in Command." Ph.D. diss., University of Maryland, 1971.

Belote, James H., and William M. Belote. *Titans of the Seas: The Development and Operations of Japanese and American Carrier Task Forces during World War II*. New York: Harper & Row, 1975.

Brown, Louis. *A Radar History of World War II: Technical and Military Imperatives*. Bristol, UK: Institute of Physics, 1999.

Buell, Thomas B. *Master of Sea Power: A Biography of Fleet Admiral Ernest J. King*. Boston: Little, Brown, 1980.

———. *The Quiet Warrior: A Biography of Admiral Raymond A. Spruance*. Boston: Little, Brown, 1974.

Buford, Rowland, and William B. Boyd. *U.S. Navy Bureau of Ordnance in World War II*. Washington, DC: Bureau of Ordnance, 1953.

Campbell, John. *Naval Weapons of World War Two*. London: Conway Maritime, 1985.

Catton, Bruce. *The War Lords of Washington*. New York: Harcourt, Brace, 1948.

Coletta, Paolo E. *Bald Eagle: Admiral Marc A. Mitscher and U.S. Naval Aviation*. Lewiston, NY: Mellen, 1997.

Cressman, Robert J., Steve Ewing, Barrett Tillman, Mark Horan, Clark Reynolds, and Stan Cohen. *"A Glorious Page in Our History": The Battle of Midway, 4–6 June 1942*. Missoula, MT: Pictorial Histories, 1990.

Dull, Paul S. *A Battle History of the Imperial Japanese Navy, 1941–1945*. Annapolis, MD: Naval Institute Press, 1978.

Ewing, Steve, and John B. Lundstrom. *Fateful Rendezvous: The Life of Butch O'Hare*. Annapolis, MD: Naval Institute Press, 1997.

Gannon, Robert. *Hellions of the Deep: The Development of American Torpedoes in World War II*. University Park: Pennsylvania State University Press, 1996.

Glines, Carroll V. *Doolittle's Tokyo Raiders*. Princeton, NJ: Van Nostrand, 1964.

Haufler, Hervie. *Codebreakers' Victory: How the Allied Cryptographers Won World War II*. New York: New American Library, 2003.

Heinl, R. D., Jr. *Marines at Midway*. Washington, DC: Historical Section, Division of Public Information, U.S. Marine Corps. 1948.

Hoehling, A. A. *The Lexington Goes Down*. Englewood Cliffs, NJ: Prentice-Hall, 1971.

Hoppes, Jonna Doolittle. *Calculated Risk: The Extraordinary Life of Jimmy Doolittle, Aviation Pioneer and World War II Hero*. Santa Monica, CA: Santa Monica Press, 2005.

Horn, Steve. *The Second Attack on Pearl Harbor: Operation K and Other Japanese Attempts to Bomb America in World War II*. Annapolis, MD: Naval Institute Press, 2005.

Isom, Dallas Woodbury. *Midway Inquest: Why the Japanese Lost the Battle of Midway*. Bloomington: Indiana University Press, 2007.

Kahn, David. *The Codebreakers: The Story of Secret Writing*. London: Weidenfeld & Nicolson, 1967.

———. *The Reader of Gentlemen's Mail: Herbert O. Yardley and the Birth of American Codebreaking*. New Haven, CT: Yale University Press, 2004.

Kernan, Alvin. *The Unknown Battle of Midway: The Destruction of the American Torpedo Squadrons*. New Haven, CT: Yale University Press, 2005.

Larrabee, Eric. *Commander in Chief: Franklin Delano Roosevelt, His Lieutenants, and Their War*. New York: Harper & Row, 1987.

Lewin, Ronald. *The American Magic: Codes, Cyphers and the Defeat of Japan*. New York: Farrar Straus Giroux, 1982.

Lord, Walter. *Incredible Victory*. New York: Harper & Row, 1967.

Love, Robert William, Jr. *The Chiefs of Naval Operations*. Annapolis, MD: Naval Institute Press, 1980.

———. *History of the U.S. Navy*. Vol. 2, *1942–1991*. Harrisburg, PA: Stackpole Books, 1992.

Lundstrom, John B. *Black Shoe Carrier Admiral: Frank Jack Fletcher at Coral Sea, Midway, and Guadalcanal*. Annapolis, MD: Naval Institute Press, 2006.

———. *The First South Pacific Campaign: Pacific Fleet Strategy, December 1941–June 1942*. Annapolis, MD: Naval Institute Press, 1976.

———. *The First Team: Pacific Naval Air Combat from Pearl Harbor to Midway*. Annapolis, MD: Naval Institute Press, 1984.

MacIntyre, Donald. *Fighting Admiral: The Life of Admiral of the Fleet Sir James Somerville, G.C.B., G.B.E., D.S.O.* London: Evans Brothers, 1961.

Middlebrook, Martin, and Patrick Mahoney. *Battleship: The Loss of the Prince of Wales and the Repulse*. London: Lane, 1977.

Morison, Samuel Eliot. *History of United States Naval Operations in World War II*. 15 vols. Boston: Little, Brown, 1947–63. See esp. vol. 3: *The Rising Sun in the Pacific, 1931–April 1942* (1948); and vol. 4: *Coral Sea, Midway, and Submarine Actions, May 1942–August 1942* (1949).

Mrazek, Robert J. *A Dawn Like Thunder: The True Story of Torpedo Squadron Eight*. New York: Little, Brown, 2008.

Nesmith, Jeff. *No Higher Honor: The U.S.S. Yorktown at the Battle of Midway*. Atlanta: Longstreet, 1999.

Parker, Frederick D. *A Priceless Advantage: U.S. Navy Communications Intelligence and the Battles of Coral Sea, Midway, and the Aleutians*. Ft. Meade, MD: Center for Cryptologic History, National Security Agency, 1993.

Parshall, Jonathan B., and Anthony P. Tully. *Shattered Sword: The Untold Story of the Battle of Midway*. Washington, DC: Potomac Books, 2005.

Peattie, Mark R. *Sunburst: The Rise of Japanese Naval Air Power, 1909–1941*. Annapolis, MD: Naval Institute Press, 2001.

Potter, E. B. *Bull Halsey*. Annapolis, MD: Naval Institute Press, 1985.

———. *Nimitz*. Annapolis, MD: Naval Institute Press, 1976.

Potter, John Deane. *Admiral of the Pacific: The Life of Yamamoto*. London: Heinemann, 1965.

Prados, John. *Combined Fleet Decoded: The Secret History of American Intelligence and the Japanese Navy in World War II*. New York: Random House, 1995.

Prange, Gordon W., Donald M. Goldstein, and Katherine V. Dillon. *Miracle at Midway*. New York: McGraw-Hill, 1982.

Regan, Stephen D. *In Bitter Tempest: The Biography of Admiral Frank Jack Fletcher*. Ames: Iowa State University Press, 1994.

Reynolds, Quentin. *The Amazing Mr. Doolittle: A Biography of Lieutenant General James H. Doolittle*. New York: Appleton-Century-Crofts, 1953.

Schultz, Duane. *The Doolittle Raid*. New York: St. Martin's, 1988.

Simpson, B. Mitchell, III. *Admiral Harold R. Stark: Architect of Victory, 1939–1945*. Columbia: University of South Carolina Press, 1989.

Smith, Peter C. *Midway: Dauntless Victory; Fresh Perspectives on America's Seminal Naval Victory of World War II*. Barnsley, UK: Pen & Sword Maritime, 2007.

Stafford, Edward P. *The Big E: The Story of the USS Enterprise*. Annapolis, MD: Naval Institute Press, 2002. First published 1962 by Random House.

Stephan, John J. *Hawaii under the Rising Sun: Japan's Plans for Conquest after Pearl Harbor*. Honolulu: University of Hawaii Press, 1984.

Symonds, Craig L. *Decision at Sea: Five Naval Battles that Shaped American History*. New York: Oxford University Press, 2005.

Taylor, Theodore. *The Magnificent Mitscher*. Annapolis, MD: Naval Institute Press, 1991. First published 1954 by Norton.

Thomas, Lowell, and Edward Jablonski. *Doolittle: A Biography*. Garden City, NY: Doubleday, 1976.

Tillman, Barrett. *The Dauntless Dive Bomber of World War II*. Annapolis, MD: Naval Institute Press, 1976.

———. *Wildcat: The F4F in WWII*. 2nd ed. Annapolis, MD: Naval Institute Press, 1990.

Weisheit, Bowen P. *The Last Flight of Ensign C. Markland Kelly, Junior, USNA, Battle of Midway, June 4, 1942*. Baltimore: Ensign C. Markland Kelly, Jr., Memorial Foundation, 1993.

Wildenberg, Thomas, and Norman Polmar. *Ship Killer: A History of the American Torpedo*. Annapolis, MD: Naval Institute Press, 2010.

Willmott, H. P. *The Barrier and the Javelin: Japanese and Allied Pacific Strategies, February to June 1942*. Annapolis, MD: Naval Institute Press, 1983.

————. *Empires in the Balance: Japanese and Allied Pacific Strategies to April 1942.* Annapolis, MD: Naval Institute Press, 1982.

Winton, John. *Ultra in the Pacific: How Breaking Japanese Codes and Cyphers Affected Naval Operations against Japan 1941–45.* London: Cooper, 1993.

Wolf, William. *Victory Roll! The American Fighter Pilot and Aircraft in World War II.* Atglen, PA: Schiffer Books, 2001.

## Articles

Earnest, Albert K., and Harry Ferrier. "Avengers at Midway." *Foundation* 17, no. 2 (Spring 1996): 48–53.

Hudson, Alec [Wilfred J. Holmes]. "Rendezvous." *Saturday Evening Post*, August 2, 1941, 9–11, 70–72, and August 9, 1941, 30–32, 71–75.

Knott, Dick. "Night Torpedo Attack." *Naval Aviation News*, June 1982, 10–13.

Linder, Bruce R., "Lost Letter of Midway." *U.S. Naval Institute Proceedings* 125, no. 8 (August 1999): 29–35.

Lundstrom, John B. "A Failure of Radio Intelligence: An Episode in the Battle of the Coral Sea." *Cryptologia* 7, no. 2 (1983): 97–118.

Parshall, Jonathan. "Reflecting on Fuchida, or 'A Tale of Three Whoppers.'" *Naval War College Review* 63, no. 2 (Spring 2010):127–38.

Pineau, Roger. "The Death of Admiral Yamamoto." *Naval Intelligence Professionals Quarterly* 10, no. 4 (October 1994): 1–5.

Schorreck, Henry F. "The Role of COMINT in the Battle of Midway." *Cryptologic Spectrum* 5, no. 3 (Summer 1975), 3–11.

Schultz, Robert, and James Shell. "Strange Fortune." *World War II*, May/June 2010, 58–65.

Vote, Robert. "The Death of Admiral Yamamoto." *Retired Officer*, November 1979, 27–30.

Wildenberg, Thomas. "Midway: Sheer Luck or Better Doctrine?" *Naval War College Review* 58 (Winter 2005): 121–35.

Worthington, Joseph M. "A Destroyer at Midway." *Shipmate*, January 1965, 4–8.

# INDEX

career, 361; quoted, 357; mentioned, 5, 17, 23,
26, 35, 49, 75, 209, 358; photo, 14
Norris, Benjamin, 242–43, 335n
North American airplanes. *See* Mitchell bomber
*Northampton* (American cruiser), 18, 82
*Nowaki* (Japanese destroyer), 310

O'Flaherty, Frank W., 313n
O'Hare, Edward (Butch), 79–81, 79n; photo, 80
Ōi Atsushi, 38
Okada Jisaku, 302
Okada Keisuke, 28
Okaga Tametsugu, 224
*Okinoshima* (Japanese minelayer), 156
*Oklahoma* (American battleship), 6
OP-20-G (code and signals section), 135–36,
182–83, 185
Opa-Locka Naval Air Station, 61–62
Operation AL. *See* Alaska
Operation K, 206–11, 288; photo, 207; map, 208
Operation MI. *See* Midway
Operation MO. *See* Port Moresby
Operation RY (attack on Ocean and Nauru
Islands), 108
ordnance, American, 52, 262. *See also* torpedoes
ordnance, Japanese, 221. *See also* torpedoes
Osbourne, Edgar, 127
Osmus, Wesley Frank, 320
Ōtorojima. *See* Wake Island
Owen Stanley Mountains, 85
Owens, James C., 268
Ozawa Jisaburō, 35

Paramushiro Island, 199
Parks, Floyd, 226–27
Parshall, Jonathan, 104, 181, 302
PBY. *See* Catalina
Pearl Harbor, Hawaii: Japanese attack on, 7,
17–18, 25, 36–37, 42, 91
Pederson, Oscar (Pete), 59, 156, 166; at Midway,
281–82, 283; manages air battle, 313–15, 319
Penland, Joseph, 300
*Pennsylvania* (American battleship), 143
*Pensacola* (American cruiser), 323
Pensacola, Florida (naval training facility), 47,
60–61
pilots, American: training of, 60–62;
characteristics of, 62–63, 124
pilots, Japanese: training of, 40–42; losses of,
174–75, 360; exhaustion of, 328

"Plan Dog," 21–22
Plan Orange, 19, 32
*Phelps* (American destroyer), 172
*Plunger* (U.S. submarine), 13
Point Luck, 197, 212
Port Moresby, New Guinea, 97, 106; Operation
MO, 108, 109, 145–46, 153
Powers, John J., 168–69
Prange, Gordon, 4, 216
*Prince of Wales* (British battleship), 43, 74, 95
Purple (Japanese diplomatic code), 137
Pye, William S., 84; described, 15; and Wake
relief expedition, 16–17

Quam, E. R. (Bud), 325

Rabaul, 76, 85, 143, 155; air battle near, 77–81, 97
radar, 125; described, 78; in the Coral Sea,
165–66, 169; at Midway, 313, 319
Rainbow Five (war plan), 22
Ramsey, Dewitt (Duke), 47
Ramsey, Logan C., 211, 224
*Ranger* (American carrier, CV-4), 45
Redman, John R., 137–38, 147, 182, 365; photo,
138
Redman, Joseph R., 138, 365
Reid, Jewell (Jack), 212–13, 214, 215n; photo, 213
*Reina Mercedes* (American training ship), 46
*Repulse* (British battlecruiser), 43, 95
Richards, William L., 216
Richardson, Gil, 387
Richardson, Robert C., 186
Ring, Stanhope C.: characterized, 246–48; and
the flight to nowhere, 248–49, 255, 258–63,
389; misses first strike against *Hiryū*, 331–32;
attacks destroyer *Tanikaze*, 345–47, 346n;
attacks Japanese cruisers, 351–52; held back
from final attack, 354; career after Midway,
364, photo, 246
Rochefort, Joseph J.: described, 135–39, 141–42;
relations with Layton, 143–45; and the Coral
Sea, 147–48, 159, 165, 170–71, 181–82; and
Midway, 182, 185, 186–88, 186n, 214; career
after Midway, 365; mentioned, 5, 387; photo,
136
Rodee, Walter: and the flight to nowhere, 255,
262–63, 390; attacks Japanese cruisers, 351,
354; mentioned, 329, 331
Roberts, Owen, 10
Robison, Samuel S., 14